PENGUIN BOOKS

THE NEW SPANIARDS

John Hooper was educated at St Benedict's Abbey in London and St Catharine's College, Cambridge. At the age of eighteen, he travelled to Nigeria during its civil war to make a television documentary. Since then, he has spent more than twenty years as a foreign correspondent, working for – among others – *The Economist*, the *Guardian*, the *Observer*, BBC, NBC and Reuters. For several years in London, he was a presenter of BBC World Service's 'Twenty Four Hours' current affairs programme. Hooper has reported from more than thirty countries, including various war zones – most recently Kosovo and Afghanistan. He developed a special affection for Spain and its people after being posted to Madrid to cover the country's eventful transition to democracy, and later returned there. This book draws on his experiences of nine years living in Spain. Hooper is currently Rome correspondent of *The Economist* and the *Guardian*. He is married to a fellow-journalist, Lucinda Evans.

The forerunner of this book, *The Spaniards*, won the Allen Lane award for 1987.

JOHN HOOPER

THE NEW SPANIARDS

Second Edition

PENGUIN BOOKS

PENGUIN BOOKS

Published by the Penguin Group
Penguin Books Ltd, 80 Strand, London WC2R ORL, England
Penguin Group (USA) Inc., 375 Hudson Street, New York, New York 10014, USA
Penguin Group (Canada), 90 Eglinton Avenue East, Suite 700, Toronto, Ontario, Canada M4P 2Y3
(a division of Pearson Penguin Canada Inc.)
Penguin Ireland, 25 St Stephen's Green, Dublin 2, Ireland
(a division of Penguin Books Ltd)
Penguin Group (Australia), 250 Camberwell Road,
Camberwell, Victoria 3124, Australia (a division of Pearson Australia Group Pty Ltd)
Penguin Books India Pvt Ltd, 11 Community Centre,
Panchsheel Park, New Delhi – 110 017, India
Penguin Group (NZ), 67 Apollo Drive, Mairangi Bay, Auckland 1310,
New Zealand (a division of Pearson New Zealand Ltd)
Penguin Books (South Africa) (Pty) Ltd, 24 Sturdee Avenue,
Rosebank, Johannesburg 2196, South Africa

Penguin Books Ltd, Registered Offices: 80 Strand, London WC2R ORL, England

www.penguin.com

The Spaniards first published by Viking 1986
Revised edition published in Penguin Books 1987
New and completely revised edition published under the present title 1995
Second Edition 2006

Copyright © John Hooper, 1986, 1987, 1995, 2006
All rights reserved

The moral right of the author has been asserted

Set in 10/12 pt Monotype Bembo
Typeset by Palimpsest Book Production Limited, Grangemouth, Stirlingshire
Printed in England by Clays Ltd, St Ives plc

FOR LUCY

Contents

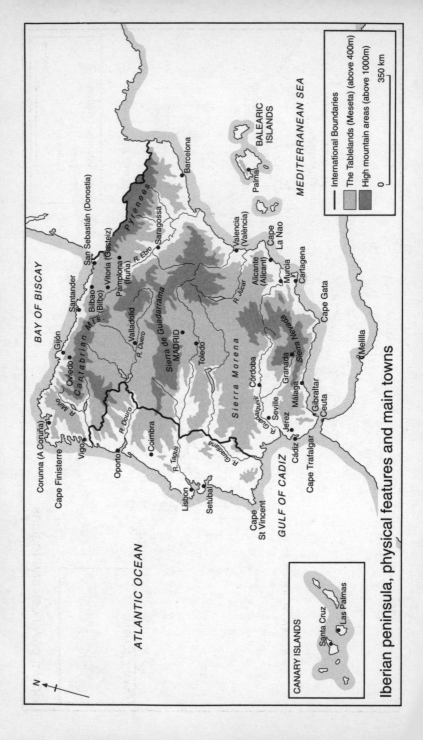

Iberian peninsula, physical features and main towns

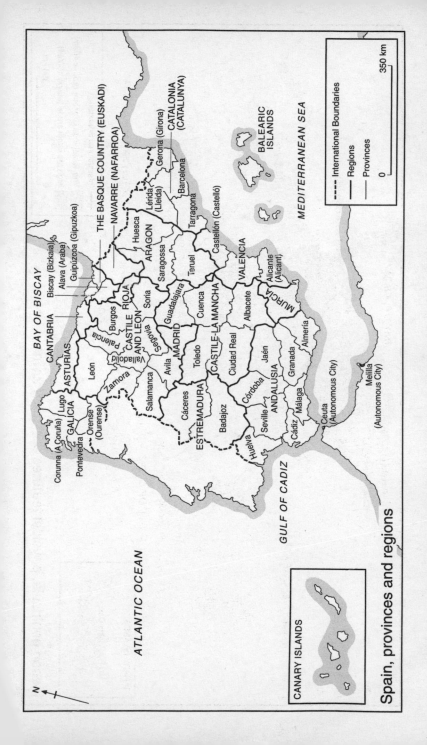

Spain, provinces and regions

Acknowledgements

On the first of my research visits to Spain for this edition, Derek Ive, Concha Perez-Sedeño and Ed Owen extended generous hospitality. In Madrid, Pedro J. Ramírez, of *El Mundo*, agreed to let me base myself in his newspaper and Jorge Fernández somehow managed to create a space for me in *El Mundo*'s already crowded newsroom.

Alan Rusbridger, the editor of the *Guardian*, kindly agreed to my taking a month away from my duties as Rome correspondent to write much of the new material in this edition.

To an even greater extent than its predecessor, this edition of *The New Spaniards* has been produced by a method not unlike that used to make sherry: part of what you are about to read has been retained from a previous version and part of that originated in an earlier work, *The Spaniards*. So it seems only right that those who helped in the preparation of these forerunners should continue to appear in the list that follows, alongside those who have contributed on this occasion.

In alphabetical order, and without distinguishing between the living and those who have died since I began accumulating obligations more than twenty years ago, I am indebted to Tesni del Amo, Ruben Amón, Joaquín Arango, Miguel Angel Bastenier, Kees van Bemmelen, Nancy Benítez, Fernando Bermejo, Rafael Borrás, Peter Bruce, Irma Caballero, Anselmo Calleja, Ana Camarero, Joaquín Carazo, José Cardona, Gustavo Catalán, Ramón Cercós, William Chislett, Kate Connolly, José and Jane Criado-Pérez, Juan Cruz, Pedro Cuartango, Aubrey Davies, Amador Díaz, Giles Dickson, Juanita Eskubi, Alvaro Espina Montero, Angel Fernández, Luis Fidalgo, Alicia García, María Carmen García, Francisco García de Valdecasas, Emilio

García Horcajo, Dionisio Garzón, Iñaki Gil, Enrique Gimbernat, Pere Gimferrer, Antonio Gómez, Miguel Gómez, Javier Goñi, Pedro González Gutiérrez-Barquín, José Luis González Haba, Luis Gordon, Vicky Hayward, Borja Hermoso, Margaret Hills, Alex Hucklesby, Elvira Huelbes, Amado Jiménez Precioso, Nick Kay, Pedro Miguel Lamet, George Lewinsky, Manuel Llorente, Francisco J. López, José Antonio López de Letona, Begoña Luaces, Bill Lyon, Isabel Mancheño, Julio Miravalls, Professor Aina Moll, Rafael Moyano, John Muller, Andrés Ortega, María Luz Padilla Franco, Campbell Page, Mariano Alvaro Page, John Parker, Lluis Pasqual, María Peral, Charles Powell, Peter Preston, Lola Requena, Rafael del Río, Sir Ivor Roberts, Ana Romero, Pilar Rubines, Marta Ruiz, Carlos Sánchez, Harry Schapiro, Victor de la Serna, Harriet Sherwood, Professor Colin Smith, Frank Smith, Francisco Sosa Wagner, Bernard Tanter, Dr Don Tills, Jorge Tinas Gálvez, Professor Antonio Tovar, Giles Tremlett, Ann Treneman, Rosa Tristan, Francisco Velázquez, Luis Antonio de Villena, Jane Walker, Paul Webster, Martin Woollacott, Ian Wright, Sir Stephen Wright and Agustín Yanel.

Thanks too to my able and determined researcher, Laura Barnett, for ferreting out all manner of facts and figures.

I owe special debts to my agent, Gill Coleridge, and her colleague, Lucy Luck, who helped steer this project through to its conclusion, and to Simon Winder of Penguin who supported it enthusiastically from its inception. Once again, though, it was my wife Lucy who was decisive in persuading me to embark on the revision of a book that has once again benefited greatly from her copy-editing skills.

J.H.
Rome
January 2006

Note on the Spelling of Place Names

Wherever an anglicization exists which involves a change of spelling, I have used it. Thus Castilla has become Castile. But where the anglicized form merely involves the loss of an accent (as in Aragon or Cordoba), I have stayed with the accented Spanish version.

Note on Exchange Rates

Currency conversions have been made at the average rate for the relevant year.

Introduction: The Change in Spain

One of the people I interviewed while preparing this book is a journalist who specializes in reporting on the media, particularly television. We spoke for half an hour or so about satellite channels, digital platforms and other products of cutting-edge technology. Then just before we parted I mentioned that I was going to Estremadura for a few days. He said he had been born there. But he did not have an Estremaduran accent.

'No,' he said. 'I was brought up in Old Castile. My father was a transhumance shepherd. He used to take the flock down to Estremadura in the summer, which is why I was born there.'

When I got to Estremadura, I stayed at the house of a woman in her forties. She explained how, when she was a child, her father, who owned one of the very few cars in Trujillo, used sometimes to drive the family to Lisbon for a long weekend.

'In those days, the road to Portugal was barely more than a lane,' she recalled. 'In spring, it would be overhung on either side by mimosa. One of my childhood memories is of falling asleep listening to the swish of the mimosa branches on the windscreen. When we got back to Trujillo, the car would be completely yellow.'

I returned to Madrid and saw a friend who, while we were talking about education, mentioned a man she knew who had been to school as a child at one of the very few progressive institutions allowed to operate in the Spain of the 1960s.

'He told me that, before the school inspectors arrived, all the children were told by their teachers to separate, so the girls would be on one side of the classroom and the boys were on the other.'

This book is about change. What makes contemporary Spain such a fascinating place is the immense, frenetic, sometimes perilous, change that it has undergone and that has, in effect, produced a new country. In less than half a century, a predominantly rural, agricultural society has been transformed into a mainly urban and technological one. A dictatorship has become a democracy. One of the world's most centralized states has been made into one of the most decentralized. A society that was intensely sexually repressed has become a notably permissive one. There has been a revolution in the roles of men and women. And, just as it seemed as if the pace of change might be dropping off, Spain experienced a surge in immigration that has turned it, in the space of just a few years, into a multi-ethnic society.

Other countries have undergone several of these transformations. But I know of nowhere that has experienced them all – and in such a brief time-span. That impression is borne out by academic research. Since the 1980s, social scientists at universities around the world have been conducting interviews with representative samples of the inhabitants of their respective societies to build up a comparative view of the values they hold. One of the aims of the World Values Survey, as it is known, is to monitor social change by measuring the gap between the attitudes held by people at different points on the age scale.

'Spain', according to the project's chief co-ordinator, Professor Ronald Inglehart of the University of Michigan, 'shows the largest differences between the basic values of the younger and older generations among the more than 80 countries surveyed.' Those differences help explain why José Luis Rodríguez Zapatero and his government, who have a predominantly young voter base, have put such an emphasis on social reform since coming to power in 2004, to the point that Spain is increasingly being talked of as a future 'Sweden of the Mediterranean'.

The invisible changes may be immense, but the visible ones are scarcely less so. New buildings are rapidly altering the skylines of Spain's major cities. Perhaps the best-known of these startlingly contemporary structures is Frank Gehry's shimmering Guggenheim museum in Bilbao. But for all its uniqueness, it is just one of many audacious projects in a country that craves to be part of the future, maybe because it is so keen to escape from the past. There is Jean Nouvel's 33-storey Torre Agbar tower in Barcelona, Richard Rogers's extension to Barajas airport outside Madrid, the striking new Valencia opera house and Bilbao's elegant Sondika airport, both by the

Valencian-born engineer-architect, Santiago Calatrava. Arguably the most remarkable of all, though, is the new Hotel Puerta America in Madrid, each of whose twelve floors has been designed by a different, internationally renowned architect.

Yet this dizzying urban renewal is taking place in a country, parts of which have only just edged into the last century. Pardamaza is a village 250 miles north of Madrid. All but the last twenty miles from the capital can be driven on a motorway. Pardamaza first got electric street lighting in 2004. Its inhabitants did not have electricity of any sort until 1996.

Progress has not just changed the way that Spain looks. It has actually changed the way that Spaniards look. You can see this in many families today, where there are three distinct physical types. The grandparents, born in the 1930s or 1940s, are likely to be much shorter than their children. Spaniards born in the 1960s and 1970s, though they had more access to protein and especially dairy products, tend to be quite slim because they were brought up on a version, albeit an ample version, of the traditional Mediterranean diet. Crown Prince Felipe and his wife Letizia are representative of this exceptionally fine-looking generation. But now prosperity has begun to exact a price, and the Spaniards who are growing up today are likely to be the fattest in the history of a traditionally lean people. Juvenile obesity has spread like an epidemic since the mid-1980s, and today one Spanish child in every six is 20 per cent or more overweight.

Sometimes the pace of change, the need for adjustment, just gets too much for people. After the death of Spain's dictator, General Francisco Franco, there emerged a phenomenon among young Spaniards that, as far as I am aware, was unique. It grew up in the generation that was born at the start of Spain's 'economic miracle' in the early 1960s. The members of this generation, whose parents most likely migrated from the countryside to one of the big cities, reached adolescence just as the sexual customs and conventions that had prevailed in Spain for centuries were being overturned. They were approaching school-leaving age when a recession bit into the job market and Spain's first democratic, post-Franco elections were being held, so that – unlike their elder brothers and sisters – they had no obvious economic or political role to fill. There were no jobs to go to and no demonstrations to join. So a lot became what were called *pasotas*.

In so far as they used drugs and tried to put as much distance as possible between themselves and the rest of society, they were like a cross between hippies and punks. But there the similarities ended, for the *pasotas* had none of the mystical aspirations of hippies, nor any of the angry nihilism of punks. In fact, the whole idea of being a *pasota* was not to participate in any way at all, but to 'pass', as in a game of cards (which is how the term came about). The spirit of *pasota*-ism was best exemplified by the way they spoke. The words were mumbled and their vocabulary was pared to a bare minimum so that things, of whatever kind, were *chismes* and situations or activities were dismissed as *rollos*.*

The *pasotas* have long since disappeared (though some of their slang lingers on), but the need to find a way of coping with Spain's social transformation remains. It is, I think, no coincidence that, as will be explained later, today's Spaniards have an exceptionally high susceptibility to addictions of all kinds.

Their country has altered with such bewildering speed that non-Spaniards too have had difficulty keeping up. Twenty years ago in my first book on Spain† I wrote that people's ideas were 'still based to a great extent on what was written during or about the period leading up to Franco's takeover'. That is no longer the case.

The majority of non-Spaniards have come to realize that Spain is not nowadays a land of conservative religious beliefs and rigid moral conventions, of vast social divisions and violent political conflicts. There is a much greater readiness to accept that it is an economically and politically advanced society with many of the problems that implies. Yet something else I wrote in *The Spaniards* remains true – that, in different ways, it is 'the best-known and the least-known of the major European nations'. Every year, more than 50 million people visit Spain. Yet the vast majority are holidaymakers who spend most, if not all, of their time at coastal resorts quite untypical of the country as a whole. Flying directly to and from the *costas*, the Balearic or Canary Islands, they have little chance to see the everyday Spain of the ordinary Spaniard.

---

* *Un rollo* (literally a roll of paper, a scroll) had long been used to mean 'a bore' and specifically 'a long-winded explanation'. The English word rigmarole carries a similar meaning and has a similar derivation.

† *The Spaniards* (Viking, 1986; Penguin, 1987).

Spain is the second largest country in the European Union, after France, and, with almost 40 million people, it is the fifth most populous. If non-Spaniards have any picture at all of the land that lies behind the *costas*, then it is probably that of the *meseta* – the tableland which encompasses Old and New Castile, León, La Mancha, Estremadura, parts of Aragón, Navarre and La Rioja. Vast and arid, stark and lofty, it has little in common with the balmy coastline the package tourists visit. Much has been written about its role in forging the character of the Spanish people, and especially that of the Castilians who have been the dominant community for much of the country's history. It may well be that the *meseta*'s testing climate – searingly hot in summer and bitterly cold in winter – has given the Castilians a stern and sober streak you will not often find among other Mediterranean people; that the immense expanses and serrated horizons of the *meseta* have made Castile a land of dreamers, of mystics and conquerors.

If Castile and the *meseta* fail to conform to outsiders' expectations of Spain, the same is true of much of the rest of the country.

Galicia, the north-westernmost region, which sits atop Portugal, is as wet and lush and mournfully beautiful as the west of Ireland. The dominant colours there are the green of its gorse and the grey of its granite. Like Brittany and Ireland, it gets a lot of rain and much of it finds its way back to the sea along valleys that have subsided over millennia to the point where their seaward ends have sunk below the level of the ocean, leaving only the valley sides visible in the form of great promontories. These half-submerged valleys or *rías* are an abundant source of shellfish – crabs, lobsters, oysters and, above all, the scallops which the pilgrims who travelled to Santiago de Compostela in medieval times adopted as their emblem. The dish of scallops cooked with mashed potato and grated cheese which the world knows as Coquilles Saint-Jacques is by origin a Galician delicacy copied by the French.

Further along the coast, Asturias with its wild countryside and abandoned coal-mines is more akin to South Wales than anywhere in the Mediterranean. Next door, Cantabria has soaring peaks with villages on their slopes that are cut off for weeks on end every winter, and deep potholes among which were found the famous cave paintings of Altamira. Much of the farming is pastoral and the sound of cowbells is never far away. You could be in Switzerland.

The Basque country also has an Alpine look to it. The typical Basque farmhouse with its broad eaves is virtually indistinguishable from a Swiss chalet. But whereas Switzerland is mountainous, the Basque country – although frequently described in the press and elsewhere as 'mountainous' – is in reality a land of odd-looking, steep-sided, flat-topped hills that tower over the valleys between them. The countryside in most areas is of a uniquely intense shade of green – a green so dark that it sometimes appears unnatural. In fact, it is a result of the rain that pours down in the Basque country day in day out, week in week out, during the winter.

In the foothills of the Pyrenees, in Navarre and Aragón, you could almost be in the Highlands of Scotland, but in both regions the landscape changes dramatically as you move southwards away from the French border. In Navarre you go through a stretch of splendid undulating countryside around the capital, Pamplona, before entering a more typically Mediterranean district where there are extensive vineyards. In Aragón you descend gradually towards the vast, flat, depopulated Ebro valley and then rise again into the bare uplands around Teruel.

Catalonia and Valencia are perhaps the regions that the majority of people regard as being most typically Spanish, yet a clear majority of Catalans and a sizeable minority of Valencians do not even speak Spanish* as their first language. Nor, whatever they may think, have many of the foreign holidaymakers who have visited Spain's east coast been for a holiday on the Costa Brava. The term *costa brava* means 'rugged coast' and is used by Spaniards to describe the rocky shoreline that begins around San Feliú and extends to the French border. Resorts such as Lloret de Mar which tour operators habitually

---

* The use of the word 'Spanish' instead of 'Castilian' to describe Spain's most widely spoken language is unfortunate in that it implies that the others (Basque, Catalan and Galician) are either un-Spanish or less Spanish. It is rather like calling English 'British', but with less justification since vernacular languages are far more extensively used in Spain. Hispanic Latin Americans tend to use the term *castellano* as much as, if not more than, *español*. Within Spain itself, the use of the word *español* rather than *castellano* is a recent phenomenon and one which was encouraged by the nationalistic dictatorships of Primo de Rivera and Franco. The first Dictionary of the Royal Academy with 'Spanish' in its sub-title was not published until 1925. Both the 1931 and 1978 constitutions referred to the official language of the nation as 'Castilian'.

describe as being on the Costa Brava are on flat, sandy land further to the south.

Beyond Valencia lies Murcia – hotter, drier and flatter. But beyond Murcia lies Almería, which is sufficiently reminiscent of Arizona for it to have been used as the setting for a string of Westerns in the 1960s. By the coastal route, Almería forms the gateway to Andalusia – Spain's Deep South. Here again, the contrast between image and reality is considerable. The Andalusia of legend is an undulating expanse of corn fields and olive groves divided up into a small number of large estates. That is indeed true of the more northerly and westerly of the eight provinces that make up the region – Huelva, Cádiz, Seville, Córdoba and Jaén. But Málaga and Granada are hilly – and, in parts, even mountainous – provinces where smallholding has always been the rule rather than the exception. As for Almería, much of it is as barren as the Sahara.

Many people are ready to accept that Spain is among the largest countries in Europe, but few would think of it as one of the highest. Yet the average height of the ground is greater than in any European country except Switzerland. If you look at a relief map you will see that, with the exception of the Guadalquivir and Ebro valleys and a relatively narrow coastal strip, the whole of Spain is upland. The *meseta* varies in altitude from 2,000–3,000 feet as one craggy mountain range succeeds another. This gives to it one of its most distinctive characteristics – the almost painful brightness of the light. Not only is Spain a land of huge expanses, but one where you can as often as not see to the furthest limits of those expanses. 'In Spain,' wrote the author and journalist Manuel Vicent, 'there is a lot of sun and an excess of light, so that everything is all too clear. It is a country of emphatic claims and denials where historically doubt has been put to the torch – to that sinister clarity.'

This alone has made Spain seem a forbidding place to the foreigner. But then Spain is a difficult country to come to grips with from almost any angle. For a start, it contains several different cultures. What is true of most of Spain need not be true of the Basque country, or of Catalonia or Galicia. Partly for this reason, anyone who sets out to study Spanish history will soon discover that lengthy stretches of it are dauntingly complicated. Some of the country's finest artists and writers – Murillo and Calderón, for example – deal largely with themes that are peculiar to their time and place, while a lot of the popular culture derives from traditions – Arab, Jewish and Gypsy – that are alien to the experience of the majority of Europeans. Non-Spaniards appreciate the spectacle of flamenco, but few could tell good from bad. Even the cuisine, with its ardent spices and outlandish ingredients like pigs' ears and bulls' testicles, requires an adventurous spirit.

Yet it is precisely the difficulty of getting to know Spain that makes the task so appealing, for it is that which makes it so challenging and rewarding.

What I wrote at the start of *The Spaniards* applies to this book too: apart from Part One, which briefly describes the economic trends and the political events that have moulded Spain into the nation it is today, this is not a book about economics or politics; nor does it concern itself with labour relations. Once again, my aim has been to paint a picture of contemporary Spanish society.

Ernest Hemingway thought it was 'probably a good system, if one has to write books on Spain, to write them as rapidly as possible after a first visit as several visits could only confuse the first impressions and make conclusions much less easy to draw'.

But then Hemingway didn't follow that advice. And neither have I.

PART ONE

The Making of a New Spain

CHAPTER I

From Hunger to Prosperity

Although Franco's regime was frequently referred to as a fascist dictatorship, the description was never wholly correct. Spain's fascist party, the Falange, was only one of several factions and institutions which rallied to the officers who rebelled against the elected government in 1936 and which thereby earned the right to a share in the spoils when, three years and half a million lives later, their side emerged victorious. In addition to the Falange, there was the army (or rather that section of the officer corps which had sided with the rebels), the Church and the monarchists, including both those who favoured the restoration of the heirs of Alfonso XIII – the king who had left Spain in 1931 – and those who supported the cause of the Carlist pretenders whose claims to the throne had twice provoked civil war during the previous century.

It was not unusual for membership of these 'families', as they have been called, to overlap. There were generals who belonged to the Falange, just as there were devout Catholics who wanted the restoration of the monarchy in some form. But there were also irreconcilable differences, notably between the Falangists, who wanted to set up a fascist republic, and the Alfonsine and Carlist monarchists. To ensure that their rivalries did not undermine the war effort and to assert his control over their activities, Franco – who emerged by a mixture of chance and design as *Generalísimo*, or Commander-in-Chief, of the rebel forces – fused the political parties representing these three groups into a single entity with the tongue-twisting, catch-all title of Falange Española Tradicionalista y de las Juntas de Ofensiva Nacional-Sindicalista (FET de las JONS). This odd coalition, which came to be called the Movimiento Nacional, was from then on the only lawful political entity in Franco's Spain. Throughout his rule, there was usually at least one member of each 'family' in the cabinet and the number of portfolios held by a particular faction was usually a good indication of the extent to which it was in or out of favour with the *Caudillo*.*

The army enjoyed a brief heyday in the immediate aftermath of the war, but it was the Falange which later became the dominant influence on Franco. Neither the Church nor the army was capable of providing a programme for running the country, and the monarchists of both camps stood for a solution that could only be put into effect if Franco were to give up the position which he had by that time acquired as Head of State. In any case, the Blueshirts (for blue was to Spain's fascists what brown was to Italy's and green to Portugal's) appeared in 1939 to represent the future.

Over the next few years the Falangists took over the Movimiento and laid the foundations of Franco's regime. As soon as it became apparent that the Axis powers might not after all win the world war that had begun within months of the end of Spain's civil war, Franco reduced the number of Falangists in his cabinet by giving non-fascists the ministries which had most contact with the outside world. Nevertheless, Falangists continued to hold most of the economic and social portfolios and Falangist ideas dominated the regime's thinking.

This was partly because fascist political philosophy, with its emphasis on economic independence and on agricultural rather than industrial development, dovetailed conveniently with the course of action forced upon Franco by events. During the Second World War, Spain had remained technically neutral while actively favouring the Axis. At the end of the war she found herself in an acutely uncomfortable position. Unlike Britain and France, she was not entitled to the rewards of victory. Unlike Germany and Italy, she was not at risk from the encroaching power of the Soviet Union. The Allies therefore had no incentive for giving Spain aid and a very good reason for denying it to her. In fact, they went even further than that and actually punished the Spaniards for having been taken over by a right-wing dictator. In December 1946 the newly created United Nations passed a resolution recommending a trade boycott of Spain.

* This was Franco's other title, equivalent to *Führer* or *duce*. In Spain it has – or had – heroic overtones because it is the word most commonly applied to the native chieftains who led the guerrilla war against the Roman occupation.

Coming on top of the deprivations brought about by the civil war, which had cut real income *per capita* to nineteenth-century levels, the boycott was a disaster – not so much perhaps because of its direct effects, but because it made it unthinkable that Spain should benefit from the Marshall Plan for aid to Europe which got under way six months later.

All the European nations suffered deprivation in the post-war era, but Spain, where the late forties are known as the *años de hambre* or years of hunger, suffered more than most. In the cities, cats and dogs disappeared from the streets, having either starved to death or been eaten. In the countryside, the poorer peasants lived off boiled grass and weeds. Cigarettes were sold one at a time. The electricity in Barcelona was switched on for only three or four hours a day and trams and trolleybuses in Madrid stopped for an hour in the morning and an hour and a half in the afternoon to conserve energy. But for the loans granted by the Argentine dictator, General Perón, it is possible that there would have been a full-scale famine.

The UN-sponsored blockade was lifted in 1950, but the Falangists' insular and ineffective doctrines continued to hold sway. For this, Spain was to pay dearly. In spite of the Falangists' exaltation of the rural economy, agricultural output fell to a level even lower than at the end of the civil war. Industry, immured from the outside world by a wall of tariffs and quotas, unable to buy the foreign technology it needed to modernize or to seek out new markets for its goods, bound on all sides by government regulations, could only grow at a painfully slow pace. National income did not regain its pre-civil-war level until 1951 and it was not until 1954 that the average income returned to the point it had reached in 1936. In the early fifties an attempt was made to ease trade restrictions and stimulate private enterprise, but although it eventually succeeded in boosting industry it opened up a trade gap that rapidly absorbed the country's foreign reserves. In the meantime, bungling in other areas of the economy led to bursts of rip-roaring inflation.

To the villagers in the poorer parts of Spain – and particularly Andalusia which had been the scene of desperate poverty even before the civil war – the deprivations of the post-war era were the final straw. Individuals, families and in some cases entire villages packed up their belongings and headed for the industrial centres of the north

– Barcelona, Bilbao, Oviedo and Saragossa – and for Madrid which, with the deliberate encouragement of a regime which feared the economic prowess of the Basques and Catalans, had ceased to be a purely administrative capital. Once they reached the cities the migrants settled like besieging armies on the outskirts. With nowhere else to live, they built *chabolas* or *barracas* (shacks) out of whatever they could scavenge – some breeze blocks from a building site, an unwanted door, a few empty cans and boxes and a sheet of corrugated iron or two to serve as a roof, weighted down with lots of heavy stones to make sure it did not blow away. The shacks were suffocatingly hot in the summer and bitterly cold in the winter. None had running water, so there was no question of sewerage. Since the shanty towns had sprung up without official permission it was usually several years before the municipal authorities got around to supplying them with electricity, let alone the more sophisticated amenities such as refuse collection or access roads. With grim humour, one of the shanty towns outside Barcelona was nicknamed 'Dallas – Frontier City'.

The whole idea of migration to the cities ran counter to the Falangist dream of a populous countryside inhabited by peasant farmers each owning a modest but adequate plot of land. At first the authorities tried to put a stop to the exodus by force. Policemen were sent to the railway stations with orders to collar anyone with a dark complexion and a battered suitcase and put him on the next train out of town. But it was like trying to turn the tide. In any case, migrants already living in the shanty towns saw in it a way of returning home for a holiday courtesy of the government – all they needed to do was put on their scruffiest clothes, travel a few miles out of town and catch a train coming up from the south.

The authorities later turned to a more sophisticated and successful approach, which was to limit the number of shacks by licensing those that had already been built and giving them numbered plaques. Those that did not have a plaque were liable to be torn down by the teams of municipal workmen – the dreaded *piquetes* which usually arrived in the middle of the morning or afternoon when the men of the shanty towns were out working, or looking for work. Although the number of licences had to be increased bit by bit, the system made the building of a shack such a hazardous enterprise that their numbers started to stabilize towards the end of the fifties.

By then Franco's regime was virtually bankrupt. The foreign exchange account was in the red, inflation was heading into double figures and there were serious signs of unrest among both students and workers for the first time since the civil war. It took a long time to persuade Franco that a radical change was required. But in February 1957 he reshuffled his cabinet and gave the Trade and Finance portfolios to two men, Alberto Ullastres Calvo and Mariano Navarro Rubio, who were representative of a new breed in Spanish politics – the 'technocrats'. The typical technocrat came from a well-to-do background, had had a distinguished career in academic or professional life and – this was the *sine qua non* – belonged to, or sympathized with, the secretive Catholic fellowship, Opus Dei.

As its title – 'Work of God' – suggests, the central belief in Opus Dei's philosophy is that of sanctification through work. Like others before him, Opus's founder, Josemaría Escrivá de Balaguer, had noted with dismay that wherever and whenever there was economic progress the Roman Catholic faith seemed to lose ground. Instead of seeing capitalist development as a threat, though, he regarded it as an opportunity: if only devout Catholics could be imbued with a 'work ethic', they could take a hand in the process of economic development at an early stage and use their control of it to spread their ideas through the rest of society that way. A rise in the GDP need not lead automatically to a fall in the numbers of the faithful.

Whether the Opus technocrats also had a political agenda is still a matter for debate. They and their admirers always insisted that its aim was to prepare for democracy. In 1966, General Jorge Vigón, who had entered the cabinet as a result of the 1957 reshuffle and was close to the technocrats in outlook, wrote that 'freedom begins as of the moment when the minimum earnings of each citizen reach $800 per annum'. However, critics of the regime and of Opus Dei have argued that the technocrats saw improving the standard of living as a way of delaying the restoration of democracy. It has been noted that in subsequent references to General Vigón's formula the target figure was repeatedly increased. But whatever the intent, the *effect* of the technocrats' reforms was wholly beneficial for Francoism, for it ensured the survival of a regime which had seemed doomed by its economic failings.

It was not until two years after their appointment that the new team began its all-out assault on the economy. The short-term aim was to tackle inflation and redress the balance of payments. The long-term objective was to free the economy from the restrictions that had been placed on it by the Falangists. The so-called Stabilization Plan introduced in July 1959 was intended to achieve the first of these goals. Public spending was cut, credit was curbed, wages were frozen, overtime was restricted and the peseta devalued. The Plan achieved what was expected of it. Prices levelled out and the deficit in the balance of payments was transformed into a surplus by the end of the following year. But the cost in human misery was considerable since real earnings were slashed. As a result, many Spaniards set off to find work abroad. Measures to liberalize the economy, and thus achieve the second of the technocrats' goals, were introduced over a longer period beginning at the time of the Stabilization Plan. Spain was opened up to foreign investment, much of the red tape binding industry was cut away, restrictions were lifted on imports and incentives were offered for exports.

The performance of the economy during the years that followed was dramatic. Between 1961 and 1973, a period often referred to as the *años de desarrollo* or years of development, the economy grew at 7 per cent a year – faster than any in the non-communist world except Japan's. Average annual income quadrupled and as early as 1963 or 1964 – the exact moment is disputed – it passed the $500 mark, removing Spain from the ranks of the developing nations as defined by the UN. By the time Spain's 'economic miracle' had ended, it was the world's ninth industrial power and the wealth generated by its progress had led to substantial improvements in the standard of living.

Spaniards had a better diet. They ate less bread, fewer potatoes and more meat, fish and dairy products. During the sixties, the number of homes with a washing-machine rose from 19 per cent to 52 per cent, and the proportion with a refrigerator leapt from 4 per cent to 66 per cent. When the boom started only one in every hundred Spaniards owned a car; by the time it ended the figure was one in ten. Telephones ceased to be the prerogative of offices, factories and a few wealthy or influential individuals, and became commonplace in private homes – a fact that had a considerable impact on relations between the sexes, which was in turn mirrored in the pop songs of the day. The number of university students tripled, and by the early seventies the infant mortality rate in Spain was lower than in Britain or the United States.

It should be pointed out, though, that one reason why the proportionate increases in all areas were so impressive was that the starting-points were so low. Even in 1973 per capita income was still lower than in Ireland, less than half the average for the countries of what was then the EEC and less than a third of the average in the United States. Moreover, *pluriempleo*, the practice of holding several jobs, which became widespread in Spain during the boom years, showed that Spaniards often had to work harder for their prosperity than other Europeans.

The principal reason why the economy was able to continue growing after 1959 in a way that it had not after the reforms at the beginning of the fifties was that ways were found of bridging the trade gap which opened up as soon as Spain's economy began expanding – a consequence of the fact that Spain had to pay more for the fuel, raw materials and capital equipment which it needed to feed its industrial expansion than it could get for the goods and produce it sold abroad. Throughout most of the period from 1961 to 1973, imports outstripped exports in a proportion of about two to one, but the deficit was amply covered by invisible earnings in the form of receipts from tourism and the money sent back to Spain by Spaniards who had found work abroad. At the same time, growing foreign investment ensured that Spain's reserves increased rather than decreased over the period.

In all these areas, the government had played an important role. It had eased the conditions for foreign investment, provided financial incentives for Spaniards to seek work abroad and, while tourism had been growing steadily throughout the fifties, it was not until 1959 when the government stepped in to abolish the requirement for visas for holidaymakers from Western Europe that the industry really took off. It is equally true, however, that none of this cash from abroad would have been forthcoming in such quantities had the other countries of the West not been enjoying a period of growth and prosperity. It was this which created the surplus funds that found their way to Spain, which made the companies of north-western Europe thirsty for cheap foreign labour and enabled individuals in north-western Europe to contemplate holidays abroad. To this extent, Spain's economic miracle was a by-product of the sixties boom in Europe as a whole.

The way that Spain acquired its vital foreign income had an immense impact on the country's lifestyle. Oddly-spelt names that Spaniards found difficult to pronounce, such as Chrysler, Westinghouse, John Deere and Ciba-Geigy, began to appear on hoardings and in the press. The young businessmen recruited by the new foreign companies picked up their employers' habits and attitudes and passed them on to their counterparts in Spanish-owned firms. Soon, a new breed of *ejecutivos* began to emerge – clean-shaven, wearing button-down shirts, casual suits and sometimes a pair of black-rimmed spectacles. Their speech, liberally sprinkled with English words and phrases, came to be known as *ejecudinglish*. The archetypal representative of these Americanized Spaniards is the singer Julio Iglesias.

Between 1961 and 1973 well over a million Spaniards received assistance to go and work abroad. By the time the boom ended there were some 620,000 in France, 270,000 in West Germany, 136,000 in Switzerland, 78,000 in Belgium, 40,000 in Britain and 33,000 in Holland – a veritable army of Spaniards all sending back about a quarter of their earnings to swell the deposit accounts of their homeland.

Spain's Mediterranean coastline was transformed out of all recognition. It is hard to believe now that when the novelist Rose Macaulay drove along it in the summer of 1947, she 'encountered scarcely any travelling compatriots and saw only one GB car'. Her main complaint was that 'on these lovely shores as elsewhere in Spain the inhabitants stare and point'. Between 1959 and 1973 the number of visitors to Spain leapt from under 3 million to over 34 million. Land by the coast which, because it was usually either rocky or sandy, was regarded as virtually worthless and was frequently bequeathed to the least-favoured offspring, suddenly became valuable. On the Costa del Sol, at San Pedro de Alcántara, a plot of undeveloped land next to the beach which changed hands for 125 pesetas per square metre in 1962 was sold eleven years later – still undeveloped – for 4,500 pesetas per square metre.

The material benefits of the tourist boom were considerable – not only for property developers, but also for shopkeepers and the ordinary people of the villages near the coast who became waiters and chambermaids in the tourist hotels. But that is not to say that the tourist boom was an unmitigated blessing. The development took place in an environment which had not changed very much since the eighteenth century – a world of thrift and deprivation which had its own strict moral code. Overnight, its inhabitants were confronted with a new way of life in which it seemed as if the men had more money than they could cram into their wallets and the women walked around virtually naked. Accustomed to measuring time in hours, they were suddenly expected to think in minutes. They had to come to grips with new concepts like credit cards and complicated machines like dishwashers. The result in many cases (although, for some reason, less among women than among men) was shock. Not in the metaphorical but the literal sense of the word – the most common symptoms were insomnia, listlessness and breathlessness. In the mid-sixties, the Civil Hospital in Málaga enlarged its psychiatric wing by adding a ward specifically to cater for young patients. It immediately became known as 'the waiters' ward'. According to a study carried out in 1971, 90 per cent of all non-chronic mental illness in the rural parts of the province of Málaga was among teenage males who had gone to work on the coast.

Tourism, emigration and the arrival in Spain of multinational firms all served to bring Spaniards into contact with foreigners and in particular with other Europeans, thereby whittling away the xenophobia which had always been a characteristic of the Spanish, and never more so than in the early years of Franco's rule. Spain did not, as the technocrats had hoped, become a member of the EEC. Her application, submitted in 1962, was ignored, although she did manage to wheedle a preferential trade agreement out of Brussels eight years later. On the other hand, her best soccer team – Real Madrid – had succeeded between 1956 and 1960 in carrying off the European Cup five years in a row (a feat which has never been equalled), and in 1968 a Spanish vocalist, Massiel, won the Eurovision Song Contest with a suitably anodyne offering entitled '*La, La, La*'. These victories probably made as much of an impression on the average Spaniard as anything on the diplomatic level would have done. They showed Spaniards that not only could they gain acceptance in 'Europe' (the Spanish, like the British, often talk about Europe as if it were somewhere else) but also hold up their heads while doing so.

The 'economic miracle' changed the nature and volume of internal migration. Poverty-stricken villagers from Andalusia continued to flood into the cities, but they were joined in increasing numbers by migrants from Galicia and the regions of the *meseta* – Castile, León, Estremadura and Aragón. Whereas the typical migrant of the fifties was a landless labourer forced to move by hunger, the migrants of the sixties were likely to be craftsmen or shopkeepers whose standards of living had dropped because of the falling population in the countryside, or peasant farmers who were still able to make a meagre living from the soil but were lured to the city by the promise of a less arduous and more varied existence. An American anthropologist, Dr Richard Barrett, who carried out a field study in the Aragonese town of Benabarre between 1967 and 1968 noted that the girls there were unwilling to marry the sons of peasant farmers if they intended to stay and work their fathers' land – to such an extent that young farmers were driven to advertising in the press for brides from the poorer regions of the country. The dream of the girls of Benabarre was to marry a factory worker – or at least a boy who was prepared to leave home in an attempt to become one.

Come the sixties, the original migrants were beginning to move out of their shanty towns and into cheap high-rise accommodation. Since shack-building was by then practically impossible, the new arrivals either had to buy a shack from a family which was moving on to better things or pay for accommodation in the apartment of a family which had already done so. From the point of view of the first wave of migrants, selling a shack became a way of getting the down payment on a flat. Taking in lodgers was a way of finding the monthly instalments.

While the cities were rapidly becoming overcrowded, the countryside was equally quickly becoming depopulated. In 1971 Dr Barrett returned to Aragón and visited seventeen hamlets near Benabarre. By referring to the 1950 census figures he discovered that during the intervening twenty years they had lost 61 per cent of their population. Four were completely deserted and in some cases the depopulation had taken as little as six years. Today anyone driving through Spain who is prepared for a bumpy ride off the main road will sooner or later come across one of these deserted hamlets. Perhaps the most forlorn of all are those that are almost, but not quite, abandoned – where the last inhabitants, who are too old to leave and too young to die, keep their livestock in what were once their neighbours' cottages.

Before the civil war, the Catalan politician Francesc Cambó had described Spain as a country of oases and deserts. Migration made this even more evident. By the end of the boom, the table of population density by provinces showed a steady gradation from most to least densely populated, but what was striking about it was the size of the gap between the two extremes. At one end there was Barcelona with more than 500 people per square kilometre – which made it as crowded as the industrial centres of north-western Europe – and at the other end there were eleven provinces with fewer than 25 inhabitants per square kilometre – a figure comparable with countries like Bhutan, Nicaragua and Burkina Faso. The process of depopulation has gone so far in some parts of the country that it is difficult to see how it can be reversed. In 1973, as the flood of migration began to abate, Teruel became the first province in Spain's history in which there were more deaths than births. Since then, several provinces with elderly populations have joined Teruel. Even if migration from these areas stops altogether, they will continue to lose inhabitants.

The increasingly uneven distribution of Spain's population encouraged an even more unequal allocation of the country's wealth. Any attempt at regional planning while Franco was still alive ran up against the problem that the areas into which the country would have to be divided for planning purposes were precisely those whose demands for recognition were anathema to the dictator and whose identity he had been at great pains to erase. The technocrats' answer was a so-called 'pole' policy. The idea was to select a number of towns in underdeveloped or semi-developed regions and offer incentives to firms to set up businesses there, in the hope that the resulting prosperity would spill over into the surrounding countryside. The criteria used for deciding which towns and firms should benefit from the scheme were never made clear and it is suspected that a good deal of corruption surrounded their selection. But the most serious flaw in the 'pole' project was that the incentives were not offered for long enough for entrepreneurs to be confident of success. By and large, investment did not live up to expectations and what investment was generated was relatively unsuccessful in creating new jobs. Of the twelve towns chosen as 'poles', only Valladolid fulfilled the hopes placed in it. By the early seventies it was well on its way to becoming a sizeable industrial centre.

With the exceptions of Valladolid and Madrid, new businesses tended to set up shop in the Basque and Catalan provinces, which had become industrialized in the previous century, or in places like Oviedo, Saragossa, Valencia and Seville – big cities which had already had some industry before the civil war. In 1975 five provinces – Barcelona, Madrid, Valencia, Biscay and Oviedo – produced 45 per cent of the country's total output. Most of the prosperity was concentrated in the north and east of the country. Of the fifteen peninsular provinces with the highest average incomes, all but two lay along the River Ebro or to the north of it. The two exceptions were Madrid and Valladolid. Average earnings in the poorest provinces of Andalusia, Estremadura and Galicia were less than half those in the richest – Madrid, Barcelona and the three Basque provinces. The disparity in wealth was mirrored by a disparity in the provision of amenities and services. There were 80 doctors per 100,000 inhabitants in Jaén, but 230 per 100,000 in Madrid.

As the boom progressed, the migrants became potentially one of the most influential classes in Spain, having virtually engulfed the old highly politicized urban working class. Unlike the workers of the thirties, the militancy of whose socialism and anarchism was famed throughout Europe, the vast majority of migrants had very little interest in, or experience of, politics. In rural Spain only a tiny number of people had the time or money to take an interest in political developments outside the village, and they were the rural notables – landowners, merchants and professional people who controlled, through their economic influence, the destinies of the labourers, tenants, sharecroppers and smallholders in patron–client relationships. During the periods in which Spain was a democracy, the clients usually voted the way they were told to by their patrons (which was one of the main reasons why democracy was so widely despised and therefore so vulnerable). The migrants who arrived in the cities during the fifties and sixties were not so much right-wing or left-wing as simply apolitical, although they were highly receptive to the go-getting materialism and individualism which, to a greater or lesser extent, affected every level of society during the *años de desarrollo*. In the shanty towns, acts of great kindness coexisted with an almost total absence of class solidarity; once they had found their way out of those ramshackle purgatories the migrants were understandably reluctant to do anything, such as striking or demonstrating, that might cause them to return. Nevertheless, their initial submissiveness tended to obscure the fact that migration had broken for ever the hold that the rural upper and upper-middle classes had once exerted over the rural lower-middle and lower classes. What is more, it was clear – although not at first to the migrants themselves – that their interests were not those of their employers. Indeed, whenever they were pressed in polls and surveys to define their views, the sort of ideal society that their answers implied was distinctly more left-wing than right-wing. By the start of the seventies, they were beginning to become politically more aware and to develop an outlook that was, if not radical, then certainly progressive.

Although the 'economic miracle' changed almost everything about Spain – from how and where people lived to the way in which they thought and spoke – one of its paradoxes was that what it changed least was the economy itself. It grew, of course, but its shape and character remained virtually unaltered. When the boom ended, there were still far too many small firms (over 80 per cent of all Spanish companies employed fewer than five workers) and it was as difficult as it had ever been to get long-term credit. Between them, these two factors ensured that far too little money was spent by industry on researching new products or training skilled workers. Productivity remained low (half the EEC average), unemployment was comparatively high (certainly much higher than the official figures suggested), and the traditional gap between imports and exports was widening rather than narrowing.

The political effects of the boom were far greater, both in number and complexity. The most popular explanation of recent Spanish history goes roughly as follows. The reason why democracy did not take root in Spain in the late nineteenth and early twentieth centuries was that Spain did not have a middle class. The 'economic miracle' was responsible for redistributing the country's wealth and creating a 'new middle class'. Together, these two factors helped to remove, or rather to bridge, the gulf which had existed up until then between the 'two Spains', and which had been responsible for the civil war. By healing this historic breach in Spanish society between the upper

23

and lower classes, the boom was thus responsible for Spain's relatively smooth transition from dictatorship to democracy.

There is an element of truth in this. Unquestionably, the 'economic miracle' in the sixties helped to smooth the way for the political transformation of the seventies. But the mechanism of cause and effect was a little more complex than is usually made out. In the first place, Spain – as we have already seen – had long had a middle class. But from the point of view of consolidating a democracy, what matters is not so much the existence of a middle class *per se* as the existence of an urban rather than a rural one. What happened during the boom years was that a substantial section of the Spanish middle classes was lured away from the countryside and into the towns for much the same reasons as the working classes. As they moved from one environment to the other, they – or more often their children – abandoned many of the conservative attitudes and prejudices which are typical of rural elites everywhere. The idea that the boom helped to level out wealth is quite simply a myth. Apart from a few radical Falangists, Franco's supporters were not ones to worry about redistributing income. The *Caudillo* himself had once cheerfully admitted that the civil war was 'the only war in which the rich became richer'. During the sixties, the technocrats were content to see the gulf between the richest and poorest in society grow even wider. It was not until the seventies, when the illegal trade unions seized the initiative from Franco's worker–employer *sindicatos* and started to flex their muscles, that the gap began to close. Even so, by the time Franco died, the top 4 per cent of households accounted for 30 per cent of total income.

But although the way the cake was cut did not change all that much, the size of the cake grew enormously. Greatly increased buying power enabled just about everyone in society to jump up a class in absolute as distinct from relative terms. To that extent, the 'miracle' did indeed create a 'new middle class' from the ranks of what one might call the upper-lower class – mainly craftsmen and peasants. Far more importantly, though, the same process decimated a class which had been destabilizing Spanish society for well over a century – a lower-lower class of landless, unskilled pariahs whose misery and desperation encouraged them to throw in their lot with any messianic demagogue who promised them salvation in this world rather than the next.

On the day following the first general election after General

Franco's death, the newspaper *Diario 16* published an article comparing the number of votes cast for right and left in 1977 and 1936. The percentages were almost identical. Poignantly, the article was entitled 'Forty Wasted Years'. The consolidation since then of a two-party system only serves to underline the point – to the extent that there were 'two Spains', they survived the *años de desarrollo* intact. What the boom years did was to make both of them wealthier and therefore more content and more tolerant.

The miracle ended with the same dramatic suddenness with which it had begun. The European boom had started to run out of steam towards the end of the sixties and the first people to feel the effects were the emigrants. As the expansion of the other Western European economies began to slow down, the number of jobs available declined and the need for foreign labour diminished. After 1970 the number of Spaniards leaving the country to work abroad dropped off. Soon, even those who were already working abroad began to find that they were no longer wanted. France, for example, offered emigrants an indemnity of 150 times their average daily wage – payable as soon as they reached their country of origin. In 1973 the emigrants began to return and in 1974 the amount of money they sent home started to fall. The same year also saw tourist earnings drop for the first time as Europeans tightened their belts and marshalled their resources. Even so, Spain's invisible earnings would have been enough to cover her trade deficit had it not been for the increase in oil prices following the war in the Middle East. Spain depended on oil – almost all of it imported – for two-thirds of its energy. The OPEC price rises doubled the size of Spain's trade gap and unleashed the inflationary pressures that had been simmering away below the surface of the economy throughout the boom years. During 1974 the cost of living rose by more than 17 per cent. The following year, an estimated 200,000 Spaniards returned from abroad in need of work. Then, on 20 November 1975, General Franco died, and for the second time in a century Spaniards were left with the unenviable task of restoring democracy in the depths of a worldwide recession.

CHAPTER 2

From Dictatorship to Democracy

At first light on 21 November 1975, the day after Franco's death, a detachment of artillerymen trundled three massive cannon into a park on the outskirts of Madrid and began firing a last salute to the late dictator. The sound of the guns echoed through the city all day, heightening the sense of apprehension that had taken hold of the capital and the nation.

For thirty-six years all the important decisions had been taken by one man. His disappearance was of itself enough to justify a feeling of trepidation among supporters and opponents alike. But Franco had also left behind him a perilous gap in expectations between the people and their rulers. It was plain to anyone with eyes to see and ears to hear that Spaniards wanted a more representative form of government. Even among those who had once supported the dictatorship – and their numbers were consistently underestimated by foreign observers – there was a widespread recognition that Francoism had outlived its usefulness. Yet until his dying day, Franco had restricted the exercise of power to those who had refused to countenance change – collectively nicknamed the *bunker* – or accepted the need for change but were only prepared to introduce it slowly and conditionally – the so-called *aperturistas*. The country's illegal opposition parties, meanwhile, were united in calling, quite unrealistically, for a clean break with the past – what, in the jargon of the times, was known as a *ruptura*. However, since they had no political power, the only way that they could put pressure on the authorities was to call for street demonstrations, which invariably turned into riots as soon as the police arrived.

Of the many prophecies circulating on that chilly November morning, one of the gloomiest yet most plausible was that the government would sooner or later be overwhelmed by an outburst of popular frustration. At that point, the armed forces – which had much to lose and little to gain from the introduction of democracy – would step in to 'restore order', possibly in the name of a higher authority. From then on, so the theory went, Spain would settle into a pattern well known to the Latin American nations (and which was set in Spain during the previous century) – phases of limited reform alternating with outbursts of savage repression.

If Spain were to avoid such a fate it was clear that much would depend on the role played by the young man who had succeeded Franco as Head of State. Franco had always implied that he was a monarchist at heart. Ever since 1949, in fact, Spain had in theory been a monarchy, even though Franco ensured that he was made acting Head of State for life and given the power to appoint his own successor. It was no surprise that, six years before he died, Franco should have named as his 'heir' a member of the royal family. But instead of selecting the legitimate heir to the throne – Alfonso XIII's son, Don Juan – Franco chose a young man over whom he had been able to exert enormous influence – Don Juan's son, Juan Carlos.

Juan Carlos was hardly someone in whom Spaniards who aspired to a modern, democratic state could have much faith. Ever since the age of ten, when he had come to Spain for his education, the young Prince had been projected through the media as a loyal son of the regime – passing with distinction his *bachillerato* (including a compulsory paper on the Formation of the National Spirit), going on to attend all three military academies and doing a sort of internship in the administration. In recent years he had rarely been seen except in Franco's shadow, standing behind the old dictator on platforms and podiums at official ceremonies. On such occasions he invariably looked a bit gormless, an impression which was reinforced by the awkward way in which he delivered speeches. The overall impression was of a nice enough chap but with not enough intelligence or imagination to question the conventions of his background.

Few people can have been so universally misjudged as Juan Carlos, for his rather gauche manner belied a penetrating and receptive mind. To the *Caudillo*, Juan Carlos was the son he never had. The young Prince fully reciprocated his affection – to this day he will not permit anyone to speak ill of the old dictator in his presence – but he had formed the opinion long before Franco's death that Spain could not and should not continue to be governed in accordance with the principles laid down by his mentor. Starting in the sixties, Juan Carlos made it his business to get to know as many people from as many walks of life and of as many shades of opinion as possible. By then, he was living in a small palace near Madrid guarded by police. Several of the people he wanted to meet had to be smuggled in. Some entered in the boots of cars. The future NATO Secretary-General and EU foreign policy chief, Javier Solana, then an activist in the clandestine opposition, went in on the pillion of a banker's motorbike, wearing a crash helmet that obscured his features.

Whether Franco knew or guessed what his protégé was up to will probably never be known, but he certainly restricted the freedom and influence that Juan Carlos would enjoy after his accession. On the day after he had been named as successor, the Prince was made to take an oath in front of the members of Franco's rubber-stamp parliament. Kneeling down, with one hand resting on the New Testament, he swore loyalty to Franco and 'fidelity to the principles of the Movimiento Nacional and the fundamental laws of the realm'. In a speech afterwards he hinted broadly at his true beliefs. 'I am very close to youth,' he told the ranks of elderly timeservers in front of him, 'I admire and I share their desire to seek a better, more genuine world. I know that in the rebelliousness that worries so many people there can be found the great generosity of those who want open horizons, often filled with unattainable dreams but always with the noble aspiration to a better world for all.' Nevertheless, the public oath he had just sworn meant that his freedom of movement would henceforth be severely restricted. If the apparatus of Francoism were to be demolished it would have to be done according to the rules that Franco had himself devised. This in turn meant that whoever was in charge of the government would need to be both firmly committed to the restoration of democracy and extremely knowledgeable about the structure of the dictatorship – an apparently impossible combination.

For most of his rule, Franco had been Head of Government – in other words, Prime Minister – as well as Head of State. But in June 1973 he relinquished his grip on the premiership and conferred it on one of the few men he ever really trusted – Admiral Luis Carrero Blanco. Franco evidently hoped that Carrero, a formidably able politician, would still be in the saddle when Juan Carlos succeeded to his throne. Carrero's assassination by Basque terrorists six months later was thus immensely helpful to the young Prince, because it allowed him a degree of manoeuvre which he would never have enjoyed had the Admiral still been around. The best man Franco could find to take over from Carrero was a supremely uncharismatic lawyer, Carlos Arias Navarro. Arias was the most cautious kind of *aperturista*. Dimly aware that the nation was clamouring for democracy, yet temperamentally and ideologically committed to dictatorship, Arias was incapable of moving with any determination either forwards or backwards. Even before the *Caudillo*'s death he had begun to cut a helpless figure, but not one for which anyone felt much sympathy. Juan Carlos himself had little time for Arias and their relations became still worse after Arias tried to resign during the delicate period just before Franco's death in protest at the Prince's decision to hold a meeting with the armed forces ministers without first telling him.

Under the constitutional system devised by Franco, the monarch could only choose his Prime Minister from a list of three names drawn up by the Council of the Realm, a seventeen-man advisory body consisting almost entirely of Franco diehards. Knowing that he stood no chance of getting a suitable candidate from the Council, the King reluctantly confirmed Arias in office after General Franco's death. In the eyes of the public it did him no good at all. Whenever young demonstrators took to the streets during the early days of King Juan Carlos's reign, their favourite chant was:

España, mañana
Será republicana

(Spain, tomorrow
Will be republican)

In January 1976 Arias outlined a programme of limited reforms. But it did nothing to reduce the level of violence on the streets. In March five workers were killed in Vitoria when police opened fire on a crowd of demonstrators. The following month Arias made things worse with a broadcast to the nation in which he seemed, even more than before, to be harking back to the past. In May the government pushed through the Cortes (parliament) a law making it possible to hold meetings and demonstrations. The month after that, the centrepiece of Arias's programme – a bill for the legalization of political parties – was passed by parliament. But hours later the same assembly threw out the legislation needed to put the bill into effect. It was eventually rescued, but the incident showed that Arias could not even carry with him his old friends and colleagues in the Francoist establishment. On 1 July the King called him to the palace and told him that things could not continue like this. Arias, who had never enjoyed being Prime Minister, seized the opportunity to tender his resignation and the King accepted at once.

It was realized that the country had reached a turning point in its history. Arias's cabinet contained three men with modestly progressive reputations – Antonio Garrigues at the Justice Ministry; Manuel Fraga, the Interior Minister; and José María Areilza, the Foreign Minister. Even the most conservative *aperturistas* had been dismayed by the effects of Arias's dithering and could be persuaded of the need for a firm policy of some kind. Most commentators were convinced that if the King, who was entitled to call for up to three lists, was prepared to hold out he could ensure that the name of at least one of these ministers would turn up.

When the King's choice eventually became known, the reaction was of stunned disbelief. The man he had chosen to succeed Arias was one Adolfo Suárez, who at forty-three was the youngest member of the outgoing government. Everything about Suárez except his youth seemed to be at variance with the spirit of the times. He had spent his entire working life serving the dictator in a variety of posts of which the most important and recent had been the General Secretaryship of the Movimiento Nacional, a post which entitled him to an *ex officio* seat in the cabinet. Not surprisingly, he filled his first government with men of his own age whom he had met on his way up through the state apparatus. A report in the liberal daily *El País* on the composition of Suárez's first cabinet listed the main characteristics of its members as 'an average age of forty-six, a classic Catholic ideology and good relations with certain banking institutions'. On the same day the newspaper carried what was destined to become a notorious commentary by one of Spain's leading historians, Ricardo de la Cierva. His response to the King's choice of Suárez and Suárez's choice of ministers had been the same as that of most democratically minded Spaniards and was summed up by the headline: 'What a mistake! What an immense mistake!' The period immediately following the change of government, the King has since admitted, was the worst of his life – 'Nobody trusted me. They didn't even give me a twenty-day margin to see if I had made the wrong choice.'

His choice of Suárez was not, as some observers had suspected, simply a matter of taking the best name on offer from the Council of the Realm. It was the culmination of months of assiduous conspiracy. During the last months of Franco's life, Juan Carlos had asked a number of politicians and officials for their opinions on how the country could best be transformed. One of the most detailed and realistic appraisals came from Suárez. The more the future king considered him, the more Suárez seemed to fulfil the apparently contradictory requirements of the Prime Minister whose job it would be to change Spain from a dictatorship into a democracy. He had an intimate knowledge of the workings of the administration, yet he accepted that its reform could not be partial or gradual. What is more, he had enough personal appeal to be able to survive once democracy had been restored – he was from an inoffensively middle-class background, he was strikingly handsome, immaculately dressed, affable and thoroughly versed in the use of the media, having been Director-General of the state television and radio network. It was at the suggestion of the King's former tutor and close adviser, Torcuato Fernández-Miranda, that Arias included Suárez in his team. Soon afterwards, the King made up his mind that Suárez was indeed the man for the job. He tried to forewarn him while they were watching a football match between Saragossa, which at that time had a young chairman, and Real Madrid, which was still run by the venerable Santiago Bernabeu. The King expressed the view that older men had to make way for younger ones 'because the life of the country is changing fast in every respect'. After Arias resigned, Fernández-Miranda, whom the King had manoeuvred into the chairmanship of the Council of the Realm, wangled Suárez's name on to the list of candidates as a makeweight. He received fewer votes than either of the other two and the members of the Council were as astonished as everybody else when the King chose him.

Suárez recognized that he would have to move with great speed. By November, three months after the swearing-in of his government, he had laid before the Cortes a political reform bill which would introduce universal suffrage and a two-chamber parliament, consisting of a lower house, or Congress, and an upper house to be called the Senate. His resoluteness caught the old guard in disarray. They had no leader and no alternative and only the most purblind could believe now that the nation did not want reform. In parliament, the role of the redoubtable Fernández-Miranda, who was also the Speaker of the Cortes, was once again decisive. He arranged for the bill to be sped through its committee stages so that there was no chance for it to be watered down. Outside parliament, it was made clear to the members of the Cortes – many of whom were now old men looking forward to a comfortable retirement or a remunerative sinecure – that the way they voted on the bill was bound to affect such matters as who sat on which committees and whether the administration turned a blind eye to certain untaxed accounts. Finally, the entire proceedings were to be broadcast on radio and television and each of the deputies was to be called upon by name to stand up and say either *sí* or *no* to reform.

By the time the bill came to be debated in the Cortes, it was widely expected that the government would win. Even so, when the vote eventually came to be taken on the evening of 18 November, it was difficult to believe that it was happening. As one by one the members of the Cortes – generals and admirals, ex-ministers, bankers and local bigwigs – stood up to endorse a measure that would put an end to everything they had spent their lives supporting, it became clear that the majority in favour of reform was going to be much, much bigger than anyone had imagined. In fact the vote was 425 to 59, with 13 abstentions. On that night Spaniards began to realize that the long nightmare of Francoism really had come to an end. On 15 December the political reform bill was overwhelmingly endorsed in a referendum. Of the votes cast, the 'yes' votes totalled 94.2 per cent and the 'no' votes only 2.6 per cent. It was conclusive proof of the extent to which support for Franco's system of government had dwindled.

The speed of events dumbfounded not only the Francoists, but also the opposition. Divided among themselves and mistrustful of the new Prime Minister, they failed to take up an offer from Suárez of talks until after the referendum. By that time Suárez was beginning to acquire considerable prestige as the man responsible for engineering the return of democracy, whereas the opposition politicians – most of whom had misguidedly called for abstention during the referendum campaign – had suffered a humiliating rebuff when more than three-quarters of the electorate turned out to vote. Further reform measures came thick and fast. Early in 1977 the cabinet endorsed a procedure for the legalization of political parties more agreeable to the opposition than the one devised by Arias's cabinet. The Socialists were legalized in February and the Communists in April. In March, the right to strike was recognized, trade unions were legalized and the following month the Movimiento was abolished. Since by that time the government and opposition had agreed on how the elections should be conducted and votes counted, a date was set: 15 June.

The problem for Suárez and the members of his administration was that while they now enjoyed tremendous popularity, they did not belong to any of the political parties that were shaping up to contest the election. The point on the political spectrum that appeared to have most appeal for the voters was what at that time passed for the centre – the frontier between those who had worked for the old dictatorship and those who had worked against it. To the right of it were the most progressive *aperturistas*, including Suárez and his ministers. To the left of it were the most moderate opposition parties – a plethora of Christian Democrat, Social Democrat and Liberal groups, some of which amounted to little more than dining clubs. The mood of the moment was reconciliation, and it was clear that whichever party could embrace supporters as well as opponents of Francoism would stand a good chance of winning the election.

The first serious attempt to create such a party was made in November 1976 when a group of *aperturistas* from inside as well as outside the government launched the Partido Popular. It was headed by José María Areilza, whose fellow-minister in the first government of the monarchy, Manuel Fraga, was busy forming the more conservative Alianza Popular (AP). In January the Partido Popular absorbed another *aperturista* group and changed its name to the Centro Democrático. From then on, like a snowball rolling down a hill, it gathered to it one after another of the minor opposition parties. As it became apparent that the Centro Democrático was the coming force in Spanish politics, Suárez approached some of its most senior figures with a deal: he would lead them into the forthcoming election, thus virtually assuring them of victory, if they would agree to two conditions. First, they must ditch Areilza, the only member of the party who could have seriously challenged the Prime Minister for the leadership. Second, they must accept into their ranks the ministers and officials whose help Suárez would need if he were to continue ruling the country. They agreed, and in March Suárez joined the party, which was subsequently renamed the Unión de Centro Democrático.

The UCD emerged from the election as the biggest party, but with only 34 per cent of the vote and 165 of the 350 seats in the lower house. By far the largest opposition party was the Partido Socialista Obrero Español (PSOE), which won 121 seats with some 29 per cent of the vote. The PSOE had been gaining strength ever since 1972, when control of the party had been wrested from its ageing and increasingly out-of-touch exiled leadership by a group of young activists inside Spain led by a lawyer from Seville, Felipe González. González was even younger than Suárez and, in a different way, just as attractive both in manner and appearance. During the run-up to the election he had managed to appear responsible and realistic while remaining aggressively anti-Francoist. Neither the Alianza Popular on the right, nor the Spanish Communist Party (PCE) on the left, did as well as they had expected, winning only 16 and 20 seats respectively.

The Spanish were already signalling a marked preference for a two-party system. But, as it turned out, what had yet to be decided was which two parties would form it.

CHAPTER 3

The Centre Falls Apart

During the final months of the dictatorship and the first years of the monarchy, Spain was gripped by what was sometimes called *fiebre autonómica* (autonomy fever). All of a sudden, it seemed, everyone wanted home rule. Not just those with a distinct language and culture such as the Basques, Catalans and Galicians, but also the inhabitants of areas such as Estremadura, Andalusia and the Canary Islands, whose Spanishness had never previously been questioned.

The designs of half-forgotten regional flags were unearthed and sported in defence of every conceivable cause. The regional officials of Madrid-based political parties, fearful of the rapidly growing support for regionalists and nationalists, lobbied for as much real or apparent autonomy as their headquarters would allow them. The Andalusian branch of the Communist Party thus became the Communist Party of Andalusia, almost as if Andalusia were a separate country.

Spain's medieval history, which had hitherto been depicted as a predestined process of unification, was now presented as the story of several independent nations coerced into reluctant cooperation. In fact a lot of liberal- and radical-minded young Spaniards stopped talking about Spain altogether and began referring solemnly to 'the Spanish state'. To some extent Spain's *fiebre autonómica* was merely the belated manifestation of a wider phenomenon. Regionalism had been having a heyday throughout Europe. But the pressure for home rule acquired a special intensity in Spain as a result of additional, entirely domestic, factors.

The fact that Franco had been such a diehard centralist, and his most vigorous opponents had been ETA's separatist gunmen, created a powerful association in the public mind between national unity and repression on the one hand and regional nationalism and freedom on the other. Towards the end of the dictatorship, dislike of totalitarian rule was frequently expressed in terms of distaste for centralism, especially among the young. It was also noticeable that, outside the three regions that had had active nationalist movements before the dictatorship, nationalist or regionalist sentiment was strongest in areas that had been particularly badly neglected by Franco. Thus there was more anti-central government feeling in Andalusia and the Canary Islands, both regions which had severe economic and social problems, than there was in, for example, Aragón or the Balearic Islands, whose claims to a distinct identity on historical and linguistic grounds were more firmly based.

Under the dictatorship, the clandestine and exiled oppositions had worked on the assumption that Franco's system of a unitary state divided into fifty provinces was unsustainable, and that when he went a measure of decentralization would be necessary. What they envisaged was the re-introduction of self-government in some form for the Basque country, Catalonia and Galicia. However, during the months between Franco's death and the holding of the first general election, it became obvious that to have granted home rule only to those regions which had had statutes of autonomy under the Republic would have been seriously at odds with the mood of the times. By the time that democracy returned to Spain the following year, there was a consensus among politicians of all parties, except Manuel Fraga's Alianza Popular and the extreme groups to the right of it, that when a new constitution was drawn up, every region that wanted it ought to have access to at least a limited degree of autonomy.

But a new constitution was still some way off; in the meantime, the unsatisfied demand for home rule in the Basque country, Catalonia, and to a lesser extent elsewhere provided a convenient pretext for agitation. Soon after the general election of June 1977 Suárez decided that the regions with the best claims to separate treatment needed something to be getting on with. He began with Catalonia, an area for which he always felt a special affinity and from which several of his closest advisers hailed.

Unlike the Basques, the Catalans had abolished their government-in-exile as soon as it became apparent that the victors of the Second World War had no intention of invading Spain and overthrowing Franco. They did, however, keep alive the title of President of the

Generalitat, Catalonia's former home-rule government, as a single, symbolic link with the past. In 1954 the mantle of that office settled on the broad and lofty shoulders of one Josep Tarradellas, an exile and once a minister in Catalonia's republican administration. He was still the incumbent when democracy was restored to Spain twenty-three years later.

A high-handed, self-opinionated but charismatic old man, Tarradellas refused to return to his native land until the *Generalitat* was re-established. Yet he was stubbornly opposed to the efforts being made by younger nationalists to negotiate its restoration, on the grounds that by doing so they were usurping the *Generalitat*'s rightful powers. Sensing an opportunity to put himself in control of the situation, Suárez made contact with the ageing exile and at the end of June 1977, in a spectacular *coup de main*, flew him back to Spain to take over a 'provisional' *Generalitat* set up at the stroke of a pen. The younger nationalists were furious, but there was little they could do.

Tarradellas, whom even they regarded as the very embodiment of Catalonia's survival as a nation, arrived back in Barcelona to an ecstatic reception. For a man who must often have wondered whether he would see his homeland again and who only managed to do so by outwitting an array of political opponents half his age, his first words on Catalonian soil were splendidly appropriate – '*Ja soc aquí*', which roughly translates as 'I made it!'

The provisional *Generalitat* was the first of a succession of 'pre-autonomous governments' set up in the regions, most of which were made up of local deputies and senators. They had no real power, but they helped to get people used to the idea of regional government before it became a reality after the introduction of a constitution.

Since the beginning of the previous century, Spain had had no fewer than eleven. The main reason why none had worked was that each had been drafted and imposed by one particular group with little or no regard to the views of anyone outside it. This time, however, the job of drawing up a new constitution was entrusted to a parliamentary commission representing all the major national parties and the more important regional ones. The document they produced, which was passed by the Cortes in October 1978, was exactly what one would expect of a committee made up of people with very different political outlooks. It was far too long, often vague and sometimes contradictory. But it was nevertheless something in which all the major parties had a vested interest and which until recently they have been reluctant to amend, let alone replace. The new Spanish constitution is among the most liberal in Europe. Spain is defined as a parliamentary monarchy, rather than just a constitutional monarchy. There is no official religion. The death penalty is forbidden and the voting age fixed at eighteen.

However, the outstanding innovation of the 1978 constitution was the sharing of power with the regions. The basic unit of the state envisaged by the constitution was the Autonomous Community, which could be made up of a single province or several neighbouring provinces.

Each Autonomous Community was to have its own President, government, legislature and Supreme Court. The exact powers of the Autonomous Communities were to be defined later in their respective statutes, but the constitution laid down certain guidelines, albeit somewhat ambiguous ones. Firstly, it specified the areas of government which could be handed over to the Autonomous Communities, of which the most important were housing, agriculture, town and country planning, sport, tourism, and health and social services (although with the proviso that in several of these areas the actions taken by the regional governments would have to fit into a framework constructed in Madrid). Secondly, the constitution listed the fields for which the central government held 'exclusive responsibility', among which were foreign affairs, external trade, defence, the administration of justice, merchant shipping and civil aviation. However, in several cases the constitution added that this or that sphere of activity was given to Madrid 'without prejudice' to whatever powers might be granted to the Autonomous Communities. These grey areas, together with those such as education which were not specifically allotted to either central or regional government, and those such as the environment which were rather vaguely divided between the two, provided a means whereby the statutes of the various Autonomous Communities could be varied substantially.

Except in the cases of the Basque country, Catalonia and Galicia – the so-called 'historical nationalities'* – where all that was needed was for the existing pre-autonomous governments to notify the central government, the process whereby a region achieved home rule began when a provincial council (*diputación*) decided that it wanted the province it represented to become an Autonomous Community in its own right or join with others to form one. Thereafter, the constitution set out two paths by which a region could attain self-government. The normal procedure was laid down in article 143.

The second route offered by the constitution was available to the 'historical nationalities' and any other region where the proposal for home rule was capable of securing the endorsement of more than half the votes in a regional referendum. Regions seeking home rule under this option, which was mapped out in article 151, could lay claim in their draft statute to the powers which the constitution deliberately refrained from allotting to either the central or regional governments. However, the constitution also stipulated that the text, once approved by the Cortes, had to be endorsed by the regional electorate in a further plebiscite. The challenges involved in pursuing this route may have been greater, but then so were the powers to be gained. Unwittingly, what the authors of the constitution had done was to create a sort of regional virility test and, as will be seen, this was to have a dramatic effect on Spain's fortunes over the next few years.

In December 1978 the constitution was overwhelmingly approved by the public in a referendum. Then, early in the new year, Suárez dissolved what had in effect been a constituent Cortes and called another general election for March. It produced a result almost identical to the previous one.

Immediately after the 1979 election, Suárez set up a new Ministry of Territorial Administration whose principal task was to oversee the transfer of power to the regions. The granting of home rule to Basques and Catalans was achieved with speed and generosity. Both communities gained control of education and won the right to set

---

* (from p. 38) This is, to my knowledge, the only way of translating the phrase '*nacionalidades históricas*', which was first heard soon after Franco's death and has since become common usage. It needs to be pointed out, however, that the word '*nacionalidad*', like its counterpart 'nationality', had always previously been used to describe a condition rather than an entity. It started to be used out of context in an attempt to satisfy the claims of the Basque country and the other regions to national status without actually having to call them nations. 'Historical nationality' may not be English, but then '*nacionalidad histórica*' is not Spanish.

up their own police forces and radio and television stations. The first elections to the new Basque and Catalan assemblies were held the following year. The two statutes, known as the statutes of Guernica and Sau, were overwhelmingly endorsed at referendums held in October 1979 and came into effect two months later.

Galicia's home-rule statute, the statute of Santiago, gave the Galicians powers that were almost as extensive as those granted to the Basques and Catalans. However, when it was submitted to a referendum in December 1980, less than 30 per cent of the Galician electorate turned out to vote and of those who did so almost one in five voted 'no'. It was a moral victory for those, especially on the right, who regarded the process of decentralization as unnecessary as well as dangerous.

By and large, though, it was not the 'historical nationalities' but the other regions that presented the government with its worst headaches. For local politicians, the pressure to demonstrate their loyalty to, and faith in, their region by supporting home rule under article 151 was immense. By the end of 1979 only two of the seven regions where the issue had been decided had opted for the normal route.

At the beginning of the following year, Suárez ill-advisedly tried to deter the Andalusians, who had been the first to opt for the more demanding but rewarding path to self-government and whose enthusiasm for autonomy gave them a genuine claim to preferential treatment, from going ahead with their plans. The attempt backfired on him when they overwhelmingly endorsed the autonomy initiative in the referendum called for by the constitution. The government was beginning to get the distinctly uncomfortable feeling that the experiment was getting out of hand.

The other outstanding challenge it faced was to ensure that the transition from dictatorship to democracy was reflected in people's daily lives. Divorce and abortion were still forbidden; the administration, the army, the police, the judiciary, the health and welfare services, the state broadcasting network, and the schools and universities were all imbued with the spirit of a totalitarian regime. A thoroughgoing reform programme was needed to sweep away the authoritarian institutions and practices that had survived in every corner of society. But it soon became apparent that Suárez and his party were incapable of meeting the challenge. To some extent, this was a consequence of the Prime Minister's own personality. All politicians are a blend of ambition and conviction. In Suárez's case, however, the element of belief seemed to be limited to a single premise – that democracy was preferable to dictatorship. Once the transition from one to the other had been completed, he appeared to have no aspiration to inspire him or any ideology to guide him. By contrast, the problem for the UCD was an excess of aspirations and ideologies, many of which were in conflict with one another. The parties which had formed the basis of the union ranged on the conventional European spectrum from a point just to the left of centre to one quite a long way to the right, and contained an ill-assorted mix of the secular and confessional. By the summer of 1980, a gap that was to prove unbridgeable had begun to open up between the Social and Christian Democrats within the UCD over the government's plan to legalize divorce. As for the men and women who had been inserted into the union at Suárez's insistence in early 1977, it was not their differences but what they had in common that proved to be the problem. Having come up through the old Francoist administration, most of them found it genuinely difficult to see the need to do more than tinker with Franco's legacy and, true to their political origins, their first impulse, whenever an apparent misdemeanour or injustice came to the surface, was to cover up rather than investigate. Within the party, they found it difficult to come to terms with the idea that in a democratic institution policy initiatives can come from the rank and file as well as from the top brass.

It was only in the very last months of Suárez's premiership that he began to reveal – or perhaps discover – his true sympathies. But far from making things better, it only made them worse; the Prime Minister was seen to be siding with the most liberal wing of his party, and to lead a coalition as diverse as the UCD from anywhere but close to the centre was virtually impossible. Not surprisingly, therefore, the revolt against Suárez's leadership, when it came, was mounted by the Christian Democrats. But it drew considerable strength from the discontent in every sector of the party over lack of consultation. In January 1981 Suárez resigned from the premiership and in recognition of his services the King bestowed on him the highest honour in his gift: a dukedom.

One of the least satisfactory aspects of Spain's new constitutional arrangements is that an unusually lengthy period is allowed to elapse between governments. It was during the uncertain month between Suárez's resignation and the swearing-in of his successor, Leopoldo Calvo Sotelo, that all Spain's nightmares came true.

From the very beginning, the most serious threat to democracy had come from the predominantly reactionary officers of Spain's armed forces. In 1978 a conspiracy was found to have been hatched in a Madrid café, and on more than one occasion the UCD's defence overlord, Lieutenant-General Manuel Gutiérrez Mellado, was openly insulted by fellow-officers. By early 1981 a group of senior officers had persuaded themselves that the country faced political and economic turmoil and that the unity of Spain, whose preservation had been entrusted to the armed forces by the constitution, was at risk from the government's regional policy.

On the afternoon of 23 February, a lieutenant-colonel in the Civil Guard, Antonio Tejero Molina, who had been demoted for his part in the 1978 plot, marched into Congress with a detachment of his men and proceeded to hold almost every politician of note in Spain at gunpoint for the best part of twenty-four hours. Tejero was what he appeared to be – a naive fanatic. But he was merely the puppet of more senior officers – in particular, the commander of the Motorized Division at Valencia, Lieutenant-General Jaime Milans del Bosch, and a former military instructor and personal secretary to the King, Major-General Alfonso Armada. The coup was cut short mainly because of Juan Carlos's quick wits and steady nerve. Using a specially designed communications centre which he had had installed at the palace to enable him to talk directly to the country's eleven captains-general, he assured them that Tejero's action did not – as the plotters were claiming – have his backing. Any captain-general who showed signs of wavering was commanded to obey.

The abortive coup persuaded the incoming government to try to appease the military. The army was given a token role in the trouble-some Basque country and plans for reform in a number of areas were either diluted or abandoned. Perhaps inevitably, regional policy was the principal casualty.

In July 1982, the UCD and PSOE signed an agreement setting limits to the decentralization process. It stipulated that, with the exception of Andalusia, which was already so far down the road mapped out by article 151 that it was pointless to try to do anything about it, the regions which had yet to be granted a statute should attain home rule in the normal way. What is more, it was agreed that none of them should get more than the minimum powers set out in the constitution. Any other powers granted during the negotiation of the statute would have to be listed under a separate heading and put into cold storage for at least three years from the date the statute came into effect. The only exceptions to this rule were the Canary Islands and Valencia, for which special laws would be passed giving them rather greater powers than the others, and Navarre which – uniquely – had enjoyed a kind of autonomy under Franco and merely required a law to update its existing arrangements.

In just over four years, one of the most centralized nations on earth had been carved into seventeen self-governing administrative units, each with its own flag and capital.

How to describe the resulting set-up was a problem. Although the powers granted to some of the Autonomous Communities were greater than those enjoyed under a number of existing federations, there had not been that ceding of sovereignty which typifies a federation. Nor was the British word 'devolution' appropriate. In many cases, authority had not been handed back to the Autonomous Communities in the way that it might have been to Scotland or Wales, but had been given to a new entity for the first time. Eventually, therefore, the new arrangement came to be known by another grammar-bending term. It was deemed to be an *estado de las autonomías* (a state of autonomies).

Despite the drive towards homogeneity after the coup, the most striking aspect of the new system was the degree to which the powers granted to the autonomous governments varied from region to region. Yet if one were to award points to each of them on the basis of their historical, cultural and linguistic singularity, as well as their degree of enthusiasm for home rule, the result might well be a ranking which would correspond to that of their relative autonomy – the Basques and Catalans pre-eminent, followed at a short distance by the Galicians and Andalusians, and at a longer distance by the Canarians, Valencians and Navarrese, with the rest an equal last.

Somewhat, I think, to their own surprise the Spaniards had provided themselves with a system of regional government which reflected comparatively accurately not only Spain's diversity, but also the degree of variation from the mean in each of its component parts.

Within the UCD the coup initially had the effect of forcing the warring factions to close ranks. But the truce was short-lived and as soon as the government had to face an important policy decision the familiar divisions reappeared. Each time, during the eighteen months between the coup and the next general election in November 1982, the new Prime Minister Calvo Sotelo tried to shift the balance of his programmes to left or right in an attempt to accommodate a rebellious faction on one wing of his party, he would invariably provoke defections from the other. In this way, the UCD spawned a Social Democratic Party (which linked up with the PSOE), a Christian Democratic Party (which linked up with the AP) and a Liberal Party. In 1982, the Duque de Suárez delivered what many saw as the *coup de grâce* to the party he had founded, when he himself left it to found the Centro Democrático Social (CDS). By the time a general election was called, the UCD had lost a third of its deputies in Congress. The loss of its support in the country was even more dramatic and this was in part because of the coup. The Centrists had topped the poll at two elections by selling themselves in much the same way as one might sell a contraceptive – by persuading the electorate that they represented 'the safe way' to democracy. If, voters reasoned, you got a coup even with the UCD in power, what was there to lose by going for broke with a party that had a much more genuine commitment to reform? The door was thus open at last for Felipe González and the PSOE.

Ever since the 1979 election González, like Suárez but with greater success, had been trying to drag his party towards what the polls indicated was the political fulcrum of Spain – the centre-left. At one point he went so far as to resign the leadership in a bid, eventually successful, to force his supporters to drop Marxism from the party's definition of itself. At the 1982 election, standing on a platform of exceptional moderation, the Socialists won over 10 million votes – 4 million more than the Centrists in 1979. Their 201 seats gave them an ample majority in Congress. To the PSOE's left, the Communists' tally of seats fell dramatically from 23 to 5. On the right, the Alianza

Popular emerged as by far the biggest opposition party, with 105 seats. But the UCD, which had run the nation for five years, picked up only 11. And as for Suárez – the mastermind of the transition, the man who had led the nation for much of its eventful journey along the path from dictatorship to democracy – his Centro Democrático Social won precisely 2 seats.

CHAPTER 4

Socialist Spain

On the night of the Socialists' landslide, I was chatting about the result to a Spanish journalist, and at some point I must have described it as a triumph for the left or a defeat for the right. 'Careful,' she said. 'This isn't a victory by the left over the right. It's a victory by the young over the old.'

The Socialists' campaign slogan had been '*El cambio*' ('The change'). But they had not explained, except in the vaguest terms, what it was they intended changing, or how. Virtually their only substantial commitment was to create 800,000 new jobs.

For the most part, the PSOE's moderation was explained to the rest of the world by foreign correspondents reporting the campaign as a purely tactical and pragmatic move. Spanish democracy had just survived an attempted *coup d'état* and the Socialists were keen not to upset reactionary officers in the army. In any case, the economy was in deep recession and the incoming administration would need to generate wealth before it could redistribute it. Thanks to Francoist corporatism, it was already heavily nationalized, so a conventionally socialist programme to extend state ownership was unnecessary.

All this was true. But it missed the point. The PSOE did not need to promise to change anything because its voters were already convinced that they were going to change everything. Just by being who they were – young men and women unencumbered by the intellectual baggage and ballast of a totalitarian past – they would be able to bring about a revolution in Spanish society when they applied to the nation's affairs attitudes regarded as normal in the rest of democratic Europe. Alfonso Guerra, Felipe González's lifelong friend who became his deputy Prime Minister, caught the spirit of the moment when he promised the Socialists would change Spain 'so that even its own mother won't recognize it'. For a while it seemed as if they would.

The Socialists swung into office with dazzling energy and set about implementing reforms in almost every area over which the government exercised control. It was a 'first hundred days' in the style of John F. Kennedy and his team. They soon demonstrated that they had learnt the lessons to be read from the UCD's failure to cope with the military: that the soldiers would tolerate, even admire, toughness. When a general publicly justified the 1981 coup attempt, he was sacked within the hour. They tackled with vigour and resolve the challenge posed when Spain's largest privately owned group, RUMASA, threatened to collapse and bring down much of the banking system with it. In a controversial move, the new government expropriated the group and sold off its component parts.

The promise – and evidence – that the Socialists could give Spain a bright new future helped them to get away with a much-needed shake-out of Spain's older industries. But the job-shedding caused by what was euphemistically known as 'industrial reconversion' led to outbreaks of street violence like that which took place round the doomed Sagunto steel works in Valencia. And instead of creating new jobs, the austerity policies applied by the Socialists pushed up the unemployment rate inexorably – from 16 per cent when the PSOE came into office, to over 22 per cent when it peaked at the beginning of 1986. In a society with virtually no tradition of saving and in which entitlement to unemployment pay was severely limited, the effects were dire. The fall from relative prosperity to utter destitution could take just months, even weeks.

An important reason why the government was able to hold to its course was the cooperation it received from the country's labour leaders. Recognizing that Spain's ability to compete had to be improved ahead of entry into what was then the European Community, the trade unions, sometimes with the employers' representatives, signed a number of agreements in which they accepted wage restraint and job losses. But it was on the implicit (and sometimes explicit) understanding that when the economy began growing again the administration would ensure the wealth generated was more evenly distributed. In particular, the government pledged an increase in the proportion of jobless workers eligible for unemployment pay. The target figure, modest enough by the standards of the rest of Western Europe, was 48 per cent.

The Spaniards who had cast their votes for Felipe González and his team in 1982 had not opted for red-blooded socialism, and it would be unfair to judge their performance in government on that criterion. What the electorate wanted was modernization. But they expected it to be modernization infused with a progressive spirit. During the Socialists' first term of office, painful measures of economic adjustment were effectively counterbalanced by an energetic programme of social reform. They also benefited enormously from the fact that Spain's application to join the EC came to fruition during their mandate. The prospect of entry was – quite rightly, as it turned out – a cause for hope that things would get better. But by the time Spain became a member at the start of 1986, there was a growing realization that the Socialists had brought with them into office a number of attitudes and practices at variance with what many of those who had voted for them had assumed they represented.

When power passes from one party to another in Spain, it is the signal for a clear-out even more comprehensive than that prompted by a change of president in the United States. In the last century, incoming Spanish governments swept clean the administration down to the level of clerk. The practice went into abeyance under Franco because, having packed the bureaucracy with loyalists at the outset, he saw no reason for change every time he reshuffled his cabinet. Nor did it attract much debate under the UCD because to a large extent the Centrists were content to work with men and women who had served Franco. Yet by the time the Socialists came to office, the degree of patronage available to a govern-ment had grown enormously. Franco had set up quasi-independent government organizations galore, and had founded a multitude of state-owned enterprises, all run by political appointees. After the return of democracy, the granting of autonomy to the regions created an additional layer of executive activity between central and local government.

According to *España 2000*, a working policy document published by the PSOE in 1988, 40,000 party members – almost one in every three of the membership – took up 'institutional posts' following the Socialists' victory. More than 26,000 were elected to office as mayors or councillors when the PSOE went on to sweep the board at the 1983 local elections. But most of the rest were appointed.

By giving in to the temptation to put party members in charge of everything from the state holding company to the smallest city museum, the Socialists perpetuated a tradition which diminished their claim to be the party of change. Indeed, it was not long before their critics were drawing pointed comparisons between the PSOE and the old Movimiento Nacional.

With so many of the party's members dependent for their livelihood on the goodwill of its leadership, few were ready to challenge directives from the top. This was particularly significant in view of the immediate past. The Socialists had just seen how in-fighting had wrecked the UCD (which was in fact wound up altogether during the PSOE's first term of office). The lesson they drew was that unity was paramount. Over the next few years the PSOE was to change into one of the most secretive and disciplined parties in Western Europe. The media began to be excluded from all but the opening and closing sessions of its Congresses. Members who spoke out against government policy were speedily and effectively removed from public life. If they had been appointed, they were dismissed. If they were elected, their names were struck off the list of candidates for the next election.

The most striking thing about Spain's new oligarchy was its youth. The Socialists' victory signalled the rise to power, for the first time in Europe, of the 'Generation of '68'. A junior minister at the Interior Ministry found himself giving orders to a policeman who had arrested him for rioting against Franco. Very few of the PSOE's older members had survived in positions of responsibility after González had wrested power from the exiled leadership. The average age of the ministers in his first cabinet was forty-one. One of the directors of the telecommunications monopoly, Telefónica, took his seat on the board at the age of thirty-two.

Another characteristic of Spain's new rulers was the high percentage who came from the educational world. A survey of the delegates to the PSOE's 32nd Congress in 1990 was to show that more than one in five had been teachers at school or university. But many were so young that they had not had time to acquire a reputation before entering full-time politics.

Spain had certainly the youngest, and arguably the cleverest, ruling class in Europe. But it was also the least employable outside politics. A worrying number of Socialist office-holders who subsequently left government went on to set up consultancies and the like which were primarily dependent on official contracts. The effect was to create a crony network that extended far beyond the administration itself.

The power of this new Socialist establishment was considerably reinforced by the absolute parliamentary majority it had just won, and which it was to enjoy for another eleven years. It had always been assumed that a system of proportional representation would give rise to a succession of 'hung' parliaments. So the commission which drafted the 1978 constitution decided that it would be safe, as well as fair, if membership of all sorts of new institutions was determined by the balance of forces in parliament. The Socialists' outright majority thus gave them automatic control over such key bodies as the council which runs the judiciary and the board in charge of the state-owned radio and television network.

The arrival of the Socialists also tilted the balance of influence from north to south in a country where regional differences are profound. Both González and Guerra came from Seville. Several other ministers and numerous officials were drawn from Socialist strongholds in Spain's poor south. It is perhaps no coincidence that southern values should have seized hold of Spain after 1982. Bullfighting began to regain favour. And within a few years of a Seville-born Prime Minister taking office, there was a craze for dancing *sevillanas*.* Seville is to Spain what Naples is to Italy. The Andalusians contributed verve, flair and eloquence to public life. But they also imported a tendency to clannishness and a preoccupation with loss of 'face' that led them to see admitting to mistakes as a sign of weakness rather than strength.

For many Spaniards, the watershed of Socialist rule was the referendum on NATO membership. Spain had joined the alliance, with a minimum of debate, under the UCD in 1982. The Socialists, who had been critical, had pledged in their electoral manifesto to hold a referendum on withdrawal; but before long they were persuaded that Spain's continued membership was a necessary condition of belonging

* The *sevillana* is the dance most often presented to non-Spaniards as flamenco. It is actually on the fringe of the flamenco canon and many authorities consider it not to be flamenco at all.

to the Western 'club'. In the event, the electorate was offered a choice between pulling out of NATO and continued membership outside the integrated military command. But ahead of the referendum, held on 12 March 1986, the full weight of party discipline was brought to bear on members to change their minds – or at least to keep quiet if they were opposed to government policy. The fact that so many Socialists did so disillusioned pro- and anti-NATO voters alike. The poll, though, came up with the result the government wanted. The vote in favour of membership was more than 9 million to less than 7 million.

Against such a background, it was hardly surprising that when a general election was held in June the PSOE lost more than a million votes. The results could well have been worse but for evidence that a leaner, fitter Spanish economy was already benefiting from entry into the EC. Foreign investment had been pouring into the country since the previous year, and unemployment began to fall just a few months before polling.

The Socialists' tally of seats in Congress dropped to 184, but that still left them with a comfortable outright majority. Manuel Fraga's Alianza Popular, standing with allies under a new label, the Coalición Popular, held on to 105 deputies, but failed to pick up any of the seats left vacant by the collapse of the UCD. These, and more, went to Suárez's CDS, whose representation in Congress soared from 2 to 19. The United Left, an alliance which included the Communist Party, but also a number of non-Communist groups and individuals, won 7 seats.

A year of turning points also saw the death of a Socialist who embodied many of the values that had brought the PSOE to power. None of the academics who struggled during the Franco years to impart forward-looking ideas to their students inspired quite as much devotion as Professor Enrique Tierno Galván. By the end of the dictatorship, he was affectionately known throughout Spain as 'the old teacher'. The small party of intellectuals which he had once led merged with the PSOE before it took office. Although some of his acolytes went into government after 1982, he himself remained mayor of Madrid, a post to which he had been elected three years earlier. The record of his administration was exemplary – efficient, imaginative and caring. A million people, one in three of the city's population, turned out for his funeral. It has sometimes been remarked since, in the knowledge of what was to come, that on that day Spain's Socialists buried the spirit of their young ideals along with the body of their old teacher.

During 1986, the rate of growth in the economy averaged 3.3 per cent, and it was accelerating as the year drew to a close. Spain had embarked on a boom fuelled by the effects of joining the EC. Between 1986 and 1991, its economy was to grow faster than that of any other country in the Community.

CHAPTER 5

Not-so-Socialist Spain

Throughout the developed world in the 1980s, the creation and enjoyment of wealth shed the distinctly unfashionable air that had attached to it in the serious seventies. But in Spain, social attitudes towards money underwent a revolution. A nation whose historic poverty had led it to build an entire value system around non-materialistic virtues – dignity, austerity and sobriety – all of a sudden flung itself into the business of earning and spending money with, it seemed, scarcely a backward glance.

Things rarely happen by halves in Spain, but it is worth remembering that its recession had been deeper and longer than any in Western Europe. It had cut deeper because the country's previous leaders, beset by the problems of the transition, had failed to react vigorously enough to the challenges presented by the OPEC oil 'shocks' and the information technology revolution. It had lasted longer because the Spanish economy was still being restructured in the early eighties and was thus in no fit state to benefit from the first post-recessional upswing in world growth: by 1984 average real incomes in Spain were fractionally lower than they had been in 1975 when Franco died. After so many years of deprivation, it is not surprising that Spaniards were in a mood to celebrate prosperity.

What made Spain's eighties boom exceptional, and more entertaining than in many other countries, was the degree to which serious money became associated with style, glamour and, ultimately, scandal. The recently completed Torre Picasso office block on Madrid's Paseo de la Castellana provided Spaniards with a suitably phallic symbol of thrusting eighties values. Mario Conde, the elegant son of a customs official, who became Chairman of Spain's most aristocratic bank,

Banesto, offered them an immaculately groomed archetype of the new, classless financier.

Conde, his associates and rivals were soon taking pride of place in the gossip magazines over the familiar cast of starlets, entertainers and royals. Among the oddest characters to emerge from among the balance-sheets were the 'two Albertos'. Cousins, brothers-in-law, name-sakes and neighbours, Alberto Alcocer and Alberto Cortina delighted in highlighting the similarities between them by wearing identical raincoats. They were also business associates, being Chairman and Vice-Chairman respectively of ConyCon, the centrepiece of a £1.5 billion conglomerate which was to play an active role in the restructuring of Spanish banking in partnership with the Kuwait Investment Office.

Unfortunately for the 'two Albertos', ConyCon was almost wholly owned by their wives, Esther Koplowitz, the Marchioness of Casa Peñalver, and Alicia Koplowitz, the Marchioness of Real Socorro. Their empire was first rocked in 1989 when Alicia Koplowitz broke up with her husband after publicity given to Cortina's relationship with one Marta Chávarri, the daughter of the government's Chief of Protocol and herself a marchioness by marriage. Subsequently, Alcocer's name was linked to that of his secretary and he too separated from his wife, Esther Koplowitz. The sisters then took spectacular revenge by ousting their estranged husbands and taking their places in a boardroom revolution.

Wealth exerted a fascination on every section of society, including the government. One of the Socialists' earliest tasks had been to enlist the support – or at least encourage the tolerance – of the Madrid banking community. In Spain, as in Germany, the banks own and run vast swaths of the rest of the economy. A lot of early introduc-tions were effected by Miguel Boyer, the Socialists' first Economics and Finance Minister. After resigning his job in 1985, he divorced to marry one of the country's foremost socialites, the Philippines-born beauty, Isabel Preysler, formerly wife of the singer Julio Iglesias, and then of a marquess.

Boyer and his new wife, Boyer's successor, Carlos Solchaga, and his wife, together with a number of other Socialist luminaries, came to be photographed regularly at high-society parties in Madrid and in the up-market Costa del Sol resort of Marbella. The press snidely dubbed them '*los beautiful people*'.

The reaction would have been less sour if it had not been Boyer who had demanded such sacrifices of the rest of the population during his three years in charge of the economy, or if, under Solchaga, the benefits of growth had been spread more evenly. But the 800,000 jobs promised by the Socialists in their first manifesto were not created until the middle of 1988; by then, because of a steep rise in the number of job-seekers, unemployment was still running at well over 18 per cent.

It became clear, moreover, that a lot of the wealth so flamboyantly on display was, to a greater or lesser extent, unearned. Much of it stemmed from the sale of family businesses to overseas investors. Much of it derived from speculation in stocks and shares which throughout the period was a much more profitable activity than trying to run a business, because the Socialists kept interest rates high and the national currency strong in order to attract foreign investment. A lot more of the money came from a boom in land and property prices that was also, in large part, attributable to government action. A law passed in the early years of Socialist rule intended to encourage rentals had had the effect of attracting to the housing sector vast sums kept secret from the tax authorities. When this so-called *dinero negro* (black money), invested by tax-dodging upper-middle-class Spaniards, met the ready cash being flourished by foreigners keen to establish themselves in Spain after it 'joined Europe', prices soared – first in Madrid, then in Barcelona, and finally in Seville and the other major regional capitals. In a country with a high level of owner-occupancy, the effect was not as socially disastrous as it might have been. Indeed, it enriched a broad swath of the new middle class. But it also meant that those who lived in the bigger cities and did not have savings invested in bricks and mortar at the start of the boom ended it with precious little chance of ever owning their own home.

What really inspired outrage, though, was the fact that a number of Spain's new rich owed their wealth to straightforward graft: civil servants who had accepted bribes in return for awarding public contracts, elected representatives who had managed to divert public funds into their own pockets. It would have been surprising if such an abrupt surge in the country's economic fortunes had not been accompanied by increased corruption. But the Socialists showed little interest in changing things, and there were even hints that the omission was deliberate: that some in the Socialist leadership believed corruption could actually promote economic growth in Spain by getting round the bottlenecks created by its antiquated bureaucracy.

From the very beginning, González entrusted control of the economy to his party's most conservative faction. Boyer, Solchaga and most of the junior ministers given economic portfolios were drawn from among the so-called 'social democrats'. In the sense that they followed a policy of deficit financing and consented to the use of government spending for job creation by means of public works, they were neo-Keynesians. They allowed more money to be spent on health and education. They pursued tax evasion with greater vigour than their UCD predecessors. And they did not go in for true privatization (under the Socialists, although shares in public enterprises were sold off, the government almost invariably retained effective control).

But what distinguished Spain's 'social democrats' from their counterparts in the rest of Europe, was their reluctance to countenance a policy aimed at the deliberate redistribution of wealth. The consistent goal of economic policy under González's governments was absolute growth, in the expectation that wealth would spill down the social pyramid without the need for government intervention.

For several years, growth – and growth on an impressive scale – is what the Socialists managed to deliver. By 1992, Spain had become about 40 per cent richer in real GDP terms than it had been in 1980. The result was that the majority of its people were considerably better off than they had ever been before.

The tough-minded economic policy adopted by Spain's 'social democrats' was similar to what was tried in other parts of Western Europe in the late eighties. Elsewhere, though, *laissez-faire* doctrines were being applied to countries that already had comprehensive systems of welfare provision. González's team began pursuing similar policies in a nation where only slightly more than a quarter of the jobless were entitled to full unemployment pay. The promises made to the trade unions in this respect were forgotten after the growth rate leapt.

The highest priority in government planning was given to enhancing the country's infrastructure. This was partly to create new jobs, partly to enhance Spain's competitiveness, but also partly to meet the demands imposed on the country by the events planned for 1992.

Seville was to be the venue for the world fair, Expo '92. Barcelona was due to host the Olympic Games. Madrid was going to be European Capital of Culture. And events in various parts of Spain were scheduled to mark the 500th anniversary of Columbus's voyage to America.

In mid-1988, the González government was confronted with a potentially catastrophic scandal. Soon after the Socialists came to power, an organization calling itself the Grupos Anti-Terroristas de Liberación (GAL) had made itself known and gone on to claim responsibility for the murder of twenty-four people in the south-west of France. Most of its victims were exiled members or supporters of the Basque terrorist movement, ETA. But some were not.

Subsequent press investigations, notably that carried out by the newspaper *Diario 16*, accumulated a wealth of evidence to suggest that GAL had been organized by two Spanish detectives, Chief Superintendent José Amedo and Inspector Michel Domínguez. Both men were committed to prison to await trial. But the key question of whether they were acting on their own initiative or on orders from above remained a mystery. The chief of the Spanish police testified that a trip on which they were alleged to have recruited mercenaries had been paid for out of secret government funds. But attempts by the investigating magistrate, Baltasar Garzón, to find out more about these funds were blocked by the Interior Ministry. The result was a showdown between the judiciary and the executive of a kind never before seen in democratic Spain. In the end, though, the council which administers the legal system backed down, and the government's claim to executive privilege was upheld.

The GAL affair came in the wake of a succession of petty scandals involving Socialist politicians and officials. In all of them, the issue at stake was the Socialists' inability, or unwillingness, to draw a line between what they were entitled to in their private and official capacities. Concern had first been voiced as early as 1985 when Felipe González took his family holiday on board Franco's old yacht, the *Azor*. It revived when his deputy, Alfonso Guerra, commandeered a military jet to avoid a traffic jam on the way back from his Easter holidays. Then in October 1988 the government-appointed head of the state radio and television monopoly, Pilar Miró, was accused of using the corporation's money to buy clothes and jewellery for herself and presents for her friends.

Ms Miró was later acquitted of all the charges against her, but it was against a background of rising public anger that the trade unions, having made numerous unsuccessful attempts to get the government to honour its earlier pledges, called for a one-day general strike on 14 December 1988. The outcome exceeded all forecasts, including the trade unions' own. Some two-thirds of the nation's work-force stayed out. The government's response was to allow a special debate to be held in the Cortes at which González explained why it was impossible to satisfy most of the unions' demands. A youth employment scheme to which they had objected was withdrawn. And that appeared to be that. However, after allowing a decent interval to elapse, Felipe González's ministers very slowly and cautiously resumed contact with the unions and, over a period of many months in lengthy and tangled negotiations, the government gave in to many of their demands.

Not that the Socialists had a lot to worry about from their political rivals. Communism was being discredited and dismantled, and the parties to the right of the PSOE were both led by men whose prospects were undermined by their Francoist past. Adolfo Suárez seemed unable to act on the notion that a democratic politician must do more than go to the hustings at election time. Manuel Fraga had played an almost equally valuable part in the transition. By throwing himself into the democratic game with evident gusto, he had persuaded most of the more reactionary elements in society that they had nothing to fear from it. But his authoritarian manner was a constant reminder of his totalitarian past. After the 1986 election, he and his party had come to the reluctant conclusion that they would never win power under his leadership. After unsuccessfully trying out two candidates to succeed him, he opted in 1989 for José María Aznar, a young former tax inspector who had put in an impressive performance as head of the regional government in Old Castile and León.

In the run-up to the general election of October 1989, the Socialists' message to the electorate was unchanged. Felipe González told a rally that Spain was enjoying greater international prestige than at any time since the reign of the Emperor Charles V in the sixteenth century. His claim was possibly true, but it brought criticism that he and his ministers were becoming prey to delusions of grandeur. In a newspaper interview, the Communist leader Julio Anguita also resorted for inspiration to Spain's Golden Age, but compared the state of the country to a Habsburg caravel – its glitteringly decorated façade concealing the rottenness within.

His critique of the government seemed to strike a chord with voters, for when the results started coming in it was clear that the United Left had defied a Europe-wide trend away from Marxism. It doubled its share of the vote and increased the number of its seats in Congress from 7 to 17, overtaking the CDS whose representation fell from 19 to 14. The United Left's success robbed the Socialists of an overall majority. The PSOE was left with exactly half the seats in Congress, although it remained able to pass legislation without support from the opposition.

On share of the vote, Aznar's conservative party, renamed the Partido Popular, did slightly worse than the Coalición Popular had done under Fraga in 1986. But it picked up an extra seat and the result was seen as reflecting well on a leader who had only been confirmed after the campaign began. When Fraga was elected head of the regional government in his native Galicia in December, he was able to bow out again in the knowledge that his party had at last found a leader who could credibly offer moderate conservatism to the electorate.

Polling was scarcely over when the Socialists found themselves faced with a scandal of quite different dimensions to the Miró affair. Alfonso Guerra's younger brother, Juan, was shown to have occupied a government office in Seville for several years, during which he at no time held a government appointment. Allegations were also made that he had used his links with the administration to amass a personal fortune by peddling influence.* His brother stepped down as deputy Prime Minister – though not as deputy General Secretary of the party – at the start of 1991. His departure deepened a rift which had been growing for some time between the Socialist party machine, which remained loyal to the rhetoric, if not the practice, of orthodox socialism, and a Socialist government increasingly seduced by neo-liberalism.

* Juan Guerra was acquitted in four of the cases subsequently brought against him. In a fifth trial involving violation of planning laws he was barred from public office for six years. The sixth case led to his being given a two-year jail sentence – later suspended – for tax fraud.

The growth of a new class of intermediaries had been rumoured for some time, and in 1989 a deputy in the Madrid regional parliament had claimed he had been offered 100 million pesetas to change his allegiance by a 'Mr Fixit' operating on behalf of the PP. Juan Guerra was so intimately linked to the highest level of the ruling party that questions began to be asked about whether he was in fact acting on his own, or the PSOE's, behalf.

Anyone who had attended its election rallies, equipped with state-of-the-art sound and lighting effects, could be forgiven for wondering how a party ostensibly belonging to the workers could possibly afford them. Part of the answer was that the PSOE, in common with other Spanish parties, was running up huge debts. But there were growing suspicions that it was not the whole answer.

In theory, the PSOE was bound by the provisions of a law on party financing which had come into effect in 1987 and which made it illegal for political parties to draw funds from any source other than public subsidies, members' dues and strictly limited donations. In practice, the only check was a tribunal whose members were appointed by a parliament in which the PSOE enjoyed an overall majority.

In the event, though, it was the PP, and not the PSOE, which was first caught up in a cash-for-favours scandal. Early in 1990, transcripts of telephone conversations recorded by the police – the by-product of an investigation into drug trafficking – were leaked to the press. They revealed senior officials of the PP, including two successive national treasurers, discussing in language more appropriate to the Mafia how they 'collected' from property developers for the privilege of not having their projects obstructed at local and regional council level.*

It was inevitably suspected that the affair had been brought to light at the instigation of the Socialists. If that was the case, then the edge they gained was short-lived, for in 1991 the so-called FILESA affair burst on to the front pages of the newspapers. It arose when an aggrieved Chilean accountant by the name of Carlos Alberto van Schouwen took out a case for wrongful dismissal against the owners of a Barcelona-based group of companies of which FILESA formed part. In the documents he presented to the court, he asserted that

---

* The case against them was subsequently dismissed after the tapes were ruled to constitute inadmissible evidence.

the real business of the group was to raise funds for the PSOE by charging big companies for non-existent consultancy work.

By the time the Socialists had to go to the country again in the local elections of May 1991, the opinion polls carried two alarming messages for them. One was that the right-wing vote was consolidating behind Aznar and his remodelled PP. The CDS put up a disastrous showing at the local elections, and immediately afterwards the party's leader, Adolfo Suárez, resigned. It was the beginning of the end of his involvement in politics.

The other warning sign for the PSOE was that its supporters were increasingly to be found among the least politically aware sections of the population. More and more, the Socialists found themselves reliant on elderly, rural voters, especially those in the poor south. Their vulnerability was underlined when they were ousted from power in Seville, the home town of González, Guerra and several of their closest associates, and a city on which the Socialists were lavishing cash in order to prepare it for its role during 1992.

'Spain's year', as it began to be known, had come about almost by accident. Although Expo '92 was identified with the Socialists because of their leaders' links with Seville, it was first conceived – before they came to power – as one half of a unique twin-based world fair, the rest of which was to have been held in Chicago to mark the 500th anniversary of the 'discovery' of America. When the Americans backed out, the Spanish decided to press ahead.

At the same time, the authorities in Barcelona were pursuing an entirely separate initiative to host the Olympics. When they succeeded, it seemed only fitting that Brussels should offer Madrid the consolation prize of being European Capital of Culture during 1992. Thus Spain found itself responsible for staging a unique extravaganza.

Certainly, 1992 allowed Spain to make a spectacular re-entry after the isolation of the Franco years. But I think it is fair to say that had it not been for the resoundingly successful Barcelona Olympics, Spain might have been judged to have tripped and stumbled a bit as it stepped back on to the world stage. The best that can be said of Madrid's stint as European Capital of Culture is that it was unexceptional. Both Expo '92 and the Quincentenary proved extraordinarily accident-prone. A specially commissioned replica of the first vessel to circumnavigate the world sank as it left the slipway. The flotilla that retraced Columbus's voyage to the New World suffered a mutiny. Expo '92's centrepiece pavilion burned to the ground. And on the night before the exhibition opened, police opened fire with live ammunition on demonstrators in Seville, thereby recalling precisely the image of Spain that the events of 1992 were meant to dispel.

The Prime Minister, Felipe González, said when it was all over that the Spaniards had laid the ghost of Spanish inefficiency and shown they were as capable as anyone of staging major events. In fact, I suspect that Spain's success the year before in hosting the Middle East peace conference at short notice did far more to convince the world of the Spaniards' abilities as organizers.

What did come as a revelation was the abruptness with which Spain's *fiesta* ended. Even before 1992 was over, the country was plunging into recession. As if symbolically, the Kuwait Investment Office, the biggest single foreign investor in Spain's eighties boom, closed down its operations after its holding company applied for receivership.* In fact, the boom had run out of steam much earlier – some would argue as early as 1989. What the government then did was to pass a couple of expansionary budgets designed to get the country ready for 1992. A lot of building was done, which helped to generate economic activity in general and keep people off the dole queues in particular. But the collapse, when it came, was correspondingly more abrupt.

What I wrote in an earlier chapter about the rapid growth between 1961 and 1973 was also true of the brief but giddy boom of the eighties: what it changed least was the shape of the economy. By the early nineties, Spain still suffered from the traditional problems of high unemployment and costly borrowing. Investment had been considerable, but a lot of it had been speculative rather than productive. In fact, after Spain joined the European Exchange Rate Mechanism in mid-1989, holding pesetas became a one-way bet – the real rate of return on deposits was greater than the maximum depreciation allowed by the ERM. A lot of firms were modernized, often after being taken over by foreigners, but industry as a whole

---

* The KIO has since said it lost $1 billion in Spain.

had not resolved the problem of how to compete effectively with European rivals.

In many areas, improvements in the quality or quantity of output had been offset by a rise in the cost of labour. Spain was no longer a cheap place for manufacturing, certainly not compared with the new democracies of Eastern and central Europe. Nor, by and large, could it offer products to match those of the more advanced nations of Western Europe.

The government's travails were compounded by the continuing investigation into FILESA. In 1993, government auditors submitted a 500-page report to the Supreme Court which upheld all the main accusations and detailed irregular payments totalling 997 million pesetas (£5 million or $7.5 million). González reacted by threatening to resign unless someone in the party agreed to take responsibility. When the party bosses led by Guerra refused to oblige, the Prime Minister called an election instead.

The 1993 general election campaign was the most exciting Spain had yet witnessed. It began with a sensation. It emerged that the candidate who was to stand immediately behind Felipe González as no. 2 on the Socialists' slate in Madrid was to be Judge Baltasar Garzón, the same investigating magistrate whose probing into the GAL affair had caused the government such embarrassment five years earlier. Critics of the government were incensed and bitterly accused the judge of bartering his moral authority for personal advancement.

During the campaign, polls showed the lead being swapped almost daily between the two leading parties. Such was the pace on the hustings that the leader of the Communist-dominated United Left, Julio Anguita, ended the campaign in a hospital bed. It was also the first general election contest in Spain to see American-style television debates. In the first of them Felipe González, who had been thought unbeatable in any sort of face-to-face confrontation, was thrown into confusion by a better-prepared José María Aznar. It was only in the second of their two encounters that the Prime Minister regained the upper hand.

What seemed to tip the balance in the last few days before polling, though, was the Socialists' resort to blatant scare tactics. At various times, they compared Aznar with Hitler, Franco, and the leader of the abortive

1981 coup. Their constant emphasis on the need to support the 'left' against the 'right' stemmed the loss of votes to Anguita's alliance.

In the event, the PSOE won 159 seats in Congress against the PP's 141. The United Left, with 18, gained only one seat more than in 1989. The CDS did not win any.

On the night of the election, the Prime Minister promised his jubilant supporters '*un cambio sobre el cambio*' ('a change on top of the change'). It was a conscious invocation of the spirit of '82, and indeed the figures implied that the PSOE had won the support of a lot of erstwhile abstainers who had voted for the PSOE eleven years earlier in order to prevent a return to right-wing dictatorship, and were persuaded they ought to do so again.

However, everything González did afterwards suggested that, having solicited and secured the left-of-centre vote, he was determined to stick to right-of-centre policies. The election left the Socialists seventeen seats short of an absolute majority. González ruled out a coalition with the United Left on the grounds that the former Communists' opposition to the treaty of European Union, signed at Maastricht the year before, made them incompatible. He opted instead for a minority government relying on *ad hoc* support from the main Catalan nationalist party, which is centre-right. His new cabinet was one purged of the more orthodox faction loyal to his erstwhile friend and deputy, Alfonso Guerra. A third of its members did not even belong to the PSOE. The 'independents' in the cabinet did not, however, include Baltasar Garzón, the judge whose 'Mr Clean' image may even have saved Felipe González from outright defeat. Garzón was instead given the distinctly modest consolation prize of being allowed to run the national drugs programme.

The cabinet formed in 1993 included some talented ministers who drafted some useful legislation, some of it referred to later in this book. But the merits and demerits of the government's programme soon became irrelevant, because almost immediately it was swamped by a tide of scandal.

Some of the controversy was not of the Socialists' making. But it involved men who embodied the cash-and-glamour spirit of the González years. Six months after the election, the Bank of Spain took control of Mario Conde's bank, Banesto, after an audit revealed a vast shortfall. Then, in May 1994, police arrested Mariano Rubio, the man who had run the Bank of Spain for most of the Socialist era. He and his beautiful wife, the Uruguayan author, Carmen Posadas, had done as much as anyone to sprinkle the period with a certain stylish allure. Rubio was charged with making some $1 million (£650,000) from <u>insider trading</u>. The accusations levelled at him were particularly shocking to the ordinary Spaniards because he was meant to have been among those safeguarding the integrity of their financial system. His signature was on their banknotes.* By the end of 1994, Conde too was behind bars, as was the Kuwait Investment Office's representative, Javier de la Rosa.† Rubio's fall eventually brought down the former finance minister, Carlos Solchaga, who left parliament.

Almost every day, it seemed, the press carried new allegations of corruption. The head of the agency responsible for printing official publications was accused of taking kickbacks from paper suppliers and later of fraudulently obtaining valuable paintings by pretending on the telephone to be the Queen or Felipe González's wife. But nothing came even remotely close in scale to the greed of – irony of ironies – the man put in charge of the Civil Guard, a body founded in the early nineteenth century which, though often criticized for its severity, had always prided itself on a certain austere rectitude. In the seven years following his appointment in 1986, Luis Roldán amassed a personal fortune of 5 billion pesetas ($40 million or £26 million) in kickbacks on the construction of Civil Guard premises and facilities. After being dismissed from his post, Roldán fled the country and was eventually tracked down in Laos.‡ The scandal prompted

* Rubio was released on bail and his case never came to trial. Posadas, who satirized the antics of Spain's jet set in her writings, won the country's top literary prize in 1998. Her husband died of cancer the following year.

† Conde was found guilty of fraud and embezzlement in 2000 and sentenced to eighteen years in jail. In 2005 he was allowed out on day release. De la Rosa was remanded in custody until 1995 when he was released on bail. In 1998, he was put in prison for a further fifteen months while an investigation was carried out into the collapse of KIO's operations. In 2002, he was given a twenty-month sentence for attempted fraud, and in 2004 another of five and a half years for embezzlement. At the time of writing he was again on trial.

‡ After being extradited to Spain, Roldán was tried and in 1998 sentenced to twenty-eight years in prison. His chief alleged accomplice, one Francisco Paesa, who was accused of laundering more than $125 million (£80 million) in bribes and illegal commissions, also fled Spain. In 1999, he was reported to have died in a Thai monastery. In 2005 he was discovered to be living in Paris. By then, the offences of which he was accused had been 'timed out' by a statute of limitations.

the resignation of the then Interior Minister, Antonio Asunción. But worse – much worse – was just around the corner. In May 1994, the formidable Judge Garzón decided to bring to an end his brief and disillusioning experience of politics and return to the bench. Within months, he had reopened the so-called GAL case,* a fundamentally more serious affair than the instances that had emerged of corrupt personal enrichment or illegal party funding. The GAL case was about death squads, not ill-gotten cash. And while it could be argued that the other scandals derived from individual 'rotten apples' or the need of a left-wing party for financing to which its right-wing rival would have had easier access because of its contacts in the business world, the GAL case suggested an ingrained contempt for the law at the highest levels in government.

That, at least, was the suggestion. There was still no proof. On the contrary, there was a court ruling that the suggestion was unfounded. In 1991, the two police officers directly involved in organizing the GAL, Amedo and Domínguez, had been tried, convicted and sentenced to more than 100 years each. But the judges had absolved the state of any responsibility for, or involvement in, the detectives' activities. Aware, no doubt, that the two men felt they had been made scapegoats, Garzón called them to give evidence in another case. They seized the opportunity to incriminate a string of more senior officers and politically appointed officials. With the evidence he collected from these new suspects, Garzón in January 1996 brought charges against the Interior Minister at the time of the GAL murders, José Barrionuevo.†

By then, further evidence had emerged of the Socialists' complicity in a 'dirty war' against ETA. It transpired that in 1983 two suspected terrorists had been kidnapped in France and brought across the border to San Sebastián where they were tortured to death by Civil Guards under the command of one Colonel Enrique Rodríguez Galindo. Yet,

* See above, p. 57.

† He and another Socialist Interior Minister were tried and eventually found not guilty on the grounds that there was no proof either had known about the use of government cash to fund the GAL. However, Barrionuevo spent time in jail and a number of politically appointed officials, including a junior minister, were convicted and sentenced to prison.

some months after the facts came to light, Galindo was promoted to general without the government objecting.*

It was not the only evidence that parts of the state apparatus had slipped out of the government's control. Officers of the intelligence service, CESID, were found to have eavesdropped illegally on a number of public figures, including the King. What is more, the service's deputy chief had handed over some of the tapes to the disgraced banker, Mario Conde, allegedly so he could try to wriggle out of his predicament. The resulting scandal forced out González's Defence Minister and his deputy Prime Minister, Narcís Serra, one of the longest-serving and most highly respected members of his team.

Sleazy bureaucrats. Crooked bankers. Death squads run with the connivance of the authorities. And sections of the intelligence service plotting against the government. Spain, by the middle of 1995, was starting to look alarmingly like one of the less stable Latin American republics. The Socialists had suffered a string of setbacks in European, regional and local elections, and their low standing in the eyes of the electorate was beginning to be transferred by association to the Catalan nationalists who were keeping them in power. In September, Jordi Pujol, the President of the *Generalitat*, seized on a rift over abortion law to withdraw his support, forcing Felipe González to bring forward the date of the general election, which he set for the following March.

In retrospect, it is hard to believe the 1996 general election was any sort of a contest. Apart from the scandals enveloping the Socialists, the conservatives enjoyed the not inconsiderable advantage bestowed by an unsuccessful terrorist attack the year before on their leader, José María Aznar. An unimposing man with a Chaplinesque moustache (it hides a scar on his upper lip), Aznar had shown himself to be pugnacious and persistent. But he had failed to inspire much affection or respect among voters. ETA's car bomb generated widespread sympathy for its intended victim and Aznar's reaction to it, coolly taking command

---

* Galindo was subsequently tried, convicted and given a sentence of more than seventy-five years. He entered prison in 2000, but four years later after suffering serious heart problems he was released from jail to serve out the rest of his sentence under house arrest.

in the seconds that followed the explosion, showed he possessed real qualities of leadership. People began to see him in a new light.

The campaign should have been a walkover for the PP. But it was not. The Socialists resorted to even cruder scare tactics than in 1993. And they worked. Up to a point. The conservatives failed to win an outright majority. With 156 seats, they had only 15 more than the Socialists and it was clear they would be as dependent as their predecessors on the support of the Catalan nationalists. The United Left, which had been expected to profit handsomely from the Socialist collapse, won just 21 seats.

The results underlined what opinion polls had consistently suggested: notwithstanding the spectacular venality of the Socialists, their abuse of power and disregard for legality, the centre of political gravity in modern Spain remained stubbornly lodged at a point just to the left of centre. Large numbers of voters were still profoundly reluctant to vote for a right they continued to associate with Francoism. At the same time, if the conduct of moderate left-wing politicians became so utterly reprehensible as to be impossible to ignore, these progressive, moderate Spaniards were more willing to abstain than to give their votes to an ideologically discredited far left.

A vast mass of votes that naturally belonged to the Socialists disappeared in 1996. It remained hidden for a further eight years. But when it resurfaced, it did so with an effect that was to send shock waves around the world.

CHAPTER 6

Conservative Spain

The first challenge facing José María Aznar was how to create a stable government out of the slim majority he had been given by the voters. In arduous talks with the Catalan nationalist leader, Jordi Pujol, he held out for a more binding deal than his predecessor had achieved. Pujol again baulked at a coalition, but agreed to provide the PP government with a guarantee of support in parliament that was to enable it to see out an entire, four-year legislature.

The new Prime Minister showed similar strength of purpose on the issue that was to dominate his first term: the forthcoming introduction of the euro. Four years earlier at Maastricht, the European Union's member states had agreed to a set of entry conditions designed to ensure the stability of the proposed new currency. It had been widely assumed they would prove too demanding for the less robust economies of southern Europe, which were often in those days referred to patronizingly as 'Club Med'. By the time the PP came to power, for example, Spain met only one of the five criteria. It looked highly likely that, together with Italy, Spain would agree to go into a second group whose members would be given more time to get their affairs in order before adopting the single currency. Six months after the election in Spain, the then Italian Prime Minister, Romano Prodi, flew to Madrid to make sure this was indeed the case. He got the shock of his political life.

Aznar was aware by then that neighbouring Portugal had a good chance of meeting the Maastricht criteria despite – or rather, because of – the fact that it was poorer. Portugal's welfare spending was so low it would have little difficulty fulfilling the key condition, which was that candidates should have a budget deficit of less than 3 per cent of their gross domestic product. Aznar realized that if little Portugal – a country on which Spaniards had always rather looked down – were to go into the euro while Spain was kept out, it would deal a blow to the nation's pride from which he would never recover.

He told his Italian guest bluntly that his government intended to do everything in its power to ensure the Spanish entered the new arrangements at the beginning with their heads held high, and that if the Italians preferred to slink in later, well then that was their affair.

Aznar's bold decision was to bring huge benefits to the economy, his government and his party. The need for 'convergence' with the leading economies of the EU allowed him to demand and secure sacrifices from his compatriots that put the economy on a much sounder footing and stimulated rapid, steady growth.

The most important of these sacrifices took shape in a deal brokered by the government between the unions and employers in 1997 that freed up the labour market. The two sides agreed to a new sort of employment contract. It was originally intended for first-time employees and older workers who otherwise faced indefinite unemployment, but it gradually became standard. The new contract offered employers two important incentives to take on extra workers. It eased the burden of the social security contributions that they had to make on behalf of their new workers in the period immediately following their engagement. And if, later on, any of the workers was laid off or fired, then he or she was entitled to a more modest pay-off from the employer than that offered under the old rules.

As Charles Powell has noted in his history of contemporary Spain,* the real breakthrough was that a new generation of union leaders had accepted something their predecessors never would – that easier firing made for easier hiring, and would eventually reduce unemployment, the scourge of post-Francoist Spain. This is precisely what happened. The jobless rate fell from 23 to 15 per cent between 1996 and 2000 and, among the young, the effects were even more dramatic. The proportion of under-25s without a job plunged from 42 per cent at the start of Aznar's first administration to 26 per cent by the end. Lower unemployment, in turn, cut the bill for welfare spending and increased the volume of contributions to the social security system, helping the government to pull off the remarkable feat of cutting

* *España en democracia, 1975–2000*, Plaza & Janés Editores, Barcelona, 2001.

income tax rates during a period in which its top priority was to reduce the budget deficit. Lower taxes, in turn, fuelled economic growth that was already being stimulated by other effects of the drive for convergence: lower inflation, lower borrowing and lower interest rates. In the four years from 1997 to 2000, annual economic growth never fell below 4 per cent.

A lot of Spaniards who voted for the left in 1996 would no doubt have been ready to believe that a conservative government could deliver strong economic growth by applying neo-liberal remedies. But polls showed that what worried many was the fear that an incoming PP government would slash welfare benefits and pensions. Aznar wisely chose to prove that fear unfounded. On the contrary, he agreed to raise minimum pensions and tie future annual revisions to increases in the cost of living.

The PP was beginning to give substance to its claim that it could reach across class divisions to be the party of the majority of Spaniards. One question, however, that was asked from the outset was how many Basques that would include. ETA's attempt to kill him had not surprisingly made Aznar deeply hostile to radical Basque nationalism. It soon became clear that his government's policy would be to attempt to stamp out armed separatism without any sort of negotiation with its political representatives. In 1997, ETA appeared to play right into his hands with a spectacularly cold-blooded action – the kidnapping of a young PP town councillor from the Basque country, Miguel Angel Blanco. His abduction brought people throughout Spain on to the streets in unprecedented numbers to beg for his life. When the terrorists went ahead and murdered him instead, many of those demonstrators reached the conclusion that the government's hardline policy was justified.

One reason why the Spanish had been ready to hand the leadership of the country to a colourless, slightly pompous former tax inspector was that he was untainted with corruption. After the excesses of the Socialist era, Spain needed to have its public life cleaned up. It also needed its democracy strengthened and deepened. Aznar and his party continued to use state-owned television in the same, shamelessly partisan way as had the Socialists. But he showed more respect for parliament than his predecessor had done, and the overall level of controversy over corruption fell off sharply during Aznar's first government.

As was to be expected, the pace of privatization picked up and there was criticism of the way the government often seemed to put members and friends of the PP in charge of the resulting, publicly quoted corporations. One such nominee, the Telefónica chairman, Juan Villalonga, who had been at school with Aznar, even found himself at the centre of a full-blown scandal over alleged insider trading. But Villalonga denied any wrongdoing and stock market regulators found no evidence of irregularity.*

That did not stop the Socialists putting the affair at the centre of political debate. But then they were keenly in need of an issue to distract attention from their own internal wrangles. A year after their defeat in the general election, Felipe González had resigned the leadership. It went first to a former minister, Joaquín Almunia, but the following year he was replaced by another leading figure from the González era, José Borrell. In 1999, he too stepped down after two of his former collaborators were charged with financial wrongdoing. Borrell acknowledged 'errors of judgement' and the party's powerbrokers gave the leadership back to Almunia, whom polls had suggested would be a less popular candidate.

For all that, the common expectation before the 2000 general election was that the PP would not emerge with an outright parliamentary majority. And, perhaps because of that, it did. The turnout was low by Spanish standards. Analysts concluded that a lot of left-leaning voters had taken it for granted that the PP would win without an absolute majority and so, deciding their votes were unnecessary, had stayed at home. In fact, when the results were in, the conservatives had 184 seats to the Socialists' 125. The United Left won eight. Aznar and his conservatives could govern alone. The vote put an end to seven years in which the centre-right Catalan nationalists had been in the comfortable position of holding the keys to power without having to take responsibility for the actions of the government. The 2000 election also established the PP for the first time as a truly nationwide party. Even in Andalusia, the Socialists' stronghold, the conservatives came out top in four of the eight provinces.

The first effect of their unexpectedly decisive victory was felt in the PSOE. Almunia gave up the leadership and a new congress was

*In July 2000, it was reported that they had restarted their inquiry and Villalonga resigned. A week later, the investigation was called off.

called to find a successor. Instead of choosing yet another former González lieutenant, the party opted for a clean break with the past and plumped for José Luis Rodríguez Zapatero, who had yet to turn forty and was virtually unknown to the general public. Zapatero had been born in Valladolid and educated in León, where he worked briefly as a university lecturer before turning to full-time politics. Like Aznar, therefore, he was a product of Spain's austere heartland, the northern Meseta. But, unlike the Prime Minister, the new leader of the opposition had a relaxed manner and a ready smile.

When he came into office, José María Aznar had promised to make Spanish politics boring. For most of his first term, he was as good as his word. But his next spell in office was to be a very different affair. He and his ministers were to lurch from one drama to the next until they met their fate in a nightmare of carnage and reproach.

Aznar's hatred of ETA terrorism was widely shared. But it seemed gradually to infect the whole of his thinking about regional nationalism. He became impatient to draw a line under the process of decentralization that had begun after Franco's death, and increasingly prone to see the shadow of violent separatism in any suggestion that it be extended. Those who were not Spanish centralists, but had never contemplated a resort to arms, found his attitude deeply offensive. Back in the mid-nineties, Aznar and Pujol had sometimes chatted together in Catalan. By the early 2000s, they were not on speaking terms of any kind.

It was just one example of a new inflexibility that was apparent in many areas of public life. The government's relations with the trade unions deteriorated to the point at which in 2002 it was confronted with a general strike against plans for a reform of unemployment benefit. The plans were subsequently withdrawn. Its dealings with the opposition also became progressively testier, partly because the cabinet took to ramming controversial legislation through parliament by attaching it to the budget.

Aznar's own personality became an issue of growing importance as his second term of office progressed. Pedro J. Ramírez, the editor of *El Mundo*, which was generally supportive of the PP, saw the change at first hand. He later described how 'The consummate reformer, aware of his limitations, who weighed up each of his moves after listening to this one and that, and who was not afraid to admit and rectify mistakes, changed gradually into a sulky puritan, disdainful of criticism.'

That creeping haughtiness which Ramírez saw in Aznar spread to other members of the cabinet. Freed by their outright parliamentary majority to act as they pleased, the conservatives became increasingly arrogant and more aggressively rightist. In many respects, they continued to make a good job of governing Spain. If the rate of economic growth dropped off in their second term, that was largely because of a Europe-wide downturn. Spain, throughout the period from 2001 to 2004, continued to out-perform the EU average by a handsome margin.

Many Spaniards were ready to acknowledge that their government was made up of competent men and women. The problem – a big problem in a democracy – was that growing numbers of voters found them insufferable. And not only that. Many began to suspect that the people running the country were not keeping them informed. This was particularly the case when things went wrong, when it seemed always to be the fault of someone, or something, else.

The issue of relations between the government and the governed was first brought to a head by Spain's biggest environmental disaster. On the afternoon of 13 November 2002, the *Prestige*, a patched-up oil tanker carrying 60,000 tonnes of crude, began to leak its cargo into the waters off the coast of Galicia. The Galician premier, Manuel Fraga, and the cabinet minister responsible, Francisco Alvarez-Cascos, both learned of the disaster while out shooting – an unfortunate reminder of the Franco era when the *Caudillo* spent much of his spare time with a shotgun in his hand. That would no doubt have been forgotten had the authorities subsequently managed the crisis with skill and sensitivity. They did anything but. They gave an impression of trying to play down the gravity of the accident. They changed their minds. They seemed always to be one step behind the pace of events. And, finally, Spaniards became so incensed with their performance that they took matters into their own hands, first in Santiago de Compostela in a demonstration called by an *ad hoc* group calling itself *Nunca Máis* (Galician for 'Never Again'); then in other Spanish cities. Most humiliatingly for the government, the demonstrations spawned a volunteer movement to clean the Galician coastline, an operation the authorities seemed incapable of organizing by themselves. All over the country, young men and women appeared by the roadsides holding placards seeking a lift to the north-west to join others shovelling tar off the beaches.

The reaction to the *Prestige* disaster might have been less forceful had it not been for the fact that so many Spaniards already felt their voices were not being listened to on the overriding international question of the day. Polls showed a growing majority of Spaniards was opposed to war in Iraq. Like many Europeans, they were unconvinced of a link between Osama bin Laden's fundamentalist terrorism and Saddam Hussein's secular authoritarianism. *lack of true representations*

José María Aznar, on the other hand, was soon passionately committed to the view that the Iraqi leader was making weapons of mass destruction that could one day fall into the hands of al-Qaida. His critics always suspected he believed what it suited him to believe. Right from the start of his mandate, he had wanted closer links with the United States and made considerable progress towards achieving them. When, in 2001, George W. Bush made his first visit to Europe after being elected President, he began his tour in Madrid (though the compliment he implicitly paid his host was somewhat undermined when he referred to him as Prime Minister 'Anzar').

Gradually, moreover, it became apparent that the PP's leadership saw better relations with the US, not just as an end in themselves, but as a means of securing a more prominent role for his country in world affairs. 'Spain must play in the first division, not in the second, having others decide for it,' Aznar once told an interviewer. This was never going to be an easy policy to sell to the electorate. Franco's foreign policy accustomed Spaniards to international isolation. He kept them out of the Second World War. He gave up his country's few colonies without a fight. And his regime's pariah status in the West as well as the East meant it could play no more than a passive role in the Cold War. Since his death, many Spaniards have come to accept that full membership of the international community requires Spain to take a more active part in world affairs. But surprisingly large numbers are unconvinced that that role has to be played at America's side. The US prompts grim historical memories among many Spaniards. Traditionalists recall that it was the US that put an end to the Spanish empire in 1898, wiped out its fleet and deprived it of Cuba, Puerto Rico and the Philippines. Progressives remember it was Washington that helped Franco out of his international isolation in exchange for military bases in Spain. And because of close ties with Latin America, Spaniards have tended to be more aware than other Europeans of the ugly sides of US foreign policy there.

Misgivings are just as strong about America's role in the Middle East. Casting around for allies, Franco forged strong links with the Arab world, and sympathy with the Palestinian cause was widespread in Spain long before it developed in the rest of Europe. As war approached, polls found that more than 80 per cent of Spaniards, including many PP voters, were opposed to an invasion of Iraq. Even Spain's ambassador in Baghdad came out publicly against his own government's policy, and handed in his resignation so as not to have to represent it.

But Aznar, who had announced that he would not be standing for re-election, ignored public opinion. Spain co-sponsored the draft UN resolution that was meant to rally support for a war. Aznar acted as a roving ambassador to try to persuade other governments to back it. And he proudly joined President Bush and Britain's Prime Minister, Tony Blair, at the summit in the Azores that called for military action without UN backing. It was not until two days before the start of hostilities in March 2003 that he ruled out the dispatch of Spanish combat troops.

Aznar's dogged stance did not do him the political damage that had been predicted. At least not at first. Regional and local elections were held in May, a month after the fall of Baghdad, and the PP emerged almost unscathed. However, it is worth recalling that polling took place at a time when evidence of the horrors of Saddam Hussein's dictatorship was coming to light every day, stirring doubts among many who had opposed the invasion. As the security situation in Iraq deteriorated, those doubts receded and criticism of the government's policy focused on its subsequent decision to put troops into Iraq without consulting parliament. Zapatero committed his party to withdrawing Spain's forces if it won power.

Nevertheless, by the time a general election was called for March 2004, the PP still had good reason to believe their new leader, Mariano Rajoy, would be Spain's next Prime Minister. A Galician with broad experience of government – he had at different times been Minister for Culture, Education and Interior – the bearded Rajoy was a more appealing candidate to floating voters than the prickly Aznar. And the PP had a superb economic record to set before the country.

The conservatives had guided Spain successfully into the new European single currency. They had created half of all the new jobs in the EU during the eight years they were in power. And they had made Spaniards not just richer, but richer relative to other Europeans.* Their clampdown on ETA's support network in the Basque country was yielding results. In 2003, only three people had died in ETA terrorist attacks. And while there were claims that the PP was not as free of corruption as it maintained, none had been proved.

The biggest financial scandal of the second conservative government was the €93 million collapse in 2001 of an investment fund, Gescartera. Some of the fund's executives had links to senior figures in the governing party, and there were claims that the PP and its friends had obstructed inquiries into the affair. Conservative Spain had spawned its own high society, for which the press coined a bizarre Anglo-Gallicism. It was called *la nouvelle society* and was peopled in the main by powerful financiers with young, decorative wives. At times, it was hard to tell the difference between the members of *la nouvelle society* and their Socialist-era equivalents, *los beautiful people*.

Opinion polls indicated that, as the campaign entered its final straight, Zapatero and his Socialists were closing on the PP. But it seems unlikely that they would have won if it had not been for what happened in Madrid on the morning of 11 March 2004. Ten bombs exploded almost simultaneously on commuter trains, killing 191 people and injuring more than 2,000 in Spain's worst terrorist attack. It was clear the slaughter could prove disastrous for the PP if it turned out to have been organized by Arab militants in retaliation for Spain's support of US policy in the Middle East. Opponents of Aznar had long warned that his backing for the US stance on Iraq could have violent repercussions at home.

The Prime Minister and his representatives did everything they could to throw suspicion on to ETA – without categorically stating that they were responsible. 'No negotiation is possible or desirable

* GDP per capita as a percentage of the average in the EU of fifteen increased from 79 per cent in 1996 to 89 per cent in 2004.

with these assassins who so many times have sown death all around Spain,' Aznar declared soon after the bombings. His Interior Minister, Angel Acebes, said it was 'absolutely clear and evident that the terrorist organization ETA was looking to commit a major attack'.

But, as the media – and particularly the media sympathetic to the Socialists – produced evidence to suggest that the bombings carried out on '3/11' might in fact have been the work of Islamist extremists, the public became increasingly concerned that the government was hiding the truth. Hundreds, in some cases thousands, of people gathered outside PP offices around the country, demanding to know what had really happened. First, the government acknowledged that the Islamist lead was worth pursuing, even though, it said, it was not the most important one. Then, on the night before polling, Acebes announced that seven people had been arrested a few hours earlier on suspicion of involvement – and that three of them were Moroccans. The government's case that the bombings were the work of ETA was in ruins.

As far as their opponents were concerned, Aznar and his ministers had been trying to delude the nation about the true consequences of a wrong-headed policy. For the government's supporters, it was a perfectly understandable mistake since there were signs that ETA had been preparing a similar operation only months earlier.* What precisely went through the minds of Aznar and those around him in the hours following the attacks is likely to remain a subject of debate for years to come. But, at the very least, they were guilty of bestowing an aura of certainty on a hypothesis that was far from proven.

The effect of the bombings and the government's reaction to them was to bring out the hidden deciders of Spanish politics – those left-leaning voters whose natural preference is for abstention but who can be roused to vote if they perceive that fundamental principles or interests are at stake. On 14 March 2004, they turned out in force to punish the government for its refusal to listen over Iraq and what they saw as a mendacious attempt to deny the consequences.

The turnout was 77 per cent and the result was the biggest electoral upset in Spain's modern democratic history. The PSOE won

---

* On Christmas Eve, 2003, two alleged ETA members were arrested on suspicion of planning to blow up a crowded Madrid-bound train.

164 seats to the PP's 147. The United Left took five – fewer than several regional nationalist parties, including Esquerra Republicana Catalana (ERC), a more radical Catalan nationalist group than the one that had kept, first, the Socialists and then the PP in power in the nineties. Zapatero lacked an outright parliamentary majority, but was able to win a vote of confidence in parliament with the help of the most left-wing array of parties to line up behind a Spanish government since the days of the Republic. It included the ERC, the United Left and another left-wing regional nationalist party, the Galician Nationalist Bloc.

Zapatero's victory was not just unexpected. It was hugely controversial, and on a global scale. Many, particularly in the US, saw it as evidence that the Spanish electorate had capitulated to terrorism. That is an over-simplification. The voters who changed their intentions in the three days between the bombings and the election were, above all, bent on ridding themselves of a government that had defied the wishes of the electorate and then, as they saw it, tried to evade responsibility for what happened as a result. A more pertinent question perhaps is whether, in the circumstances, that was the most important consideration. For, whatever the voters' subjective intentions, the objective effect of their actions was to send out an immensely dangerous message: that terrorism, if applied in sufficiently horrendous doses, can change the outcome of a democratic election.

The people who had voted the Socialists back into office were inevitably jubilant, but also wary. Even the youngest among them knew the last Socialist government had ditched its idealism and ended its days in a welter of sordid corruption scandals. When a mainly young crowd gathered in Madrid to cheer Zapatero and his victory, an odd chant went up: one that explains, as much as the nature of the PSOE's parliamentary support, the unexpected radicalism of his government's early months. What the crowd was shouting by the time the new Prime Minister appeared was '*No nos falles*' ('Don't let us down').

CHAPTER 7

Legacies, Memories and Phantoms

On the eve of the twenty-fifth anniversary of General Franco's death, almost 2,000 people gathered in the Plaza de Oriente in the centre of Madrid for a commemoration of the *Caudillo*. There is a rally of this sort every year and it normally passes off without much fuss. This time, though, there was a violent counter-demonstration by left-wingers, who were eventually baton-charged by the police in a re-run of the street clashes that marked the dictator's last years. Elsewhere, there was considerably less passion. A survey published by *El País* found that the most common reaction prompted by his name was one of indifference.

Francoism has not survived as a political movement. And since the history taught in schools usually ends with the civil war, a lot of younger Spaniards have only the haziest idea of who he was. A number of schoolchildren interviewed on radio for a programme in 1992 to mark the centenary of his birth were under the impression Franco had belonged to the then governing party, the PSOE. Those who have grown up since the end of the dictatorship are baffled, and even annoyed, by the way foreigners continue to refer to the country in which they live as 'post-Franco Spain' more than thirty years after his death.

But then foreigners can often see more clearly than Spaniards what it is about Spain that is distinctive. And they know, or sense, that many of its distinguishing traits are the result of its having been ruled by one man, not for five or ten or even twenty years, but for thirty-six. Franco's signature can still be read all over the country he ruled. Spain is unique in being the only country in Europe which developed into a technologically advanced society under the aegis of an ultra-right-wing dictatorship. As we shall see, ordinary Spaniards first acquired prosperity in a society in which taxes were low, but in which they were expected to buy their own houses, provide for their own futures and pay for their own health care; a society in which trade unions, collective bargaining and strikes were all illegal.

The Opus Dei technocrats who masterminded Spain's economic 'take-off' did not perhaps succeed in replacing altogether the Spaniards' traditional disdain for labour with a new – Catholic, rather than Protestant – work ethic. The two attitudes can be seen in daily conflict. But they certainly did succeed in superimposing the one on the other, and in infusing society with an element of the 'stand on your own two feet' ethos.

Spaniards tend not to expect from the state the sort of cushioning which is regarded as normal in the rest of Western Europe. They look astonished when you say it, but of all the societies in Europe, theirs is the one where attitudes to the role of the state are closest to those in the United States. Closest yet furthest, for the technocrats were not writing on a blank slate. They were imposing their liberal ideas on a society which had already been profoundly affected by the fascism of Franco's earliest days. One of the ideas that characterized fascism, as it did communism, was a belief in the benefits of state ownership and intervention. The remnants of Falangist economic and social thinking can be seen in the inflexible labour market and huge public sector Franco bequeathed to his successors. It can be glimpsed too in the corporatism that is still to be found in the civil service and the liberal professions.

Franco's rule made Spaniards more reliant on themselves and on the state. But not on each other. Their reluctance to associate had been noted long before Franco. 'The Iberians', declared the nineteenth-century traveller, Richard Ford, 'never would amalgamate, never would, as Strabo said, put their shields together – never would sacrifice their own local private interest for the general good.' Spanish thinkers reached similar conclusions. For Ortega y Gasset, writing in 1921, Spain was 'invertebrate'.

What is undoubtedly true is that it has traditionally been deficient in voluntary associations – trade unions, mutual societies, political clubs, pressure groups, charitable foundations and the like. The origins of the phenomenon may indeed lie in the nature of Spanish society or the character of the Spanish people, but by making it difficult – and in many cases illegal – to create such groups, Franco's dictatorship ensured its persistence. Ironically, Spain's continuing 'invertebration' may be one reason why it has proved so easy to change. The authorities have not had to contend with the normal array of well-organized interest groups which in other countries might have questioned and obstructed their reforms.

Even more important has been a legacy which, all the evidence suggests, Franco had no intention of bequeathing: a generous tolerance which has become the hallmark of modern Spanish society.

Franco himself was obsessively vindictive. Several months before the end of the civil war, he promulgated a Law of Political Responsibilities which made it an offence not only to have fought against the Nationalists but also to have refrained from joining their rebellion; and not only to have been on the wrong side during the civil war but also to have been on the other side before it even broke out.

Historians are still wrangling over the numbers, but it is generally reckoned that between 50,000 and 100,000 'reds' and alleged 'reds' were executed by Franco's followers during the conflict. Some were put before firing squads by the rebel authorities. Others were hauled from their homes by gangs and told they were going for a *paseo* (stroll), from which they never returned. Some were killed in retaliation for atrocities committed by the Republican side. Others were murdered for reasons that had nothing to do with the war: as a way of settling the kind of festering enmities that spring up easily in small towns and villages. The right's most celebrated victim, the playwright and poet Federico García Lorca, seems to have been murdered more for being gay than for being left-wing.[*] It is conservatively estimated that a further 30,000 people were executed after the war. I remember meeting a man in Aragón, a lawyer, who told me that, when he was a schoolboy in the 1940s, he always knew when it was Wednesday because his route to school took him past the walls of the prison in

---

[*] Conscious of Lorca's worldwide renown, the Franco regime denied its followers' involvement in his murder right up until the 1970s when the true facts were unearthed, not by a Spanish author, but by an Irish one, Ian Gibson. His findings were first made known through a Paris-based publishing house, Ruedo Iberico, in 1971. They were later published in English as *The Assassination of Federico García Lorca*, W. H. Allen, London, 1979.

Saragossa and Wednesday was the day they carried out the executions. He usually got to the prison just as the shots rang out. There is evidence that killings continued until as late as 1949. Many of the victims lie in unmarked graves.

The inhabitants of the two most populous Basque provinces had a 'punitive decree' passed against them. The leader of the Catalans was shot. And though Franco's regime was to become progressively less active in the persecution of its opponents, some remained unconvinced that it was safe to emerge from hiding. One of the most remarkable developments in the years immediately following Franco's death was the reappearance of a string of so-called *topos* (moles) who had stayed in hiding within Spain for more than three and a half decades. By ensuring that the wounds left by the civil war remained open so long, though, Franco seems to have inoculated his fellow-Spaniards against the very intolerance he came to symbolize.

Spaniards were to need all the tolerance they could muster in the years following Franco's death. Unlike Portugal's right-wing dictator, António Salazar, he succeeded in keeping his army loyal, perhaps because he refused to let himself be lured into colonial warfare. That ruled out a revolution of the kind that disgruntled officers launched in Portugal in 1974. In fact, it ruled out a revolution of any kind, because the army – still broadly loyal to the memory and ideals of its *Generalísimo* – would have seized on any evidence of a return to pre-Francoist chaos as a pretext for intervention. Spaniards, predisposed by their folk memory of the civil war towards evolution rather than revolution, were thus given an extra incentive for bringing about change in a more conciliatory way. The word they hit upon to describe the process was 'transition'. This was a special – perhaps unique – process and it endowed the country which emerged from it with special, and perhaps unique, characteristics.

It has become customary to talk of Spain's 'peaceful transition' from dictatorship to democracy, as if peacefulness were its defining characteristic. It was not. Politically motivated violence took the lives of more than twenty people between Franco's death in November 1975 and the first democratic general election in July 1977. The toll later rose to almost 1,000, principally because of the activities of ETA.

What made Spain's transition special was the lack of a clean break with the past. In essence, the transition was achieved by an unwritten, and for the most part unspoken, pact. The Francoist establishment acknowledged that the time had come for a change and undertook to wind up its operations on condition that reprisals were never taken against any of its members.

In the event, those who had served Franco escaped, not just retribution, but refutation. In the years immediately following Franco's death, politicians were eager to extol the virtues of the new arrangements. But because of the continued threat from the armed forces, they were not so keen to recall the evils of the old ones. Spaniards were often told that democracy was good, but only rarely that dictatorship had been bad.

The spirit of the transition is sometimes described as being that of 'forgive and forget'. That is not entirely correct. Since no one in Spain was ever judged, no one was ever deemed guilty. And since no one was ever deemed guilty, forgiveness never entered into it. It was just a matter of forgetting. Spain never had anything like the Truth and Reconciliation Commission that brought such a necessary catharsis to South Africa after apartheid. Instead, things were left to take the course of least resistance.

Franco's birthplace, El Ferrol, ceased after a few years to be called El Ferrol del Caudillo. But his statue still commands the city centre. Elsewhere, there are towns and villages that still sport his vainglorious title, attached to the end of their names – places like Alberche del Caudillo in La Mancha and Guadiana del Caudillo in Estremadura. Streets named after the iconic figures or victorious battles of the winning side in the civil war have been replaced, but only when the left has taken control of the local authority, and then only after indignant protests from the right. Francoist symbols still adorn official buildings and town squares, particularly in rural areas. Thousands of plaques and inscriptions vilifying the losing side have been left in place. Official records written in the same abusive vein have never been altered.

It was perhaps inevitable that the Valle de los Caídos, Franco's pharaonic mausoleum near Madrid, which he had hewn out of a mountainside after the civil war by forced labour, should remain a tourist attraction. It was perhaps inevitable too that his relatives should re-emerge as gossip magazine celebrities. But it was by no means unavoidable that notorious torturers from the Franco era should have been allowed to remain in the police and, in some cases, climb to the highest levels in the service. Nor was it unavoidable that journalists who once profited handsomely from their collaboration with the Franco regime should have been allowed to carry on seamlessly to become commentators and editors, only too ready to offer their views on how best to run a democracy.

Starting in the early 1990s, the Socialists talked about the civil war and its aftermath at election time. But they did so to depict the PP as a band of unreconstructed Francoists whose hidden agenda was to restore a dictatorship. And that was scarcely a contribution towards establishing the truth of anything.

The PP was indeed the brainchild of a Francoist minister, Manuel Fraga. As you would expect of a conservative party, many of its leading members are from well-to-do families that sided with the Nationalists when Spanish society split down the middle in 1936. But, when it was in power, the PP never gave the slightest hint of wanting to play by any other rulebook than that of democracy. And when it lost power, in a hugely controversial election, its leaders never gave the slightest indication that they might call on the armed forces to keep them in power, as had so many Spanish governments in the past. Aznar's conservatives felt themselves to have been 'robbed' every bit as much as the US Democrats in 2000. And by terrorists, what is more. But when the time came for them to go, they went. They grumbled. They protested. They seethed. But they went. Indeed, Spain had by then become so totally bound up in democratic Europe that any other response would have been greeted with almost as much derision as alarm.

The PP years proved, even to the poor, elderly, rural voters at whom the Socialists had aimed their scare tactics, that Aznar's party was not, in fact, a threat to freedom. This could explain an apparent paradox, which is that when the phantoms of the civil war were finally conjured up, it was not, as you might expect, under a left-wing government but under a right-wing one.

A wave of books and documentaries about the civil war and its aftermath has broken over Spain since the late 1990s, and it has been accompanied by increasingly vociferous pleas for the rehabilitation of Franco's victims. So-called 'historical memory' groups have sprung up in many parts of the country demanding the right to unearth the bodies of those who were executed so that they can finally be given a decent burial. The first such exhumation was carried out in 2000 at Priaranza del Bierzo near León. These and other groups, meanwhile, have pressed for a proper recognition of the military status of all those who took up arms against Franco. The earliest step in this direction was taken when parliament voted for the removal from public records of terms such as 'bandits' to describe the insurgents who in 1944 launched an unsuccessful guerrilla campaign against the Franco regime over the Pyrenees.

The conservatives' reaction to all this was hesitant. In 2000, the PP let through parliament a motion describing Franco's rebellion as a 'fascist coup', but the following year it used its parliamentary majority to defeat another that condemned it. Aznar's government agreed that local authorities could use public money to fund exhumations. But whether they did so often depended in practice on whether the left or right was in control. In 2002, campaigners appealed for support from the United Nations, which has a working group on forced disappearances. The PP said it would abide by any decision the UN made, even though it was under no legal obligation to do so. The following year, the working group asked Spain to provide information on disappearances after 1945.

The arrival of Zapatero promised to change the situation radically. The new Prime Minister's own grandfather, a captain in the army, was shot for refusing to join Franco's rebellion. One of the government's first moves after coming into office was to set up a commission under Zapatero's deputy, María Teresa Fernández de la Vega, to study the entire range of issues bequeathed by the civil war and its aftermath, a move the PP always resisted. But the task has proved more difficult than expected, and the government has conceded it could take years to complete.

A vast amount remains to be done before Spaniards can achieve the 'closure' they obviously need. No one has even touched the mass graves, each with more than 1,000 bodies, that campaigners say are to be found in several parts of the country. The biggest, near Mérida, is reckoned to hold the remains of 3,500 men and women. Then, there is the hugely sensitive issue of how to treat the civil war and the Franco regime in school textbooks. Up to now, it has been avoided because events after 1936 were considered too recent to constitute history.

But that argument is starting to wear thin. Finally, there is the question of whether to extend this process of coming to terms with the past to more recent years. No one has so far suggested that Manuel Fraga, for example, should be brought before a tribunal to explain his conduct in the years when he sat in Franco's cabinet. But there are thousands of people – I know some personally – who harbour deep and unresolved feelings over the way they or their loved ones were treated, often for espousing the very values of democracy and freedom that are now universally embraced by society. One of the questions to be resolved by Fernández de la Vega's commission is whether they deserve recognition or compensation and, if so, in what form.

Curiosity about the later years of the dictatorship is, if anything, greater than about the early years. One of the effects of Spain's collective, voluntary amnesia is that the quite recent past can seem a lot more remote than it does in other countries. 'Spaniards', said an *El Mundo* editorial written at the time of Franco's centenary, 'look at the Franco era as if from an enormous distance.'

This goes some way towards explaining a phenomenon of recent years – the extraordinary success of Televisión Española's *Cuéntame cómo pasó* ('Tell me how it was'), a drama series following the story of a middle-class Spanish family, the Alcántaras, from the late sixties, through the transition and into the eighties. Interestingly, the scriptwriter, Patrick Buckley, is someone more used perhaps than most Spaniards to looking at their society with detachment. He is the son of an English father, a former Reuters correspondent in Madrid, and a Catalan mother.

In an entertaining way, the series cuts through the 'authorized version' that has grown up in Spain around the later Franco years and which, for example, has it that everyone but a few ageing hardliners was waiting impatiently for the *Caudillo*'s demise. There was also fear about what might come afterwards and in *Cuéntame cómo pasó* that is reflected by the character of Antonio, the father, who is worried about the end of the Franco era because he has known nothing else. The seeds of change are there too, though. His rebellious daughter Inés, who works on a women's magazine, goes to London and acquires a long-haired English boyfriend. In the first episode, she is discovered to have contraceptive pills in her bedside table.

In 1968, when the series opens, that would have been transgression indeed, for Spain then was – to an extent that is today almost unimaginable – in the sway of the institution that has done more than any other to shape its character and destiny.

PART TWO

Private Domains

CHAPTER 8

Belief and the Church: Emptying Pews

In the late sixties, the workers at one of the great sherry houses of Jerez mounted what became a prolonged and bitter strike. Among their demands was that they should be given two days off every year for christenings. One of the leaders of the strike later recalled that the head of the firm had asked them why 'a bunch of commies' should need time off to go to church. 'We said that that was different. You might not believe in God, but you had to believe in baptism otherwise your kids would be Moors, wouldn't they?' he said.

Spain, like Pakistan, became a nation in the aftermath of a religious segregation. Christianity came to be considered as essential to Spain's nationhood as Islam was to be to Pakistan's. As the Jerez sherry-worker's remark shows, saying that you were a Christian could be as much a claim to national identity as a profession of religious belief.

And if being a Spaniard meant being a Christian, in Spain being a Christian meant being a Catholic. The *reconquista* had barely ended when the Reformation began, and after centuries of fighting the infidel, Christian Spaniards were in no mood to put up with heretics or dissenters. Spain was the undisputed leader of the Counter-Reformation. A soldier-turned-priest from the Basque country, Ignacio de Loyola, provided the movement with its spiritual shock troops, the Jesuits, and Spanish commanders such as Alba, Spinola and the Cardinal Infante Fernando led the military offensive against the Protestant nations of the north.

At home the Inquisition made sure that by 1570 there were virtually no Protestants left in Spain. Abolished in 1813, during the War of Independence, the Inquisition was reconstituted the following year by Fernando VII and was only finally suppressed in the 1830s. Even after that – except under the two Republics – religious freedom was usually more notional than real. Brave souls like George Borrow, author of that exuberantly idiosyncratic classic *The Bible in Spain*, set out to break the stranglehold of Popery but only succeeded in creating the odd prayer group.

Franco, while not actually banning other forms of worship, outlawed their external manifestations. Services could not be advertised in the press or on signboards and since none but the Catholic Church had legal status, other denominations could not own property or publish books. The Second Vatican Council's historic declaration on freedom of conscience forced the regime to abandon this policy and in 1966 a law was passed which, while retaining a privileged status for the Catholic Church, freed other creeds from the constraints that had been placed upon them. But it was not until the 1978 constitution took effect that Spaniards secured an unambiguous right to worship as they pleased.

One result of the virtual absence of Protestantism was that disagreement with the doctrines of Catholicism, which in other parts of Europe was channelled into Lutheranism or Calvinism, tended to take the form of Freemasonry in Spain. Many of the nineteenth-century *pronunciamientos* were the result of Masonic conspiracies. Persecuted by Franco more than any other group except possibly the Communists, the Masons were effectively obliterated from Spanish life by his dictatorship. Though Freemasonry is nowadays legal, it has made scant impact on the country that has emerged since Franco's death.

Throughout much of Spanish history, then, Roman Catholicism has been not so much *a* religion as *the* religion. This tradition of untrammelled supremacy helps explain the angry and indignant reaction of the Church hierarchy to the policies of José Luis Rodríguez Zapatero's newly elected Socialist government. Within a few months of coming to office, it had announced a string of measures at odds with Roman Catholic teaching: bills to make divorce and abortion easier, to legalize stem-cell research and enable homosexuals to adopt children. But what appalled the Roman Catholic hierarchy and the Vatican more than anything was the new government's determination to make good on its campaign promise to legalize gay marriage.

The idea that Spain – 'Catholic Spain' as it was often known in the past – should be introducing such a reform, before even countries like Sweden, caused plenty of astonishment elsewhere. At the Vatican,

Pope John Paul protested that the 'living roots of Christianity' in the country were being 'ripped out'.

In fact, largely unnoticed by the rest of the world, those roots had been withering for years. When Zapatero made his move on gay marriages, he did so in the knowledge that he had the support of a largely secular society. Opinion polls suggested that about two-thirds of Spaniards were in favour of equal rights for all couples.

It is still the case that the vast majority of Spaniards – more than 90 per cent – are baptized Roman Catholics. But that does not mean they consider themselves Catholics or that, if they do, they fulfil the requirements of their faith. A survey carried out by the Spanish government's Centro de Investigaciones Sociológicas in 2004 found that fewer than three-quarters of those interviewed described themselves as Roman Catholics. But several studies have indicated that the proportion of the population that goes to church at least once a month is below a fifth. That is still quite a high share compared with church attendance in the other countries of the European Union. Only Ireland, Poland, Italy and Hungary have proportionately more churchgoers. It nonetheless represents a huge fall since the end of Franco's dictatorship when more than three times as many Spaniards claimed that they went regularly to Mass.

This steady decline may be about to end. But not because of any re-evangelization of the native population. A lot of the immigrants who have poured into Spain in recent years are devout, observant Catholics from Latin America who are beginning to fill some of the many empty pews in Spain's churches. What remains to be seen is whether they will make more than a temporary impact on the church attendance figures. The experience of other countries indicates that, as immigrants become integrated into their new homelands, they – and, to an even more marked extent, their children – abandon the beliefs and practices of the society they left behind.

The process of secularization among native Spaniards has inevitably led to a fall in the number of Roman Catholics in Holy Orders as progressively fewer Spaniards have applied to become priests, monks and nuns. A drop in the number of priestly vocations was first noted as far back as 1963 and the total seminary intake has been dropping, albeit fitfully, ever since. In 2002, it was reported that some seminaries had begun the academic year with not a single new student.

As in many other countries, the ranks of the priesthood and the religious orders have been further depleted by priests, monks and nuns giving up Holy Orders, usually because of objections to the Church's policy on celibacy. According to COSARESE, a body representing the secularized clergy, almost 3,000 parish priests, more than 6,000 monks and nearly 10,000 nuns opted to leave Holy Orders in Spain between 1960 and 1990.

The Spanish Church today, like that of many other traditionally Catholic countries, is both elderly and shrunken. By 2002, the number of monks and nuns was down to 64,000 from 109,000 two decades earlier and the number of parish priests had fallen to 18,500 from 23,000 in 1982. Between 10 and 15 per cent of Spanish parishes had no priest to look after them, but then many had scarcely any worshippers.

Some of those who have left the Roman Catholic Church have done so to embrace other denominations or religions. The number of Protestants in Spain has approximately quadrupled since the end of the dictatorship. The Protestant churches claim a following of around 350,000,* including both members and those – mostly children – who belong to their 'area of influence'. But even counting up the number of Protestants by this rather generous method, they account for less than 1 per cent of the population.

The evangelical churches have been swelled by the conversion of large numbers of Gypsies. The Alianza Evangélica Española reckons that between 10 and 15 per cent of all Spanish Gypsies are now Protestants and that they and their families number around 150,000. However, one of those figures has to be wrong if the official government estimate of the total Roma population – 650,000 – is accurate.

Spain's remaining Protestants are overwhelmingly middle-class. The biggest concentrations are in Madrid and Catalonia, and in coastal areas of the country where foreign influence has been strong. Andalusia, for example, is thought to have a disproportionate number of Protestants because of Gibraltar.

Small numbers of Spaniards have also switched to non-Christian

---

* In addition, it is reckoned that some 800,000 Protestants from elsewhere in the EU live in Spain for more than six months of the year.

faiths, and in particular to Islam. Conversions began to gather momentum in the early eighties and were especially pronounced in those parts of the country once ruled by Moslems. There is a community of several hundred converts in the Albaicín, the old Moorish quarter of Granada. But if Spain today has a Moslem population of some 500,000, that is overwhelmingly due to immigration, particularly from North Africa. The same is true of Spain's tiny, 14,000-strong Jewish community.

In the main, native Spaniards who give up Roman Catholicism do not take to another religion. However, it would seem that astonishingly few lose their faith in God. The CIS survey cited earlier found that just 0.6 per cent of Spaniards described themselves as either atheists or agnostics, though almost 20 per cent said they were not religious, and that figure may hide a lot of people who do not, in fact, have any kind of belief in God. Nevertheless, it left more than 50 per cent of the population who regarded themselves as Roman Catholics, but who were non-practising.

Notwithstanding the rows of empty pews, then, there is still a large reserve of latent belief in Catholicism and a deep reluctance among Spaniards to dissociate themselves wholly from it. All this is worth bearing in mind when considering the claims by senior clerics that Roman Catholicism in Spain is, in effect, becoming a persecuted faith in what was once one of its heartlands.

'We are hounded on all sides, but they can't deal with us,' the Archbishop of Pamplona, Fernando Sebastián, told a congress of Catholic lay people held in Madrid in 2004. 'We are persecuted, but we shall never be annihilated.'

This is rhetorical nonsense. For a start, the Church – diminished though it may be – is still a very large institution and one with the means to exert a huge influence on what Spaniards think. The Bishops' Conference owns a 50 per cent stake in one of the country's main radio networks, Cadena Cope, and one Spanish child in every seven goes to a school owned by a religious order or association. Most importantly of all, perhaps, the Church oversees religious education in all of Spain's schools, including even those it does not own.

As a result of its influence, Spanish society is shot through with instinctively Catholic attitudes, just as the Spanish language is crammed with phrases drawn from Catholic practice and dogma. When, for example, a Spaniard wants to convey the idea that something or somebody is reliable, trustworthy, 'OK' in the widest sense, he or she will say that that person or thing '*va a misa*' ('goes to Mass'). When some terrible thing like multiple sclerosis or nuclear war is mentioned in conversation, in circumstances where an English-speaker might say, 'It doesn't bear thinking about', a Spaniard – even an ostensibly irreligious one – will often say, '*Que Dios nos coja confesados*' ('Let's hope God catches us confessed'). And when the first baby to be conceived through *in vitro* fertilization was born, that eminently secular periodical *Cambio 16* headlined its report with the words 'Born without Original Sin'.

Far from being persecuted, the Church is merely starting to get a measure of normal treatment after centuries of being showered with privileges. As the *reconquista* pushed forward the limits of Christian Spain, the Church acquired immense tracts of land, especially in the southern half of the peninsula. No sooner were they confiscated in the 1830s than it was felt that the state had to make amends. In a pact, or Concordat, drawn up between Madrid and the Vatican in 1851, the government undertook by way of indemnity to pay the clergy's salaries and meet the cost of administering the sacraments. This extraordinary commitment was honoured by every government until 1931, when it was renounced by the authors of the Republican constitution. But two years later, when a conservative government came to power, the subsidy was resumed.

Franco not only continued to pay it, he also provided government money to rebuild churches damaged or destroyed in the civil war and passed a series of measures bringing the law of Spain into line with the teachings of the Church. Divorce, which had been made legal under the Republic, was abolished; the sale (but not, for some reason, the manufacture) of contraceptives was banned, and Roman Catholic religious instruction was made compulsory in public as well as private education at every level.

In return, the Vatican granted Franco something that Spanish rulers had been seeking for centuries: effective control over the appointment of bishops. Cooperation between the Church and the regime became even closer after the end of the Second World War when Franco needed to turn a non-fascist face to the world. Several prominent Catholic laymen were included in the cabinet and one of them, Alberto Martín Artajo, succeeded in negotiating a new Concordat with Rome.

Signed in 1953, it ended the diplomatic isolation to which Spain had been subjected ever since the Allied victory. Franco was happy to make whatever concessions were necessary to clinch it. The Church was exempted from taxation and offered grants with which to construct churches and other religious buildings. It acquired the right to ask for material it found offensive to be withdrawn from sale, yet its own publications were freed from censorship. Canonical marriage was recognized as the only valid form for Catholics. The Church was given the opportunity to found universities, run radio stations and own newspapers and magazines. The police were forbidden to enter churches except in cases of 'urgent necessity'. The clergy could not be charged with criminal offences except with the permission of their diocesan bishop (in the case of priests) or the Holy See itself (in the case of bishops).

It was the Second Vatican Council which first brought the terms of this cosy relationship into question. The Council, which came down unambiguously in favour of a clear separation between Church and state, invited all those governments which had a say in the appointment of ecclesiastical officials to give it up. But nothing could persuade Franco to surrender what he regarded – correctly – as an immensely powerful instrument of control. Because of it he was able to block the elevation of numerous liberally minded priests upon whose heads Pope Paul VI wished to place a mitre. Throughout the last years of Franco's life, ministers and officials were flying to and from Rome with suggested revisions of the Concordat. But all attempts to rewrite it foundered on the ageing dictator's point-blank refusal to give up his power over the appointment of bishops.

His death and the disappearance of his dictatorship created a very different political background for relations between Church and state. In its draft form, the 1978 constitution did not mention the Catholic Church at all, and it was only after a determined campaign that the bishops succeeded in having a reference to it included. Even so, this reference looks like what it is – an afterthought. Having specifically rejected the idea of an official religion, the constitution went on to say: 'The authorities shall take into account the religious beliefs of Spanish society and maintain the appropriate relations of cooperation

97

with the Catholic Church and the other denominations.' There was no explicit affirmation that the majority of Spaniards were Catholics, nor that the state should take into account – let alone be guided by – the teachings of Catholicism.

In the meantime, preparations had been made for a revision of the Concordat. In 1976, King Juan Carlos had unilaterally renounced the privilege of being able to name Spain's bishops and in August of that year an agreement was signed formally restoring to the Church the power to appoint its own leaders in Spain. In December 1979 a partial revision of the Concordat appeared to prepare the ground for a financial separation between Church and state. Referring to the state's lengthy atonement for the confiscations of the previous century, it was agreed that 'the state can neither ignore nor prolong indefinitely juridical obligations acquired in the past'. So, tacitly acknowledging that the Church was incapable of going it alone overnight, the agreement proposed a transitional period of six years divided into two three-year stages. During stage one, the government would continue to pay the usual subsidy. But during stage two there would be a new system of finance. Taxpayers would be able to state on their returns whether they wished a small percentage of their taxes to go to the Church and the government would then hand over the resulting sum to the bishops. The press immediately dubbed it the *impuesto religioso* (religious tax), but this was a rather inaccurate label since it was never conceived of as a separate or additional charge. Whatever the individual taxpayer decided would make no difference to the size of his or her tax bill.

And not only that. Under the revised Concordat, the state undertook to ensure that during this second phase of the transition to self-financing the Church would get 'resources of similar quantity' to those it was already receiving. However few or many taxpayers expressed a desire to help the Church, therefore, it would make no difference to what it obtained from the state.

The transitional procedure seems to have been intended to accustom people to the idea that the Roman Catholic Church's expenses were going to have to be paid for by ordinary citizens. Because of the state subsidies the Church had for so long been receiving, the faithful in Spain were not used to the idea of having to put more than a token sum into the collection plate.

In fact, the arrangements in the Concordat have been only partially, and belatedly, implemented. Stage one lasted, not for three years, but for nine. It was not until 1988 that taxpayers were asked to decide whether they wanted a share of their contribution to be given to the Church or spent on 'objectives of social interest' (i.e. charities). But the share – 0.5239 per cent – was based on an estimate of the percentage of total revenue that would be needed to equal what the Church had received from the state in the year before the new arrangements were introduced. Therefore, only if every single taxpayer opted for the Church would the sum initially allocated to the bishops constitute the 'resources of similar quantity' the state had promised.

In the event, 35 per cent marked their forms in favour of the Church and 12 per cent in favour of the 'objectives of social interest'. But since the government promptly made the total up to the 14,000 million pesetas the Church could have expected to receive had nothing been changed, the whole exercise was pointless. It still is, because while the deadline for the transition from stage one to stage two was postponed, the deadline for the transition to full self-financing was simply ignored. A Church which has been formally disestablished thus continues to receive a sizeable amount from government funds under a deal that was meant to have become obsolete in 1986. And every year Spaniards go through the same illogical ritual, earmarking funds for the Church, often unaware that it makes no difference to how much the Church will receive.

One effect of this is that Spain's atheists, Protestants, Jews and Moslems are still having to pay for the upkeep of a religion they do not share. To compensate, the government has undertaken to provide funds to other faiths too, but it means that, rather than shed its obligations to one religion, the new Spain has assumed responsibility for several.

If Roman Catholicism is in poor shape in Spain then it is certainly not because the Church is in some way being hamstrung by politicians, but because it is failing to offer people a form of religion with which they wish to associate. One huge obstacle separating the Church from its potential congregation is the Vatican's teaching on contraception, seen – and not just by Spanish Catholics – as a prime example of the way in which the Church is out of touch with the realities of modern life. But there is at least one other factor, and that is the repeated failure of the Spanish Church to make of itself a truly national institution. Again and again, when the country has split, the Church has sided all too readily with the forces of conservatism. On occasions, it has tried to reach across the recurring division of Spanish society. But each time it has pulled back and succumbed to the temptation to throw in its lot with the half of society with which it feels more at home.

The Church that had spearheaded the Counter-Reformation was quite incapable of coming to terms with the new ideas that flooded into Spain during the nineteenth century, and took refuge in a forlorn hope that the old order of things could be re-established. The identification of the Church with reaction created by implication a mirror-image alliance between radicalism and anti-clericalism. During the late nineteenth and early twentieth centuries, whenever the right lost its grip on the levers of power there were frenzied outbursts of violence directed against Catholicism and its representatives. Churches were burned or desecrated. On occasion, priests were killed and nuns raped. The civil war provoked the worst atrocities of all – accounting for the lives of 4,000 parish priests, over 2,000 monks and almost 300 nuns.

The atrocities perpetrated by the Republicans make it a little easier to understand the Church's attitude to the Nationalists. Spanish prelates blessed Franco's troops before they went into battle and were even pictured giving the fascist salute. In a famous broadcast to the beleaguered defenders of the Alcázar in Toledo, Cardinal Isidro Gomá y Tomás – a future Primate of Spain – inveighed against 'the bastard soul of the sons of Moscow and shadowy societies manipulated by semitic internationalism'. On the day of his victory, Franco received from Pope Pius XII a telegram of congratulation which read: 'Lifting up our hearts to the Lord, we rejoice with Your Excellency in the victory, so greatly to be desired, of Catholic Spain.'

Yet within twenty-five years of that telegram, the Spanish Church was providing some of Franco's most vocal critics. To an extent it was a reflection of the diminishing support throughout society for the dictatorship. It was partly, too, a question of morality. The gap between what the regime promised and what it delivered in the way of social justice grew wider every year and was quite soon demonstrably at variance with Christian ideals. In addition, the Spanish Church, like every other Catholic Church, was deeply influenced by the liberal spirit which began to emanate from the Vatican as soon as John XXIII was elected Pope and which took shape in the measures adopted by the Second Vatican Council. But perhaps the main reason for the change was, ironically enough, Franco's own victory.

Just as the Church's political conservatism had helped to forge an alliance between anti-clericalism and radicalism, so the anti-clericalism of the radicals had ensured that the Church remained conservative. The death and exile of so many Freemasons, anarchists and Marxists effectively destroyed anti-clericalism as a force in society and gave the Church a freedom of manoeuvre which had been unthinkable previously. Among other things, it encouraged the Church to fish for souls in the traditionally anti-clerical urban working class. In the early fifties, the leaders of the Vatican-inspired lay organization, Acción Católica, set up three new societies – Hermandades Obreras de Acción Católica (HOAC), Juventud Obrera Católica (JOC), and Vanguardias Obreras Juveniles (VOJ) – to proselytize among the working classes, particularly the young.

In the event, the urban working classes were to have a much greater effect on the Church than the Church ever had on the urban working classes. The result of the experiment was to raise the social consciousness of, first, the laity and then the clergy more than the religious consciousness of the people they had set out to convert. By the early sixties, a sizeable element within the Church was at odds with the regime. This was the heyday of the *curas rojos* (red priests), who took advantage of the privileges and immunities granted to the Church by Franco to allow strike meetings in the vestry and sit-ins in the nave.

The younger clergy's antipathy to Francoism was further fuelled in some areas by the regime's hostility to regional nationalism. This was especially true of the Basque country, the most observant part of Spain. There, the clergy had identified closely with demands for the restoration of traditional rights and privileges, although during the nineteenth century this had tended to take the form of support for reactionary Carlism.* In contrast to what happened in the rest of Spain, the Basque clergy sided with the Republic during the civil war and paid the price for their choice after Franco's victory when

* See below, pp. 228–9.

sixteen of their number were executed. Understandably, therefore, many Basque priests were sympathetic to the resurgence of militant nationalism.

The revolt within the Church, particularly in the Basque country, reached such proportions that a special priests' prison had to be created at Zamora. At first, the radicalism of the rank and file appalled the hierarchy. But towards the end of the sixties, the hierarchy itself began to show signs of dissent. In 1972 the Church got a 'red bishop' to add to its many 'red priests' – Bishop Iniesta, who was appointed to Vallecas, a working-class suburb of Madrid.

The publicity given to the 'red' bishops and priests of the Franco era tended to give the impression that the Church had become more radical than was in fact the case. By the end of the dictatorship it consisted, in Bishop Iniesta's words, of 'a minority right wing, a minority left wing and a majority belonging to the centre'. Cardinal Vicente Enrique y Tarancón, the Archbishop of Madrid, who had been elected President of the Bishops' Conference in 1971, was the embodiment of this ecclesiastical centre. A friend and admirer of Pope Paul VI, he shared the late pontiff's cautious but realistic approach to the modern world. He was, in short, the ideal man to preside over the Spanish Church during the transition.

Rarely can a Church have been in such an ideal position to make itself a force for reconciliation and unification as the Roman Catholic Church in Spain in the years following General Franco's death. Its opposition to the dictatorship had given it widespread credibility among that vast majority of Spaniards who were looking forward to democracy, albeit with a degree of trepidation. Many of the young, emergent politicians of the post-Franco period had belonged to the lay organizations formed by the Church in the fifties, yet the Church was not aligned with any specific party.

The forces of Christian Democracy had been split into pro- and anti-Francoist factions under the dictatorship and were unable to sink their differences in time for the 1977 elections. Some Christian Democrats stood for the AP, others for the UCD, while a third group who entered the lists as Christian Democrats pure and simple suffered a crushing defeat. The fall of the UCD and the rise of the PP served to concentrate most of them into a single party, but they remained a minority within it.

At the same time, the laity were scattered more or less evenly across the political spectrum. More than half the country's practising Catholics and a fifth of its daily communicants voted for the Socialists at the 1982 general election. Although the leadership of the PSOE was overwhelmingly agnostic, a study by its Grupo Federal de Estudios Sociológicos in the eighties found that over 45 per cent of members described themselves as believers. Less than 20 per cent of those who had joined during the Franco era were Catholics, but among those who had joined since, the proportion had been increasing each year until among the most recent entrants it was 50 per cent. Two of the ministers who served in Felipe González's governments had been seminarists and one of his junior ministers was a former priest. Two of the PSOE's regional presidents had also worn the cloth at an earlier stage in their lives.

So how did the Church react to this remarkable opportunity? Guided firmly from the Vatican under Pope John Paul II, it gradually, haltingly shifted itself to the point at which it was, and is, seen by many as the People's Party at prayer: an institution reflecting the outlook of only one half of Spanish society. To some extent, those who view it in that way are wrong. The Spanish Church is too big and heterogeneous an organization to be neatly pigeonholed. There are thousands of parish priests whose outlook remains solidly Tarancónist. Spain's religious orders are, on balance, distinctly more progressive than reactionary. But, since the early 1980s, the Vatican has taken care to ensure that the leadership has been rigidly conservative.

When in 1983 Tarancón reached the age of seventy-five and was obliged to submit his resignation from the Archbishopric of Madrid, Pope John Paul replaced him with the Archbishop of Santiago de Compostela, Angel Suquía. In 1987, Suquía – by then a cardinal – was elected President of the Bishops' Conference. The Suquía era was marked by repeated and corrosive disputes with the Socialist government. In 1990, relations hit perhaps their lowest point when the Church hierarchy attacked a government campaign promoting condoms to prevent the spread of AIDS. Suquía's General Secretary at the Bishops' Conference called it 'disastrous', adding that it was what you would expect from a 'materialistic, agnostic and atheistic political enterprise'. Felipe González returned the compliment by refusing officially even to meet Suquía. The cardinal once described modern Spanish society as 'sick' and, under his leadership, it seemed the bishops could find nothing positive in the direction it was taking. At one point they even appeared to question the merits of democracy, arguing that the 'dialectic of majorities and the power of the vote' had supplanted ethical criteria.

In 1994, when Suquía retired, the Pope gave the key Madrid Archbishopric to Antonio María Rouco Varela, the man who had taken over from Suquía in Santiago de Compostela where he had impressed the Pope with his organization of a successful world youth gathering in 1989. Five years after getting to Madrid, Rouco Varela, who had been given a cardinal's hat in the meantime, was chosen to head the Bishops' Conference and has since governed the Spanish Church with the same unwavering approach as Cardinal Suquía.

The steady conservatism of the hierarchy was accompanied by a concentration of Roman Catholic politicians into the PP, and the favours they bestowed on the Church after the PP won power only strengthened the impression of a link between Roman Catholicism on the one hand and the right on the other. A law passed in 2001 gave the Church and offshoots like the charitable organizations Caritas and Manos Unidas a status that critics argued went beyond the provisions of the 1979 Concordat and effectively freed them of the obligation to answer for their actions. The following year, the government accorded a unique 'offshore' status to Cajasur El Peñón, the Gibraltar subsidiary of a bank based in Andalusia which is partly owned by the Spanish Church and which provides it with the funding for many of its activities.[*]

The PP years also saw the return to government of that intensely controversial product of Spanish spirituality, Opus Dei. At least four of José María Aznar's ministers were either members of the movement or had very close links with it. The *Obra* (Work), as it is known in Spain, today claims some 85,000 members in sixty countries. By far the biggest concentration is in Spain itself, where more than 30,000 people belong to the organization. Opus Dei's latest triumph – and latest controversy – came in 2002 with the canonization of its founder,

---

[*] Its chairman, Father Miguel Castillejo Gorráiz, is among the most singular figures in either the ecclesiastical or the financial world. According to an article in *El Siglo*, published in 2002, he was covered by a life insurance policy worth €2.9 million.

Monsignor Josemaría Escrivá de Balaguer. Escrivá, who died in 1975, was declared a saint against a background of sustained protest from liberal Catholics. His canonization, one of the fastest in the history of the Church, was approved despite allegations that he was vain, snobbish, misogynistic, and even – according to a former senior member of Opus – an apologist for the Nazis.

The son of an Aragonese shopkeeper, Escrivá founded Opus Dei in 1928 and in 1939 published his most famous work, a collection of maxims entitled *Camino* (Way). Like the Jesuits before him, he realized the benefits to be derived from gaining a foothold in the educational world and using it to build up support among the elite. In 1941 José Ibáñez Martín, a friend of one of Escrivá's closest associates, was made Minister of Education. By the time he left the job in 1951, it was reckoned that between 20 and 25 per cent of the chairs at Spain's universities were held by Opus members and sympathizers. The year following Ibáñez Martín's departure also saw the foundation by the Opus of a college near Pamplona, the Estudio General de Navarra. In 1962 it achieved the status of a university and has since been responsible for educating some of Spain's highest achievers. In addition, Opus Dei set up a business school, the IESE, in Barcelona and an administrative college, the ISSA, in San Sebastián. As the young people whose sympathies the Opus had won at university and college moved up in the world, they spread the organization's influence into every area of Spanish life. They became – and remain – powerful in the media and in business.

Parallels have been drawn between Opus Dei and any number of other groups and creeds. Its hierarchical – or at least compartmentalized – structure has inspired comparison with Freemasonry. Its exaltation of work is reminiscent of some of the more po-faced forms of Protestantism. Its induction methods have been compared with those of modern-day cults and sects. But in one respect, Opus is unique. In so far as its most committed members live in communities and/or are bound by undertakings of poverty, chastity and obedience, they form a religious order. Unlike the majority of monks and nuns, though, Opus Dei's initiates do normal jobs, work normal hours and wear normal clothes. It is this which has enabled them to attain such influence – and, I suspect, caused them to inspire such misgivings – in secular society. The Jesuits, to take the example of their most implacable enemies, are no doubt capable of exerting immense behind-the-scenes influence. But you are not likely to discover one day that the editor of, say, a financial journal for which you have been writing, or the chairman of an engineering company with which you have been negotiating, is also a member of the Society of Jesus. Nor is it conceivable that Jesuits, Dominicans or Benedictines would be appointed Spanish cabinet ministers.

You do not expect, but you may well find, especially if you live in Spain, that someone you work alongside, or over, or under, does not go home at night to a family, or a partner, or flatmates, but to a community in which there are lengthy periods of silence; that for two hours each day he or she is wearing a *cilicio*, a chain with pointed links turned inwards, on the upper thigh (so that neither it nor the wounds it inflicts can be seen); and that, once a week, your colleague whips his or her buttocks with a *disciplina*, a five-thonged lash, for as long as it takes to say the prayer *Salve Regina*.

Opus Dei's uniqueness has twice been recognized by the Vatican. In 1947, it became the Roman Catholic Church's first – and, for some time, its only – secular institute. In 1983, it became its first – and remains its only – personal prelature. Known in full as the Prelature of the Holy Cross and Opus Dei, the organization comprises two groups, one clerical, one lay. The Priestly Society of the Holy Cross is for the priests and deacons who make up less than 3 per cent of the membership but wield immense power over it. The lay group, Opus Dei itself, is divided by gender into men's and women's sections, and by vocation or availability into various categories.

Numeraries are invariably university graduates, and either have a doctorate or are believed to be capable of acquiring one. They are always celibate and mostly live in Opus houses. Whatever they do not need for the sober lives they lead they hand over to the director of the community in which they live. Since the majority have well-paid jobs, this is an important source of income. Below the numeraries come two categories of lesser standing, neither of which live in Opus communities. Associates (once referred to as oblates) are celibate, supernumeraries are not. In addition to its members, Opus recognizes a fourth category of so-called co-operators who can be non-Catholics, or even non-Christians, but who provide the organization with help and support.

In the dying years of the Franco dictatorship, Opus Dei, for all its political influence, was still a minority pressure group within the Spanish Church as a whole – marginalized both by its relatively small numbers and by its theological conservatism. But by the mid-2000s, after more than a quarter of a century of John Paul II's papacy and the 'silent apostasy' by liberal Catholics that accompanied it, the *Obra*'s heterodoxy had become something closer to orthodoxy in a Church with a different centre of gravity. At the same time, in Spain at least, Opus Dei's increased membership gave it far greater relative weight in a Church of reduced dimensions. Two of the statistics cited earlier in this chapter are worth looking at again in this context. The membership of Opus Dei in Spain was equivalent to very nearly half the number of Spaniards in religious orders. Barring a radical change in the orientation of Roman Catholicism under Pope Benedict XVI, it is likely that Opus Dei and other conservative groups, such as the Italian-inspired Comunione e Liberazione, will come to make up the mainstream in a Spanish Church that is more reactionary, but also more homogeneous.

Long before then, though, the Church in Spain will have paid a huge price in terms of popular sympathy. Indeed, it has already begun to do so. The pollsters who carried out the CIS survey mentioned earlier asked interviewees to say how much they trusted various institutions. There were seven in all. The Church emerged as the second most widely *dis*trusted. Barely a third of respondents said they had 'a lot' or even 'some' confidence in it. Only television, at a time when Spaniards' screens were awash with so-called *tele-basura* (junk telly), fared worse.

CHAPTER 9

Sex: From Francoist Prudery to Gay Marriages

As they drive around Spain, tourists are often puzzled to see buildings at the side of the road whose outlines are picked out in vividly coloured neon strip-lighting. These occasional bursts of gaiety are all the more incongruous because they usually adorn rather grim-looking houses, standing alone in the middle of the countryside. Outside, there will always be a car park, and sometimes it will be packed with vehicles. The buildings are roadside brothels. Inside, the motorist will find a bar crammed with heavily made-up *señoritas* who will be only too willing to join him for a drink and, at the right price, accompany him upstairs or wherever the bedrooms are to be found. Other, similar, though slightly less eye-catching, 'clubs' are to be found in every large Spanish town, often on the same street or in the same district.

According to the Civil Guard there are about 1,000 of these *bares de alterne* in Spain and in 2001 some of their owners formed an association, known by its initials as ANELA, to represent their interests and press for regulation of the sex industry. Prostitution is not illegal in Spain, but pimping and coercing women into prostitution are. ANELA says its members simply provide sex workers with the facilities with which to carry on their profession. They make their money, not from a share of the prostitutes' earnings, but from admission charges, the selling of drinks and the hiring of rooms.

The *bares de alterne* – by no means all of which operate according to the high standards set by ANELA – are just one branch of a vast industry. Other prostitutes operate on the streets or from apartments and houses. Their advertisements occupy considerable space in even the most respectable of Spanish newspapers. The Barcelona daily, *La Vanguardia*, for example, is the august and stolid journal of the

Catalan upper-middle classes. During the dictatorship, it was pro-Franco. Nowadays, it tends to be identified with the moderate Catalan nationalists, many of whom are stoutly traditional Roman Catholics. Yet flick to the back and you will find column after column of ads such as this one: 'MARINA will introduce you to sado. and humil., rain, transv. and enemas.'

The number of prostitutes at work in Spain is vast. Most recent estimates have put the figure at between 250,000 and 350,000. The sex industry's turnover has been reckoned at between €12 billion and €17 billion. A survey by the Instituto Nacional de Estadística (INE) in 2004 found that 27 per cent of the men it interviewed, who were between the ages of fifteen and forty-nine, acknowledged having had sex with a prostitute. This was by far the highest figure in any European country. One in fourteen Spanish males said he had visited a prostitute in the previous year.

If all of this strikes you as symptomatic of Spain's experimentation with new freedoms since the end of its dictatorship, then think again. If anything, it is indicative of how little – or rather, how slowly – things have changed in Spaniards' private lives. The resort to prostitution is more indicative of repression in society than liberation. The blatancy with which call-girls and red-light bars make themselves known to the public is a product of a new, more relaxed attitude, but the phenomenon they represent was even more prevalent under Franco than it is today. The earliest *bares de alterne* date from the 1930s and the estimated number of prostitutes in the last year of the dictatorship was 500,000 – one in twenty-seven of the adult female population.*

Apart from the overall fall in the number of prostitutes, two things have changed since. One is that far fewer Spanish women sell themselves nowadays. It is reckoned that between 70 and 80 per cent of all the prostitutes in Spain are foreigners, and that at least half are in the country illegally. Several town and city councils have quietly undertaken rehabilitation programmes, sometimes offering Spanish ex-prostitutes jobs, most commonly as gardeners. Probably the most dramatic change has been wrought in Barcelona, in what was once

---

* This would be consistent with one of the very few official statistics available. Shortly after the civil war, a census of prostitutes in Madrid indicated that one in every twenty-five women in the city was 'on the game'.

Spain's most notorious red-light district, the *barrio Chino*. As recently as the late eighties, the maze of alleyways and tenements depicted in Jean Genet's *Journal du voleur* was still both dangerous and stupefyingly squalid. By the early 2000s, it boasted a museum of contemporary art, several university faculties, bookshops, boutiques and a sprinkling of commercial art galleries.

Another big change has been a decline in the number of men who lose their virginity to prostitutes. The first comprehensive investigation of Spanish sexual attitudes and customs, carried out in the mid-sixties, found that almost two-thirds of the men interviewed had had their earliest experience with a professional. Yet a poll for the Instituto de la Juventud in 1987, the most recent that I have been able to find, suggested that that figure had dropped to just 9 per cent. Clearly, this suggests a greater readiness among young Spanish women to have sex with their boyfriends. But it would be a mistake to believe that the advent of democracy had led to a surge in sexual activity among the young. There has been an increase, certainly. But it has been gradual. Back in 1975, a survey for the weekly magazine *Blanco y Negro* found that 42 per cent of Spanish women had lost their virginity by the age of twenty. By 1987, according to the Instituto de la Juventud, 56 per cent had had sex by the age of eighteen. Unfortunately, I know of no recent survey in which an exactly comparable calculation was made. But the INE poll mentioned earlier found that the average age at which women between the ages of eighteen and forty-nine had lost their virginity was nineteen (for men, it was eighteen). What you see in those figures is a trend, unquestionably, but something a good deal less than an overnight revolution.

Perhaps the INE's most interesting finding was that 56 per cent of the women it interviewed – and 24 per cent of the men – said they had only ever had one partner. My personal impression – and I think anecdotal evidence counts for as much as pollsters' statistics in this most private of areas – is that a lot of Spaniards still have a preference for lengthy, steady relationships before marriage, not so different from the traditional *noviazgo*, or engagement, which often lasted many years. In fact, you frequently hear young Spaniards refer to their boyfriend or girlfriend as '*mi novio*' or '*mi novia*', even though they are not formally engaged. Since, in the old days, it was pretty much unthinkable that either party should back out of a *noviazgo*, the parents of the *novios* were sometimes prepared to turn a blind eye to sexual relations between them. It would be fascinating, though doubtless impossible, to know just how much the level of sex before *noviazgo*, as distinct from the level of sex before marriage, has really altered over the years.

A recent WHO report comparing various countries on the basis of polls among schoolchildren carried out in 2001–2 perhaps offers a clue. It looked, among other things, at the number of fifteen-year-olds who had already had sex. In Spain, the figures were 18 per cent for boys and less than 15 per cent for girls. The overall figure for both sexes was the third lowest among the thirty countries surveyed. Interestingly, the only countries that produced lower figures were Croatia and Poland, both countries where the Roman Catholic Church has had a powerful impact on society.

In the same way as the other Catholic countries of the Mediterranean, Spain has been subject to the doctrines of a religion which, ever since St Paul, has been deeply suspicious of physical enjoyment of any kind. To the monks and nuns in charge of many of Spain's private schools, the penis was the 'diabolic serpent' and the vagina 'Satan's den'. There is of course a direct link between attitudes of this sort and the Spaniards' traditional enthusiasm for the mortification of the flesh. As Monsignor Escrivá, the founder of Opus Dei, wrote: 'If you know that your body is your enemy and the enemy of God's glory, why do you treat it so gently?'

For the Church, sex was, and to some extent still is, strictly for the purpose of procreation within wedlock. Incredible as it may seem now, the Roman Catholic Church in Spain had great difficulty in agreeing to any form of physical contact between *novios*. As late as 1959, the Spanish bishops' 'Norms of Christian Decency' stated unequivocally that '*novios* walking along arm-in-arm cannot be accepted'. A Capuchin friar, Quintín de Sariegos, writing in the early sixties, had reconciled himself to the fact that *novias* would not only touch their *novios*, but might even kiss them. But he offered this advice – 'Whenever you kiss a man, remember your last communion and think to yourself, "Could the Sacred Host and the lips of this man come together on my lips without sacrilege?"'

For almost forty years, moreover, the Church was able not merely to advocate but to enforce its ideas with the assistance of a regime that depended upon it for its legitimation.

The Church was involved in official censorship at every level and was particularly responsible for deciding on matters of sexual propriety. As the decree which created Francoist Spain's board of film censors, the Junta Superior de Orientación Cinematográfica, put it: 'on moral questions, the vote of the representative of the Church shall be especially worthy of respect'. The cinema was of particular concern to the Church. Fr Angel Ayala, the founder of the Catholic pressure group ACNP, described it as 'the greatest calamity that has befallen the world since Adam – a greater calamity than the flood, the two World Wars or the atomic bomb'. In spite of its representative's privileged status on the Junta, the Church was apparently unconvinced that the Francoist authorities were sufficiently rigorous in their approach; four years later it set up its own Oficina Nacional Permanente de Vigilancia de Espectáculos, whose officials watched the films passed by the Junta after they had been censored and gave them a rating on a scale that went from one ('suitable for children') to four ('gravely dangerous'). Although it had no official standing, the Church's 'moral classification' was invariably printed alongside each film in the listings section of the newspapers.

But not even that was enough to satisfy the more zealous members of the clergy. Sometimes, after one of those 'gravely dangerous' films had slipped through the net, parish priests would take it on themselves to put up a notice in the foyer of the local cinema which said: 'Those who watch today's programme are committing mortal sin.' One bishop, outraged by the authorization of a film to which he objected, went so far as to arrange for groups of pious ladies from Acción Católica to wait at the entrance of the cinema. Whenever someone approached the box office, the leader would cry out: 'Say an Our Father for the soul of this sinner!' and the others would fall to their knees in prayer. It cut down the audiences no end.

Under the Church's guidance, censorship attained extraordinary heights of puritanism. Professional boxing matches were kept out of newsreels on the grounds that they showed naked male torsos. Photographs of the bouts did appear in the press, but with vests painted in by the *retocadores* (retouchers) who were employed by every newspaper and magazine until the fifties. Among their other duties was to reduce the size of women's busts. In later years, producers at state-run Televisión Española had to keep a shawl handy in case a starlet turned up for a show with a dress that was too décolleté. A similar horror of the female mammary glands led TVE's censors to cut from a Jean-Luc Godard film a glimpse of a magazine advertisement for brassières, and to reject *Moana*, Robert J. Flaherty's classic documentary about Polynesia, on the grounds that it included too many shots of bare-breasted native women.

In the forties and fifties it could be argued that the moral climate had at least some foundation in the nature of society. Sexual repression may have been severe, but then society was very traditional. During the sixties and seventies, however, the gap between what was considered acceptable by the authorities and what was considered acceptable by the public markedly widened. Official attitudes changed, but not as quickly or as much as those of society at large.

In 1962 the Ministry of Information and Tourism, the department primarily responsible for censorship, was taken away from Gabriel Arias Salgado, the religious bigot who had run the Ministry since its inception eleven years earlier, and given to the more pragmatic and secular Manuel Fraga Iribarne. The changeover ushered in a period in which some of the more absurd restrictions were lifted. Even so, it was not until 1964, for example, that the censors allowed a woman in a bikini (Elke Sommer, as it happened) to appear on the cinema screens.

After Franco's death, it was the publishing world which first breached the established taboos. In February 1976 a Spanish magazine called *Flashmen* (*sic*) carried a photograph of a model in which her bare nipples were plainly visible. Whether by accident or design, it was overlooked by the censor and thereafter *Flashmen* and others of its ilk set about pushing back the frontiers of the permissible inch by inch and curve by curve. Most of the nude models in the early days were foreign girls, but a previously obscure revue artiste called Susana Estrada won enduring fame by becoming the first Spanish woman in modern times to appear bare-breasted in the pages of a Spanish magazine.

Estrada became a symbol of what Spaniards dubbed the *destape*,* a

---

* *Destapar* is to take the lid off (something).

revolution in the depiction, discussion and appreciation of sex. All the big Spanish cities soon acquired clubs with striptease shows and bars with topless – Spanish – waitresses. The real turning point came in 1978. That was the year in which Spain got its first sex shop, *Kitsch*, which was opened in Madrid. The authorities closed it down five months later, but it had set a trend that was unstoppable, and soon even Burgos, that dour grey bastion of Catholic orthodoxy, had one. It was also the year in which the fashion for topless bathing, which was to change for ever the Spanish attitude to nudity, reached the holiday *costas*. At first, the Civil Guards did their best to halt it, sometimes by charging offenders with not being in possession of their personal documents. But by the beginning of the following season they had come to realize that it was an impossible task. They began to turn a discreet blind eye, and going topless soon became fashionable among Spanish women as well. Finally, 1978 saw the release of Spain's first-ever 'home-grown' soft-core porn movie, an embarrassingly dreadful production called *El maravilloso mundo del sexo*. The boyfriend of one of the actresses walked out on her halfway through the première.

The situation as far as hard-core films were concerned was somewhat anomalous, as were so many things at that time. The importing of explicit movies for private viewing was banned, yet hard-core one-reelers were being churned out by the dozen by a Spanish production company called Pubis Films.

Attempts to promote a hard-core movie business were encouraged by a belief that the administration was about to legalize a new kind of movie-house for the showing of explicit sex films. Officials have since said that between 1977 and 1978 the government was deterred by the activities of an Italian group suspected of connections with the Mafia, which was thought to be trying to take control of the Spanish market. Plans for the legalization of blue movie cinemas were shelved, killing off the fledgling Spanish hard-core film industry. When in 1984 Spain's first 'X' cinemas eventually opened for business, having been licensed by the new Socialist government, they relied mainly on US-based productions.

The years following Franco's death also witnessed important changes in the law that helped to narrow – although not, as we shall see, to close – the gap between what was actually happening and what was officially condoned.

The first of these was the legalization of contraceptives. In practice the ban had never been total under Franco. Condoms could always be obtained, albeit with some difficulty, in red-light districts and street markets. The invention of the Pill opened up further possibilities, because – in addition to its purely contraceptive effects – it could be used to treat certain hormonal disorders, such as severe premenstrual tension. The first packets of Schering's Anovial arrived in Spain in June 1964. Thereafter, a small but growing number of doctors were prepared to prescribe the Pill on therapeutic grounds for women who in fact wanted it for contraceptive purposes. It has since emerged that a few stood trial for doing so. By 1975, according to an official report leaked to *Cambio 16*, the Pill was being used by more than half a million women.

Nevertheless, the demand for contraceptives was vastly greater than the supply. If, by the end of Franco's rule and in spite of official exhortations to the contrary, there were on average only 2.5 children per family, it was also due to a good deal of self-restraint – *coitus interruptus*, *coitus reservatus* and simple abstinence.

The articles in the Penal Code which made the sale of contraceptives illegal were quietly revoked in 1978. It can be argued that few developments have had as great an impact on the nature of contemporary Spain. As we shall see in succeeding chapters, the increasing availability of effective contraception has had far-reaching effects. It has tilted the balance between the sexes, helped change the structure of family life, and exerted a profound influence on Spain's welfare and education systems.

At first, little was done to ensure that the contraceptives made legally available to Spaniards were used safely and reliably. While the UCD remained in power, there was no sex education in schools and the only family planning centres to be set up were financed, not by the central government, but by local authorities (invariably those run by the left).

All that changed after the Socialists took office. But probably the most important factor in raising awareness of contraception has been AIDS. The Instituto de la Juventud survey in 2002 found that nine out of ten people between the ages of fifteen and twenty-nine considered themselves well-informed about contraception and 85 per cent had used some kind of artificial contraceptive method the last time they had sex. However, among the relatively few – roughly one in six – who admitted to having casual sex, 40 per cent were not using contraception at all. The existence of this reckless minority would help to explain the soaring numbers of Spanish women using 'morning after' pills, which became legal in Spain only in 2001. Within two years, sales were running at well over 300,000 packets a year – a figure which, when it became known, prompted calls for more information campaigns on the risks of both pregnancy and infection by sexually transmitted diseases.

Still, Spain has come a long way in a relatively short time. The greater availability of both sex education and contraception has not just helped contain the spread of AIDS, but also contributed to a better enjoyment of sex, particularly among women. A succession of learned inquiries in the latter years of the dictatorship suggested that between 60 and 80 per cent of married Spanish women routinely obtained no pleasure from sexual intercourse. In *Las españolas en secreto: Comportamiento sexual de la mujer en España*, Dr Adolfo Abril and José Antonio Valverde concluded that 'no more than 20 per cent of the (female) population is able to use the word "orgasm" properly, another 30 per cent has heard or read the word "at some time" and the rest – half the (female) population – half of all Spanish women – have never heard the word and do not of course know what it means'. Compare that with the findings of a recent survey by the Federación Española de Sociedades de Sexología in which 84 per cent of Spaniards described themselves as sexually content.

Among the most remarkable paradoxes of Franco's supposedly Catholic Spain was that it had one of the world's highest pregnancy termination rates. It was never possible to arrive at an exact figure because the abortions were of course illegal, but a report by the Supreme Court prosecutors' department, the Fiscalía del Tribunal Supremo, in 1974 while Franco was still alive put the annual total at 300,000. By the time contraception was legalized, it was generally reckoned that the total was closer to 350,000.

In addition, the seventies saw a huge rise in overseas abortions. The favourite destination was London, which by 1978 was catering for more than 14,000 Spanish women every year. Overall, it would seem that the number of abortions as a proportion of all pregnancies was around 35 per cent.

The prevalence of abortion contrasted dramatically with the stiff penalties for practitioners. In 1979 the case of eleven Bilbao women charged with carrying out abortions became a *cause célèbre*. In the days leading up to their trial, 300 women occupied one of the main court buildings in Madrid and were violently evicted by the police. More than 1,000 women, including several well-known actresses, lawyers and politicians, published a document announcing that they had had abortions, and a similar number of men, including other well-known personalities, signed another document declaring that they had helped to arrange abortions. Whether or not as a result of this pressure, when the case came to court it was thrown out by the judges on the unprecedented grounds that the defendants had acted out of necessity. Their verdict did not, however, put an end to the prosecutions. Shortly afterwards another abortionist was sentenced to twelve years, and a girl who had had an abortion in London was fined.

Nevertheless, the outrage felt among middle-class intellectuals at these sentences tended to distract attention from the fact that a clear majority of the Spanish electorate was opposed to abortion on demand, although polls showed that the level of opposition was much higher among older voters than among younger ones, and that in the youngest age groups the 'pros' and 'antis' were more or less evenly balanced. On the other hand, abortion in special cases, such as after a rape or when the foetus was deformed or the mother's health was in danger, commanded more support – that of about two-thirds of the electorate, in fact. The Socialists in their winning manifesto promised to introduce a bill legalizing abortion in these three circumstances.

It was obviously going to be a political hot potato even so, and the Socialists gave the distinct impression of wanting to put off the introduction of a bill for as long as possible. The pressure which forced them to take action came from a most unlikely quarter: the courts. During the first few weeks of the Socialist government, the provincial court in Barcelona handed down a succession of judgements in which the judges, while reluctantly passing sentence on defendants who had clearly been involved in abortions, criticized the government for its failure to change the law.

At the end of January 1983, the government decided to bring forward its plans for legislation. Apparently unconvinced of the government's resolve, the Barcelona courts kept up the pressure and in March an attorney, acting not for the defence but for the prosecution, found an even better way of holding the law up to ridicule.

As the law then stood, the only mitigating circumstance which could be taken into account in abortion cases was where the defendant had undergone an abortion 'to hide her dishonour'.* It was such an archaic formulation that it had long since fallen into disuse, but when this particular attorney found himself in the position of having to prosecute a woman who was charged with having an abortion, he argued – doubtless tongue in cheek – that she was just such a case. At all events, the judges accepted his plea and reduced her sentence to one month.

It was clear that unless something was done, every liberally minded judge in the land would soon be handing out nominal sentences to defendants in abortion cases on the grounds that they had been defending their honour, and that this in turn could make Spain look ridiculous internationally. In fact, the original case went unnoticed outside Spain, but by the end of the year the Socialists' bill had passed through both chambers of the Cortes. It became law in 1985.

On paper at least, the new act was the most restrictive anywhere in the EU outside Ireland, where abortion was completely unavailable. However, Spain's law contained a loophole. It provided for pregnancies to be ended in circumstances where there was a threat to the mental as well as the physical health of the mother, and it left it entirely to the medical profession to decide if such a threat existed.† In practice, a lot of doctors proved ready to give the go-ahead for an abortion on the basis of little or no real evidence of a risk. In recent years,

* Defence of one's honour was also a mitigating circumstance in cases involving the murder of an illegitimate child. It applied not only where the child had been murdered by its mother but also in cases in which it had been put to death by the mother's father (with or without the mother's consent).

† Under this heading, moreover, there is no time limit. France, by contrast, has abortion on demand, but only up to the tenth week of gestation. In the mid-1990s, doctors in Spain, and particularly in Catalonia, began to exploit this difference between the laws of the two countries by offering abortions to French women who had missed the deadline, often because of delays in getting doctors' appointments. Some hired French-speaking staff and produced glossy leaflets in French to advertise their facilities. Thus, the EU state with ostensibly the least liberal law became a destination for 'abortion tourism'.

about 95 per cent of legal abortions in Spain have been carried out on these grounds.

That said, many other doctors, for reasons of conscience, refused to perform or authorize abortions even in circumstances allowed for by the law. Since, moreover, abortion was not normally available on the state health service, women who lacked the funds to pay a clinic (often because they did not want to ask their parents) may have been tempted to go for cheaper, illegal terminations.*

A comparative study published in 1999† using official data for European countries from 1996 showed Spain as having one of the EU's lowest abortion ratios – 12.6 for every 100 known pregnancies.‡ Only Belgium, Holland and, of course, Ireland, had lower ratios. However, the number of legal abortions in Spain has risen steeply since then, from 51,000 to more than 77,000 in 2002, and the official statistics make no provision for illegal abortions.

Here, you enter into a very foggy area indeed. The authors of the study just mentioned estimated that 100,000 illegal terminations were being carried out each year in the whole of southern Europe. But in 2000, Spain's Federación de Planificación Familiar reckoned there were 100,000 in Spain alone.§

Which of these estimates is right is absolutely crucial to assessing the prevalence of abortion in Spain and the impact made by the legalization of contraception and the spread of sex education. In the first case, assuming Spain accounts for, say, a third of the southern Europe total, the number of all abortions as a proportion of all pregnancies would have fallen from an estimated 35 per cent in 1978 to just over 20 per cent. But if the Federación de Planificación Familiar is right, then the true abortion ratio in 2000 would have been nearly 30 per cent, only slightly lower than it was in the last year in which the sale of contraceptives was banned. The uncertainty over the true

* In 1999, police arrested two Chinese women in the south of Madrid who were carrying out abortions in unsanitary conditions for a third of the price charged by a top-class clinic.

† Stanley K. Henshaw, Susheela Singh and Taylor Haas, 'Recent trends in abortion rates worldwide', in *International Family Planning Perspectives*, 25 (1) (March 1999).

‡ Live births plus legal abortions.

§ Proportionately, that would nevertheless represent a big drop on the official estimates of almost a decade earlier. In 1991, the government's Instituto de la Mujer reckoned that 70 per cent of all abortions in Spain were illegal.

situation only helps to fuel the impassioned debate between the pro- and anti-abortion camps. Over the years, the proportion of Spaniards in favour of a less restrictive law has increased steadily. But all efforts to introduce changes have so far foundered.

` The earliest such attempt played an important role in ending modern Spain's first experience of Socialism. Felipe González had promised to relax the abortion law in the 1993 election campaign. But after the vote he was dependent on the support of Jordi Pujol's Catalan nationalists, who were opposed to reform. The Socialists' decision in 1995 to try to change the law without the nationalists' agreement signalled the end of their alliance and made inevitable the early poll of the following year at which González and his government were removed from office. In the event, the Catalan nationalists joined forces with the People's Party to stop parliament holding a vote.

Four attempts to change the law were nevertheless made while the PP was in office. They all failed by slim margins in a parliament each time besieged by raucous demonstrations for and against reform. In February 1998, the opposition's bill was rejected only after three successive ballots yielded an exactly equal number of votes for and against the proposed measure. After returning to power, the Social-ists were planning to try again with a measure that would provide for abortion on demand in the first twelve weeks of pregnancy. The new abortion bill was one of a series of measures tabled by José Luis Rodríguez Zapatero's government that infuriated the Vatican and astonished many outsiders who had come to assume that Spain would always be somewhere in the rearguard of social reform. Another bill would do away with the previous government's restrictions on assisted reproduction and stem-cell research. In 2003, the PP had passed a law that limited to three the number of eggs that doctors could fertilize for a childless couple. The Socialists' bill would lift that restriction. More controversially, it would introduce a limited degree of embryo selection. Parents of children with incurable, genetically based illnesses would be allowed to conceive new embryos and then choose from among them to have another child so as to harvest its genes and save its sick sibling. The proposed new measure would also scrap restrictions imposed by the conservatives that had made human stem-cell research in Spain effectively impossible.

But the legislation that really caught international attention was that which made Spain only the third country in the world to institute gay marriage.* A law passed in June 2005 gave homosexual couples the same rights as heterosexual ones, including the right to adopt. The move reflected a shift in public attitudes towards gay people that, typically of modern Spain, has been as rapid as it was radical.

Under the dictatorship, the north-eastern coastal town of Sitges was an enclave of tolerance in a society otherwise severely repressive of homosexuals. Franco's contribution to gay rights was to make homosexuality illegal by including it in the 1970 *Ley de Peligrosidad Social* (literally, 'Law of Social Dangerousness'). It was this that led to the founding of a Movimiento Español de Liberación Homosexual. Throughout the late seventies, the Movimiento was responsible for organizing demonstrations on 28 June (International Gay Pride Day).

The first lesbian movement to be formed in Spain, the Catalonia-based Grup de Lluita per l'Alliberament de la Dona, did not come into existence until 1979. Even after that, the lesbian movement tended to keep a very low profile indeed. Its first demonstration was staged as late as 1987 and was prompted by the arrest of two gay women for kissing in public. That year, on 28 June, lesbian activists staged a 'kiss-in' in the Puerta del Sol, the square which has always been Madrid's rallying-point, and it became an annual event.

In 1979, homosexuality had been removed from the terms of the *Ley de Peligrosidad Social* by decree. Gay associations were legalized in 1980 and, as soon as the Socialists came to power, police raids on clubs virtually ceased. By the middle of the eighties, Madrid had a large gay quarter, the Chueca district in the centre. Nonetheless, public attitudes were, on balance, conservative and many gay Spaniards were still reluctant to 'come out'. A study in the early nineties found that only 2.8 per cent of men and 1.4 per cent of women were prepared to describe themselves as gay. Yet 9 per cent of both sexes acknowledged that they had felt desire for members of their own sex.

But by then attitudes in the rest of society were changing fast and, as the decade progressed, many Spaniards felt sufficiently confident to declare openly that they were gay. Among them were a priest and an army lieutenant-colonel.

---

* The others were Holland and Belgium. Sweden and Denmark have 'civil union' laws for same-sex couples, but have not legalized gay marriages as such.

In 1997 the Centro de Investigaciones Sociológicas published the results of a poll that showed for the first time that a majority of Spaniards was in favour of giving homosexual couples equal – or almost equal – rights. The exception was the right to adopt. The following year, the Catalan autonomous government introduced a measure that gave legal status to same-sex unions. Regional authorities in the Basque country, Valencia, the Balearic Islands, Navarre and Andalusia all followed suit over the next four years. Navarre, long regarded as one of the most traditional areas of Spain, went further and legalized adoption.

As for public opinion, it was now firmly on the side of gay marriages. A CIS survey in 2004 indicated that two-thirds of the population were in favour. What is more, it showed that, on the issue of whether to extend to gay couples the right of adoption, the balance of sentiment was, for the first time, in favour. To some extent, therefore, the Socialists were simply giving legal expression to something that most Spaniards backed and which was already a reality in several parts of the country.

CHAPTER 10

Men and Women: Machismo Meltdown

Because no one really expected José Luis Rodríguez Zapatero to win the 2004 election, very few people studied the Socialists' manifesto. So the impact, when they started to deliver on their radical promises, was that much greater.

Long before the vote, Zapatero had said he would give women an equal opportunity at ministerial level. But that was anyway something less than a clear-cut pledge, and no one outside Spain expected him to unveil a cabinet in which half the ministers were women. The only other European country where such a team had been formed was Sweden, and it was Zapatero's 'fifty-fifty' cabinet more than anything that prompted talk of Spain as a 'Sweden of the Mediterranean'.

It was pointed out that there was a certain amount of gender bias in the distribution of portfolios. The 'heavyweight' departments such as Foreign Affairs, Defence, Interior and Industry all went to men while women got the 'social ministries' such as Education, Health and Housing. Nevertheless, Zapatero's senior Deputy Prime Minister was a woman, María Teresa Fernández de la Vega, as was the new holder of the infrastructure portfolio, who had very real power and a large budget. The symbolic importance of the announcement was incalculable. It was a message of empowerment and encouragement to every woman in Spain.

In fact, that message had been growing louder and clearer ever since the return of democracy and regardless of the political orientation of the country at the time. There had been only one woman minister in the five years the UCD was in office. But there were five in the fourteen years of the González era, and ten in the eight years the PP was in power. In 2000, both houses of a conservative-dominated parliament had elected women to be their speakers and José María Aznar had made a woman, Ana Palacio, his Foreign Minister. At the 2004 election, 126 of the 350 deputies elected – 36 per cent of the total – were women. That was a higher proportion of female parliamentary representation than in Germany and a much higher one than in Britain, France or Italy.

But then, wherever you look in Spanish life today, you will find women in positions of responsibility. According to the World Bank, in 2000 women accounted for almost half of Spain's liberal professionals and a third of its managers. The figure for managers may have been slightly below the EU average, but that for the professions was exactly in line with it.

It is hard to overstate the magnitude of the transformation represented by those statistics, for the status of women has changed more rapidly and substantially in Spain than in perhaps any country on earth.

It is no coincidence that a Spanish word, _machismo_, should have come to be adopted internationally to signify what American feminists dubbed male chauvinism.* The discrimination to which women in all European countries were subjected acquired an especially keen edge in Spain. This was maybe partly because of its sustained experience of Islam. Or perhaps because the seven centuries of conquest and settlement that it took to remove Islam from the peninsula bred among its Christian population a special emphasis on, and reverence for, traditionally masculine values. For centuries, moreover, women in Spain, as in other parts of southern Europe, were the prisoners of a code of moral values at the core of which was a peculiar conception of honour. It was regarded not as a subjective measure of self-esteem, as it was in northern Europe, but as an objective, almost tangible, asset that a man could lose, not just by his own actions but also by those of others, and in particular those of his female relatives.

A wife could strip her husband of his honour by cuckolding him and a daughter could forfeit her father's honour by losing her virginity before marriage. If the girl were betrothed there was a good chance that the marriage could be held earlier than planned, at which point the loss of honour could be minimized; but if she had had

* However, the word '_machismo_' originated in Mexico.

sex without even getting engaged the sanction was horrific, because the only way in which the family could save itself from dishonour was by removing the cause, which in this case was the girl herself. Expelled from home, single mothers were usually unable to find any respectable employment in a society where it was difficult enough for women to acquire a training, let alone a job. As a consequence many drifted into prostitution. In this way, Latin society has divided women into whores and madonnas, not just in theory but in practice. For the father of the child, on the other hand, the fact of having had sex before marriage – whatever the circumstances – was as much a distinction as a disgrace.

This was consummately unjust, since men, it could be argued, had less excuse for pre-marital dalliance. Unlike women, they could always resort to prostitutes. But then the reason why frustrated young men were able to afford the services of prostitutes was that they were cheap, and the reason they were cheap was because they were numerous. That in turn was because their numbers were constantly being replenished by cohorts of unmarried mothers who had themselves been unable to withstand the pressures imposed by the taboo on pre-marital sex. Thus the Latin way of sex always had a sort of iniquitous internal logic.

The division of women into the stereotypes of whore and mother is deeply embedded in the Castilian language and especially its slang. *Hijo de puta* ('son of a whore') is a serious insult, yet *de puta madre* ('whore-motherish') means 'great', 'superb', 'fantastic'. The allegation, in *hijo de puta*, that one's own mother might be a whore is intolerable, but the abstract notion of a woman combining both erotic and maternal qualities is nevertheless thought to be highly appealing.

This whole complex of social and moral values had been sustained and encouraged under Franco's dictatorship. As a way of promoting the growth of a population which had been reduced by civil war, Franco instituted a system of incentives for large families – but the prizes were given to the fathers, not the mothers. Although divorce and contraception were outlawed within a matter of months of the end of the civil war, there was no law to ban brothels until 1956, and even then it was never implemented. At a time when Franco's censors were busy covering boxers' chests and trimming actresses' busts, they were quite content to give their imprimatur to a novel, *Lola*, whose heroine was a prostitute-spy.

It has been said that towards the end of Franco's rule the only European country in which there was a comparable degree of institutionalized discrimination against married women was Turkey, and that on several counts the status of wives in Turkey was actually higher. The assumptions underlying the Spanish civil code were summed up in article 57: 'The husband must protect his wife and she must obey her husband.' At the crux of their legal relationship was the concept of *permiso marital* (marital permission). Without her husband's agreement, a wife could not embark on any sort of activity outside the home. She could not take a job, start a business or open a bank account. She could not initiate legal proceedings, enter into contracts, or buy and sell goods. She could not even undertake a journey of any length without her husband's approval.

Under the Spanish system, the property owned by a married couple is divided into three categories: that which the husband has brought into the marriage, that which the wife has brought into the marriage and that which they have acquired since (their so-called *bienes gananciales*). But whereas the man did not need his wife's permission before selling, lending or mortgaging the property he had brought into the marriage, she required his for a similar transaction. Not only that, but the wife had no control whatsoever over their *bienes gananciales*, even when she had been partly – or entirely – responsible for earning them. As if that were not enough, the wife did not have proper control over her children either, because, unlike the husband, she did not enjoy what was called the *patria potestad* or paternal authority.

Leaving the family home for even a few days constituted the offence of desertion, which meant – among other things – that battered wives could not take refuge in the homes of their friends or relatives without putting themselves on the wrong side of the law. And although adultery by either sex was a crime, punishable by between six months and six years in prison, there were different criteria for men and women. Adultery by a woman was a crime whatever the circumstances, but adultery by a man only constituted an offence if he committed it in the family home, or if he was living with his mistress, or if his adulterous behaviour was public knowledge.

The first significant reform of this system was approved shortly before Franco died. In 1975 Spain abolished *permiso marital* – fifty-six years after Italy and thirty-seven years after France. The laws against adultery were revoked in 1978 and those articles of the civil code which put women at such a disadvantage with regard to their children and the family finances were replaced in 1981.

Since then, women have made up so much ground in Spain that it can seem as if the restrictions on them were lifted, not in the last few decades, but centuries ago. If the social revolution of the seventies was about sex, the social revolution of the eighties and nineties was about gender. It was the decade in which Spanish women flooded into higher education and on to the labour market.

By the start of the academic year 1987–8, there were more female than male students in Spain's universities. In 1981, women had accounted for less than a quarter of the total active population. By 1991, they accounted for a third.

Women worked their way to positions of prominence in every walk of life, including even bullfighting. In 1993, Cristina Sánchez, a former hairdresser, became the first woman (in modern times at least*) to kill all six bulls in a *corrida*.†

Almost as striking was the incorporation of women into Spain's military, and paramilitary, services. The first Civil Guards to wear skirts entered service in 1989, having begun their training a year earlier – at the same time as the military academies opened their doors to women seeking to enter the non-combatant branches of the armed forces as NCOs or officers. It was not until the following year that the government permitted women to apply for admittance to the fighting units – and only then at the insistence of a schoolgirl.

Ana Moreno, from Denia on the east coast, had been inspired by a teacher, a retired pilot, to dream of becoming one herself. At the age of seventeen, she wrote asking to enter the Military Aviation Academy at San Javier in Murcia; in reply, she had a letter telling her

---

* A ban on women fighting bulls on foot was lifted in the year of Franco's death. It had been in force since 1908. Before that, Spain produced a number of female bullfighters. The most extraordinary was perhaps Martina García, who fought in her last *corrida* in 1880 – at the age of seventy-six.

† She retired in 1999 complaining, it should be noted, of discrimination in the allocation of fights.

there was no law to say she could. Taking the attitude that there was no law to say that she could not, she appealed to the courts and in 1988 the High Court in Madrid ruled that her case was a violation of the constitution which guarantees equality of the sexes. It took a year for the government to issue a decree to regularize the situation, but in 1989 women who wanted to join fighting units were allowed to sit the common entrance examination for Spain's three military academies. Thirty-six did so. None passed, though this was hardly surprising since they had had only a few months in which to prepare, compared with several years in the case of the men.

A further change in the regulations in 1992 allowed the recruitment of soldiers, sailors and air force personnel who had not done military service, thereby enabling women to join the ranks.* The first offer of places in the armed services after the amendment elicited some 12,000 applications. The Ministry of Defence was astonished to discover that almost a fifth came from women.

The arrival of vast numbers of women in the labour market has transformed the Spanish language. Because women had never before occupied certain jobs, the words used to describe those jobs existed only with masculine endings. So the choice has been between inventing new words with feminine endings, and using the existing masculine noun with a feminine article. The dilemma is still unresolved. It is now agreed that a woman who belongs to the cabinet is *una ministra*, but a female doctor is *una medico*. Most people referred to Cristina Sánchez as *la torera*, yet she herself preferred to be known as *la torero*. For the most part, practice has actually gone further than would seem necessary. Words ending in 'e', which were never gender-specific, have also been changed. Usually, 'the boss' – if a woman – is not *la jefe*, but *la jefa*.

One battle in which Spaniards do not have to engage is whether a wife should use her own or her husband's name: it has always been customary for married women to retain their surnames. However, Spanish women are still hampered by the rigid division of their numbers into *señoras* and *señoritas*, nor is there an obvious Spanish equivalent of Ms.

---

* The only areas initially barred to women were the Legion, the Parachute Brigade, submarines and small craft.

The vast changes in the status of Spanish women have stirred astonishingly little public controversy. Women's liberation groups sprang up in the seventies as similar movements emerged in other parts of the world. But their voices tended to be drowned out in the louder, wider debate over how best to build a democratic Spain. Feminism nevertheless came to be seen as part of a wider process of liberation in society, and it was not long before it was embraced – some would say smothered – by officialdom.

The UCD's contribution to the women's cause was to set up within the Ministry of Culture a women's department whose most memorable initiative was a series of television advertisements aimed at drawing attention to sexism in society. One opened with a handsome (male) executive striding down the street towards a group of women of about his own age. As he drew near, the women looked him up and down and then broke into whistles and catcalls interspersed with suggestive remarks. It was hilarious – though none the less effective for that. The Socialists took a more vigorous approach. Soon after they came to power for the first time, they set up a well-funded Instituto de la Mujer, which attracted many of the activists in the existing feminist movement. It has since remained a key point of reference and source of initiatives.

Perhaps because of this, the cause of women's rights in Spain never developed that combination of mannishness and anti-maleness which was characteristic of radical feminism in the English-speaking world. This too may help to explain why the progress of women towards equality in Spain has been so short on acrimony. If there was never a Spanish Norman Mailer, it could be because there was never a Spanish Kate Millett.

If anything, there was a tendency to link women's liberation with heterosexual permissiveness. Carmen, as portrayed in Carlos Saura's film version, is a promiscuous, predatory troublemaker. Yet when the film came to be shown on television in Spain, the listing in one of the newspapers that day began: 'Carmen, a liberated woman ...'

In 1990, the Instituto de la Mujer carried out an extensive investigation into male attitudes. One element of the exercise was to identify different categories by their reaction to certain statements in the questionnaire. For example, the 'household monarch' was someone who agreed with the statement: 'A woman's place is in the home.'

One of the statements was: 'For the good of the marriage, it doesn't matter if the woman has the odd fling.' The men who agreed with it were classified as 'feminists'.

Why women's liberation should have become so closely linked to sexual permissiveness in Spain can only be guessed at. My personal theory is that it has a lot to do with the peculiarities of Spain's recent economic and social history. Elsewhere, moves towards sexual equality followed progress towards sexual freedom. That is what happened in Spain too. But the influx of millions of foreign tourists in the sixties allowed Spanish men to indulge in pre-marital relationships without involving Spanish women. The *sueca* (literally 'Swedish woman', but a term which came to be applied to all northern European females) soon figured prominently in Spanish popular legend. One result was that Spanish women were left feeling they had some catching up to do on the men as soon as they had the opportunity.

In a way, Spain has leapt from pre-feminism into post-feminism without having really experienced the feminist upheaval which elsewhere took place in between. Spanish society was never lectured by a Gloria Steinem or a Germaine Greer. As a consequence, profoundly sexist attitudes have survived into an era in which women are acquiring much genuine freedom and equality.

It is also the case that women in Spain continue to be at a disadvantage both at work and in the home. The boom of the eighties saw women brought into the labour market on an unprecedented scale. Yet almost two decades later, barely half of all Spanish women between the ages of twenty-five and sixty-five had a job. Unemployment among women was nearly twice as high as among men, suggesting that employers were still deeply reluctant to give them work. Women were more than six times as likely to have a temporary contract and, partly because of that, they earned far less than their male counterparts. According to the International Labour Organization in 2003, the disparity between the earnings of Spanish men and women doing equivalent work was 28 per cent, double the EU average.

As in other countries, but to an even greater extent, women in Spain have reacted to discrimination by carving out niches for themselves within the labour market. It is reminiscent of the way the Jews turned to certain trades when they were forbidden to bear arms or own land in parts of medieval Europe. The favoured areas are health, education and the law. Official figures for 2003 showed that women accounted for more than 40 per cent of Spain's judges and doctors, 65 per cent of its schoolteachers (but only 35 per cent of its university teachers), and 70 per cent of its chemists. Yet while plenty of women were managers, their presence in boardrooms was negligible. Less than 3 per cent of the directors of Spain's biggest publicly quoted companies, those included in the IBEX-35, were women.

Once they have secured a job, Spanish women – or, to be precise, Spanish mothers – have the advantage of more extensive nursery-school facilities than exist in many other parts of Europe.* However, they have to contend with a problem that more than offsets it: the attitude that most Spanish, indeed most Latin, men continue to hold about their role in the home.

For this, women themselves – or rather, earlier generations of women – are partly to blame. The Spanish *madre* may not have fussed over her sons to the same extent as the Italian *mamma*. Even so, the degree to which boys have traditionally been pampered and privileged by their mothers in Spain can be difficult for outsiders to credit. One Spanish woman I know says that she discovered that she was a feminist as a child when one of her brothers mentioned he could do with a glass of water. 'You heard him,' her mother said. 'Go and fetch your brother a glass of water.'

Reared in accordance with such a set of values, Spanish men are often feminist in word but not in deed. In the winter of 1976–7, an extensive survey was carried out on the initiative of a multinational advertising agency among young city-dwellers in nine European countries. Asked whether they agreed that 'a woman's place is in the home', only 22 per cent of the young Spaniards said 'yes', compared with 26 per cent in Britain, 30 per cent in Italy and 37 per cent in France. The only countries that returned a lower figure than Spain were the Scandinavian ones. By 1990, the young men who had been interviewed in that survey would mostly have married and would thus have qualified to take part in a study conducted by the Spanish government's polling institute, the CIS. This found that the number of husbands who helped with work in the home varied from 15 to 20 per cent for everything except preparing breakfast (36 per cent)

---

* See below, pp. 313–14.

and home repairs (70 per cent). Little seems to have changed since then. A study carried out by the Instituto de la Mujer in 2004 found that, on average, men spent 43 minutes a day on domestic tasks while women spent 5 hours and 23 minutes.

Childcare also fell almost entirely to women. The same body found that over the period 2000–2003, the percentage of households in which the father, rather than the mother, took leave from work after the birth of a child rose, but from 1 per cent to 1.5 per cent. This, however, was partly because the law granted Spanish men such meagre paternity leave. A Spanish father was entitled to just two days, compared to fourteen in some Scandinavian countries.

In an effort to reverse the trend, an MP introduced a clause into the 2005 divorce law putting pressure on men – or at least those who had a register office wedding – to do more of the household chores. The legislation altered the civil marriage ceremony so that it now includes an undertaking by the groom to do his share. And if he does not then, if the marriage fails, it will count against him in the divorce court. Judges will have the power to order that men who refused to do their part be given less frequent access to their children.*

The fact that the changing role of Spanish women has so far made so little difference to the traditional habits of men is, I think, an important reason why there has been so little conflict between the sexes. Women have begun to assume new responsibilities in society, yes. But in addition to, rather than in place of, the ones they already had. To a greater extent than most of their European counterparts, they are trying to fulfil three roles at once – those of partner, mother and wage-earner.

The degree to which they are aware of their predicament was highlighted in 1990. The magazine columnist Carmen Rico-Godoy published a novel called *Cómo ser una mujer y no morir en el intento*, a humorous account of the travails of a middle-class Spanish woman with a high-powered job and an unconsciously, but irredeemably, *machista* husband. It became an instant best-seller.

The unusually difficult circumstances in which women have been

---

* The same year, a Spanish designer, Pep Torres, offered a more direct solution to the problem when he created the first washing machine in the world that shares out domestic tasks. His invention, named 'Your Turn', scans the fingerprints of the user to see if it is being loaded by the same person as the time before. If so, it shuts down.

joining the labour market help to explain the outstanding demographic change since the return of democracy: the drop in Spain's fertility rate (the number of children per woman of child-bearing age). Nothing – no change of government, no boom or recession, no revolution in attitudes – nothing, except perhaps the death of General Franco itself, has had such a vast effect on modern Spanish society. As will become apparent later in this book, it has conditioned everything from the nature of the family to immigration policy.

Since 1975, the fertility rate has more than halved. Not long after the Socialists came to power for the first time in 1982, it sank below 2.1, which is the level demographers reckon is necessary for the regeneration of the population. Ever since then, Spain has been doomed to become an ageing nation. In the nineties, Spain 'overtook' Italy, which was undergoing a similar process, to become the country with the world's lowest fertility rate. In 1998, the rate fell to 1.15. Since then, it has picked up slightly, but entirely because of immigration.

Male attitudes are clearly not the only reason for this remarkable drop. Other factors have undoubtedly played a role: a reluctance to have children outside marriage, combined with a sharp fall in the marriage rate; the increased use of contraception, and also, it has been suggested, a growing preference for material comforts – a nice home, a good car and expensive holidays – rather than a big family. The evidence strongly suggests, however, that the main reason is that Spanish women have been taking up full-time employment without significant changes in the division of domestic work between the sexes. As has been seen in other countries in southern Europe, women who do not wish to give up their jobs and cannot spread the burden of domestic tasks react by cutting down, or cutting out, their third role – as mothers. The fertility rates in Portugal and Greece have also dropped sharply and are close to that of Spain.

There is nothing to say that fertility rates must go on declining inexorably, though. Quite the reverse. As the conditions affecting women improve, as changing social attitudes and labour legislation provide them with more help at work, in the home and with children, so they recover their freedom of manoeuvre. Ironically, it would seem that the longer Spanish men cling to traditional attitudes towards women, the greater the damage they will do to that most traditional of Spanish institutions, the family.

CHAPTER 11

Family Values and Home Truths

It was the Saturday before Christmas. A typical Madrid winter's day – piercingly cold and bright.

The *Gordo* ('fat one'), one of the world's richest lotteries, was being drawn that morning and had just showered 10,000 million pesetas (then worth about $100 million or £55 million) on staff at a Madrid department store. It was in an up-market part of town, so assistants who had spent weeks catering to the caprices of Madrid's rich had just been handed a present bigger than any they had sold. In a bar across the street from the store, the ladies from perfumery were toasting their luck with champagne. One of the men sharing a drink with them had bought several shares in the winning ticket and stood to gain 40 million pesetas (about $400,000 or £220,000).

What was he going to do with it? Buy a house and a car and spend the change on a round-the-world cruise?

'No,' he said. 'I come from a big family, you see. There are six of us, so each of my brothers and sisters will get five million, and my in-laws will have to have another five, so that should leave my wife and me with ten million to pay off the mortgage and put something aside for the future.'

'And what does your wife think about it?' I asked.

'Oh, I've phoned her and she's overjoyed,' he replied, wholly missing the point of the question.

Survey after survey has shown that what matters to Spaniards above all else is not an ideal or a belief. It is no longer God or Spain, but the family.

Back in the 1990s, as Spain became embroiled in the first Gulf war, it was clear the country's long isolation from foreign conflict was coming to an end and that soon some Spaniards might be called upon to lay down their lives for their country or an ideal, such as freedom or democracy. *Cambio 16* carried out a survey to see if people were, in fact, prepared to do so. The results were extraordinary. Only 8 per cent said they would give their life for their country, while ideals such as love and freedom scored a mere 3 per cent. No other cause commanded more than 8 per cent among those interviewed – except their immediate family. Fully 54 per cent said they were ready to lay down their lives for 'a close relative'.

More recent polls have all indicated that the Spanish continue to accord the family more respect than any other institution or principle. In 2003, for example, the research department of the savings bank, La Caixa, conducted an inquiry in which respondents were asked to rate a series of values on a scale of 1 to 10. The one that scored highest was 'Having a good relationship with your family'. It was considered more important than good health, earning money or success at work.

The reliance Latins place on the family has sometimes been criticized as a weakness rather than a strength. Favouring the interests of your relatives can breed favouritism, corruption and an 'us against the rest' mentality that stands in the way of a society in which things are done for the common good. The family has nevertheless played an invaluable role in Spain in recent times. It has helped mitigate the crisis of values in society caused by the transition from dictatorship to democracy and the decline in influence of the Roman Catholic Church. What is more, in a country whose economy has been consistently unable to generate enough jobs, family solidarity has made up for many of the shortcomings of a modest welfare system and prevented high unemployment becoming a source of political instability.

In so far as the family is concerned, then, it would seem that the stereotyped view that outsiders have of the Spanish is correct: they are indeed a family-minded people, and their family values have given them a much-needed anchor with which to ride out the political and economic storms that have assailed them. That said, it is worth taking a closer look at what exactly Spaniards are talking about when they refer to the family, because what they mean today is very different from what they meant just a few decades ago.

It is all too easy, on a brief visit, to get a distorted view of family life in modern Spain. Typically, holidaymakers go out to a restaurant at lunchtime on a Sunday, see a group of Spaniards of all ages sitting round a table and form the impression that large but close families, all living under the same roof, are still the norm. Sunday lunch is indeed an important way for members of a family to keep in touch. But what you are most likely to see grouped around a restaurant table are the members of several different, though interrelated, nuclear families who are unlikely to see each other again for weeks, or perhaps months. And if grandma and grandpa are there, the statistical probability nowadays is not that they will be going back to a son's or daughter's house, but to their own home or an old people's residence. As with so much in Spain, appearances can be deceptive.

What has happened over recent decades is that the nuclear family has shrunk in one direction while expanding in another. On the one hand, contemporary Spaniards are increasingly reluctant to share their homes with elderly parents. Not so very long ago, it was the norm. Today, it is very much the exception. In 1970, 71 per cent of people over the age of sixty-five lived with a member of their wider family. By 1992, that figure had plunged to 23 per cent.

Traditionally, no Spanish home was complete without a silver-haired *abuelo* or *abuela* dozing in a corner by the fire. Now, the place of the somnolent grandparent is more than likely to be occupied by a young man or woman of what was once considered marriageable age. Spain has become a society of stay-at-home offspring. The 2001 census showed 75 per cent of twenty-five-year-olds – and even 35 per cent of thirty-year-olds – still living with their parents. In both cases, the proportions were more than double what they had been twenty years earlier.

This dramatic rise is conventionally explained in economic terms. The surge in property prices that began in the eighties, coming on top of high unemployment, particularly among the young, staunched a tendency that was evident in other societies for children to leave the parental home once they had finished their education, and move into shared accommodation with people of their own age. But there are, I suspect, other factors at work, just as there are in other Mediterranean societies that have experienced the same phenomenon.

One is that parents and children in Latin countries get on pretty well. I don't mean to deny that there are individual cases of children who fall out with their parents or that there have been differences – at times, sharply defined – between the overall views of younger and older people on issues ranging from sex to politics. But there has never been anything like the drastic generational conflicts that split Anglo-Saxon societies back in the fifties and sixties of the last century. Latin cultures have produced very few iconic young rebels of the kind portrayed by James Dean and, in the years since, there have not been any Latin Johnny Rottens or Kurt Cobains. The notion that bad and wild equals independent equals admirable is one that just does not square with the Latin, family-based value system. The other factor that I think is worth bearing in mind is that most of today's Spanish parents take a vastly more tolerant approach to sex than did their own, and that has removed an important incentive for leaving home.

'We let our boys stay out late and we let them bring girls home for the night,' said a friend whose four sons were all still living with the family. 'I don't know about you, but the reason I left my parents was because I wanted the freedom to sleep with girls. My sons have that – and they still have their mother to wash their clothes and cook their meals. No wonder they don't want to go!'

The reluctance of the young to leave the family home is an important additional reason for Spain's low birth-rate. Because Spaniards are waiting longer to set up homes of their own, whether inside or outside marriage, they are waiting longer to have children, and thus having fewer. This is ironic: while still keen on the idea of family, Spaniards are increasingly slow to form families of their own.

In 2000, the average age at marriage was 28 for women and 30 for men. In the year following Franco's death, the corresponding figures were 24 and 26. Ever since the beginning of the twentieth century, the annual rate of marriages in Spain had fluctuated between about 7 and 8.5 per 1,000 inhabitants. But in the late seventies it began to drop like a stone and, in the early nineties, Spain's marriage rate was the lowest in Europe. This is no longer the case, but the marriage rate has nevertheless continued to fall. In 2002, it was just over 5 per 1,000.

One reason for this, though, has been an increase in the popularity – and acceptability – of unmarried partnerships. In the 16–29 age group, more than a fifth of Spanish couples in 2002 were unmarried. That was still below the EU average of more than 30 per cent. But it was double the rate to be found in Portugal or Italy, the other traditionally Roman Catholic countries of southern Europe.

Another important qualification to the rose-tinted picture of Spanish family life most foreigners carry away with them is to be found in statistics pointing to a <u>level of violence in the home</u> that is at least as great as that to be found in other societies.

Cruelty to children is a good deal more common than is generally believed. The view that the Spanish and other Latin nations do not have organizations for the protection of children because they do not need them is simply bunk. They do not have them because for years – for centuries, indeed – it has been more or less taboo to interfere in family affairs. Child abuse exists in Spain just as it exists elsewhere, and as elsewhere it is most often found among the most disadvantaged sectors of society.

But the form of domestic violence that has most attracted public concern in recent years is that perpetrated by men against women. Inevitably, partner abuse came to be known in Spain as *violencia machista*. Since long before Franco, the whole subject had been ignored. Under his dictatorship the law said a woman must obey her husband. How he went about compelling obedience was his business. Right up until the late 1960s, there was no legal impediment to mistreating a wife. Even after that, it was not classified as a crime, but as a mere infraction. By and large what went on between husband and wife was not a matter for the police, let alone the courts – until, on occasions, it was too late, and the emergency services were called to the scene of a murder. It was not until 1983 that officials even began collecting statistics on *violencia machista*. There was a parliamentary inquiry in the late eighties, but nothing much was done and the issue sank to somewhere near the bottom of the political agenda.

What changed things was a regional television programme. In 1997, a sixty-year-old Andalusian woman called Ana Orantes gave an interview in which she described the nightmare of her existence. Her husband repeatedly beat her, yet the courts had ordered they should continue to live together. The interview put a name and a face to the victims of what people knew was happening within the four walls of many a home, and in the courts of complacent, or complicit, judges. Unfortunately, though, the programme did more than that. A few days later, Orantes's husband took revenge. He attacked and beat her again. Then he tied her to a chair, doused her with petrol, set her alight and left her to die. The publicity given to her death set off a national debate that has yet to abate.

Over the next five years, the number of specialized help-desks in police stations and courthouses doubled. The number of shelters for battered women increased by well over half. Newspapers, meanwhile, kept track of each year's tally of deaths as it rose, ensuring the issue was never far from the minds of Spain's lawmakers.

One of the problems of dealing effectively with *violencia machista* was the slowness of the Spanish courts. Sometimes, women died before getting a restraining order against their partners. A package of legal reforms brought in by the Aznar government* gave battered spouses and partners the chance to get a restraining order within a maximum of 72 hours. It also made domestic violence a full-blown crime with correspondingly stiffer penalties. But the conservatives' response fell well short of the broader – and costlier – solution that women's groups had been pressing for. Their cause gained added urgency as it became clear that, despite the government's measures, the annual death toll was not falling.

Zapatero took office promising that a more comprehensive bill to tackle *violencia machista* would be among the first measures his government approved. The Socialists' law, which came into force in 2005, offered victims of domestic violence legal, economic and psychological support. It also provided for gender education in schools and measures against sexist advertising. What remained to be seen was whether it would help in reducing the incidence of what the Prime Minister himself called Spain's 'worst disgrace'.

His choice of words was interesting, because what is exceptional about *violencia machista* in Spain is not necessarily its pervasiveness, but rather the public's feelings of embarrassment and shame about it. Men beating women is all too redolent of that 'primitive' past from which Spaniards are so desperate to escape. An EU survey in 1999 suggested Spaniards took violence of all kinds against women more seriously

* See below, p. 334.

than most other Europeans. Yet there is quite a lot of evidence to show that partner abuse is no more prevalent in Spain than elsewhere in Europe. Women's groups claim this is simply because much of it still goes unreported. But two polls carried out by the Instituto de la Mujer and the University of Paris and published in 2000 tried to get at the truth by asking women themselves if they had had experience of male violence in any form, from mild psychological aggression to actual bodily harm. The surprising result was that the level of all forms of violence was slightly lower than in France. An area in which the figures cannot be distorted by a failure to report is murder. Here again, the Spanish total of around 100 deaths a year, or 2.5 per million, horrific though it is, is comparatively slight when set against the 4,000 women, or 15 per million, who die every year at the hands of their partners in the US. It may seem perverse to say so, but the concern about *violencia machista* in Spain is actually quite encouraging – a sign that sensibilities are changing and approximating to those in the rest of Europe.

It can be argued that it is only now, in fact, that the Spanish family is really being put to the test because until relatively recently it was kept together by the force and sanction of the law. There was no divorce.

Under Franco's dictatorship, there were two kinds of marriage – civil and canonical. But if only one of the partners was a Catholic* they had to have a canonical marriage. Not the least of the injustices of this system was that Protestants and non-Christians who wanted to marry a Spaniard had no choice but to undergo a Catholic ceremony, often against the dictates of their conscience. The law was changed after Franco's death to allow Catholic – or at least nominally Catholic – partners to have a purely civil marriage. Since then, register office weddings have grown in popularity to a surprising extent. By 2002, they represented a quarter of all marriages in Spain.

Since there was no divorce under Franco – the Republican divorce law passed in 1932 had been revoked by the Nationalists six years later while the civil war was still in progress – the only way that a marriage contracted in Spain could be dissolved was by means of an

---

* The law defined as a Catholic anyone who had been baptized in a Catholic church. In 1969 it became possible for baptized Catholics to renounce their faith by notifying the civil and ecclesiastical authorities.

annulment. The circumstances in which a marriage can be annulled in accordance with the laws of the Roman Catholic Church are, on the face of it, highly restrictive. The grounds only extend to such contingencies as one of the partners being physically unable to have intercourse, being under age at the time of the marriage, or not having given his or her genuine consent.

These strictures did not, however, prevent several thousand Spaniards obtaining an annulment before the introduction of divorce. Annulments had always been possible, but became more common in the years leading up to the end of the dictatorship. Ordinary members of the public could not help but notice that the people who got the annulments were invariably rich and either famous or influential. Suspicions were increased still further when some of those who had obtained annulments on the grounds of impotence remarried and had children. Perhaps the most extraordinary case was that of the singer Sara Montiel who had not one but two marriages annulled, to become one of the very few Spanish women up to that time to marry three times.

For those unhappily married Spaniards who could not get an annulment the only solution was a legal separation. But the process of obtaining one was a nightmare. In the first place, there was no guarantee of any kind that the courts would grant a separation at the end of it all. The parties and their lawyers had to prove, rather than merely state, that the marriage had fallen apart while the aim of the judge and the court officials (especially the so-called *defensor del vínculo* or 'defender of the link') was to contrive a reconciliation. Secondly, blame had to be apportioned before a case could be settled. Witnesses had to be called, statements had to be taken. More often than not private detectives had to be hired and on occasions even the police were involved, bursting in on couples *in flagrante delicto*. Nor was the question of guilt simply a matter of personal pride. Whichever party was found guilty not only forfeited custody of the children but also the right to alimony.

In normal circumstances it took between two and three years to obtain a separation, but it could take up to eight years. The expense was therefore considerable – in the mid-seventies it cost about 300,000 pesetas. In theory it was possible for couples with low incomes to apply for a separation and have the cost borne by the authorities, but cases of this sort were virtually worthless to the lawyers, and in practice they were postponed indefinitely.

When the dictatorship came to an end there were some half a million people whose marriages had broken down and who were legally separated, but many more were living in misery with partners whom they were unable to leave. Not surprisingly, therefore, some 71 per cent of Spaniards, according to an official survey carried out in 1975, were in favour of divorce.

Its opponents argued that the effect would be to leave thousands of middle-aged women lonely and impoverished as their husbands set off in pursuit of younger wives. But a timely study of the workings of the previous, 1932 Act – Ricardo Lezcano's *El divorcio en la Segunda República* – showed that more than half the petitions during the first twenty-two months that the act was in force were submitted by women. In no fewer than sixteen provinces – of which, interestingly, the vast majority were rural – *all* the petitions came from women.

By the time the drafting of a divorce bill began in 1977, the question was not whether Spain would have a divorce law, but of what kind. A bill passed through the cabinet without incident in January 1980 and was submitted to parliament later that year.

However, the *proyecto Cavero* (Cavero Bill), as it was called after Iñigo Cavero, the Justice Minister, was considerably less progressive than the mood of the nation. In the summer of 1980 Suárez reshuffled his cabinet and handed the Justice portfolio to Francisco Fernández-Ordóñez, who had already provided Spain with the foundations of a modern tax system. One of his earliest moves was to withdraw the *proyecto Cavero* from parliament and order the drafting of an entirely new bill. This new bill, inevitably called the *proyecto Ordóñez*, halved the period in which a divorce could be obtained to between one and two years. It allowed marriages to be dissolved without one of the partners having to be blamed, and in effect, if not in name, it offered divorce by mutual consent.

The Christian Democrats in the UCD were less than happy with it. The Speaker of Congress, Landelino Lavilla, who was one of the leaders of the Christian Democrat wing of the party, succeeded in postponing any further discussion of the bill in parliament until after the UCD's national conference, which was due to be held in January of the following year, in the hope that by then the Christian

Democrats would have regained their ascendancy within the party. During the run-up to the conference, their attitude hardened still further and it was generally felt that the intensification of their campaign against the bill reflected the hostility towards it of the new pontiff, John Paul II.

The long-awaited UCD conference was pre-empted by Suárez's decision to resign – a decision which was at least in part the result of the pressures to which he had been subjected by the constant warring between Christian and Social Democrats over divorce. The choice of Leopoldo Calvo Sotelo as Suárez's successor and the shock of the abortive coup in February both helped to shift the UCD to the right, but not far enough for Fernández-Ordóñez to be removed from the Ministry of Justice.

The bill survived its first debate in Congress more or less intact, but then the leadership of the UCD agreed under pressure from the Christian Democrats that it should be amended in the Senate so as to give judges the power to refuse divorce in certain circumstances. However, on 22 June 1981, in the final, historic and tumultuous debate in Congress, the amendment was removed with the help of the votes of at least thirty UCD deputies who defied the party line. The bill passed but the session broke up in disorder with one Centrist deputy declaring prophetically: 'We may be a coalition but never a party – the models of society that the Christian Democrats and Social Democrats have are just too different.' It was the beginning of the end of the UCD. In less than eighteen months it would be deserted by its founder and decimated by the electorate. The issue which, above all others, sealed its fate was divorce.

So when the dust settled, what sort of divorce law had Spain acquired? The answer was, a relatively liberal one. Either partner could petition for a divorce one year after obtaining a legal separation and the separation itself could be obtained without citing grounds, provided both partners agreed. With such a backlog of unhappily married couples, one could have predicted that the divorce rate would soar. Yet, as so often with Spain, one would have been hopelessly wrong.

By 1990, Spain's divorce rate – with 0.6 divorces per 1,000 inhabitants – was a quarter or less of that in some EU nations. By 2001, it had edged up to 1 per 1,000, which was well under half the rate in Britain. It was higher than in Italy, which had a more restrictive law, but substantially lower than in Portugal, where it was 1.6 per 1,000. So the evidence suggests that Spaniards remain profoundly reluctant to break up the families they have formed. Or does it?

What went virtually unnoticed – or at least unremarked – while it was being debated was that Spain's divorce law had a gaping loophole. There were no penalties for the non-payment of alimony. It is difficult to see this as anything other than unmitigated *machismo* on the part of those responsible for framing and drafting the bill. Only in 1989 was the gap plugged, non-payment being made punishable by suspended jail sentences and fines of between 100,000 and 500,000 pesetas. But that still left the problem of getting a court order out of one of the world's slowest judicial systems. And it was not until two years later, in fact, that an ex-husband was actually punished by the courts for failing to pay for the maintenance of his ex-wife and their children. In 2004, the penalty was increased to between three months and a year in jail.

The extent of the problem remains a subject of heated debate. Women's groups have claimed that the rate of default is as high as 80 per cent, but an organization representing separated fathers has argued that such claims are based on a misreading of official statistics and that the true level is nowadays closer to 15 per cent. At all events, it is clear that a lot of alimony has gone unpaid over the years since Spain acquired its divorce law. This, together with a certain social stigma that still attaches to divorcés (and particularly divorcées), explains the number of couples who have opted for what is sometimes known as *divorcio a la española*. The partners separate rather than divorce because the wife does not believe she will ever get maintenance from her husband and cannot see the point of spending a lot of time and money on formally ending their marriage.

At all events, Spain's low divorce rate is offset by a high separation rate. Government figures show 60 per cent of marriages fail. To bring the law more into line with social reality, the Zapatero government passed legislation in 2005 making divorce easier and faster. As a result, couples who are in agreement will not have to wait for more than two months, while, in contested cases, the divorce will take effect in a maximum of six months. The concept of fault disappeared altogether and, for the first time in Spain, the law allowed for shared custody of the children.

CHAPTER 12

Living on the Edge

Depending on your point of view, coffee-drinking may be considered a pleasure, a necessity, a bad habit or a health risk. In Spain it comes close to being an art form. There are so many ways of imbibing it that it can take some considerable time to explain to a waiter exactly how you want it served.

You can have it *solo* (black), *cortado* (with just a drop of milk) or *con leche* (white). Each of the three varieties can be served with single or double measures of coffee, in either a glass or a cup. The strength can be varied by asking for your coffee to be *corto de café* (short on coffee) or *largo de agua* (long on water), a *solo largo de agua* being known as an *americano*. In the case of *café con leche*, you must decide between a large, medium or small cup or glass, with corresponding amounts of milk added to bring it up to the brim. And with *café cortado*, you have the choice of either hot or cold milk. By my reckoning, that makes for seventy-two basic permutations, though it could be argued that a single *largo de agua* is the same as the corresponding double, *corto de café*.

It does not stop there. There are the various forms of instant coffee – universally known as Nescafé, even if of another brand – and of *café descafeinado* (decaffeinated coffee). Both can be mixed with either milk or water or both. Then there is *café helado*, which is chilled black coffee served with crushed ice and a straw, and not to be confused with *café con hielo* which consists of hot black coffee in a cup served together with a glass full of ice cubes. Finally – I think – there are the alcohol-laced variations. A *carajillo* (a *café solo* with a shot of Spanish brandy) is usually, though not always, partially burnt off before serving and customarily, though not always, served in a glass. There are at least two more elaborate regional varieties of flambéed coffee – Catalan *cremat* and Galician *queimada* – which are prepared with locally made *aguardiente*, coffee beans, sugar and spice. Add to these at least half a dozen imported liquor-enhanced brews – Irish coffee is immensely popular in Spain – and you have almost twenty further ways in which coffee can be ingested.

Most of the coffee served in bars and restaurants comes from Colombia. But simply roasting and grinding one of the world's stronger varieties and serving it in generous measures is not enough to satisfy the Spaniards' requirement for something that enables them to remain alert while getting up early, staying up late and often drinking significant quantities of alcohol in between. The coffee you will normally be served in Spain is known as *torrefacto*, which has been double roasted and finely ground until it is the gastronomic equivalent of Semtex.

The Spaniards' addiction to *torrefacto* is all of a piece with a nation in which there is very little that is bland, gentle or reassuringly soft. So is the way in which they use the word *descafeinado* in a wider, and universally pejorative, sense to mean 'watered-down', 'artificial' or 'bloodless'.

Their seemingly instinctive enthusiasm for whatever is bold, strong and decisive has bedevilled their history, turning it into a succession of abrupt changes in direction. The relatively smooth transition from dictatorship to democracy has often been adduced as evidence that Spain's bloody past has cured the Spanish for good of their propensity for destructive excesses. But it is also true that the transition did not prevent – and in several respects actively promoted – excesses of a different kind.

After Franco's death, the Spanish became a bit like the archetypal ex-convent schoolgirl, recklessly experimenting with everything previously forbidden. The sexual emancipation of the *destape* was one aspect of this. But it was by no means the only one.

Among the first changes to be made after the return of democracy was a relaxation of the curbs that had been placed until then on gambling. It was a change that was to have far-reaching effects on Spanish society.

The Spanish are born gamblers. Risk-taking, of course, is at the heart of the quintessentially Spanish activity of bullfighting. But what few readers are likely to know is that Spain's most popular indigenous card game, *mus*, also provides for a 'moment of truth' — a defiant, reckless, all-or-nothing fling known as the *órdago*.

Gambling also helps fuel the fond belief of many Spaniards that a fortune can be made *sin dar golpe* (roughly, 'without slogging'). Just as Spanish entrepreneurs have traditionally lived in hope of the *pelotazo* (the 'long ball' or 'big kick'), that single stroke of luck or genius which will bring them a fortune overnight, so the ordinary Spaniard can get by on the hope that one day '*me toca la lotería*' (literally, 'it is my turn to win the lottery').

Franco had allowed Spaniards to put money on horse-racing (through on-course betting and a restricted form of off-course betting called the *Quiniela Hípica*). He had agreed to a football pool, officially described as the *Apuesta Deportiva* but familiarly known as the *Quiniela Futbolística* or just the *Quiniela*, which was used to finance sporting activities. He also consented to a lottery for the blind, the *Cupón pro-ciegos*. And like every Spanish ruler since the start of the nineteenth century, he raised no objections to the state lottery, the *Lotería Nacional*.

But in 1977 a decree enacted by the then UCD government legalized casinos (which had been outlawed since the dictatorship of General Primo de Rivera), bingo and gambling machines. As in other countries, the appeal of casinos proved to be limited. In the early 2000s, they accounted for no more than 6 per cent of the gambling money staked in Spain.

Bingo proved to be a very different matter. What had started life in most of the rest of the world as a parlour game for large families and had grown into a compulsive distraction for bored housewives became, in post-Franco Spain, a craze that engulfed people of all types and classes. Hundreds upon hundreds of bingo halls sprang up. Variations in the price of entry and the cost of a card soon established social differences between the various halls. Those at the top of the scale became meeting-places for the rich, the fashionable and the influential. For a foreigner, one of the oddest — and most amusing — experiences to be had in late-seventies Spain was a visit to one of these establishments, where men in immaculately tailored suits and women decked out in jewels could be seen hunched over their cards, solemnly covering up the numbers as they were shouted out by the caller. The gaming went on deep into the night.

Although the running of bingo halls was meant to be confined to charitable institutions, irregularities were soon rife. Many of those who were put in charge were former owners or managers of red-light bars and the like. Within a year of the decree which legalized them, forty-nine bingo halls in the province of Madrid were closed down on the orders of the Civil Governor, but more sprang up to take their places. In 1980, almost half the bingo halls operating in and around the capital had their licences suspended for failing to submit accounts.

The wild days of Spanish bingo have since been brought to an end by tighter regulation and surveillance. Meanwhile, the passage of time has sorted out the dilettantes from the devotees. Nowadays, bingo accounts for less than 15 per cent of total gambling outlay.

The habit that has stuck is the playing of 'one-armed bandits', initially known in Spain as *tragaperras* ('peseta-swallowers'). After their legalization, they multiplied like sex-crazed robots until their tiresome bleeping and clicking and their mournfully jolly jingles polluted the air of almost every bar and club. In 2003, four out of every ten euros gambled in Spain went into the slot of a 'one-armed bandit', which was more even than Spaniards paid for lottery tickets.

Spain's state lottery, the *Lotería Nacional*, was the brainchild of one Ciriaco González de Carvajal. A court official in Nueva España, the Spanish colony which included present-day Mexico, he had been struck by the success of the state-run draw that had been held there since the eighteenth century. On his return to Spain, he presented a bill to the Cortes of Cádiz, the parliament set up during the War of Independence, which proposed a similar project in Spain. It was approved with not a single vote against, and the first lottery was held in 1812. The *Lotería Nacional* soon came to be regarded by governments as the only way to get Spaniards to pay taxes.

Almost half the money gambled on the *Lotería Nacional* is spent on the first and last draws of the year. The *Niño* ('child') is so called because it is held on the eve of Epiphany, the day on which Spanish children traditionally receive their Christmas presents. The *Gordo* ('fat one'), which takes place just before Christmas, is as good a name as any for one of the world's richest draws. It has become one of the most important rituals in the Spanish year. The winning numbers are sung out in the style of Gregorian plainchant by children from the

San Ildefonso school for the blind, reinforcing the point that chance itself is blind. The whole performance is broadcast nationwide over several hours. Go where you may on 23 December – to shops, offices or cafés – you will be unable to escape this haunting litany of fortune. And for a truly terrifying experience, take a cab ride that day with a driver who has a radio in his taxi and a stake in the draw.

The *Lotería Nacional* advertises itself as *la lotería* ('*the* lottery') and used to be, if not the only lottery, certainly the only state lottery. But in 1985, the government launched the misleadingly named *Lotería Primitiva* ('Original Lottery'), and followed it up with the *Bonoloto* in 1988. Both were attempts to respond to the mounting popularity of the draws of an organization that was to acquire huge influence in the Spain of the eighties and nineties.

The Organización Nacional de Ciegos Españoles (ONCE) was created by General Franco's Nationalist government in 1938 to provide employment for the blind, whose numbers had been swollen by the civil war. As a way of financing it, Franco agreed to an idea that had first been tried out during the Second Republic when blind people had banded together to organize local raffles. The new, provincially based, daily lotteries were exempted from tax (which was the least the authorities could do, since ONCE was relieving the state of what would otherwise have been a considerable financial burden). The blind man or woman, standing on a corner, draped with strips (*tiras*) of lottery tickets and crying '*Iguales para hoy*'* soon became an integral part of Spanish street life. The *Cupón pro-ciegos* did what was expected of it and in 1950 ONCE was able to set up a proper welfare system for its members.

After Franco's death, it was several years before the spirit of democracy was extended to the organization. But in 1981 a decree was passed which more or less freed it of state interference and enabled the members of ONCE to hold elections the following year for a new ruling body. Control was won by a left-wing alliance whose leader, Antonio Vicente Mosquete, became the organization's first democratically elected Chairman.

Mosquete took over at a time when the organization's income was no longer big enough to finance its burgeoning commitments. What is

---

* 'Equals for today.' ONCE tickets are divided into equal shares for sale.

more, it was in danger of being eroded by the newly legalized casinos, bingo halls and fruit machines. In 1984, he secured permission from the government to launch a single nationwide lottery in place of the various provincial draws held up until then. So popular was the new lottery that huddles of devotees were soon forming at ONCE points of sale, even before the vendor arrived to start work.

Then in 1987 the ONCE Chairman met a violent and controversial end: he fell down a lift shaft in one of the rare moments when he was without a bodyguard. The police decided it was an accident, but all kinds of sinister rumours circulated about the death of a man whose courage and imagination had given him immense financial power.

The reshuffle that followed brought into the management team, as Director-General, the man who was to mastermind a second ONCE revolution. Blind from birth, Miguel Durán started life in a poor family in Estremadura. He distinguished himself at school, emerging top of his year for the whole country in the Spanish *bachillerato*, and went on to enjoy a glittering career at university. By the time he took over the running of ONCE, its vendors were earning almost double the average national wage. Its senior executives were being driven around in bullet-proof limousines. They had become the administrators of a financial empire with potentially awesome influence.

Until 1988, however, virtually all ONCE's rapidly accumulated wealth was in fixed-interest securities. It had become like a millionaire with his money locked up in 'gilts'. With the consent of two successive chairmen, Durán shifted a growing proportion into equities, which carried a greater risk but promised higher returns. ONCE bought sizeable holdings in some of Spain's biggest banks, in supermarket chains, tourist projects and above all, the media.*

In 1985, the Socialists had promulgated a decree that put government officials back on to its ruling body and made ONCE answerable to a cabinet minister. The organization was frequently accused of wielding its prodigious influence on behalf of the Socialists in areas, particularly TV and radio, where the government in a free-market economy ought not to have any place. As Durán launched himself into the conquest of a media empire, some in the press suddenly began to take a more jaundiced view of his activities, dubbing him '*Al Cupón*'.

---

* See below, pp. 368–9.

It soon became apparent, moreover, that ONCE was a double-edged weapon for the government, for it had shown itself to be rather more successful than the state in holding its share of the overall lottery market. The last straw was Durán's decision in 1991 to go ahead with the launch of another lottery – the *Cupón-abono* – despite a warning from the Socialist government that it was illegal. The cabinet ordered the project to be scrapped. Its ruling was the first serious setback ONCE had suffered, and heralded a more cautious phase in its history, which began in 1993 with Durán's retirement.

What with high-life – and low-life – bingo and blind men falling down lift shafts, the freeing-up of gambling in Spain was nothing if not eventful. But has it left an enduring mark? The answer would seem to be 'yes'; that it has turned Spaniards into even more inveterate gamblers than they were before. International comparisons in this field are few and far between, but two I have seen that refer to the early and mid-nineties suggest that proportionately – taking into account relative income levels – the Spanish bet about twice as much as either the British or the Americans.* The sharp rise in living standards since then has been accompanied by an even sharper increase in gambling. The total bet in 2003 was 40 per cent higher than in 1996. By the end of the period, the average adult Spaniard was gambling around €855 (£590 or $965) a year and losing some €275 (£190 or $310). To put that in perspective, what Spaniards spent – that is to say, lost – on legal gambling alone was more than they spent on fresh milk and fresh fruit and vegetables combined.

Back in the seventies, Raymond Carr and Juan Pablo Fusi argued that Franco's dictatorship had generated a 'culture of evasion' – a habit of escaping from reality into romantic films, trivial plays, radio soap operas, football and lotteries. After Franco's death that 'culture of evasion' was replaced by a much more destructive 'culture of addiction', for Spain was to be swamped by an influx of narcotics.

A number of specific factors can be adduced to explain why this should have been the case. Spain at the time had one of the youngest populations in the EU. Because of its proximity to North Africa and

* That is without illegal gambling. Bars the length and breadth of Spain host games of cards and dominoes on which money is staked. The Basques have traditionally been enthusiastic wagerers – they even bet on poetry contests – and in the Canary Islands large sums of money change hands at illegal cockfights.

its links with Latin America, it had long been an important route into Europe for both hashish and cocaine. None of this, though, explains why such large numbers of young Spaniards took to heroin, which reaches Spain in the same way as it reaches other European countries, from the Middle and Far East.

Clearly, the new sense of freedom that democracy brought had a lot to do with it. It soon became the prevailing belief that what you did with your body was your own business, and yours alone. In 1988, a book was published in France that provided detailed information on available drugs and how they could help to improve physical, intellectual and sexual performance. In France, it caused a scandal. The government described it as an attack on public health and its publisher was put on trial. The following year, the same book was launched in Spain. It carried an enthusiastic introduction by a popular intellectual, and was put on sale with a virtual absence of controversy.

The impression throughout the eighties was that 'anything goes'. Spain's Socialist administration, it should not be forgotten, was the first in Europe to be recruited almost entirely from the 'generation of '68'. One of its earliest measures, in the year after coming to office, was to legalize the consumption of narcotics both in public and private.* It was not until 1992 that the government modified its policy and made public, but not private, consumption an offence.

From time to time, in the years before the ban was re-imposed, you could be sitting in an up-market restaurant and a client would finish lunch or dinner and light up a spliff as if it were the most natural thing in the world. In the seedier quarters of the bigger cities, it was not at all unusual to see heroin addicts sitting in doorways injecting themselves.

The government's attitude towards hard drugs could seem peculiarly complacent. It was not until 1990 that the authorities began offering heroin addicts the alternative of methadone. Campaigns aimed at deterring youngsters from taking to drugs, for the most part, seemed to pull their punches. As for rehabilitation, the resources invested by the state were paltry in comparison with the scale of the problem Spain faced.

* So far as cannabis was concerned, the reform did no more than reaffirm a previously little-known peculiarity of the law. Even under Franco, the possession of small quantities for personal consumption was not an offence.

Although ministers and officials would, from time to time, assure the public of their concern about the drugs problem, their avowals were nearly always accompanied by an assertion that legal drugs did more damage than illegal ones. There is truth in this, of course. The number of heroin victims was in the hundreds each year whereas several tens of thousands die, year in, year out, from tobacco and alcohol. But the official view rather missed the point that heroin addicts tend to die a good deal earlier in their lives than the victims of tobacco and alcohol, and of more directly attributable causes. It also overlooked two other factors that were to acquire a considerable, and sinister, importance for the rest of society.

One was the role that heroin addiction played in pushing up crime rates. Since heroin users were not able to get the drug (or, at first, even a substitute) by declaring their addiction to the authorities, they routinely took to prostitution or crime – often violent street crime – to finance their habit.

The other factor was the role of intravenous drug taking in spreading AIDS. By 1992, almost two-thirds of Spain's AIDS sufferers were heroin addicts who were believed to have contracted the disease by sharing needles with other users, and more than 40 per cent of heroin users were reckoned to be HIV positive. By then, Spain had the highest AIDS rate in the EU. Given the close links between drug addiction and prostitution, and the important role that prostitution plays in sexual relations in Spain, it is not difficult to understand why 1993 should have seen the start of a steep rise in the percentage of AIDS sufferers who had contracted the disease heterosexually.

The links between criminals and heroin and between heroin and AIDS were evident in figures showing that between a quarter and a third of the prison population was HIV positive. Yet when the Socialist government was asked to provide free syringes to prisons, its response was to distribute bleach instead. A greater awareness of the risks finally turned the tide against heroin in the early 1990s. The number of fatalities fell for the first time in 1992 and the number of new AIDS cases peaked two years later.

At the same time, however, there were warnings of a serious cocaine problem taking shape below the surface of society. This was partly because Spain was reflecting Europe-wide trends. Cocaine was the 'yuppie drug'. It had become popular everywhere in the eighties.

Now, addicts were switching over from heroin to avoid the greater risks involved.

But in Spain cocaine won an exceptional degree of social acceptance and the rise in its use was particularly steep. Not the least of its attractions for the Spanish, with their fondness for staying up half the night, is that it enables users to go for lengthy periods without sleep.

Possibly for similar reasons, Spain was among the first countries to embrace Ecstasy and other, similar 'designer drugs'. Club culture first took root in Europe on the Spanish island of Ibiza and spread to the east coast, giving rise in the early nineties to one of the craziest manifestations of Spaniards' passion for living on the edge.

The first step on the so-called *ruta del bacalao** involved dosing up on a drug like Ecstasy or a home-brewed variant like *felicidad* (happiness), which offered a 30-hour trip. The next step was to dance from Saturday into Sunday in Madrid. Then it was off for a wild drive to Valencia, which is 225 miles away, to carry on revelling in the city where *bacalao* music was born. There, the dancing carried on till late afternoon or early evening, when it was time to return, exhausted but usually at very high speed, along the same busy road.

By the autumn of 1993, the *ruta del bacalao* was sufficiently established among the young of Madrid for nightclubs to have been set up along the way, in the middle of the countryside, solely to cater for those who chose to break their journey for a quick top-up of music, pills, or both. The record for young people killed in a single weekend along the *ruta del bacalao* was twelve.

Some of the most pernicious effects of heroin have abated since the early 1990s. The number of deaths from narcotics abuse in 2001 was less than a quarter of the figure ten years earlier. The total of new AIDS cases was down 70 per cent from its 1994 peak. Only a fifth of prisoners admitted to having injected heroin in the month before their imprisonment.

But the wave of addictions in Spain in the early years of its return to democracy has left a grim legacy all the same. In 2001, Spain was still reporting more new AIDS cases than any country in the EU except Portugal, and Madrid was home to Europe's biggest narcotics

---

* *Bacalao* was a super-rhythmic variety of club music.

retail point – Las Barranquillas, a wasteland between two car dumps where cocaine and heroin are sold from around 100 shacks. Though heroin consumption has fallen, UN figures cited in a report by state prosecutors leaked to *El País* in 2005 indicated Spaniards were proportionately the world's biggest cocaine users. According to an EU survey of national data from the early 2000s, the percentage of the population in Spain that had tried Ecstasy was second only to that in Britain. As regards cannabis, Spain ranked third.

More recent data, collected among fourteen- to eighteen-year-olds at the end of 2002, offers little prospect of the overall situation changing. It showed a fall in the popularity of Ecstasy, but rising use of both cannabis and cocaine. More than 3 per cent of Spanish teenagers said they had taken cocaine in the previous thirty days and 22 per cent said they had smoked a 'spliff' during that period.

The survey also showed something else of concern to the health authorities, which was that the number of fourteen- to eighteen-year-olds smoking tobacco remained unchanged from eight years earlier, despite increased publicity of the risks and growing social disapproval. Though the number of no-smoking areas has increased dramatically in recent years, breaking the Spanish of their tobacco addiction is proving a tough proposition.

There again, it involves tackling deeply rooted customs. Tobacco first reached Europe through Spain after being discovered by Columbus and gradually became an intrinsic part of Spanish life. Richard Ford in the nineteenth century felt that a Spaniard without a cigar 'would resemble a house without a chimney, a steamer without a funnel'. Right up until the mid-1970s, a good Cuban *puro* could be bought in Spain for a fraction of what it cost in the rest of Europe. Since then, Havanas have soared in price and the numbers sold have dropped sharply. These days, they are mostly smoked on special occasions, and particularly at bullfights.

Since pipe-smoking is rare, tobacco in Spain means cigarettes.* Recent years have seen traditional black tobacco rapidly ceding ground to Virginia cigarettes, which are known as *rubios* (blondes). In 1988, sales of *rubios* overtook those of *negros* for the first time.

* Literally so. If you want to ask for cigarettes in a bar or restaurant, you say '*¿Hay tabaco?*', not '*¿Hay cigarrillos?*'

Part of the appeal of *rubios* is that for many years they were kept out by the then tobacco monopoly, Tabacalera, and could only be obtained at exorbitant prices on the black market. But one cannot help suspecting that the name given to them in Spanish adds to their allure. Blonde hair continues to exercise an extraordinary fascination in Spain and one that is vigorously exploited by advertisers.*

There are several different ways of calculating tobacco consumption, but – whichever method is used – Spaniards come out as the second or third heaviest smokers in Europe. In 2001, according to the WHO, 34 out of every 100 Spanish adults were smokers. Consumption reached a peak in 1986. Since then, the number of men who smoke has fallen steadily from 55 per cent to 42 per cent. But the number of women smokers has risen, from 23 per cent to 27 per cent. Spain appears to be heading towards a pattern typical of the rest of the EU in which there are fewer smokers than in the past, but in which the number of men and women smokers is roughly equal.

A similar process of convergence is taking place with respect to alcohol. If you wind back the clock thirty years, you find a clear difference between drinking habits in the wine-producing Mediterranean nations and those in the rest of Europe (and, indeed, most of the rest of the world). The former drank greater quantities of alcohol, yet it was the beer- and spirit-drinking northern Europeans who seemed to get drunk more often. In Spain, wine-drinking started early, at the family table. Alcohol consumption could even unwittingly begin in babyhood: Spanish mothers traditionally dipped their children's dummies in *anis* (aniseed liquor) to stop them crying.

By the time Franco died, the Spaniards' average consumption of alcohol was almost twice that of the British and Americans. Though it was not as high as that of the French, what was striking was the relentless consistency of Spanish drinking.

As the foreign boss of a multinational subsidiary once said to me of his employees, 'While none of them is ever drunk, at any one time about half are less than sober.' He was in the computer business and had noticed that the quality of programming dropped as the day advanced.

---

* The cartoonist Forges once drew two yokels watching the 'box', with one saying to the other that until he got a television he had never realized the majority of children in Spain were blonde, freckled and blue-eyed.

Among manual workers, it was quite usual to start the day with a *carajillo*. At around 11 a.m. cafeterias would be packed with office workers eating the traditional late-morning breakfast, and plenty of them – male and female alike – would be rounding off their first meal with a *caña*, a small glass of draught beer. Over lunch, most Spaniards had at least one beer or glass of wine, often mixed with *Casera* (sweet gassy water). Formal business lunches were prefaced with a shot of dry sherry and sealed with a *copa* of spirits. By 6 or 7 p.m., the cafeterias were again busy with some of those same office workers taking a quick swig of vermouth, gin or whisky before knocking-off time and the chance to share in a round of after-work drinks with friends.

Spanish wine is among the strongest in Europe and spirits in Spain are poured with prodigious liberality. Yet you almost never saw people drunk to the point at which their speech was slurred or their movements erratic. Spaniards rarely drank wine without eating something, even if only some *tapas*,* and before or after tackling spirits they would usually take a strong dose of *torrefacto* coffee to offset the effects. Except perhaps in the Basque country, outright drunkenness did not evoke that humorous, conspiratorial tolerance with which it is often treated in northern Europe. In a country where personal dignity counts for so much, the loss of control which accompanies drunkenness was seen as wholly deplorable.

Much of what I have just written still holds good for many Spaniards.† But for some time now there have been clear indications of a change in the pattern of drinking towards a more 'northern' model.

Overall consumption has been dropping gradually from its peak in the mid-seventies. Spaniards in 2001 still drank more than the European average, but less than some northern Europeans such as the Irish and the Germans. What is more, they have increasingly drunk in the same way, consuming less wine and more spirits. So it

---

* These were originally titbits served on a saucer or plate set on top of the customer's glass. The word *tapa* means 'lid'.

† In 2001, the Interior Ministry published a survey that tried to identify problem weekday drinkers. Intake was only judged to be excessive in men who, on average, drank the equivalent of seven or more *cañas* in a working day. For women, the turning point was set at five.

is highly debatable whether, as they often assure you, '*bebemos menos pero bebemos mejor*' ('We drink less, but we drink better').

In addition, the Spaniards' traditional, steady drinking has little by little given way to an equally northern style of weekend binge drinking. The origins of this change can be traced back to the 1970s when Spain's newly liberated young got into the habit of *ir de copas*, going out to drink until the early hours at the weekend. By the end of the decade, even the smallest provincial capital had its *movida* (roughly, 'scene') centred on a network of *bares de copas*, usually in a specific area of the old quarter. *Copas* normally meant spirits. But they were usually being consumed after dinner at a restaurant. And drunkenness, though not unknown, was still rare.

A very different style of drinking became abruptly – indeed dramatically – apparent just before Christmas 1990 on the day that the schools broke up for the holidays. Reacting to one of those unfathomable common impulses that can move the young, tens of thousands of chanting, singing teenagers converged on the centre of Madrid, swigging from brown plastic litre bottles of beer known as '*litronas*' and blocking the traffic with their sheer numbers. For the most part, it was a good-natured occasion. But by late afternoon many were hopelessly drunk. Fights broke out, some windows were smashed and a few of the youngsters ended the day in jail or hospital. A similar number of British teenagers on the rampage would no doubt have left parts of the city uninhabitable, but it was nevertheless an extraordinary departure from normal Spanish conduct.

A *litrona* habit was soon well established throughout Spain. Teenagers would band together to buy several bottles of beer and then go in a group to drink them in the open air, usually in a park or on a square. At the end of an evening, sitting amid their discarded *litronas*, the young drinkers could look a lot like down-and-outs. It was a sight that appalled their elders.

But, instead of passing, as teenage crazes so often do, the *litrona* habit just gave way to a successor, known as the *botellón* after the big bottle in which the drinkers mixed up what was, in effect, an alcopop – a brew of some fizzy drink with either spirits or wine. Disapproval of open-air teenage drinking and the rowdiness to which it sometimes gave rise led in 2002 to an act of parliament, universally known as the *ley antibotellón*, that imposed on public alcohol consumption the same fines that had been approved ten years earlier for public drug taking.* It has been no more than a partial success.

Efforts at both the national and local level to curb the *botellón* and the country's various *movidas* often run into indignant, violent resistance. Events in the autumn of 2002 in Cáceres are typical of what has happened in several provincial capitals. The local authorities had the temerity to insist that bars in the area round the Plaza Mayor, which is also a favoured venue for the *botellón*, be shut down at 3.00 a.m. Shortly after 3.00 on the weekend that the new ordinance came into effect, between 3,000 and 4,000 young people gathered, some chanting '*No nos moverán*' (the title of a historic protest song) ('They shall not overcome'). In the ensuing clashes, three police officers were injured, and a car was burnt out. I lost track of events after the Interior Ministry in Madrid ordered in specialist riot units.

* The same law also raised the legal age for buying cigarettes from sixteen to eighteen.

PART THREE

King and Country

CHAPTER 13

An Engaging Monarchy

The terrorist attacks of 11 March 2004 so traumatized Spain that a state funeral was arranged for the victims – the first time such a service had been held for anyone outside the royal family since the restoration of the monarchy in 1975.

The streets of Madrid were eerily quiet as millions stayed at home or in their offices to watch the service on television. State funerals, like state visits, are intrinsically formal, ceremonial affairs. There were some twenty bishops in attendance and the congregation at the Almudena cathedral included the Prince of Wales, the French and Italian Presidents, the British Prime Minister, Tony Blair, and the US Secretary of State, Colin Powell.

The atmosphere on a bleak, overcast day could scarcely have been more tense. Many of the relatives present blamed the outgoing Prime Minister, José María Aznar, and his support for US policy in Iraq, for what had happened. As the head of the government walked up the aisle to his place, the angry voice of a middle-aged man rang out. 'Mr Aznar,' he shouted, 'I hold you responsible for the death of my son!'

When the service ended, the dignitaries prepared to file out, led by the Spanish royal family. But instead of leaving the relatives alone with their grief and incomprehension, King Juan Carlos and Queen Sofía, accompanied by their children and their children's partners, moved from pew to pew consoling the bereaved. Nor was this just a matter of a few muttered condolences. They clasped the hands of the bereaved, hugged their shoulders and kissed their cheeks. The King embraced a stooped old lady, and bent down to listen to her story. The Queen wept openly. Princess Cristina too sobbed as she hugged mourners.

For almost half an hour, some of the world's highest-ranking officials were kept waiting, standing, while the Bourbons sought to comfort the people for whom the service was really intended, most of them working-class people from the southern suburbs of Madrid. Their display of unselfconscious sympathy left experienced, professional royal-watchers open-mouthed. One wrote afterwards that it was 'a rare sight in the history of European royalty'. As indeed it was. It is inconceivable that any of the Windsors, for example, would have put their dignity at risk in that fashion. What those present in the Almudena cathedral saw that day was an example of the approach to monarchy that King Juan Carlos and Queen Sofía have evolved – one that sits somewhere between the extreme informality of some Scandinavian royals and the stiff-necked aloofness of the Windsors. The Bourbons do not try to give the impression of living normal lives. But nor do they let their special position in society stand in the way of making natural, human contact with the people of the country over which they reign.

Every week, the King holds civil and military audiences that enable him to get to know those who wield influence in Spain. He has an easy-going, back-slapping manner that is ideally suited to breaking the ice and getting people to say what they really think. His understanding of Spain's politicians, bankers, diplomats – and generals – was a decisive factor in steering the country safely down the road from dictatorship to democracy.

However, it was his wife, an altogether more reserved person, who first showed how the royal family could engage with the rest of society at moments of intense emotion. Back in the late seventies, there was a horrific accident involving a school bus. That afternoon, Queen Sofía took it upon herself to commandeer a helicopter and fly to the area where the accident had taken place to see if she could be of any help. It soon became clear that what she could do was comfort the relatives of the victims, as she did, not just on that occasion but on many other subsequent occasions, whenever there was some ghastly tragedy. Normally, politicians and royalty wait a few days, then make a well-organized tour of some hospital wards. Queen Sofía, by contrast, would turn up within hours of an incident, long before the casualties had been cleaned up and the passions had died down. I vividly recall a photograph of her with her arms around two grief-stricken middle-aged women, each resting their head on one of the Queen's shoulders and sobbing their hearts out. The King showed a similar sensitivity to the needs of the moment in 2002 when he became the first public figure to visit Galicia's polluted beaches after the *Prestige* oil spill.

Spaniards have come to feel that the royal couple are, to use an American phrase, 'there for them' at critical junctures. And not just the bad ones, but the good ones too.

At the Barcelona Olympics in 1992, the royal family threw themselves into the task of cheering on the Spanish team with a vigour and enthusiasm that was quite obviously unfeigned. It seemed as if every time Juan Carlos, in particular, turned up to watch an event the Spanish would win. People started joking about a 'Juan Carlos effect'. The Games too produced another of those images that have etched themselves into the iconography of contemporary Spain. It was taken at the final of the water polo and showed the entire royal family leaping out of their seats and into the air with delight at the winning, Spanish goal.

The Bourbons have unquestionably succeeded in creating a strong and healthy bond between themselves and the nation over which they rule. But, surprising as it may seem, they have not succeeded in persuading the Spanish of the virtues of monarchy. As the Spanish themselves often say, they are '*muy Juancarlistas, pero poco monárquicos*'. That is to say, they are keener on Juan Carlos as a person than they are on the monarchy as an institution.

In 2000, the government's statistics office, the CIS, conducted a survey to gauge opinions about democracy, the constitution and the monarchy twenty-five years after the end of Franco's dictatorship. It showed that the King was remarkably popular: 89 per cent agreed with the statement, 'The King has been able to earn the sympathy and affection of his subjects.' His role in the transition to democracy was widely appreciated. In fact, when interviewees were asked to assess the contribution made by a series of groups and individuals, Juan Carlos came out top. Yet nearly 75 per cent felt monarchy was 'outdated' – almost twice as many as had expressed the same view in an earlier CIS poll carried out in the late eighties.

There seems to be a paradox here. Because Juan Carlos did so much for his country during the transition, he created a powerful association in the public mind between himself and the defence of Spain's democratic institutions. Now that those democratic institutions are no longer under threat, now that no one worries any longer about the country being knocked off course by a military coup, people are more inclined to question the usefulness of a monarchy. More than three-quarters of respondents in the CIS poll agreed that 'The figure of the King is a guarantee of order and stability for Spanish people.' But a growing number of opinion-formers has questioned that claim. And during the 1990s two parties that had always been nominally republican, the United Left and the Basque Nationalist Party, became much more overtly so.

Clearly, one reason for the fragility of royalist sentiment in Spain is a lack of continuity. For almost half a century, from 1936 until 1974, the monarchy was absent from Spanish public life. But it is also the case that, with few exceptions, Spain's Bourbon monarchs, of whom Juan Carlos is the latest representative, were a pretty feckless lot whose legacy was all too often to divide the nation they ruled. Of the three institutions that have traditionally held Spain together, the 'three pillars' as they have sometimes been called – the monarchy, the army and the Church – it is the monarchy which has invariably looked the shakiest.

The Bourbons came to rule Spain, not by invitation but through a war – the so-called War of the Spanish Succession – which broke out among the European powers over who should inherit the Spanish throne after the previous (Habsburg) monarch had died without an heir. The war not only split Europe; it divided Spain too. A sizeable number of Spaniards – principally the Catalans, Valencians and Aragonese – supported the Bourbons' opponents, and when the war was over they were punished for having picked the wrong side.

It was a Bourbon, moreover, who abjectly surrendered to Napoleon's forces in 1808, and although his son was restored six years later his descendants never really lived down the fact that a monarch had shown himself to be less patriotic than his subjects. During the 123 tumultuous years that followed, dissatisfaction with the monarchy twice reached such a pitch that the ruler of the day was forced to leave the country.

The first occasion was in 1868 when an alliance of liberal generals and admirals got rid of the nymphomaniac Queen Isabel, and the

Cortes invited a member of the Italian royal family to take her place. But he abdicated soon afterwards, ushering in a brief and disorderly period of republican rule. After the failure of the First Republic, the Spaniards decided that there was nothing left to try and restored the Bourbons in the person of Isabel's son, Alfonso XII. It was his son, Alfonso XIII, who lost the throne once again.

In 1923 he connived at the seizure of power by a group of senior officers led by the flamboyantly eccentric General Miguel Primo de Rivera. By putting up with Primo de Rivera's dictatorship, the King flouted the very constitution from which the restored monarchy derived its legitimacy, and tied its standing to the success or failure of Primo de Rivera's experiment. After seven years, the experiment failed. The King survived for slightly more than a year until he allowed the local elections of 1931 to become a trial of strength between pro- and anti-royalists. As the results came in from the towns and cities, which were the only areas where a fair ballot had been held, it became clear that the King's opponents were going to sweep the board. A republic was declared in the Basque industrial centre of Eibar and it seemed certain that unless Alfonso stepped down there would be bloodshed. On the evening of 14 April, he issued a statement in which he carefully avoided abdicating but said that he did not want to be held responsible for the outbreak of a civil war. 'Therefore,' he added, 'until the nation speaks I shall deliberately suspend the use of my royal prerogative.' That night he left Madrid for exile. Spain became a republic, but the tensions between right and left that had been articulated for a brief period as support for, and opposition to, the monarchy merely resurfaced in other guises; the internecine conflict that Alfonso had been at pains to avert broke out five years later.

Alfonso died in Rome in 1941, a few weeks after his failing health had persuaded him to abdicate. His eldest son, also called Alfonso, had already given up his claim to the throne in 1933 to marry a Cuban woman. He died in a car crash five years later without leaving any children. Shortly after his renunciation, his brother Jaime, who was next in line but, being deaf, was thought incapable of assuming the responsibilities of kingship, also renounced the succession. He subsequently married and had two children, Alfonso and Gonzalo. The legitimate heir was therefore Alfonso XIII's third son and fifth child, Juan, Count of Barcelona.

Don Juan, as he came to be known, had left Spain with his father in 1931 and had been sent to the Royal Naval College at Dartmouth. In 1935 he married another Bourbon, María de las Mercedes de Borbón y Orléans, Princess of the Two Sicilies. The military uprising against the Republic the next year seemed to the young Prince as if it could be the means by which he might recover his throne and that he ought to be a party to it. A fortnight after the start of the rebellion he crossed secretly into Spain to join the Nationalist forces, but the rebels – reluctant to risk the life of the heir to the throne – put him back over the Pyrenees. Perhaps they were sincere in their motives, but it was nevertheless a singularly convenient decision for General Franco, who was proclaimed Head of State later that year.

Once the war was over, the *Caudillo* showed no intention of giving up to Don Juan his position as Head of State. The principal reason was of course that he thoroughly enjoyed the exercise of power, but it is only fair to point out that had he, say, become a mere Prime Minister under Don Juan, he might have wrecked the tenuous alliance of forces that had won the war – the accession of a monarch, any monarch, would have upset the anti-royalist Falange, while the accession of one of Alfonso XIII's sons would have alienated their Carlist rivals. Equally, Don Juan's subsequent disenchantment with Franco, although it had its roots in the *Caudillo*'s refusal to surrender power, grew in conviction as the Count, who saw the monarchy as an instrument of reconciliation, had to stand by while Franco used his power to humiliate his former opponents.

The Law of Succession to the Headship of State, which the Cortes passed in 1949, restored the monarchy in name but made Franco acting Head of State for life and gave him the right to name his successor 'as King or Regent'. Spain became, in the classic phrase, 'a monarchy without a monarch'. Shortly after the Law of Succession was passed, Don Juan's representatives entered negotiations with the exiled Socialists and Communists. These negotiations ended in the so-called St Jean de Luz Agreements whereby, if Franco fell, there would be a referendum to decide the form of state. Yet, before they were signed, Don Juan had met Franco on board his yacht to discuss the dictator's suggestion that Don Juan's sons should be educated in Spain.

Don Juan's heir, Juan Carlos, was born in Rome on 5 January

1938. He was Juan's and Mercedes's third child; they already had two daughters, Pilar and Margarita. In 1942 the family moved to Lausanne in neutral Switzerland and it was there that Juan Carlos began school. In 1946 when his parents moved to Portugal, so as to be as close as possible to Spain, they made arrangements for Juan Carlos to stay as a boarder at the Marian Fathers' school in Fribourg.

Franco's offer put the Count of Barcelona in an extraordinarily difficult position. On the one hand, he was being asked to surrender control over the upbringing of his son and heir to a man he mistrusted. Moreover, to do so would give credibility to the dictator's claim to have restored the monarchy. On the other hand, Franco undoubtedly had a point. If the monarchy were ever to be restored, it would have to have a credible representative and if Don Juan were to die before the *Caudillo*, his son would need to be up to the challenge. As it was, Juan Carlos – who had never seen Spain – spoke Spanish with a pronounced French accent. After several weeks' deliberation, Don Juan decided to accept Franco's offer and on 8 November the ten-year-old Juan Carlos, accompanied by his younger brother, Alfonso,* boarded the Lusitania Express at Lisbon for a train ride that would eventually take him to the throne.

The first few years of the Princes' stay in Spain, during which they studied in Madrid and San Sebastián, saw something of a reconciliation between the Count and the *Caudillo*. But after Juan Carlos passed his *bachillerato* in 1954 it became clear that the two older men had very different ideas about his higher education. Don Juan wanted him to go to a foreign university where he would receive a liberal 'European' education. Franco, on the other hand, wanted him to study at a military academy before entering a Spanish university. In December 1954, Don Juan and General Franco met once more, this time at a hunting lodge near the Portuguese border, and Franco once again won the day.

The following autumn, Juan Carlos began a four-year military training – two years at the army college in Saragossa to be followed

---

* Like his namesake in the previous generation, Alfonso died in tragic circumstances. In 1956, at the age of fifteen, he was shot while playing with a loaded gun at the family home in Estoril. Juan Carlos, who was with him at the time of the accident, was profoundly affected. Childhood friends say that the incident turned him from a bit of a bully into an altogether more thoughtful, sensitive boy.

by a year each at the navy and air force colleges. In 1959, Juan Carlos passed out as a lieutenant in all three services and returned to his parents' home in Estoril. Franco had decided that the next phase of Juan Carlos's education should be at the University of Salamanca, and it was only after his rooms had been chosen and his tutors selected that Don Juan seems to have realized the full implications of his son being sent to an institution that had remained intellectually fossilized for centuries. Don Juan and General Franco returned to the hunting lodge near the Portuguese frontier in March 1960 and this time it was the Count who got his way. A panel of six eminent academics was to draft a special two-year course in liberal studies for Juan Carlos. He was to take the course in Madrid, but would be taught by the academics on the panel and the lecturers and professors they selected.

The Prince's engagement to Princess Sofía of Greece was announced while he was at university. They had first met in 1954 aboard the Greek royal family's yacht during a cruise in the Aegean, but it was not until the Duke and Duchess of Kent's wedding seven years later that their romance began.

'We were alone. We were without our parents. And we more or less got engaged in London,' she later told an interviewer. 'In fact, my parents had never contemplated the possibility of my marrying into the Spanish royal family. There was a difference between the religions of our two countries.' The problem was solved by Juan Carlos's grandmother, Victoria Eugenia, who travelled to Rome to secure the Pope's personal permission for a double ceremony that included both the Latin and Greek rites.

Princess Sofía, the eldest daughter of King Paul and Queen Frederika, had been born on 2 November of the same year as Prince Juan Carlos. They shared a passion for sailing. The Princess had been her brother Constantine's reserve at the 1960 Olympics, when he won a gold medal. The Prince was later to sail for Spain in the 1972 Olympics. But initially their common interest did more to separate than unite them. 'I once went sailing with him when we were still engaged,' Sofía later recalled, 'and I shall never understand how I was able to marry him after that.'

More importantly, perhaps, the earliest memories of both were of exile. In 1940, Sofía's parents had fled Greece ahead of the Nazi invasion and settled in South Africa. When she returned to her native country at the age of eight, she had no memory of it. Like Juan Carlos, she had been packed off to boarding-school – only in her case she went later but stayed longer. This is a crucial point for understanding the way in which the monarchy has evolved since it was restored after Franco's death. Both the King and Queen were given a lesson in their early years that no member of the British royal family received – that, for a monarch, the penalty for failing to judge correctly the mood of his or her country, can be exile and debilitating irrelevance.

On 14 May 1962, Juan Carlos and Sofía were married at the Catholic cathedral in Athens before a constellation of kings, queens and presidents. Over the next few years, Sofía gave birth to three children – Elena in 1963, Cristina in 1965, and Felipe, who was born on 30 January 1968.

After university, Juan Carlos spent a few weeks in each of the ministries to understand how they worked. In December 1962, Franco had celebrated his seventieth birthday and the question of who should succeed him appeared increasingly urgent. But it was not easy to see how he could put into effect his apparent intention of restoring the monarchy.

The Carlists were a spent force. In the first place, their claim to the throne was now exceedingly tenuous. The original pretender's last direct male descendant, Alfonso Carlos, had died in 1936 without leaving a son. His closest male relative and therefore the successor to the Carlist claim was none other than Don Juan, so to keep alive the cause Alfonso Carlos had before his death adopted as his heir a remote cousin, Prince Javier de Borbón Parma. In spite of this, in 1958, several leading Carlists publicly acknowledged Don Juan's entitlement to the pretendership. Javier subsequently abdicated his claim in favour of his son, Carlos Hugo. Eight years older than Juan Carlos, Carlos Hugo was young enough to be an eligible successor to the throne and in 1964 he enhanced his credentials still further by marrying Princess Irene of the Netherlands after a runaway romance. But the Carlists' dream of a return to absolutist monarchy seemed even to Franco to be impracticable in the latter half of the twentieth century, and throughout his rule the Carlists never had more than a token presence in the government.

The problem was that the other branch of the family was represented by a man whom he neither liked nor respected. In view of Franco's disdain for Don Juan, an increasing number of Don Juan's more reactionary supporters, who had always felt that it would be better if Franco were to outlive the Count so that he could hand over to a king brought up under the dictatorship, began to toy with the seemingly outlandish notion that, even if the Count outlived Franco, Juan Carlos might succeed to the throne. The most committed proponents of the 'Juan Carlos solution' were the Opus Dei 'technocrats' who had been responsible for initiating Spain's 'economic miracle' and whose popularity with Franco was rising at about the same rate as the GNP. Their patron was Franco's old friend, Admiral Carrero Blanco.

A lot of Spaniards, though, were convinced that, given the problems, Franco would never bring himself to name a successor. The Falangists in particular hoped that he might fudge the issue by bequeathing power to a regent. The man they had in mind for the job was another old friend of Franco, Lieutenant-General Agustín Muñoz Grandes. A lifelong Falangist, he had led the Blue Division – Franco's contribution to the Axis war effort – and served as a minister in two cabinets. In 1962 Franco appointed him deputy Prime Minister, the first time he had created such a post.

Muñoz Grandes's elevation thoroughly alarmed royalists of all hues and it was at about this time that the technocrats and Admiral Carrero Blanco launched a campaign, which came to be known as *Operación Lucero*, aimed at promoting Juan Carlos's candidacy both to Franco and to the nation. In retrospect, it can be seen that Franco needed very little persuading – he once remarked to Juan Carlos that he had 'more chance than your father of becoming king'. Selling Juan Carlos to the country was a more difficult task. The technocrats had considerable influence in the media, business and the universities, but the Falange – through their control of the Movimiento – held sway over much of local government. When Juan Carlos and Sofía visited the provinces, as they did a lot during this period, at the prompting of their supporters, they were often met with either total indifference – or rotten fruit. Juan Carlos, who had been jeered by Falangists in the streets of San Sebastián when he was at school and had had to face a demonstration by Carlists when he was at university, knew how to cope. He subsequently recalled how on one occasion when he was being shown round by a local bigwig, 'I sensed that something was going to happen – something disagreeable, naturally. We were walking along, with me on the alert, looking out for the place where I thought the trouble might occur, when suddenly I took one step forward and two steps back and a tomato imprinted itself on my companion's uniform.' For Sofía, it must have been quite a trial.

The extent to which Juan Carlos sympathized with the ulterior motives of *Operación Lucero* remains a mystery. As late as January 1966 he told a visiting correspondent, 'I'll never, never accept the crown as long as my father is alive.' The first public indication that the plan was succeeding came the following year when Franco summarily dismissed Muñoz Grandes and gave his job to Carrero Blanco. The accession of Juan Carlos now began to look like more of a probability than a possibility. Feeling that regency was a lost cause, a number of Falangists reconciled themselves to the idea of a monarchy and began promoting the candidacy of Alfonso de Borbón-Dampierre, the son of Don Juan's deaf elder brother who had renounced his claim to the throne in 1933. Carlos Hugo, meanwhile, moved rapidly from the right to the left of the political spectrum in an attempt to secure the support of the democratic opposition – a move that appalled many of the traditional supporters of his cause. In December 1968, he made a speech openly attacking Juan Carlos, and five days later the police gave him and his wife twenty-four hours to leave the country.

With the Falangists and the Carlists both now clutching at straws, the succession was Juan Carlos's for the asking. In January 1969, he asked. 'I am ready', he told the official news agency, 'to serve Spain in whatever post or responsibility may be of most use to her.' The Prince's remarks took his father completely by surprise, but there was nothing he could do to stop the giddy progress of events.

On 12 July Franco called Juan Carlos to see him and in the course of a 45-minute conversation told him he intended naming him as his successor. Ten days later, Franco announced his choice to the Cortes, which endorsed it by 491 votes to 19 with 9 abstentions. To drive home the point that Juan Carlos's title to the throne derived from his being Franco's protégé rather than Alfonso XIII's grandson, he was henceforth to be known as Prince of Spain, not as Prince of Asturias, the title traditionally accorded to the royal heir.

The next day Juan Carlos swore his oath of loyalty to Franco and to the Movimiento Nacional. Don Juan, who had let it be known that he was at sea in his yacht, put in that afternoon at a little village on the Portuguese coast so that he could watch the proceedings on television in a fishermen's bar. His only comment when his son had finished speaking was, 'Nicely read, Juanito, nicely read.' Back in Estoril, he disbanded his Privy Council and issued a statement bluntly pointing out that 'I have not been consulted and the freely expressed opinion of the Spanish people has not been sought.' From then on he maintained increasingly friendly contacts with some of the leading figures in the democratic opposition, including some who had once been openly republican. Then in June 1975 he made a speech at a dinner in Barcelona lambasting Franco and his regime and was banned from re-entering the country.

As for Juan Carlos, his problems did not end with his being named successor. Neither the Carlists nor the Falangists were prepared to give up their aspirations. Carlos Hugo decided that his cause would best be served by forming a political party which espoused left-wing socialism and workers' control. The most extreme, traditional Carlists subsequently rallied to his younger brother, Sixto Enrique.*

A more serious threat to Juan Carlos emerged when, in 1972, Alfonso de Borbón-Dampierre married Franco's eldest granddaughter, María del Carmen Martínez Bordiú. As a consequence, several members of Franco's family – in particular his wife, Doña Carmen – threw their weight behind a conspiracy hatched by Falangists to put Alfonso on the throne of Spain. Doña Carmen tried to have her granddaughter's marriage declared a royal wedding and it was proposed that Alfonso should be addressed as 'His Royal Highness'. Both ideas were scotched only by Juan Carlos's personal intervention. Franco's royalism had always been in part a reflection of his own kingly pretensions,† and

---

* In 1976 when followers of Carlos Hugo made the Carlists' traditional annual pilgrimage to the top of Montejurra, a high hill near Pamplona, they were set upon by a band of armed right-wingers led by Sixto Enrique. One man died and several were wounded.

† Among other things, Franco felt empowered to hand out titles of nobility. Today more than thirty Spanish families owe their peerages to the munificence of the son of a naval supply officer. One of the aristocrats he created, Pedro Barrié de la Maza, head of the Galician hydroelectricity concern, Fuerzas Eléctricas del Noroeste Sociedad Anónima (FENOSA), was allowed to take his title from the name of his firm, becoming the Count of Fenosa.

throughout the last years of his life there was some apprehension among Juan Carlos's supporters that the *Caudillo* might change his mind and transfer the succession to Alfonso in order to make himself the founder of a dynasty.

Juan Carlos's astute conduct of affairs during the first year of his reign did much to heal the breach between him and his father. In early 1977, as it became clear that Suárez's government was heading towards the setting-up of a fully fledged democracy, Don Juan decided to give his son the public endorsement he had so far withheld. In May, at the Palacio de la Zarzuela he renounced his rights to the throne in a speech reiterating his faith in democracy. At the end of it he stood to attention, bowed deeply and declared, 'Majesty. Spain. Above all.' Don Juan will, I suspect, go down in history as one of the tragic figures of the twentieth century – the king who never was. A simple man who always said that his happiest years were spent as an ordinary naval officer, an indecisive man caught between his distaste for a parvenu dictator and his responsibility for the survival of his dynasty, he nevertheless proved himself in the end to be wise enough and humble enough to recognize that, having lost a throne, he need not lose another son.

The same year also saw the beginning of the end of another, far more momentous, division within the Bourbon family. In October, Carlos Hugo returned to Spain after nine years in exile and made it clear in his very first speech that he saw himself as the leader of a political party rather than the head of a rival dynasty. Five months later, he and Juan Carlos met and in 1979 Carlos Hugo was granted Spanish citizenship. Since then, his party has effectively disappeared from the political scene.

The tone of King Juan Carlos's reign had been set before it began. Some months before Franco's death, the Prince – as he then was – decided that when he took the throne he would not move into the residence of his ancestors, the eighteenth-century Palacio de Oriente in Madrid, but would remain in the house where he had lived since 1962.

Although extensions have been added, the Palacio de la Zarzuela, a few miles to the north-west of the capital, is no bigger than many a company chairman's home. The drawing-room can only just take a hundred people standing, so the grander official receptions have to be held in the Palacio de Oriente. Yet the Zarzuela houses not only the royal family itself but also the offices of the royal household and the living quarters of some of the people who work for it. Apart from the Zarzuela, the King and Queen also have the use of the Palacio de Marivent, a former museum overlooking a bay just outside Palma de Mallorca, where they spend August and some of their weekends during the summer. During the winter, the royal family occasionally goes skiing at Baquiera Beret, a resort in Catalonia.

To the disappointment of some of the aristocracy, they have not re-established any sort of court. On big occasions, Juan Carlos can still look a little awkward, and he has never truly acquired the knack of delivering a prepared speech with ease. It is in the slightly more informal atmosphere of audiences and receptions that the King is at his best. Outgoing and casual, he is blessed with a good sense of humour and a prodigious memory for names and faces.

The King's enthusiasms have mostly had something to do with sport. He still skis in the winter, sails in the summer and likes to play snooker after dinner. When he was younger, he was keen on, and reputedly good at, squash, tennis and karate. Those close to the palace say he has become more religious as he gets older. His faith is said to be of a very uncomplicated, unintellectual sort, and that would certainly be all of a piece with the man.

As is the case with her husband, the less formal the occasion, the more favourable the impression created by Queen Sofía. She herself has recognized that she has a distinctly forbidding 'ceremonial expression', like that of Queen Elizabeth of England. But she is capable of breaking into a dazzling smile which implies a likeable personality behind it. Sofía's charms, though, are discreet ones and in a country where forceful personalities are appreciated, reserve is all too often mistaken for coldness or slyness. It is probably fair to say that, instinctively, the Spaniard in the street takes to the Queen less than to her husband. She has said that she now feels that Spain, not Greece, is her homeland, but she has undoubtedly had problems in adapting. In an interview on her fiftieth birthday, she was asked what she most liked and disliked about the Spanish. Her response was frank: 'I admire [their] generosity, courtesy, gaiety – and pride when it is kept within bounds. I admire less – not to say detest – the exaggeration of that pride, and also covetousness.'

Over the years, the Queen's interests have become predominantly intellectual. As a young woman, she was interested in archaeology. She took part in several excavations and wrote two books on her discoveries in collaboration with her sister, Irene. She is also known to have taken an interest in subjects as varied as UFOs and the Sephardic Jews, whose history and culture she was studying at the Universidad Autónoma in Madrid when Franco died and she had to give up her course.

She has a passion for classical, and especially Baroque, music. She plays the piano and is a regular concert-goer. She has also done a lot to promote the cause of Spanish performers and composers both inside and outside the country, and in recognition of her contribution, the national chamber orchestra is named after her.

Sofía, who was once a children's nurse back in Greece, is on record as saying she would like to have gone on to be a paediatrician. But she has also said that if she had not been born a royal she would not have minded being a hairdresser. Above all, Queen Sofía gives the impression of wanting to live as ordinary a life as her circumstances will allow. 'There's only one thing I really hate about my work,' she once said, 'and that's having to try on dresses.'

She is reputed to be deeply religious but it is noticeable that she arranged for all her children to be sent to secular schools. Nothing is known for certain about her political attitudes, but her views on other subjects suggest a woman with a progressive outlook. She objects to the wearing of furs, as well as to bullfighting, and is something of a vegetarian. The schools she chose for her children are known for their progressive methods and one of the most telling anecdotes about her concerns the primary school which Prince Felipe attended. Some of the parents, who felt that the cost of meals was too high, decided to boycott them and send their children to school with packed lunches. Queen Sofía took their side and thereafter the heir to the throne turned up every morning with sandwiches in his satchel.

There is a school of thought which holds that Sofía, whose gentle looks are said to belie a will of iron, may have had as much of an impact on recent Spanish history as her husband. The young Princess, so the theory goes, was horrified by the hold that Franco and his wife exerted over Juan Carlos and set about making him into his own man, converting him to the view that no monarchy supported by the followers of a totalitarian regime could survive in the late twentieth century. How much truth there is in this will not be known for many a long year, if ever. But it is noteworthy that the future King began his secret meetings with politicians and others shortly after marrying Sofía.

Since the coup, King Juan Carlos's role has become more ceremonial and his life less eventful. He attends the various official functions his job demands and he makes overseas visits, though progressively fewer as he gets older. Perhaps the biggest challenge that he and the rest of his family have had to face is one that would be familiar to Europe's other 'royals' – how to deal with an increasingly curious press. For years, coverage of the private lives of the King and Queen, and even comment on their public roles, was virtually taboo. The King was seen as the architect of the transition, and for as long as the survival of democracy was felt to be at stake he was protected by the voluntary restraint of editors. The most they permitted themselves in print was an occasional indication of disapproval whenever the King's enthusiasm for dangerous sports brought him to grief.

But in the summer of 1990, the pact began to crumble. A news magazine published a detailed report on the tacky high-society crowd who followed the King to Mallorca, and *El Mundo* chided him in an editorial for not breaking off his holiday because of the Gulf crisis. In different ways, the two articles highlighted the same problem.

The images of the King to which his subjects had become accustomed showed him aboard a yacht or otherwise enjoying himself. In fact, he was doing a lot on their behalf. But he has never, like Queen Elizabeth, for instance, involved himself in the sort of activities which would make his endeavours more obvious to his people. Unlike her, he has never spent much time opening hospitals and touring factories.

A passage that year in King Juan Carlos's Christmas address stressing the need to balance press freedom with responsibility prompted renewed criticism from the media, who felt that, after a year in which they had helped to uncover several scandals, it was a reminder they did not need. Unhappily for the King, just two days later, he again made himself a target for censure when he crashed his Porsche while driving to a ski resort in the Pyrenees.

Then in July 1992 it emerged that the King had made two

AN ENGAGING MONARCHY

unannounced visits to Switzerland without the Queen in less than a week. The official explanation, that he had gone abroad for a rest, only served to prompt fears for his health while at the same time generating a certain degree of scepticism. The following month, *El Mundo* reported that an Italian magazine had linked the King with a Mallorcan woman who was also named at about this time in reports in the British and French press.

The publicity given to the King's private life coincided with evidence of considerable upheaval at the palace. In 1991 the head of the King's secretariat, a distinguished former ambassador, José Joaquín Puig de Bellacasa, left the Zarzuela after less than a year in the job. Puig de Bellacasa, who had served the King before he came to the throne, had been instrumental in introducing him to members of the clandestine opposition before Franco's death. Energetic, cosmo-politan, forthright and open-minded, he had been thought to be precisely the kind of person needed to steer the King towards a new role. Then, two years later, General Sabino Fernández Campos, the Head of the Royal Household, also departed in circumstances and for reasons that were equally unclear.

The often puzzling events of the early nineties proved to be no more than a 'wobble'. The royal household recovered its poise and in 1995 the nation was given a reminder that, however frivolous the King might seem when portrayed through the gossip magazines, he was still risking his life in the cause of Spanish democracy. During the summer of that year, while the royal couple were holidaying on Mallorca, the security forces discovered and foiled a plot by ETA to assassinate Juan Carlos on his yacht.* Since then, media attention has gradually shifted away from the King and Queen and towards their children, particularly as the prince and princesses have looked for partners, stirring both curiosity and controversy.

Until her marriage, Princess Elena, the eldest, had done almost nothing to attract publicity. She trained as a primary-school teacher and spent a year giving English classes. Then she went to Britain to study Education and Sociology at Exeter University before returning to Madrid where she graduated from the Comillas University with a

* Evidence of further attempts by ETA to kill the King was discovered in 1997, 2000 and 2005.

179

degree in Educational Science. She is a keen horsewoman, reputedly by far the best rider in the royal family. At the opening ceremony of the Barcelona Olympics, she touched a lot of hearts when her brother, bearing the Spanish flag, led the national team into the stadium and the TV cameras picked out Elena doing her best to smile as tears of pride rolled down her cheeks.

In 1995, in modern Spain's first high-profile royal wedding, she married a young aristocrat and banker, Jaime de Marichalar, the son of the Count and Countess of Ripalda. The King conferred on Elena and her new husband the titles of Duchess and Duke of Lugo, and they seemed destined to settle back into the comfortable obscurity from which they had both fleetingly emerged. They duly had two children, Felipe, born in 1998, and Victoria, in 2000. But in 2001, the Duke suffered a stroke while riding an exercise bike in a gym. He was partially paralysed down his left side and spent a number of weeks in hospital. The man who emerged from hospital soon appeared to many to be quite different from the one who had gone in. Sympathy for his affliction turned to criticism when he was seen around during his convalescence in the company of various people, including starlets and bullfighting personalities, who were felt to be inappropriate companions for a royal duke. Jaime de Marichalar has cultivated the eccentric habit for a Spanish male of using a fan. His consuming passions are heraldry and fashion. He regularly attends international fashion shows and in 2004 was appointed to the board of directors of the Spanish design house Loewe.

Elena's younger sister, Cristina, has made a uniquely important contribution to the monarchy's chances of survival in Spain, though perhaps without ever intending to do so. She studied Political Science in Madrid, graduating in 1989, and then did a Master's in International Relations at the University of New York. She was employed for a while at UNESCO in Paris and then went to live in Barcelona, where she began work for the cultural foundation set up by Catalonia's biggest savings bank, La Caixa. Her family may well have guided her towards Barcelona as a way of signalling to the Catalans that the restored Bourbons were not the same, insensitive centralizers that some of their predecessors had been. But what no one could have foreseen was that Princess Cristina would then meet and fall in love with a Basque.

Like most of the members of her family, she is passionately interested in sport. In 1988, she qualified as a reserve for the Spanish team at the Seoul Olympics and carried the national flag at the opening ceremony there four years before her younger brother did the same in Barcelona. At the 1996 Games in Atlanta, she met a handball player, Iñaki Urdangarín, the son of a Basque father and a Belgian mother. They married in 1997 in Barcelona cathedral. Urdangarín had lived in the city until he was sixteen, before moving to the Basque capital, Vitoria. He returned two years later to start a professional career with FC Barcelona, the club he stayed with until his retirement from handball in 2000. By then, he had become one of Spain's most successful players ever, winning bronze medals at both the Atlanta and the Sydney Olympics. Some eyebrows were raised over the Princess becoming engaged to a commoner. But it is hard to overestimate the value of her marriage in demonstrating to the public, above all in Catalonia and the Basque country, that the royal family is truly a national institution.

Since his retirement from active sport, Iñaki Urdangarín has thrown himself into sporting politics and, in 2004, he became first vice-president of the Spanish Olympic Committee. His marriage to the Princess has so far produced three sons, Juan, Pablo and Miguel, and a daughter, Irene. Since their wedding, she and her husband have only once provoked anything remotely like a stir, and that was when they were photographed kissing while on holiday in Palma de Mallorca.

As a Spanish journalist once wrote, to address the heir to the throne as 'Your Highness' is merely to do honour to the truth, for Prince Felipe is almost two metres (6' 7") tall. His height gives him an immediate advantage over all but a handful of his future subjects, though it means he can scarcely move around incognito.

Felipe made his first official appearance in 1975 when his father was proclaimed King. Two years later he was given the title of Prince of Asturias, which is traditionally bestowed on the heir to the Spanish throne. In 1980, a Prince of Asturias Foundation was set up to give awards for distinction in the arts and sciences. Its annual prize-giving ceremony, at which the Prince presides, provided an early opportunity for him to become accustomed to formal occasions. It was at one such that he gave his first public speech when he was thirteen.

By then, though, he had already had a harsh lesson in the realities of his position. At his father's insistence, he spent the whole of the night of 23 February 1981 at the King's side watching him foil the coup attempt. After that, the Crown Prince was none too gradually introduced to the duties of an heir. In 1985 he was sent to a school in Canada for a year before returning to Spain to do one-year courses at each of the three military academies. In 1988 he entered the Universidad Autónoma in Madrid to study Law and Economics, and five years later, after graduating, he did a Master's in international relations at Georgetown University in Washington DC. After he returned to Spain, he presented a series of wildlife programmes for TVE. Since then, his father has given him an increasingly broad role to play and, by the early 2000s, he was making as many official overseas visits as the King.

But, inevitably, ordinary Spaniards, aware that his wife could be their next queen, were far more interested in his private life than his public duties. And – it has to be said – his private life was rarely uninteresting.

His first serious romance began in 1989 when he started to go out with a young aristocrat, Isabel Sartorius. Rumour soon had it that his parents disapproved. Isabel certainly had a lot more experience of life. Three years older than the Prince, she had had a sophisticated and cosmopolitan upbringing, as her twice-divorced mother moved in and out of the international jet-set. The following year, though, things took an altogether more serious turn when the press linked some of her mother's friends to allegations of cocaine smuggling.

Spanish public opinion was consistently, and overwhelmingly, in favour of an eventual marriage between Felipe and Isabel. But in 1993, after months of on-off speculation, Isabel Sartorius (who had left to live in London) gave an interview to *El Mundo* in which she made it plain that the relationship was finished, though she gave no reason.

His next high-profile romance was with a Norwegian model, Eva Sannum. The Prince met her through Crown Prince Haakon of Norway in 1997, but it was not until two years later that their relationship seems to have taken wing. It soon ran up against a solid wall of hostility, tinged with derision. Sannum just did not fit the nation's idea of a possible future queen. She was beautiful and intelligent. She spoke six foreign languages. But everything else about her was considered unsuitable. For a start, a lot of Spaniards expressed a preference for a Spanish – or at least a Spanish-looking – queen. Sannum, with her blonde hair and blue eyes, was unmistakably Scandinavian. Her parents had divorced when she was ten years old and she and her sister had gone to live with their father who, at various times, worked in the government employment service and a car re-spray firm. When she became a model, her speciality was lingerie.

The King's official biographer, José Luis de Villalonga, remarked that if the Prince married Sannum it would make him 'consider the advantages of a republic'. That and other comments from people close to the King or Queen signalled that the royal couple too were unhappy about their son's girlfriend. In 2001, Sannum and the Prince appeared together for the first time in public, at Prince Haakon's wedding. She wore what the arbiters of good taste in Spain decided was an inappropriate, low-cut dress. Nevertheless, an engagement seemed to be on the cards. The press reported that Eva was even preparing to convert to Catholicism. Then, in December, Felipe astonished everyone by announcing that he and his girlfriend had come to a mutual agreement to end their romance.

Six months later, as part of his never-ending preparation for the throne, the Prince made a visit to the newspaper *El País*. Like other royals, he has had a pretty uneasy relationship with the media, and once complained bitterly about how the press sabotaged his love life. So it came as a surprise when, without anyone asking him, he told *El País*'s journalists that he had always harboured a secret desire to write for the newspapers. 'If I weren't what I am, I'd be a journalist,' he said.

With hindsight, it can be seen that this abrupt change of sentiment might have had something to do with the fact that, at exactly that time, the Prince met the journalist who was to become his wife.

Letizia Ortiz was born in Oviedo, the main city of Asturias, in 1972. Her mother is a nurse and an active trade unionist. Her father was the founder and, for many years, the director of a local radio station. He in his turn had come from a journalistic family – his mother had been a well-known voice on Spanish radio.

Letizia and her two sisters had the most normal of middle-class upbringings. She went to a state school and when, in 1987, her parents moved to Madrid because of her father's work, she went with them.

As a child she attended ballet classes three times a week and her earliest ambition was to be a dancer. But, after school, she opted to study journalism at the Complutense University in Madrid, and from then on seems never to have looked back.

In her final year at university, she worked as an intern at the daily newspaper *ABC* and on the foreign desk of the news agency EFE. After graduating, she spent a year in the provinces, at a newspaper in her home town of Oviedo, before enrolling for a Master's degree in radio and TV journalism. Former colleagues describe Ortiz as friendly, intelligent, discreet, professional – and very ambitious. But after getting her Master's degree she did something uncharacteristic of a journalist whose only interest is in getting as quickly as possible to the top. She went off for a year to Mexico to study for a doctorate while working on a paper in Guadalajara.

In the event, she never finished the doctorate. Instead, she returned to Spain to take a job on the Bloomberg financial channel, then joined CNN+, the Spanish version of the all-news channel, at its launch. Barely a year later, she moved to the state-owned TVE where her talent and telegenic good looks won her rapid advancement. She was soon presenting the main weekly current affairs programme. In 2000, Ortiz reported from Washington on the US presidential elections. The following year, she broadcast live from Ground Zero after the 9/11 attacks. In 2002, she helped cover what, for Spain, was the story of the year, the *Prestige* oil spill. After the US-led invasion of Iraq, she went to Baghdad. Her reporting won her a best young journalist award and, by September 2003, she was doing the most prized on-screen job in Spanish television journalism, presenting TVE's main evening news bulletin.

By then, she and Prince Felipe were deeply involved. Yet no one, outside a tiny circle of the Prince's closest friends, knew anything about it. This is the single most remarkable thing about their romance. We live in an age when the media is meant to be able to pry into every last corner of celebrities' lives. Yet the Crown Prince enjoyed a romance of more than a year with one of the best-known women in Spain, a woman who was herself working in the media, without anyone guessing. After the unfortunate Eva Sannum affair, the Prince apparently decided that this was the only way to do things, and an elaborate plan of concealment and deception, code-named *Operación*

Silenzio,* was devised with the help of royal aides. But it involved a considerable risk.

The debate over Eva Sannum may have been awkward and embarrassing for all concerned, but it had the advantage of signalling to the Prince and the royal household what the public felt about her. When, on 1 November 2003, Felipe announced that he was engaged, he had no way of knowing if his choice would be acceptable to the majority of Spaniards. He must have hoped that a woman who was familiar to millions of people from their television screens would be a popular future queen. But he also knew that her life before they met was not exactly a blank slate.

In 1998, she had married one of her former schoolteachers, Alonso Guerrero, after a relationship which, according to some accounts, began when she was still at school and Guerrero was teaching her literature. The marriage lasted for little more than a year and broke up soon after Guerrero finished a novel about a writer facing divorce. A few months earlier, Ortiz's parents had separated and her father has since found a new partner.

Then there was the nude painting. While she was in Mexico, Ortiz became friendly with a Cuban artist, Waldo Saavedra. After she returned to Spain, he painted a poster to go with an album produced by a Mexican group. It features a naked woman with Letizia Ortiz's face standing up to her waist in water. Although Saavedra describes her as his former muse, he has denied she ever posed nude for him.

It is not entirely surprising, therefore, that the King and Queen are said to have objected to Prince Felipe's plans to marry the beautiful young TV presenter and to have relented only after he threatened to give up the succession in order to do so. But, in this instance, the Prince had a surer instinct than his parents. After their engagement was announced, his choice of partner won overwhelming backing from the public. A poll conducted by the SER radio network found 80 per cent believed Letizia Ortiz would give the royal family a modern image – a particularly important finding in view of the 'outdated' tag hung on the monarchy by respondents in other polls. When the

* *Silenzio* (instead of *silencio*) being an allusion to the idiosyncratic spelling of Letizia's name. The normal Spanish form is Leticia. Apparently her name was put into the register of births by an Italian-born official, who wrote it with a 'z'.

Prince married his bride, in May 2004, it was reckoned that 300,000 people flocked to Madrid for the occasion.

The birth of their first child, Leonor, in October 2005, gave the monarchy a new boost, spiced by controversy over the baby Infanta's future role. In line with its efforts to promote gender equality, the Socialist government is planning to introduce legislation that would give women equality with men in the succession once Felipe ascends the throne.

So. A fairy-tale ending to a story that had, at times, risked tipping the monarchy into outright crisis. As Prince Felipe and Princess Letizia began to go about their duties together, they did so in the knowledge that they could rely on considerable public goodwill. Fewer than thirty years after the return of the monarchy in the person of 'Juan Carlos the Brief', the least historically stable of Spain's 'Three Pillars' was looking pretty sturdy. Against the backdrop of Spain's often turbulent history, that represented no small achievement. The Prince unquestionably deserves some of the credit for it. But his growing popularity should not obscure the fact that he might not even have had a throne to aspire to if his father had not acted as he did on the most dramatic night in Spain's recent history.

CHAPTER 14

The Army: Back in Step

Just as Americans remember where they were when the attack began on the Twin Towers, no Spaniard who was alive at the time will forget what he or she was doing on the afternoon of Monday, 23 February 1981. That was when a detachment of Civil Guards led by the elaborately moustachioed Antonio Tejero burst into Congress, interrupting a broadcast debate on the appointment of the new Prime Minister. The millions of people listening to the proceedings on the radio heard, first, a series of confused shouts and then a sustained burst of gunfire. The intention was to force the assembled deputies on to the floor, but to everyone listening it sounded as if a madman had wiped out the entire political class of Spain.

How many army units were meant to have risen against the government during the hours that followed will probably never be known. In the event only the Motorized Division under Lieutenant-General Milans del Bosch, based near Valencia, actually took to the streets. Cristina Soler Crespo, a resident of Valencia, scribbled down what she saw and heard as it happened. Her account, published a few days later by the newspaper *El País*, evokes something of the terror and uncomprehending outrage of that night.

As I write these lines at 2 o'clock on a cold February morning, I can see a few metres from my window on the third floor of the Gran Vía in Valencia a tank – a huge, terrifying, green tank – parked calibrating its guns ... aiming at thousands of windows, behind whose net curtains one can glimpse the terrified faces, the terrified eyes of peaceful citizens, of families with children, of old people who have seen these scenes before and are reliving the deaf, dumb, impotent panic of those who don't understand ... Lorries full of soldiers arrive. Army jeeps and police cars occupy every corner along the wide avenue and the birds take to the air, as startled as the humans. Now the lights in the garden that runs down the centre have been put out and the scene takes on the appearance of a nightmare. I can see that the three young men in the nearest tank are no more than twenty years old. Their gun is now definitely aimed at the PSOE office with its red flag opposite my window. The people at the windows above it draw their curtains and put out the lights.

The events of 23–24 February made real something that the majority of Spaniards had dreaded ever since Franco's death. The threat of military intervention had distorted almost every aspect of Spanish life, conditioning the way that politicians approached a range of issues and, in particular, regional policy, making them much more wary than they would otherwise have been. There again, by the standards of Spain's history, involvement by the army was the norm rather than the exception.

The origins of the army's enthusiasm for meddling in the affairs of state have been traced as far back as the eighteenth century, when senior officers were called upon to play an unusually prominent role in the administration. But it was the Napoleonic invasion in 1808 which created the preconditions for that persistent military intervention which became the hallmark of Spanish politics during the nineteenth century.

One of the paradoxes of the War of Independence which followed the invasion was that while the middle-class administrators and officers who filled the vacuum left by the King and his court were busy fighting the invaders, they adopted many of the ideas that the French were bent on propagating. Of these the most basic was that the monarch should be subject to the constraints of a written constitution. However, Fernando VII, who was put back on the throne in 1814, refused to acknowledge that times had changed; the result was that his reign was punctuated at frequent intervals by uprisings led by officers who had served in the War of Independence and who sought to impose a constitution. The upheavals under Fernando gave the world two new words. One, which was coined to describe the opponents of absolute monarchy, was *liberal*.* The other, first used

* Although the word is often used now to denote someone to the left of the centre of the political spectrum, it is important to understand that the nineteenth-century Spanish *liberal* would be considered a conservative in the twenty-first century. To distinguish them from modern liberals I shall continue to use italics whenever I refer to the original Spanish variety.

by Major Rafael de Riego to describe his declaration of a rebellion against the Crown in 1820, was *pronunciamiento*. At first, *pronunciamiento* was used to describe only an initial call to arms, but it subsequently came to mean an uprising in its entirety. By 1936 there would have been no fewer than forty-four of them.

Fernando died in 1833 at a time when his heir, Isabel, was not yet three years old, and Spain came to be ruled by that least authoritative form of government – a regency, exercised in this case by Fernando's widow, María Cristina. Her shaky authority was still further undermined by the dynastic wrangle that had led Fernando's brother, Carlos, to declare war on the government and recruit to his cause all those who had a vested interest in the perpetuation of absolutism. The Carlist war made María Cristina exceptionally dependent on her army, so that when her two leading generals demanded that she agree to a constitution she was in no position to refuse.

In one sense, Spain was well-suited to a two-party parliamentary democracy. From the very beginning the *liberales* had been split into two groups, which came to be known as the Moderates and the Progressives. Unfortunately, Spain's economic backwardness and political inexperience were such that the idea of one party voluntarily surrendering power to another by means of fair elections never really took root and the politicians soon got into the habit of getting the army to oust the government instead. In a society where it was demonstrably impossible to assess public opinion through the ballot box, the generals and colonels acted ostensibly as interpreters of the will of the people. Throughout Isabel's reign, power usually changed hands by means of *pronunciamientos* by officers allied to one or other *liberal* camp – men such as Espartero, O'Donnell and the indomitable Ramón María Narváez who, when asked by his deathbed confessor to forgive his enemies, is said to have refused on the grounds that 'I have killed them all.'

Perhaps inevitably it was a *pronunciamiento*, led by an alliance of Progressive generals and admirals, which finally robbed Isabel of her throne in 1868. Unfortunately for the Progressives, however, their idea of importing a more amenable ruler from abroad did not work and the initiative passed outside the *liberal* camp to those who did not want a monarchy of any kind, constitutional or absolute. The politicians who ruled Spain during the short-lived First Republic were not only anti-monarchist, but anti-militarist. They espoused several ideas which the officer corps abhorred. In particular, a significant number of them favoured turning Spain into a federal state. In this respect they had something in common with the Carlists, whose dream of putting the clock back to the eighteenth century included restoring traditional local rights and privileges. To the officer corps, whose principal task had been the suppression of Carlism, the devolution of power in any form was anathema and it was altogether appropriate that the Republic should have been overthrown by a general seeking to forestall the introduction of federalism.*

The experience of the First Republic persuaded the *liberales* that they had to make a two-party system work, and the restoration of the monarchy in 1874 ushered in a period of contrived democracy in which the opposing *liberal* factions, re-christened Conservatives and Liberals, swapped power by means of rigged elections in an effort to keep the Republicans and other radicals at bay. Almost incidentally, this system succeeded in putting an end to the *pronunciamientos*. Its failing was that the only sections of society whose interests were represented were the upper and middle classes. As parts of Spain became industrialized over the next fifty years, an ever larger and stronger urban working class was left without a voice in parliament. Therefore it frequently took its grievances on to the streets and successive governments had to call on the army to restore order.

The same period also saw a string of humiliating defeats overseas. It started with a forlorn struggle to hold on to Cuba, which ended abruptly in 1898 when the United States declared war on Spain, wiped out its fleet and deprived it not only of Cuba but also of Puerto Rico and the Philippines. Six years later, Spain received compensation of a kind when it secured two small chunks of Morocco. But almost immediately it was faced with resistance in the northern sector. From 1909 until 1925 it had to contend with a full-scale war there, waged by the tribes of the Rif mountains,† which, although it was eventu-

---

* General Pavía's coup which brought down the First Republic in 1873 almost certainly provided the inspiration for Tejero's intervention. Pavía, like Tejero, led his men into the Cortes and ordered them to fire in the air.

† The Moroccan war saw the creation of what was to become the most renowned unit in the Spanish army – the Legion, founded in 1920 by Lieutenant-Colonel José Millán Astray. Like the French Legion, upon which it was modelled, the Spanish Legion

ally won by the Spanish, was blighted by a succession of disasters for them. In the worst of these, caused by the defeat at Annual in 1921, they lost 15,000 lives and 5,000 square kilometres of territory in a matter of days. Like the leaders of many a defeated army before and since, Spain's officers sought to explain their lack of success in terms of the alleged incompetence or indifference of the politicians 'back home'. In the process, they became excessively sensitive to criticism. After the 1905 local elections, for example, the victorious party in Catalonia held a massive banquet that inspired the humorous weekly *Cu-Cut* to publish a cartoon showing a soldier asking a civilian about a group of people he saw gathered in front of a door.

'The victory banquet,' the civilian explained.

'Victory! Ah, then they must be civilians,' said the officer.

This cartoon so enraged the military that to appease them the Cortes passed a law that was to bedevil relations between the armed forces and the rest of society until only a few years ago – the *Ley de Jurisdicciones*, according to which any offence against the army or its members could be tried by a court martial.

By 1923, when General Primo de Rivera seized power and set up a dictatorship, the Spanish army officer had begun to play the roles of both policeman and judge. And whether he was serving in the hills of Morocco or behind a desk in Madrid it was obvious that the distance between him and his fellow-citizens was growing. This posed a special problem for a body of men accustomed to regard themselves as instruments of the collective will and they began to evolve the curious belief that, even though they might not reflect the circumstantial preferences of the electorate, they none the less embodied the eternal values of the fatherland. A distinction was beginning to be drawn between Spain and the Spanish which in 1936 would serve to justify a war against the majority of Spaniards

---

was meant to have been composed of foreigners and was originally called the *Tercio de Extranjeros*. In fact, foreigners never accounted for more than a minority. But the Legionnaires, with their distinctive quick march, exotic mascots and tasselled forage caps, soon became a formidable combat force with a strong *esprit de corps*. Their most distinctive characteristic was an attitude towards death that bordered on the affectionate and which perhaps owed something to the Moslem tradition of enthusiastic martyrdom that so inspired their earliest enemies. Millán Astray called them *los novios de la muerte* (the fiancés of death).

as a war in defence of Spain. Even so, it required a prolonged bout of near-anarchy under the Second Republic to create the conditions for a successful uprising.

What is so striking about the army's role during the century that elapsed between Isabel's accession and the outbreak of the civil war is not that its political outlook changed so much, but that it changed so little. At first sight, it appears that an officer class fervent in its defence of liberalism during the nineteenth century was somehow transformed into a potent force for reaction in the twentieth. But that is more than anything the result of confusion over the changing meaning of the word 'liberal'. What in fact happened was that as the centre of gravity of political life moved steadily to the left, as it did throughout Europe during this period, the officer corps stoutly continued to occupy the same area of the political spectrum, clinging to a view of politics which may have seemed radical by comparison with the absolutism of Fernando VII, but which was beginning to look somewhat conservative by the time of the First Republic and positively reactionary by the time of the Second Republic.

Having said that, it is important to stress that the area of the political spectrum occupied by the officer corps was always quite a broad one. When, as occurred under Isabel, the focus of political life fell more or less in the middle of it, its members could appear severely divided. Events during the First Republic served to make the views of the officer class somewhat more uniform than they had been, but they continued to vary significantly, as the 1936 uprising showed. By no means every officer joined the revolt and a sizeable minority – including the majority of senior officers – stuck by the Republic.

What really changed things was the outcome of the civil war. The 3,000 officers who had remained loyal to the Republic and survived the war were purged from the army, and about 10,000 young men who had joined the Nationalists as *alfereces provisionales* (temporary subalterns) and been put into the field after a brief training course were allowed to stay in. As a result the officer corps became considerably more homogeneous and reactionary, and this process continued as, with the passage of time, an increasingly large proportion of the officer class came to be made up of post-civil-war recruits – young men who had actively chosen to serve a dictatorship.

A month after his first government took power, Suárez held a meeting with Spain's most senior officers at which he set out his plans and asked for their support. The outcome was a florid communiqué, the gist of which was that the armed forces would put up with the government's reforms provided they were approved by the Cortes (which at that time was still filled with Franco's supporters). During the meeting, however, it appears that the officers got the impression that he would consult them before legalizing the Communist Party. When, the following year, Suárez was prompted by events and – it would seem – the King to legalize the PCE, the reaction within the officer corps was one of outrage. Only one of the three armed service ministers actually handed in his resignation, but the damage done to Suárez and the government's standing in the eyes of the military was immense. Thereafter, a mutinous undercurrent continued to bubble away just below the surface of army life.

What Ortega called the 'praetorianism' of the officer class was the biggest single obstacle to Spain's transformation from a dictatorship into a democracy. The man Suárez chose for the daunting task of trying to curb it was Lieutenant-General Manuel Gutiérrez Mellado who, until he was brought into the cabinet, had been Chief of the General Staff. With his pinched face, closely cropped moustache and heavy-rimmed spectacles, 'Guti', as he was nicknamed, looked the very image of a Francoist general. Indeed, he had spent most of his adult life in the service of the *Caudillo* – first as an undercover agent for the Nationalist side in the Republican zone during the civil war and later as a talented staff officer and unit commander. But his views were not those of a Francoist. 'The army', he declared in a speech shortly after Franco's death, 'is there not to command, but to serve.'

The general threw himself into the job with Herculean gusto. Working with only a modest staff, sleeping as little as three hours a night, he drafted a string of decrees that reformed pay and promotion, laid down the limits of political activity in the armed forces; abolished their jurisdiction over terrorist offences and provided them with a new set of standing orders. The existing ones had not been changed since the eighteenth century. Most importantly of all, he transformed the armed forces' command structure so that it began to resemble that of a democratic nation. Under Franco, the armed forces' most senior representatives – the Chief of Defence Staff and the three armed forces ministers in the cabinet – all had direct, routine access to the head of government. The armed forces did not come under the control of the government. They were part of it.

Gutiérrez Mellado rendered superfluous the armed services ministers by making the Chiefs of Staff the commanders of their respective services, and then did the same to the Chief of Defence Staff by transferring his powers to a newly created joint chiefs of staff committee, the Junta de Jefes del Estado Mayor (JUJEM), comprising the three service chiefs and a chairman. By early 1977 the armed forces had been put firmly under the thumb of the government and the way was open for the abolition of the three armed forces ministries, and their replacement by a single Defence Ministry immediately after the general election of June 1977.

Gutiérrez Mellado became the first boss of the new ministry, but his eventual aim was to work himself out of a job by preparing the way for the appointment of a civilian Defence Minister. After the 1979 elections, direct control of the armed forces was handed, for the first time in forty years, to someone who was not, nor ever had been, an officer: Agustín Rodríguez Sahagún. Even so, Gutiérrez Mellado retained a seat in the cabinet as deputy Prime Minister, with responsibility for security and defence. It was not until 1981 when Suárez threw in the towel that Gutiérrez Mellado also withdrew from the government, thus enabling Calvo Sotelo to form a cabinet without any military ministers.

By then, however, Spain's democratic order had very nearly been overthrown in a coup. Gutiérrez Mellado merits an illustrious place in his country's history for what he achieved, but the government of which he was a member must take a share of the blame for what happened in 1981. Its key failing was that, often, when faced with evidence of a failure to respect the new democratic order, it chose to ignore it. Between 1977 and 1982, there were several occasions on which officers were punished by the military authorities for expressing support for the constitution while others who openly abused it were let off. The 1981 coup was itself a consequence of the UCD's timidity. Both Tejero and Milans del Bosch had been caught plotting against the government, yet were allowed to continue in positions of responsibility.

The torrent of indignation unleashed by the coup must have proved to all but the most quixotic officers that, had Tejero and his masters succeeded, they would not have been able to count on a significant measure of support from the population, as Franco had done. That, as much as anything, explains why the danger of renewed military intervention has receded so quickly in the years since 1981. That, and the fact that the political attitudes embraced by most of the rest of society have spread gradually to the army.

However, it is also the case that it was not until after the Socialists took power in 1982 that the public's fear of another coup abated or that evidence of plotting in the army receded.* The man who, more than anyone, helped bring the Spanish army to heel was a bearded and bespectacled former mayor of Barcelona, Narcís Serra, who served as Defence Minister from 1982 until 1991, when he was promoted to become Felipe González's deputy Prime Minister.

Without compromising their undertakings to the electorate, the Socialists settled many of the issues which had been causing such anxiety in army messes. They gave the country the firm government it had been lacking ever since the UCD started to fall apart. They provided assurances that the granting of additional powers to the regions would not be allowed to endanger Spain's unity. And, above all, they applied to the army itself the strict discipline whose absence had so disconcerted its officers since Franco's death.

The Socialists also, of course, took Spain into the European Union. Anyone plotting a coup from that point on would have known that, if it succeeded, it could bring about Spain's expulsion from the EU and the dire consequences that that would cause. Just as important in ending the Spanish officer corps' predilection for intervening in politics has been the way successive governments have gradually altered the mission of the armed forces.

Under Franco, the only fighting the army had to do was against Spain's colonial subjects in North Africa – and there was precious little of that. The *Caudillo* was nothing if not a realist and Spain's colonial possessions were relinquished at the first whiff of trouble.

---

* For some time it was assumed that the last attempt by army officers to overthrow the elected government was one known to have been foiled in October 1982, shortly before the Socialists came to office. But in 1991 a detailed, though unsourced, report in *El País* said a plot to kill the King and Queen, the Prime Minister and the heads of the armed forces had been detected in 1985. The report did not make clear whether the conspirators were identified or, if so, whether any action was taken against them.

Spanish northern Morocco went in 1956. Spanish southern Morocco went in 1958 along with Ifni, a territorial enclave opposite the Canary Islands which had been ceded to Spain in 1868. The West African territory of Río Muni and the island of Fernando Po jointly gained their independence as Equatorial Guinea in 1968. The army's main role was to be an army of occupation and the occupied territory was Spain. Franco re-instituted the division of the country into captaincies-general, each commanded by a lieutenant-general with significant civil as well as military powers. Unlike many of his predecessors he did not use the army on the streets to break up demonstrations. But he deployed the officer corps extensively in internal repression. Most officers in the paramilitary police forces were drawn from the armed forces, as were most members of the intelligence services. In addition, officers were often called upon to try terrorist suspects at courts martial. All this inevitably created an impression among officers that their job had as much to do with controlling society as with defending its interests with the use, or threat, of force.

The obvious role for the Spanish army after Franco's death was to join the fighting forces of the rest of the West in the confrontation with communism. But within three years of Spain's NATO membership being confirmed by the 1986 referendum, the Berlin Wall came down and the Soviet Union's influence crumbled, undermining NATO's original purpose. The Socialists' response was to provide the soldiers with an additional role by involving them heavily in UN peacekeeping. In 1989, the army got its first experience of such an operation when seven of its officers donned sky-blue berets to join the mission supervising the withdrawal of Cuban troops from Angola. Just three years later, Spain had more officers serving under the UN flag than any other country in the world.

The years that followed saw a gradual shift towards involvement in the activities of a reoriented NATO. It began even before the Socialists lost power. After the signing of the 1995 Dayton Accord between Bosnia, Croatia and Yugoslavia, the Spanish troops who had been serving in the Balkans under the UN flag gave up their blue helmets to join the NATO contingent. Spain's less-than-wholehearted membership of the Alliance had already begun to seem anomalous and it looked even more so when a Spaniard and Socialist, Javier Solana, was elected to be NATO's Secretary-General. One of José

María Aznar's earliest moves was to involve Spain fully in the Alliance. But the course of events, and Aznar's view that Spain's place was at America's side, contrived to guide Spanish forces into a string of non-NATO missions. After 9/11, Aznar committed small numbers of ships, aircraft and personnel to the US's Operation Enduring Freedom. He later contributed Spanish soldiers to the international force in Afghanistan. After the US-led invasion that toppled Saddam Hussein, Aznar sent to Iraq the contingent that was subsequently withdrawn by Zapatero.

But, in some respects, the most significant operation for the Spanish armed forces was one that prompted not a few smiles, both inside and outside Spain. On 16 July 2002 – at 23.43 hours, as Spanish newspapers later reported – Aznar gave the order for troops to seize back the tiny, uninhabited island of Perejil (the Spanish word for 'parsley'). Moroccan gendarmes had earlier occupied the island, barely more than a rock, lying just 260 metres from the Moroccan coast. Helicopters landed a special operations unit that captured the six Moroccan sentries on the island and raised the Spanish flag. A photograph immortalizing the moment is vaguely reminiscent of one of the Second World War's most celebrated images – the raising of the Stars and Stripes on Iwo Jima. Ludicrous though the whole Parsley Island affair unquestionably was, it risked bringing the two countries into conflict, and represented the first unilateral military action undertaken by Spain since the return of democracy. Aznar, who hungered for a more prominent international role for his country, would doubtless have liked to be able to use the armed forces more extensively, but he was hampered by their relatively low level of operational effectiveness.

One reason for this was, to some extent, self-imposed. His government, like its predecessors, allotted a comparatively small proportion of its spending to the military. When the PP left office, the defence budget accounted for less than 1 per cent of GDP,* the second lowest proportion in NATO. The armed forces' share had remained the same since Aznar came to office although, since GDP had risen

* It was reckoned that 'hidden funding', particularly by way of research spending and loan amnesties, might have pushed the overall figure for defence spending up to as much as 1.3 per cent, but that would still be low by comparison with other NATO member states.

sharply, the money available for new and better equipment had also increased significantly.

The other constraint on a more adventurous foreign policy was that the armed forces, and particularly the army, were still in the throes of a structural overhaul that had begun more than a quarter of a century earlier. Franco bequeathed an army that was over-sized and top-heavy. In 1975, the army had a total strength of 220,000. That was far more than was needed and out of all proportion to the size of the other armed forces. The same year, the strength of the navy was 46,600 and that of the air force was 35,700. What is more, the army had 24,000 officers – more than one for every ten other ranks, and their conditions of employment actively deterred professionalism. They could not be dismissed for any reason, including even insanity. Promotion depended entirely on age and postings depended largely on how well they had done at cadet college. The most important task, once the command structure had been reshaped, was to reform this wholly ludicrous system.

Calvo Sotelo's government enacted two measures of cardinal importance. One gave the military authorities the power to remove officers from the active list for 'physical, psychological or professional incompetence', and changed the arrangements for retirement in such a way that the lower an officer's rank the sooner he was forced to retire. The other made promotion dependent in part on merit by stipulating that officers had to go through selection processes before being promoted to major and brigadier. The combined effect of these two laws, which came into force in 1981, was to allow the authorities to reduce the number of officers on the active list by removing the least talented among them – the longer it took an officer to get over the hurdles created by the second law the more likely it was that he would reach the age of retirement set for his rank by the first. The new measures were deeply resented by those officers who had come to regard the army as a meal ticket for life. Their fears were played on by the ultra-right-wing press and the campaign against the officers responsible for drafting the reforms reached such a pitch that one of them – General Marcelo Aramendi – shot himself.

The 1981 reforms nevertheless fell a long way short of what was logically required – to match the number of officers of each rank to the number of posts of corresponding importance. By the time the

Socialists came to power the following year there were still 21,800 officers in the army, of whom no fewer than 300 were generals. The Spanish army's officer corps was not only very large, but also very old. The average age for a general was sixty-two, that of a colonel fifty-eight and that of a captain thirty-eight.

The Socialists introduced legislation that allowed officers to continue working their way up the scale of ranks largely according to age, but did not guarantee them a posting. Those who failed to qualify for one were offered the chance, in effect, of retiring on full salary. And not only that; as members of the so-called 'transitory reserve', they continued to qualify for promotion and the salary increases that went with it.

By 1990, more than 4,400 officers had taken up the offer, although the numbers varied considerably according to rank. It was then that a much more controversial reform took effect. This divides the officer corps into 'fast' and 'slow' tracks according to their performance in training. Those on the 'fast track' are assured of reaching the rank of major and those on the 'slow track' that of captain. But after that, their promotion is determined by selection. And if they have not made the rank of brigadier after thirty-two years in the service, they are out, though with a generous pension. The officer corps was on its way to becoming both leaner and fitter. But what of the other ranks?

The army's NCOs were professionals. So were most of its technicians and the troops in elite units such as the Royal Guard, the Parachute Brigade and the Legion. But the bulk of the army was made up of conscripts. More than 200,000 were being called up each year.

The shift in attitudes towards military service is as good an illustration as any of the changes that have overtaken Spain in the past thirty years. There was a time when a lot of youngsters looked forward to the *mili*. It gave them a chance to see the world outside their *pueblo* and provided some with a last opportunity to learn to read and write. But long before the 1990s it had come to be seen by most young Spaniards as just a waste of time. It taught them nothing they were likely to need to know during the rest of their lives. And for early school-leavers, it could mean the loss of a hard-won job.

The main symptom of growing discontent was a rise in conscientious objection. Franco's governments had simply refused to recognize it.* In fact it was not until 1984 that legislation was passed by the Cortes that did. From that point on, the number of young men applying for recognition as conscientious objectors soared and more than 90 per cent of those who applied were recognized.

It was this upsurge in conscientious objection that eventually forced Spain to have a professional army. At first, the idea was thought utterly scandalous. Its first advocate was Colonel Amadeo Martínez Inglés, a general staff officer with a distinguished service record, whose refusal to stop advocating a volunteer army landed him in prison. It eventually led to his removal from the army. But by the mid-nineties, the situation had become untenable. Conscientious objection had long since ceased to have any but the most tenuous connection with religious beliefs. It had become a convenient, and effective, way of getting out of military service. The number of conscientious objectors registered each year was fast approaching the 100,000 mark. After the 1996 election, Jordi Pujol's Catalan nationalists made their support for Aznar's government conditional on his agreeing to do away with conscription, and by the end of 2001, there were no conscripts left in the Spanish armed forces.

The big problem ever since has been to find the volunteers to replace them. The government tried offering places in the Spanish armed forces to non-Spaniards to make up the difference. But by 2004 it had attracted scarcely 1,000, and it was decided to slash the target for the number of professionals in the three services from 102–120,000 to 70–80,000.

There are a number of reasons why Spaniards themselves are proving so reluctant to enrol. One is financial. Spain's booming economy is a problem for the armed forces because it makes it harder for them to offer pay and prospects that rival those available from civilian employers. There is the fact that young Spaniards have become so averse to leaving home.† And then there is a strong streak of pacifism that nowadays runs through Spanish society, a product perhaps of the evil folk memories stirred by anything to do with fighting and soldiers in a nation that has experienced a civil war, a military dictatorship and, most recently, an attempted coup.

---

* One poor soul, a Catalan Jehovah's Witness, spent eleven years in jail for refusing to do military service, before being pardoned in 1970.

† See above, pp. 136–7.

This underlying pacifism last surfaced in the overwhelming popular opposition to the war in Iraq. Much of that opposition had nothing to do with pacifism. Most Spaniards, including many who would be ready to countenance the use of force in other circumstances, felt the Bush administration failed to make its case that Saddam Hussein possessed weapons of mass destruction and posed a threat to world peace.

Nevertheless, there is also plenty of evidence that an unusually high proportion of Spaniards are reluctant to get involved in any war in any circumstances, even one in defence of their homeland. In 2002 the Centro de Investigaciones Sociológicas conducted a poll not unlike the one carried out a decade earlier by *Cambio 16*.* Interviewees were asked if they would be ready to sacrifice everything, including their lives, for various causes. The smallest number – less than 16 per cent – was made up of those ready to die for their country.

To some extent, no doubt, this lack of patriotism is a corollary of the strength in Spain of rival loyalties, to the family and region especially. But it is also, I suspect, a reflection of the Spaniards' profoundly ambivalent and mistrustful relationship with an entity that claims pride of place over both family and region – the state.

* See above, pp. 134–5.

CHAPTER 15

The State: More Tax, but Less Red Tape

'Since Spaniards in general feel an instinctive animosity towards the joining of associations,' wrote Fernando Díaz-Plaja in *El español y los siete pecados capitales*, 'the state – an organization to which there is no option but to belong – is viewed with suspicion. The state is an abhorrent entity which is regarded, not as the necessary link between the individual and society, but as a conglomeration of interventions trying to regulate the life of Juan Español,* with the sole aim of damaging his interests.'

As some other Spanish authors have pointed out, the nature of the relationship between the Spaniard and the state is deftly expressed in the vocabulary surrounding taxation. A tax in Spanish is an *impuesto*, literally an 'imposition'. A taxpayer is a *contribuyente*, or contributor. The impression created is not that the citizen routinely pays the state for the services he receives, but that he every so often, reluctantly but graciously, hands over some cash to make it go away. Until recently, this was not so very far from the truth. However much Spain's leaders may have longed to meddle in the affairs of its citizens, they only had the wherewithal to do so intermittently.

At first glance, weak government would appear to be the last thing Spain suffered from, having been ruled by dictators for most of the last century. But although the regimes of Primo de Rivera and Franco may have been strong in the negative sense that they were capable of preventing people from doing this and that, the fact remains that they were weak in the positive sense of being able to encourage them to do things. The police may have been brutal, the bureaucracy obstructive, but the government's capacity to intervene

* Juan Español is to Spain what John Doe is to the US.

and to regulate, to shape the pattern of society was severely limited. The contrast was particularly marked under Franco.

The avowed aim of the Nationalists when they came to power was to impose a New Order that would affect every facet of private, as well as public, life. In November 1936, a mere four months after the outbreak of the civil war and with battles raging along two fronts, the government issued a decree unconnected with rationing that stipulated the number and content of the courses to be eaten at mealtimes. 'Henceforth,' it solemnly declared, 'both in restaurants and at home the egg dish will consist of a single egg.' All such attempts at social engineering soon ran into the sand and within a few years of Franco's victory they were abandoned. In fact, towards the end of his rule one of the most striking things about Spain was the virtual absence of petty restrictions. You could park three abreast or litter the streets without fear of anyone stopping you.

It is tempting to put the whole thing down to the anarchic Spanish temperament. But there was also a sound practical reason, which was that Franco's ministers had to work with the same inefficient civil service and the same inadequate financial resources as their predecessors, going back at least until the beginning of the previous century. Spanish governments had traditionally been unable or unwilling to reform their bureaucracy or raise enough tax, and they had paid a price for these shortcomings in their inability to mould society.

One of the outstanding characteristics of Franco's regime was that with the exception of the odd working-class fascist all the *Caudillo*'s ministers came from middle-class backgrounds. They held to middle-class values and acted in middle-class interests, and this was never more evident than in their taxation policy – or rather, the absence of one.

Apart from a limited reform in 1940, successive ministers of finance left untouched a system that had been in force since the end of the previous century. It was a system which above all favoured the well-to-do. In the first place, the proportion of the government's income raised by indirect taxes, such as the duties on goods and services (which fall equally on all consumers regardless of their wealth or income), was always considerably greater than the share raised by direct taxes, notably income tax (which, by its nature, should fall more heavily on the rich than on the poor). Throughout the sixties the ratio of indirect to direct taxes was about two to one.

What is more, as far as personal taxation was concerned, an inordinately large amount derived from the charge on wages (which was usually deducted at source and was therefore difficult to evade) while only a small amount came from the separate 'personal income tax' that was paid by those who received high incomes or incomes from several sources (which was assessed and collected on an individual basis and was much easier to avoid). For those who could, the temptation to dodge taxes was overwhelming. There were very few tax inspectors and evasion was not even a criminal offence. The 'personal income tax' accounted for less than 1.5 per cent of total fiscal revenue.

Apart from being grotesquely unjust, Franco's tax system ensured that the state remained as poor as ever, because the effect was to exploit that section of the community which had least to give. In 1975, when Franco died, fiscal receipts excluding Social Security contributions amounted to just under 20 per cent of the gross domestic product (GDP). In the other nations of the 'West' – the member countries of the OECD – the average figure was 33 per cent.

If the men and women who took over from Franco agreed on anything it was that they had a historic mission to transform society. One of their highest priorities was to increase the resources at their disposal by getting Spaniards, and particularly rich Spaniards, to pay more taxes.

The first step was taken in 1977 when the then Finance Minister, Francisco Fernández-Ordóñez, steered through the Cortes an elementary tax reform law. It unified the system of income tax so that wage-earners and non-wage-earners were assessed according to the same rules, and for the first time evasion was made an offence. In the meantime, the Finance Ministry installed a battery of computers and recruited some 1,500 inspectors to deal with personal taxation. So that in the future no one would have an excuse for evading their responsibilities, a team of advisers was provided by the government and anyone who had to fill in a return was entitled to call on their services. Among those who did so was the King, who – in keeping with the egalitarian spirit of the new Spain – pays taxes like everyone else. An advertising campaign was launched around the slogan '*Ahora Hacienda somos todos. No nos engañemos.*' A literal translation would be:

'Now we are all the Treasury, let's not cheat ourselves', but it lacks the punch of the original.

The combination of carrot and stick worked, up to a point. The number of Spaniards who submitted their returns by 1 August 1978, the deadline for declaring income received during 1977, was much higher than in previous years, even though a number of them turned up on 31 July with blank forms on the principle that if the tax-men wanted the money then they would have to work for it. Of the total number of declarations, about one in ten contained arithmetical errors (the vast majority of which were, of course, in favour of the taxpayer). More seriously, however, a sizeable number contained flagrant omissions. During the weeks and months that followed, Fernández-Ordóñez put into effect a plan, dubbed Operation Red File, aimed at flushing out the worst defaulters by using the records of other government departments to confirm the ownership of shares, property or whatever else had been left off their returns.

The next step was to increase the number of people who had to fill in tax returns. In 1980, for the first time, anyone who owned or earned more than a certain amount, or who, for example, owned a house worth more than a certain amount or a car of less than a certain age, or who employed more than one servant or had a seat on a board of directors, had to fill in the hated form.

By the time the UCD left power, direct taxes had overtaken indirect ones, to make Spain's fiscal system 'progressive' rather than 'regressive' for the first time in the country's history.

It would be nice to think that the '*Ahora Hacienda somos todos*' campaign persuaded Spaniards to pay up gladly for the good of all. Needless to say, it did not. When the Socialists took office, it was apparent that the economy was still awash with undeclared assets, known in Spanish as *dinero negro* (black money).

The struggle to bring it into the light will long be associated with the bespectacled son of a Catalan baker. José Borrell was still in his thirties, though with a doctorate in economics and a professorship of mathematics under his belt, when he was made the number two at the Finance Ministry in 1984. Not a man to suffer fools gladly, he was nicknamed by one of the papers the 'Torquemada of taxation'. This, of course, was precisely the image the government wished to create.

In fact, the Socialists' efforts to cut down on tax-dodging were often ham-fisted and, in at least one instance, counter-productive. The effect of one of their earliest moves – the so-called Boyer decree* – was to drive a lot of the *dinero negro* into property at a time when the sector was still a closed book to the tax authorities.

The key reform of the Socialist years was a law passed in 1985. One of its effects was to provide an ingenious way in which tax-dodgers could launder their 'black money' and at the same time settle their debts with the Treasury. A new kind of treasury note was created which, being made out to 'bearer', could never be traced once sold. The tax due on it was levied at the time of purchase. For the government, the scheme had the additional advantage that it provided access to a new source of cheap borrowing.

The 1985 Act also forced the banks to provide more information about their customers. However, it left a loophole that was soon spotted. Insurance companies, unlike banks and other financial institutions, were not required to collect tax from their customers on the interest they earned. Throughout 1986 and 1987, a number of banks advised their customers to transfer money out of their accounts and into single-premium insurance policies run by groups under the banks' control. The wheeze, uncovered by the government in 1989, proved there was still an astonishing quantity of 'black money' in circulation. Some 4,200 billion pesetas – equivalent to £22 billion or $35 billion at the prevailing exchange rate – was eventually estimated to have been spent on single-premium policies. Eighty per cent was thought to be *dinero negro*. What the authorities had discovered was a secret hoard equivalent to 7.5 per cent of that year's gross national product (GNP). The affair also showed the degree of social respectability attached to cheating the tax-man in Spain. Some of the country's leading banks had been involved in the operation.

Unravelling the insurance scam represented a major victory for the government. Some of its other initiatives fared less well. The singer Lola Flores, for example, was put on trial for not paying her taxes. Predictably, she turned the courtroom into a stage, melted all hearts, and was acquitted.

In 1990, the government appeared to recognize the limits of its

* See below, p. 326.

ability to clamp down on evasion when it offered an amnesty. Tax-dodgers were given a choice between declaring their *dinero negro* free of the threat of a penalty, or investing it in a new series of special, low-interest government securities. The move brought to light another 1,700 billion pesetas.

Notwithstanding the introduction of VAT in 1986, the ratio of direct to indirect taxes continued to increase, albeit somewhat errati-cally, under González's governments. The reason was that personal taxation went up by leaps and bounds, just as it did under the UCD. But this was not so much because of government action as because of a phenomenon known as 'fiscal drag'. It is particularly prevalent during periods of high inflation and/or rapid growth, and Spain experienced first the one and then the other. What happens is that, as salaries increase, the people earning them move into successively higher tax brackets with progressively higher tax rates, so that the proportion of the taxpayers' income which the government takes away in tax goes up without the politicians having to lift a finger.

The arrival in office of the PP put an end to a way of thinking that had prevailed ever since the start of the transition. José María Aznar and his followers did not assume, as had their predecessors, that high taxes – and particularly high taxes on the rich – were inherently beneficial to society. Inspired by Britain's Conservatives and US Republicans rather than by the architects of the Euro-pean social model, they viewed taxation as a brake on enterprise, particularly when heaped on to what Margaret Thatcher liked to call 'wealth creators'. People who were prepared to risk their capital to set up new firms – firms that would create, not just profits, but jobs – needed to know that, if they succeeded, they could hang on to enough wealth to make the gamble worthwhile. Lower tax revenues would, of course, mean the government had less to spend, but that would just encourage it to be less spendthrift.

In 1999 and again in 2003, Spain's conservative government introduced sweeping reforms of the tax system that simplified it and reduced substantially the burden of income tax. But, as the PP's opponents never tired of reminding voters at election time, its popular income tax cuts distracted attention from the fact that the government was quietly increasing the overall tax burden by other means. In the year Aznar came to office, total tax revenue as a share of GDP was less than 33 per cent. By the time he left, it was almost 36 per cent. This was higher than in the US where the corresponding figure was below 30 per cent, but low by the standards of the European Union for which the average was over 40 per cent. Spain, in other words, was still a country whose government had relatively little cash to spend on the provision of services to the community as a whole.

But what really made it stand out in comparative tables was the low take from income and other personal taxes. This was partly because of the tax cuts made by Aznar, but partly too because the Spanish Treasury was less efficient at collecting taxes than treasuries in other developed nations. The OECD calculated that, in 2001, taxes on individuals accounted for just 7.4 per cent of GDP, which was the lowest figure in the EU after Portugal and Greece. In the US, that bastion of free enterprise and individual rights, the corresponding figure was 12.8 per cent. And in post-Thatcherite Britain it was 13.2 per cent. Spain remained, as it had been under Franco, a great place to be rich.

To a greater extent than in any of the countries just mentioned, the government relied for its income on social security contributions. When they were left out, tax receipts were less than 22 per cent of GDP. Compare that to the corresponding figure given earlier in this chapter for 1975 and you will see just how little things have really changed in this area over the years since General Franco's death. Despite all the hullabaloo that had attached to tax reform in the previous quarter of a century, despite the heated parliamentary debates, the reform bills, the catchy slogans and the social drama of millions of people having to learn how to fill out returns, the proportionate increase in taxes other than social security contributions had been a bare 2 per cent of GDP.

The problems associated with the bureaucracy go back to the days of the *pronunciamientos*, when changes of government were routinely accompanied by a full-scale reshuffle of the civil service in which the hangers-on loyal to one faction would be replaced by the hangers-on loyal to another. In an effort to protect themselves against politically motivated appointments, dismissals and promotions, groups of specialists within particular ministries – principally lawyers and engineers at first – formed themselves into corps (*cuerpos*), admittance to which was usually conditional on the holding of a particular academic or professional qualification. With time, the *cuerpos* acquired an important say in the hiring and firing of their members and often controlled promotion too. The refusal of successive governments to countenance trade unions in the civil service only consolidated the role of the *cuerpos* as the channel through which civil servants could put their demands to the minister in charge. At the same time, the absence of a pay-review body encouraged the *cuerpos* to drive a coach and horses through the hierarchy of office and scales of pay established by the government.

'Many corps,' Professor Kenneth Medhurst wrote,*

resolved the financial problems of their members by the simple expedient of abolishing the lower rungs of the career ladder and granting everybody 'artificial promotions'. The result was, for example, many officials with the rank and pay of departmental heads filling no more than clerical posts ... But even these devices failed to resolve completely the problem of inadequate pay. The corps therefore used their influence to establish a multitude of sometimes spurious bonus and incentive schemes. Ultimately these were so commonplace that for most officials the basic salary became only a fraction of the net income.

But in spite of all their efforts, the *cuerpos* were unable to ensure that civil service pay kept pace with inflation, and during the thirties, long before *pluriempleo* became a feature of Spanish society as a whole, this pernicious practice had taken root in the bureaucracy.

The *cuerpo* system undoubtedly helped to create the idea – and the reality – of a non-political civil service in Spain. But this could have been achieved by other means and the system's disadvantages far outweighed its advantages. The number of officials in a department was frequently a function of the interests of the *cuerpo* rather than the needs of the administration. Promotion was invariably by seniority rather than by merit. Rivalry between *cuerpos* meant there was very little co-ordination between departments and almost no mobility between ministries. This in turn led to duplication of effort.

Under Franco, little serious effort was put into reforming the civil service. This was partly because of the inherent conservatism of the regime and its leader, particularly where vested interests were

* Kenneth M. Medhurst, *Government in Spain*, Oxford, Pergamon, 1973.

concerned. But it also reflected the blurring under Franco of the distinction between the government (i.e. a policy-making body made up of politicians) and the administration (i.e. a policy-executing body made up of officials). Ministers under Franco were often drawn from the ranks of the bureaucracy and were themselves therefore members of a *cuerpo*. A law introduced in 1964 created a new hierarchy and reorganized, but did not abolish, the *cuerpos*, while empowering the government to prevent the setting-up of new ones. But the law was never fully put into effect and the overall situation became considerably worse.

Like a huge, untended creeper, Franco's bureaucracy sprouted myriad offshoots. Firstly, there were the *delegaciones provinciales*, each representing a particular ministry in a particular province. Together they made up a huge *administración periférica* which, by the early seventies, employed one in seven of the central government's employees. The *administración periférica* had all the disadvantages of dispersal and few of the advantages of decentralization – its staff, although only intermittently in contact with head office, were first and last servants of the central government, so all important decisions, and a lot of unimportant ones, had to be referred back to Madrid. Secondly, there were the quasi-autonomous agencies such as the state holding company INI and a plethora of *Institutos*, *Comisiones* and *Servicios* set up by different ministries to look after special areas of interest, which became increasingly difficult to control both economically and politically. At the end of the sixties there were 1,600 of them and they accounted for about a third of public spending.

Being the arm of government under a dictatorship, the Francoist civil service was effectively immune from criticism. There was nobody comparable with the Ombudsmen who operate in several European countries, nor – because of laws effectively forbidding pressure groups – could there be a body like Common Cause in the United States, set up to press for better government. Left to their own devices, Spain's bureaucrats did what bureaucrats the world over will do in similar circumstances, which is to make their life as comfortable as possible. A discrepancy, that later became standardized, developed between their notional working hours, which were 8 a.m. to 3 p.m., and their real working hours, which were 9 a.m. to 2 p.m. It also became customary whenever there was only one day between a public holiday and the start or end of a weekend to join them up by means of an extra day off called a *puente*, or bridge.

In Madrid it was – and may still be – theoretically necessary to get official permission to wallpaper a room. Yet to obtain this or any similar permit you had to put in a morning's work. First, there was the queue for the application form. Then the queue to hand it in, only to find that the application was not valid unless presented with two other documents which could only be obtained from other departments which were almost always in a different part of town. Once you succeeded in getting them, and had queued again for your permit, it was time to discover that the permit did not take effect until stamped by the head of the department and that he had gone home for the day. The whole process was made infinitely more difficult by the opening hours of the *ventanillas* (the little grilles from behind which Spanish bureaucrats used to confront the public). Not only did the opening hours vary from department to department, but they were also always as short as possible – some areas of the administration were only open to the public between 11 a.m. and 1 p.m. daily. Anything of genuine importance could take weeks, months or even years. The inefficiency of the bureaucracy has given rise to a phenomenon which, as far as I know, is peculiar to Iberia and Latin America – *gestorías administrativas*. A *gestoría administrativa* is an agency for people who have more money than time. If you want a driving licence, say, you go to the *gestoría* with all the relevant papers and, for a fee, one of its employees will do the form-filling and foot-slogging for you.

To an even greater extent than Franco's ministers, the members of Suárez's and Calvo Sotelo's cabinets were drawn from the bureaucratic elite and although they acknowledged that there was a need for change they were unable to come up with the radical reforms necessary. The civil service which the UCD handed over to González was substantially the same as that which the Centrists had inherited from Franco. According to Javier Moscoso, a former public prosecutor who took over the cabinet portfolio which carried responsibility for the civil service, it contained 290 *cuerpos* and not even his own aides could supply him with a precise figure for the number of people who worked in it. One of the difficulties of arriving at an exact total was that, in addition to the numerous bureaucrats working for the civil service in the morning and for private firms in the afternoon, there were many doing – or being paid for doing – more than one job within the administration itself. An internal survey carried out shortly after the Socialists came to power in 1982 revealed that there were some senior officials supposedly doing three official jobs and some who had never even been seen in the office where they were meant to be working.

The advent of Moscoso was nothing if not dramatic. Within weeks of his arrival he issued a circular which the press dubbed the '*reforma de los relojes*' ('reform of the clocks') that shortened the Christmas and Easter vacations and ordered civil servants to work the number of hours for which they were paid – forty-eight hours for senior officials and thirty-seven and a half hours for junior officials. The new minister also sent out instructions that the *ventanillas* should be pulled down and that every government department should be open to the public from nine until two, that information desks should be set up to guide people to the right queue, that all the official forms and stamps needed for the processing of a particular document should be available within the same building, and that members of the public should not be called on to locate and produce documents already in the possession of another government department.

Moscoso's reforms gave rise to two laws, passed in 1984. One forbade civil servants to hold a second job, whether inside or outside the administration, and gave legislative sanction to the new hours. The other was intended to give the government more power over the people who worked for it.

The first succeeded in making *pluriempleo* much rarer, but not in getting the civil service to work to the modified timetable. Soon after the new hours were introduced, it became customary to acknowledge a '*media hora de cortesía*' ('a courtesy half-hour') – i.e. to accept that rank-and-file functionaries would arrive up to thirty minutes late. It was not long before the *media hora de cortesía* became an *hora de cortesía*, and then started to be applied at the end as well as the beginning of the working day. It is often said that the biggest improvements in productivity have come from putting cafeterias on the premises so that civil servants spend less of their time walking to and from their mid-morning breakfasts.

As for the second of the two laws, it seems to have been a complete failure. A study document prepared by the PSOE and published in 1988* concluded the administration was still unable to 'appoint civil servants to the jobs it needs to fill in line with its priorities. At the same time, it is generally recognized that the disciplinary regime is effectively incapable of bringing about the dismissal of civil servants who fail to do their jobs properly.'

Successive governments have since chipped away at the bureaucracy's capacity for resisting change and the situation is no longer as dire as it once was. But a lot still needs to be done. When José Luis Rodríguez Zapatero came into office in 2004 he still felt the need to have a senior official with the title of Director General de la Modernización de la Administración.

Spain, for example, has been among the countries that have been slowest in embracing so-called e-government and the opportunities it presents for saving time and money. A study by Brown University in the US published in 2004 compared 198 governments according to their use of the internet to interact with the public. The Spanish administration came 77th. Three years earlier, according to government figures, less than 9 per cent of public employees had an office computer with access to the Internet and, on average, ministries spent just 2 per cent of their budgets on information technology. There were some excellent interactive sites, notably that run by the tax service, but there was no central page from which web users could surf to the sites of ministries and, from there, to the various bodies associated with them. Indeed, the official who had been put in charge of modernizing the administration admitted in an interview with *El País* that 'No one knows how many civil service web pages there are.' The echoes of Javier Moscoso's complaint, more than twenty years earlier, that he did not know how many people were working for the administration, are all too obvious to need stressing.

What has transformed the Madrid civil service is not so much that it has been reformed as replaced. As powers have been transferred to the regions, so too have the posts and people that go with them. By 2004, just 10 per cent of all public employees worked for the central government. Some 15 per cent was accounted for by the armed services, police forces, court administration, university staff and those

* *Aspectos y problemas de la vida política española. Programa 2000.*

who worked for other public bodies. Roughly a quarter were engaged in local government. But by far the biggest proportion, almost half the total, was made up of those employed by administrations that had scarcely existed twenty years earlier – the governments of Spain's Autonomous Communities. These are the outstanding governmental innovation of post-Franco Spain – a response to the dilemma posed by Spaniards' fierce loyalties to their native regions, which, some would insist, are nations in their own right.

PART FOUR

A Fissile State

CHAPTER 16

Centrifugal Forces

As far as many Spaniards were concerned, the fun started to go out of motoring in the year 2000. That was when the government introduced new licence plates. On the old ones, you could see clearly the province in which the vehicle had been registered. On the new plates, there was nothing to show whether it came from Huelva at one end of the peninsula or Huesca at the other. So you could no longer point at a particularly inept bit of driving and say 'Isn't that just typical of a Galician?', or 'God. Look at the speed that fool's driving. Ah! I knew it! He's Valencian. Reckless bastards!'

The motor trade was delighted with the change. Second-hand dealers said that, as more and more cars with the uninformative new plates came on to the market, sales had grown rapidly. Previously, customers had been reluctant to buy a car licensed outside the region in which they lived – and, in some cases, they were deeply averse. Beyond the Basque country, it was well nigh impossible to sell a car with Basque plates because drivers were frightened of being pulled off the road all the time by the police, on suspicion of being terrorists. Vehicles registered in Madrid were hard to sell in Barcelona because of the taint of centralism. For the same reasons, car-hire firms found it difficult to circulate their fleets.

Despite these considerable advantages for business, in 2004, a minister in the Catalan government disclosed that the new Zapatero government in Madrid was studying a proposal to change the plates again so that they would show the region, though not the province, from which the vehicle came. Montserrat Tura dismissed objections from the motor trade, saying the plan was 'reasonable and consistent with the present administrative structure of the state'. Catalan officials do everything they can to avoid uttering the word 'Spain'.

In the meantime, many of the minister's fellow-Catalans had been taking the matter into their own hands. Some had put a sticker with CAT for Catalonia next to – or, in extreme cases, over – the E for España on the new plates. Others had stuck the silhouette of a donkey on the back of their cars in response to a campaign to instate the <u>donkey as a symbol of Catalan identity</u>. *Planta't el burro*, as the campaign was called, was organized as a response to the spread of bumper stickers featuring the silhouette of a bull, also used for the huge black hoardings that are scattered across the Spanish landscape. Devised as a logo for Osborne sherry and brandy, it has come to be regarded as an emblem of Spanishness.* According to its promoters, *Planta't el burro* aimed 'to combat the homogenizing centralism expressed in symbols such as the bull and the Spanish number plate'. Not long after the campaign was launched, a new silhouette appeared. This one showed the donkey mounting the bull.

All this may be very puerile, but it highlights a fact of immense political, economic and social importance: that a lot of Spaniards put loyalty to their region, nation or whatever on a par with, or even ahead of, loyalty to their country. Regional sentiment bedevilled attempts to build a strong unitary state in the sixteenth and nineteenth centuries. And it is separatism in the form of ETA and its supporters which has posed one of the greatest challenges to the stability of contemporary Spain.

To some extent, the strength of regional feeling is simply a manifestation of the Mediterranean tendency to subjectiveness. Southern Europeans, far more than northern Europeans, tend to favour whoever is closest to them, physically or socially, regardless of their merits. This is why face-to-face contact is so important in business dealings and why favouritism towards friends and relatives is so common. The same, I think, applies to places.

Traditionally, a Spaniard's greatest affection has always been reserved for his or her native town or district, which the Spaniards themselves, in a telling phrase, often refer to as their *patria chica*, or 'little fatherland'. Next comes their region and, last of all, the state. A number of other factors – geographical, historical and cultural – have combined

---

* In 2005, a judge in Seville ruled that the bull had become a 'national symbol' and an 'artistic legacy that belongs to the Spanish peoples'. He was rejecting an attempt by Osborne to stop other companies from commercializing the image.

to divide Spaniards from each other and to produce in many of them the conviction that the region comes first and the state second – or, in some cases, nowhere at all.

By European standards at least, Spain is a big country. If you leave out Russia, the only countries in Europe bigger than Spain are France and Ukraine. It is very nearly half as large again as Germany and, at slightly less than 200,000 square miles, or rather more than 500,000 square kilometres, it is almost twice the size of Italy and four times the size of England. Yet, throughout its history, Spain's population has been modest. As a result, it was – and is – a country of widely spaced communities. Since earliest times, their isolation from one another has been made more acute by a dearth of navigable rivers. Moreover, because of the poverty which was Spain's lot, road and rail links developed only very slowly. For example, it was not until 1974, when the *puente aéreo* – the air shuttle between Madrid and Barcelona – was opened, that one could travel between the country's two largest cities with ease. Right up until the late seventies, when a lengthy stretch of motorway was built, it took about nine hours of solid driving to cover the 630 kilometres (390 miles) by car.

The *meseta*, which one might think would have drawn the country closer together, has, if anything, had the reverse effect. Apart from being a formidable obstacle to communication between the peoples of the periphery, it is itself riven by a succession of mountain ranges – 'those East-West ramparts', as Laurie Lee called them, 'which go ranging across Spain and divide its people into separate races'.

Spain's geography may not have exactly favoured unity, but it did not make it unthinkable. France is almost as varied and marginally bigger, yet the French today are a remarkably homogeneous people. What ensured that Spain would remain so divided was the course of its history.

Like much of the territory bordering the Mediterranean, the Iberian peninsula was visited by Phoenicians, settled by Greeks and finally conquered and occupied by the Romans. When Rome's power declined, the peninsula – in common with most of the rest of Europe – was invaded by tribesmen from the north and east of the continent. At the start of the fifth century, three German peoples – the Alans, Vandals and Sueves – crossed the Pyrenees. The Alans were all but wiped out when the Visigoths, a Christian people loosely allied with

Rome who raided the peninsula in a short-lived attempt to return it to the Empire. The Vandals moved on to North Africa. This left only the Sueves, and by the middle of the fifth century they were on the point of taking over the entire peninsula when it was once again invaded by the Visigoths. This time, the Visigoths, who had carved out a kingdom for themselves with its capital at Toulouse, came to stay. Soon after their invasion of the peninsula, they lost most of the territory they controlled on the other side of the Pyrenees and from then on their kingdom became a predominantly Iberian enterprise.

The task of bringing the whole of Iberia under Visigothic rule took more than a century. Successive monarchs had to contend, not only with the Sueves, who had retreated into the north-west, but also with an army of Byzantines, who – in return for helping a Visigothic pretender on to the throne – helped themselves to a large chunk of territory in the south-east. The Sueves were finally overcome in 585 and the last bit of the Byzantine colony was annexed in 624. The Visigothic monarchs continued to be plagued by uprisings among the native population, and in particular by the Basques. But there again, so had the Romans. If anything, Visigothic Iberia was rather more united than the other realms that were emerging in Europe after the collapse of the Roman Empire. Both the Visigoths and the majority of their subjects practised Christianity and spoke a form of Latin. Moreover, in the middle of the seventh century, the Visigothic monarchy imposed upon the entire country a code of laws applicable to all.

Doubtless, Visigothic rule would not have lasted for ever, but there is no reason why – barring a bolt from the blue such as the one that ended it – it could not have survived for a few centuries longer. And when it did fall, it is quite possible that the peninsula might have survived to this day as a single political entity in the way that France has. At the very least, the Visigoths would have been able to bequeath to their successors a land which was in the process of evolving a common language and way of life, so that if – like Germany and Italy – Iberia had then disintegrated into a plethora of tiny states, a strong sense of national identity could have survived.

But Iberia was not to follow the same path as the other great geopolitical entities of Europe. Her fate was being decided 3,000 miles away on the shore of the Red Sea, where a man who believed himself to be God's messenger was preaching the new religion of

Islam. Mohammed's followers burst out of Arabia after his death in 632 and by the end of the seventh century their descendants had conquered the whole of North Africa. The first Moslem incursion into Iberia was in 710, when a small reconnaissance force landed at the southernmost point of the peninsula. The following year a former slave, a Berber by the name of Tariq ibn-Ziyad, led an army of about 7,000 ashore at a point close to the huge rock which dominates the entrance to the Mediterranean (the Moslems named the rock Jabal Tariq, or Tariq's Mount, and eventually clumsy Christian tongues changed it to Gibraltar). It took no more than two years for Tariq's small force to subdue the whole of what is now Spain and Portugal. But after crossing the Pyrenees and penetrating to the very heart of France, where they were defeated by the Franks, the Moslems withdrew into the southern three-quarters of the Iberian peninsula. Most of the indigenous inhabitants fell under the rule of the Moslems, but some fled across the Pyrenees or took refuge in the line of hills and mountains that stretches along the top of the peninsula from Galicia to Catalonia.

The Moslem invasion shattered the tentative unity that had been achieved by the Visigoths. When the Christians began to fight back, they did so, not in unison, but grouped into tiny statelets that soon acquired distinct traditions. The first was formed by Visigothic noblemen who had retreated to the mountains of Asturias. Supported intermittently by some of the Basques, the kings of Asturias expanded westwards into Galicia and southwards until, in the tenth century, they were able to establish their capital on the *meseta* at León. This Asturo-Leónese kingdom was responsible for giving birth to two counties in the strict sense of the word – Castile and Portugal – which subsequently grew into kingdoms themselves.

Another miniature state was set up by the Basques in Navarre, while further to the east – but still within the foothills of the Pyrenees – a number of little counties were created of which Aragón, soon boasting its own monarchy, emerged as the most powerful. Finally, on the Mediterranean coast, an army composed largely of the descendants of men and women who had fled across the Pyrenees fought its way back into Catalonia, where another network of counties then emerged.

The arrival of the Moslems also put paid to any hope of a single language. Cut off from one another in the mountainous north and brought into much closer contact with the languages of the pre-Roman peoples who lived there than would otherwise have been the case, the descendants of the Latin-speaking refugees who had fled from Tariq's conquering army evolved no fewer than five separate new languages – Galician, Bable (the language of Asturias), Castilian, Aragonese and Catalan. In the south, the Christians living under Moslem rule developed yet another tongue – Mozarabic. With the exception of Mozarabic, all these languages have survived to the present day, although Bable and Aragonese are nowadays spoken by only a tiny number of people, most of whom live in remote areas. Together with Basque and such curious linguistic relics as Aranés (a variety of Gascon Provençal, which is spoken in the Arán Valley of northern Catalonia), they constitute a rich heritage – and a source of persistent friction. Today more than a quarter of Spain's inhabitants speak a vernacular language in addition to, or instead of, the official language of the state.

It is noticeable that all but one of the early Christian states started life in the mountains, and mountain regions – Switzerland is a prime example – tend to favour the development of representative systems of government at an early stage in their history. The indigenous inhabitants of the mountains of northern and north-western Iberia were no exception. When they moved south in alliance with descendants of the refugees from the Moslem invasion, they took with them their institutions and customs, albeit in a progressively diluted form. In the north-east, the political and social system was much closer to the feudal model developing elsewhere in Europe, but even certain sections of Catalan society were able to win from their rulers political freedoms in exchange for their financial or military contributions. For most of the Middle Ages, therefore, the inhabitants of the Iberian peninsula enjoyed far greater individual freedom and carried far greater individual responsibility than their contemporaries in other parts of Europe. As a consequence, Spaniards tend to look back at the medieval period when the regional states were at the height of their power not as a time of disunity so much as one of freedom and equality.

The *reconquista* was neither continuous nor co-ordinated. The petty Christian states spent quite as much time fighting each other as they did fighting the Moslems. Outstanding monarchs tried and occasionally succeeded in uniting two or more states either by treaty or conquest, but time and again they were persuaded by factional interests to re-divide their territories in their wills. In fact, the process whereby the various kingdoms came to form a single state lasted far longer even than the *reconquista*. In 1137, the County of Barcelona – which by then had absorbed most of the other Catalan mini-states – was joined by marriage to the Kingdom of Aragón. Together the Catalans and the Aragonese went on to conquer Valencia and the Balearic Islands during the thirteenth century. Castile, which was in the process of recovering a large chunk of Andalusia, and León, which by then took in Asturias, Galicia and Estremadura, eventually came together in 1230, having united and divided twice in the preceding hundred years. The conquest and settlement of Murcia at the end of the thirteenth century was a joint venture by the Crown of Castile (the name given to the state formed by the unification of Castile and León) and the Crown of Aragón (the state formed by the federation of Aragón and Catalonia).

The annexation of the Canary Islands, which had never formed part of the Moslem domains, was undertaken exclusively by and for the Crown of Castile. The language and culture of the native inhabitants, the Guanches, were both eventually destroyed. But the pacification of the islands, which was not completed until the end of the fifteenth century, brought within the Crown of Castile, and eventually Spain, a territory more than 1,000 miles from Madrid yet, at its closest point, less than 70 miles from the coast of Africa. The climate, vegetation and thus the economy of the Canary Islands are all quite different from those of the mainland. Over the centuries, the remoteness of the islands and their idiosyncrasies have often been a source of misunderstanding and dispute between the islanders and those charged with deciding their destinies.

The Navarrese meanwhile, whose most outstanding sovereign, Sancho III, had come closer than any of Spain's medieval rulers to uniting the Christian domains, had for several centuries been looking northwards. At its point of greatest expansion, Navarre took in a large stretch of what is now France, and its rulers became entwined by marriage with several French royal and noble families, to the extent that it came within a hair's breadth of being incorporated into France.

The members of the royal families of the three other kingdoms – Portugal, Castile and Aragón – had so often intermarried that it became inevitable that sooner or later two of these states would be united by inheritance. In the event it was later rather than sooner; it was only in 1474, when the ineffectual Enrique IV of Castile died without leaving a son, that the opportunity arose. The two claimants to his throne were Isabel, his half-sister, and Juana, the woman he claimed was his daughter, but who was alleged by opponents to be the illegitimate offspring of an affair between Enrique's wife and a courtier. The nub of the matter was that Juana was married to Afonso V of Portugal while Isabel was the wife of Fernando, heir to the throne of Aragón. Whichever of these two won the throne would determine whether the peninsula was to be dominated by an alliance between Castile and Portugal or one between Castile and Aragón. It took a war to settle the issue. But by 1479 – the year in which Fernando succeeded to the throne of Aragón – Isabel's forces had overcome Juana's. Technically, Castile and Aragón remained separate. Under the agreement worked out between Fernando and Isabel each was to reign as sole monarch in his or her own country while ranking as no more than a consort in the realm of the other. But in practice Isabel concerned herself with the domestic affairs of both countries, while her husband looked after their foreign affairs.

One of Isabel and Fernando's most celebrated joint ventures was the ten-year campaign that culminated in the surrender in 1492 of the Kingdom of Granada – the last Moslem stronghold on the peninsula. The fall of Granada marked the end of the *reconquista*. It had lasted for almost 800 years and it had had a profound effect on the characters of both the Spanish and the Portuguese, although – as more than one historian has pointed out – the fact that Portugal was fully reconquered more than 200 years before Spain meant the *reconquista* left a much greater impression on the latter than on the former. The legacy of almost eight centuries of conquest and colonization can, I believe, be seen in many aspects of Spanish life, such as an often casual acceptance of violence and bloodshed, and in the two most contradictory aspects of the Spaniards' character – their respect for firm leadership and their uncompromising faith in their own judgement and ability. It also, I suspect, gave rise to a trait which is characteristic of other frontier societies, like those of

North America and South Africa – an inordinate love for the land that has been captured and settled.

The gradual spread of the Christian peoples through the peninsula had cleared the way for a corresponding expansion of the Romance languages that had begun life in the highlands of the north. Some prospered more than others. In the west, Galician had given birth to Portuguese. In the east, Catalan had spread to the Balearic Islands and to much of Valencia. But it was Castilian that had become pre-eminent – to the point that it would come to be known in most of the rest of the world as 'Spanish'. Spaniards who speak one of the other languages tend to believe that Castilian gained its ascendancy by dint of force – by conquest in medieval times and by repression and coercion more recently. This is only partly true. An equally important reason for its expansion has been that it is a superbly efficient means of communication which, whenever it has come into contact with another language, has tended to be adopted solely on its merits. In the centre of the country, it had made inroads into the Kingdoms of León to the west and Aragón to the east, displacing Bable and Aragonese respectively, long before Castile acquired any political clout in either area. Its linguistic excellence also won it a foothold in the Basque country centuries before anyone tried to force the Basques to abandon their native tongue. It was undeniably force of arms that allowed it to spread through Andalusia. But it is significant that when Castilian clashed head-on with Catalan in Murcia, following a campaign in which the Castilians and the Catalans both took part, it was Castilian – sprinkled here and there with Catalan words and phrases – that emerged as the language of the region.

Events following Isabel's death in 1504 underlined the shakiness of the alliance between Castile and Aragón. For one thing, she had added a codicil to her will barring the Aragonese and their confederates, the Catalans and the Valencians, from trading with the New World discovered by Columbus in the same year that the Christian Spaniards conquered Granada. Isabel's only son Juan and Juan's posthumous son had both died before the death of Isabel herself, so the Crown of Castile passed to her daughter, another Juana, who, being mentally incapable of ruling, had to have a regent. Since Fernando had remarried and gone to live in Italy, the task fell to Juana's husband. It was only his sudden death in 1506 that caused Fernando to become involved once more, as regent, in the affairs of Castile. In this capacity he was responsible for the incorporation of the third of the medieval peninsular kingdoms when, in 1512, he masterminded the annexation of most of Navarre.

Fernando died two years later. Although it was Isabel who had consciously aspired to the unification of the peninsula, it was he who had done most to bring it about. Appropriately, he left his own kingdom, Aragón, to his daughter Juana's son Carlos. Rather than follow in his father's and grandfather's footsteps by becoming regent in Castile, Carlos insisted on being made king.

His accession in 1516 is traditionally regarded as marking the unification of Spain. But that is only true with hindsight. The goal had always been – and remained – the reunification of the whole of Iberia, and that was not achieved until 1580 when Carlos's son, Felipe II, annexed Portugal after its king had died on a madcap expedition to North Africa, leaving behind him no obvious heir. What then happened was that the process of unification suffered a reverse – as it had many times in the past. This time it was not the result of a will, but a war. In 1640, the Catalans and the Portuguese, both of whom had been chafing at Castile's insensitive centralism, rebelled against Madrid. The Catalans were finally beaten into submission in 1659, but the Portuguese survived as a separate nation, ruled by a new dynasty, and in 1665 they confirmed their independence by defeating the Spaniards at the Battle of Montes Claros.

Spain and Portugal were never again to reunite, although the dream of reunification through a loose confederation of the traditional regions was to persist until the twentieth century. That the six states which emerged in the north of the peninsula should have evolved into two nations – one of them made up of five of those states and the other consisting of the remaining one – was a matter of the purest chance. Had a battle here or there gone the other way; had this or that son not died in infancy; had this or that mother not perished in childbirth, the division might have been altogether different. Contrary to what the more rabid of Spain's centralists claim, there is absolutely nothing 'sacred' about the unity of Spain, because there was nothing pre-ordained about its shape.

The Habsburg and Bourbon monarchs who ruled Spain from the beginning of the sixteenth century until the end of the eighteenth were aware that their realms were circumstantial conglomerations of states that had once been independent. It did not mean, however, that they were happy with the situation in which they found themselves: several regions enjoyed political faculties and economic privileges that seriously limited the power of the central government and made the construction of a modern state virtually impossible.

The choice of Madrid as the capital was a response to the problems this created. Until the sixteenth century, the Spanish court had moved from place to place. But in 1561 Felipe II decided that the machinery of government ought to have a permanent home. In an effort not to boost the power and status of any one region, he hit on the idea of putting his court in the geographical centre of the peninsula. Madrid is almost totally devoid of natural advantages. It does not have a harbour. It does not stand by the shores of a lake or at the meeting-place of two rivers. The reason why human beings settled there is because of an escarpment that offers commanding views across the surrounding plain. Throughout the Middle Ages the military importance of that escarpment made Madrid a valuable prize for Moors and Christians alike. But with the end of the *reconquista*, the town would almost certainly have withered into insignificance had it not been for Felipe's initiative. Like Abuja or Brasilia, Madrid is an 'artificial' rather than an 'organic' capital, and until recently it did not have much of a hold over the country's affections.

The change of dynasty from Habsburg to Bourbon was marked by a lengthy and bloody war – the so-called War of the Spanish Succession, lasting from 1702 until 1713, in which the traditional regions of Spain were again split into two opposing camps, each of which supported a rival claimant. It also marked a shift in the Crown's approach to its more restive subjects. Whereas the Habsburg Felipe IV had refrained from taking reprisals against the Catalans after they rebelled in 1640, the Bourbon Felipe V, who emerged as the victor from the War of Succession, punished the Catalans, Aragonese and Valencians who had supported his opponent by annulling their laws and institutions and thus creating within the Catalan-speaking part of Spain an undercurrent of discontent that has persisted to this day.

The Spaniards' reaction to the occupation of their country by the French in 1808 highlighted a paradox: that for many Spaniards at that time patriotism and a form of regionalism bordering on separatism were not mutually exclusive. In what came to be known as the War of Independence, Galicians, Basques, Castilians, Aragonese, Catalans and Andalusians all turned on the interloper with a ferocity which proved that, however distinct they might feel themselves to be from one another, they felt a good deal more different from foreigners. Yet they did so in a characteristically independent way. The vacuum left by the overthrow of the monarchy was filled – not by a provisional central government set up in opposition to the administration installed by the French – but by a plethora of local *juntas* (committees), most of which ran their own tiny armies.

France's short-lived occupation introduced the relatively small Spanish middle class to a number of ideas about government that were then regarded as progressive. As was mentioned earlier, one of these was that the monarch ought to be subject to a constitution. Another was that a modern state ought to be uniform. It could not tolerate feudal rights and privileges. The result was that the cause of centralism in nineteenth-century Spain was taken up by the bourgeois proponents of a constitution – the *liberales* – while the defence of local laws and traditions became a cause of the supporters of absolutism, who were mostly to be found among the most reactionary sections of the aristocracy and the peasantry. Unhappily for Spain, a dispute over the succession enabled these two opposing groups to identify themselves with rival claimants to the throne. Twice in the nineteenth century the ultra-reactionary Carlist pretenders waged unsuccessful but highly disruptive wars against a monarchy which, although not progressive by instinct, was forced to turn for support to the *liberales*. The Carlist cause appealed above all to the pious, reactionary and fervently independent Basque peasantry, and when Carlism was finally defeated in the 1870s the central government penalized the Basques – including many who had stayed loyal to the central government – by abolishing their traditional rights and privileges.

As Spain entered the final quarter of the nineteenth century, the central government had succeeded in alienating precisely those regions – Catalonia and the Basque country – where conditions existed, or were about to develop, that would foster the growth of modern nationalism. In the first place, the Basques and Catalans each had a language and culture of their own (this factor alone was sufficient to stimulate the growth of a modest nationalist movement in Galicia). Secondly, these two parts of Spain were the first to become industrialized and were therefore the earliest to nurture a substantial middle class of the kind which, in many parts of the world, has been eager to support nationalist aspirations. Among the Basque and Catalan middle classes, a sentimental hankering after traditional values mingled with a feeling of superiority with regard to the hated Castilians. This feeling stemmed largely from the quite reasonable belief that Madrid was incapable of understanding the problems of advanced industrial societies such as theirs. But it was also in part the result of an instinctive desire to dissociate themselves from Spain's decline, the scale of which was to be made embarrassingly obvious by Spain's defeat at the hands of the United States in 1898.

Unfortunately for Madrid, both the Basques and Catalans live hard by the two main routes into France and in each case there are people who speak the same language as they do on the other side of the border. Rebel Basques and Catalans from Spain have never found it difficult to find refuge or supplies in France, especially since it has often proved convenient for Paris to turn a blind eye to the activities of the Basques and Catalans under French rule, as a means of undermining whoever was in power in Madrid.

The defeat of Carlism put paid to any chance that regional aspirations might be fulfilled by the accession of an absolute monarch. From then on, the best hopes of the Basques and Catalans lay with the overthrow of the *liberal* monarchy by opponents at the other end of the political spectrum. Spanish radicals had already developed an affection for federalism which came to the fore when they ruled the country for less than a year during the First Republic (1873–4). When the monarchy was once again overthrown in 1931, the pressure for home rule was immense. The Catalans were granted a Statute of Autonomy in 1932 and the Basques and the Galicians were on the verge of gaining a limited form of home rule when civil war broke out again in 1936.

Although General Franco and his allies described themselves as Nationalists, what they meant was that they were Spanish nationalists – wholly opposed to the regional nationalism which they regarded as one of the principal reasons for the turmoil that had bedevilled the Second Republic. During the early years of the dictatorship, not only was it forbidden to teach vernacular languages but serious efforts were made to stop people from speaking them. They could not be used on official premises or at official functions. Stickers were even put up in telephone booths telling callers that they had to conduct their conversations in Castilian or – to use the parlance of the regime – 'speak Christian'. A ban on the publication of books in vernacular languages did not last long, but a similar prohibition on their use in the press, and on radio and television, remained in force until after Franco's death.

Indeed, such was the intransigence of Franco's centralism that it succeeded in creating regionalist groups in areas such as Estremadura and Murcia where no one had previously questioned their Spanishness. Not perhaps surprisingly, it was nationalism in its most radical and violent form which ensured that Franco's style of government would not survive him. In 1972, his Prime Minister and chosen successor, Admiral Carrero Blanco, was blown to pieces by terrorists drawn from among the most fiercely independent minority of all – the Basques.

CHAPTER 17

The Basques

The most obvious difference between the Basques and their neighbours in France and Spain is their extraordinary language which the Basques themselves call *euskera* or *euskara*, depending on which dialect they speak. Although over the years it has absorbed individual words from both French and Spanish, the basic vocabulary and structure of the language bears absolutely no resemblance to either. One sixteenth-century Sicilian author was convinced that the Basques' strange tongue enabled them to communicate with the monsters of the deep.

A phrase taken at random from a text-book, 'The table is laid – you can bring in the food', when translated into Basque is '*Mahaia gertu dago. Ekar dezakezue bazkaria.*' The syntax is no less exotic. The definite article 'the' is not a separate word but a suffix. Nouns used with numerals remain in the singular. Auxiliary verbs vary according to the number of objects as well as the number of subjects, and what we would call prepositions are in Basque suffixes and prefixes, which alter according to whether the word to which they are attached represents something animate or inanimate. The author of the first Basque grammar could perhaps be forgiven for entitling his work *The Impossible Overcome*.

It seems always to have been assumed that Basque was a language of great antiquity. In the Middle Ages, when it was believed that the various languages of the world were the product of God's intervention at the Tower of Babel, a number of scholars argued that it was the language that Noah's grandson, Tubal, was said to have taken to Iberia and that in ancient times Basque must have been spoken throughout the peninsula. Long after the biblical explanation of the origin of languages had been called into question elsewhere in Europe this theory was stoutly defended within the Basque country itself, largely because of the immense authority there of the Church. Some Basque authors went as far as to claim that theirs had been the original language of Europe, or even the world. There is no doubt that Basque was once spoken over a much larger area than it is today – an area which almost certainly included the entire Pyrenees, since it is known to have been spoken in parts of Aragón and Catalonia during the Middle Ages. But it is unlikely to have been the language of all Iberia, much less that of Europe or the world.

Modern scholarship has, however, shown that it is an extremely old language. The touchstone of modern philology was the discovery towards the end of the eighteenth century that many European and Asian languages – subsequently given the name Indo-European – came from a common source. Throughout the nineteenth century, Basque resisted all attempts to find it a place in the Indo-European family and philologists have eventually had to reconcile themselves to the conclusion that Basque predates the migrations from the East which brought the Indo-European languages into Europe some 3,000 years ago. But there is also evidence that it may be much older even than that. It has been suggested, for example, that words like *aitzkor* (axe) and *aitzur* (hoe) derive from *aitz* (stone) and date from the time when tools were made of stone.

Attempts have been made to link Basque to other pre-Indo-European languages, such as those still spoken in the Caucasus and among the Berbers of North Africa, but no one has so far proved that a connection exists.

While linguists have been puzzling over the singularity of the Basques' language, doctors and scientists have been discovering that they have other, less evident, peculiarities. To understand these, one has to make a brief detour into the world of serology, the study of blood.

On occasions, when the blood of two individuals is brought into contact, it coagulates. This is because the blood of at least one of them contains what is called an antigen. There are two types of antigen – A and B. Some people have both and their blood is classified as A/B. Other people's blood contains only one antigen and is classified as either A or B. But there is also a third type, O, which contains no antigens at all. There are two reasons why all this is of importance to anthropologists. Firstly, antigens are hereditary – no one can have either A or B in their bloodstream unless at least one of their parents had it in his or hers. Secondly, the proportion of each blood type in the population varies significantly from place to place. As one moves across Europe from east to west, for example, the percentage of A increases while the percentage of B decreases. The Basques were found to have one of the highest proportions of type O blood anywhere in the world. What is more, the percentage of A was higher and the proportion of B lower than one would expect even for a people perched on the Atlantic coast.

In 1939 an American researcher opened up new fields for exploration when he discovered a substance in the blood of the Macacus Rhesus monkey which was also found to be present in the blood of some humans. According to whether or not their blood contained the new substance, people could thereafter be divided into Rhesus positive (Rh+) and Rhesus negative (Rh−). In Europe the percentage of Rhesus negatives is higher than in other parts of the world and for the most part varies from 12 to 16 per cent. The relevance of this to the Basques was discovered, not by researchers in the Basque country, but by an ordinary general practitioner working thousands of miles away in Argentina who was concerned with an entirely different problem − erythroblastosis. This is an often fatal illness which affects newborn children whose blood is incompatible with that of their mothers. In most cases, the problem arises because the mother is Rh− while her child is Rh+, having inherited the substance from its father. The general practitioner, Dr Miguel Angel Etcheverry, noticed that an unusually high proportion of these unfortunate mothers were, like him, of Basque descent. To test his suspicion, he took samples from 128 Argentinians who had four Basque grandparents and discovered that fully one-third of them were Rh−. After his findings were published in 1945, a series of studies in the Spanish Basque country all produced figures in excess of 30 per cent, and one, carried out in the French Basque country, put the proportion of the population who did not have the Rhesus substance in their blood at 42 per cent − the highest figure recorded anywhere in the world. As far as blood grouping was concerned, therefore, the Basques were emerging as exceptionally 'European' (by virtue of their Rhesus count) and very 'Westerly' (by virtue of their antigen pattern).

Throughout history, the Basques had been thought of by their neighbours as being bigger and stronger. A great deal of measuring and weighing by anthropologists, especially during the early part of the twentieth century, proved this to be the case. The Basques were found to be, on average, two to three centimetres taller than the average in France and Spain and, although they tended to be more muscular, their limbs – and in particular their hands and feet – were inclined to be quite delicate. The anthropologists also established that the typical Basque had a distinctive 'hare's head', broad at the top and narrow at the bottom, and that he or she was likely to have a high forehead, a straight nose and a distinctive bulge over the temples.

By themselves, these findings proved nothing. But when they were put alongside the archaeological discoveries of that period, they became very interesting indeed. Shortly after the First World War, two Basque researchers, Telesforo de Aranzadi and José Miguel de Barandiarán, had begun excavating a number of dolmens dating from around 2000 BC, the time of the Indo-European invasions. On the basis of the bones they found in them it was suggested that the people who had lived in the Basque country at that time had the same physical characteristics as the Basques of today. Even more interestingly, and controversially, a skull found in the mid-thirties by the two men in a cave near Itziar in Guipúzcoa dating from the late Stone Age – about 10,000 BC – was held to have several typically Basque traits, suggesting that the Basques of today might be the direct descendants of Cro-Magnon man.

A good deal of doubt has since been cast on the significance of these finds, but the absence from Basque folklore of any sort of migration legend, when combined with the linguistic and serological evidence, would seem to suggest that the Basques have lived where they are now to be found since the Stone Age. Secure in a homeland of steep-sided hills and valleys, much of which was covered in dense forest, they seem to have had only the most limited contact with the peoples who entered Europe two millennia before Christ and who brought with them their Indo-European languages and their distinctive blood group distribution, characterized by a high proportion of B and Rh+.

Recent genetic studies have pointed in two directions. A gene map of Europe completed by Professor Luigi Luca Cavalli-Sforza of Stanford University, California, showed the genetic make-up of the

Basques to be very different from that of their neighbours, although the boundaries were more blurred to the north, in France, than they were to the south, in Spain. However, the view of the Basques as 'Europe's aboriginals' was given a jolt in 2001 when a team of British and American scientists disclosed the results of a study that found considerable genetic similarities between the Basques and the Celts of Ireland and Wales.

The Basques enter written records with the arrival of the Romans. The Latin authors noted that there were four tribes in what is now the Spanish Basque country – the Vascones, the Vardulos, the Caristios and the Autrigones. Interestingly, each of the areas in which a particular Basque dialect is spoken today coincides roughly with an area occupied by one of these tribes. Navarrese is, or was, spoken in the area once inhabited by the Vascones. Guipúzcoan corresponds to that of the Vardulos, Biscayan to that of the Caristios, and the part of the Basque country outside Navarre in which Basque has long since ceased to be spoken was once the land of the Autrigones.

One of the most enduring myths about the Basques is that they were never subject to Roman rule. Spaniards will earnestly assure you even now that the reason why the Basques are so fiercely independent is that they were never given a taste of Roman discipline. It is true that the Romans had to contend with persistent rebellions in the Basque country, but their grip on the area was firm enough to enable them to build roads and settlements there, and even run the odd iron mine. Basque soothsayers were renowned throughout the Empire.

The collapse of Roman rule marked the last time that all Basques were subject to the same administration, although that is not to say that the Basques on both sides of the Pyrenees had formed a single administrative entity either before or during Roman rule. After the legions departed, it was left to the Romans' 'barbarian' successors to try to impose their will on the area – the Franks strove to control an area roughly corresponding to the modern French Basque country and the northern part of Navarre, while the Visigoths attempted to govern what is now Guipúzcoa, Biscay and Alava. Neither succeeded fully.

At the beginning of the seventh century the Franks set up a dependent Duchy of Vasconia, which at one stage stretched from the Garonne to the Ebro. It was shaken by a succession of violent revolts until, in 788, a Frankish army returning from an unsuccessful campaign against the Moslems was ambushed by Basques in the valley of Roncesvalles. The ensuing battle was immortalized in the *Chanson de Roland*, although its author depicted the attackers as Moors, not Basques. Soon after Roncesvalles, the Basques in the south of the Duchy declared themselves independent. The state they founded, which at first controlled no more than a small area around Pamplona, was destined to become the Kingdom of Navarre. It subsequently expanded to take in much of the French Basque country and a large area, non-Basque in speech and custom, to the south of Pamplona.

The Visigoths, meanwhile, were forced to wage repeated wars against the Basques of Alava, Biscay and Guipúzcoa, but never seem to have actually ruled all of them except for brief spells. The Visigothic nobles who founded the Kingdom of Asturias inherited the Visigoths' claim to the western Basque country. But they and their successors, the kings of Castile and León, had to contend not only with the Basques' stubborn refusal to be ruled, but also with the rival ambitions of the new Kingdom of Navarre. Next to nothing is known about the provinces of Alava, Biscay and Guipúzcoa during this period, but it was clearly a pretty wild place. It was the last area of southern and western Europe to be converted to Christianity, probably in the ninth or tenth centuries. Local legends suggest that pockets of paganism survived for quite a long time afterwards, and as late as the twelfth century nominally Christian Basques were harrying pilgrims on their way to the shrine of St James at Compostela. It was also the last region of Europe to acquire towns – the last to be civilized in the strict sense of the word. The earliest inland settlements in Guipúzcoa were not founded until the second half of the thirteenth century and those in Biscay were not established until the latter half of the fourteenth.

Treaties were drawn up solemnly allotting this or that province, or the entire area, to either Castile or Navarre, but to all intents and purposes power was held locally. The Alavese were ruled by nobles, but Biscay and Guipúzcoa retained a kind of primitive democracy in which the heads of all the families in a valley either elected or formed a council that sent representatives to a provincial assembly. The provincial assembly decided who should be responsible for taking decisions about the affairs of the province when the assembly was not in session. At different times, this power was delegated to councils of notables or to elected or hereditary lords (there was an aristocracy in both provinces, but its power seems to have been more economic and social than political).

Although the Basque country was a poor area, serfdom disappeared there more swiftly and completely than elsewhere in Spain, and by the end of the Middle Ages the liberties enjoyed by ordinary Basques would have been the envy of their counterparts elsewhere in Europe – they could bear arms, they were free to hunt and fish and they were entitled within their native district to make use of what were usually extensive common woodlands and pastures.

The Kings of Castile acquired sovereignty over the western Basques only very slowly and gradually. The Guipúzcoan notables in the thirteenth century and the Alavese aristocracy in the fourteenth century both voted to offer the Castilian Crown the overlordship of their respective provinces, while the lordship of Biscay passed to Castile by inheritance in 1379. Navarre, on the other hand, remained fully independent until 1512 when Fernando, the King of Aragón and Regent of Castile, who was at that time waging a war against the French, demanded that the Navarrese allow his troops free passage through their realm. The Navarrese refused and Fernando invaded and annexed their kingdom. In 1530 the newly united Kingdom of Spain relinquished the bulk of what had been Navarrese territory on the other side of the Pyrenees and the Spanish Basque country took on more or less its present shape.

Although nominally integrated into the Spanish state, the Basques held back a good deal of power from the central government. In Guipúzcoa and Biscay they retained intact their system of local administration. The Guipúzcoan assembly could veto laws submitted by the Spanish sovereign with the words 'we obey but do not comply' and the Biscayan elders insisted that as soon as a monarch succeeded to the throne, he or she or a representative had to go to the province and swear to uphold its laws beneath the tree in Guernica where their assembly met. The Navarrese for their part enjoyed the privilege of being ruled by a viceroy – the only one outside the Americas – and were allowed to retain their own local legislature, executive and judiciary. They also had the right to mint their own money – as late as the nineteenth century the Navarrese were striking coins depicting King Fernando VII of Spain as King Fernando III of Navarre. These political rights, together with a number of valuable economic and social privileges such as immunity from Spanish customs duties and exemption from military service outside their native province, were embodied in codes of traditional law known as *fueros*.

Nationalists tend inevitably to emphasize the extent of the Basques' independence under the Castilian Crown, but remain silent about their close links with the Castilian people. Yet one of the reasons why the Basques enjoyed such a privileged status was precisely because they had been associated for so long and so intimately with the Castilians, even if it had always been on their own terms. Basques helped the Castilians to establish their earliest settlements on the *meseta* and subsequently played a prominent role in many of the decisive battles of the Castilian *reconquista*. Under the Habsburgs, the Basque country provided Spain with some of its finest administrators, two of its greatest explorers – Pedro de Ursua and Lope de Aguirre, whose doomed search for Eldorado provided the inspiration for Werner Herzog's film *Aguirre, Wrath of God* – and two of its most celebrated religious figures, St Ignacio de Loyola and St Francisco Xavier.

Another distinguished Basque from Spain's Golden Age was Sebastián Elcano, who took command of the first expedition to circumnavigate the globe after its commander, Magellan, had been killed in the Philippines. The Basques had for centuries had close links with the sea. They seem to have learnt deep-sea fishing from the Normans and, until the eighteenth century, they were also renowned whalers. Some of their terminology was picked up by the whalers of the Azores, who passed it on to the seamen from Massachusetts who used the Azores as a supply base in the last century. The word for a sperm whale, cachalot, is ultimately of Basque origin. But although the fishing villages of the Guipúzcoan and Biscayan coast have always played a large part in the life and lore of the region, its soul lies inland where, between the end of the *reconquista* and the start of the Carlist Wars, there evolved a highly idiosyncratic society, the last traces of which can still be detected in the Basque country of today.

Its outstanding characteristic was the relatively low proportion of the population concentrated in villages and the correspondingly high proportion scattered over the countryside in homesteads. This pattern is thought to have developed in the stable and prosperous sixteenth century, at the same time as the characteristic Basque farmhouse

– called *caserío* in Spanish and *baserri* in Basque – began to take shape. The earliest *caseríos* consisted of a ground floor containing accommodation for both humans and animals and a top floor where grain was stored. In later designs the people slept upstairs, but the cooking and eating continued to take place downstairs next to the stables. With their steep roofs, the *caseríos* look very like Alpine chalets. Most of them are held on tenure (although the number of owner-occupiers has been increasing since the fifties) and they almost always stand on the land which their occupants farm. The farms are small (about six hectares on average) and invariably include a wide variety of crops and livestock. They are as a result extremely uneconomic. Traditionally, the *caseríos* housed a larger social grouping than the nuclear family – a couple, their children, an unmarried brother or sister, the parents of either the husband or wife and one or two servants, all living under the same roof.

The status of Basque women has always been relatively high and it could well be that this is a last distant echo of the matriarchies which are thought to have existed throughout northern Spain in prehistoric times. The rural Basque country is also one of the few areas in Europe where there has never been more than a minimal division of family wealth. In much of the region this was achieved by transferring the *caserío*, the land attached to it and the family's entire wealth to the first-born (in some parts, regardless of whether the eldest child was male or female). Elsewhere, the parents chose whichever child appeared most capable.

Like many historically poor peoples, the Basques are renowned for the excellence of their cuisine and for eating to excess whenever they have the opportunity. The traditional Basque drinks are beer, cider and an acid 'green' wine called *txacolí*, but in recent times they have had increasing access to the excellent wines of the Rioja. Drunkenness does not incur quite the same fierce social disapproval that it does in the more southerly parts of Spain.

Another distinctive trait of traditional Basque society is the important role accorded to sport. The Basques have invented numerous games. The most famous is *pelota*, a game not unlike squash, which dates back to at least the sixteenth century when it was played by between eight and ten players wearing gloves and when, long before the development of professional sport in the rest of the world, there were semi-professional *pelota* players touring the Basque country giving demonstration matches. Since then, it has undergone numerous changes and several variants have evolved. The name of one of them, *Jai-Alai*, is sometimes used to describe the sport as a whole. The arm basket or *txistera* which is used in one form of the game – and which allows players to throw the ball at the wall at extraordinary speeds – is not as traditional as is sometimes assumed. It only made its appearance in the middle of the nineteenth century. Some of the other sports which still thrive in the Basque country are caber-tossing, wood-cutting, stone-lifting, tug-of-war, and one (*sokatira*) in which oxen are made to drag huge lumps of stone over short distances – often across town squares. There also used to be games similar to golf (*perratxe*) and cricket (*anikote*), but they have died out. Not surprisingly in view of where they live, the Basques are celebrated hill-walkers and rock-climbers, and their mountaineering clubs have traditionally been a breeding-ground for radical nationalist sentiment.

Perhaps because of the importance attached to sport, gambling has always played a big part in Basque life. It is not unusual to see a blackboard in a Basque bar smothered with wagers struck between the customers. Even the folk culture of the area has a competitive edge, exemplified by the *bertsolariak* or poetry competitions – in which the participants improvise in accordance with a given metre, each taking his cue from his rival's poem. But then the way in which most of the arts are expressed or practised in the Basque country is quite different from in the rest of Spain. Basque art is unusually symmetrical, for example. The music has none of the sinuousness of flamenco and it employs several instruments unique to the region. One is the *txistu*, a kind of flute with two finger-holes at the top and one at the bottom which is played one-handed, allowing the musician to beat a drum with his other hand. Then there is the *trikitrixa*, a small accordion, and the *alboca*, which is made from a bull's horn and sounds like the bagpipes. The songs are unusual within Spain in that each note corresponds to a syllable, and the dances, which include equivalents of the Greek glass dance and the Scottish sword dance, are more athletic than sensual, the object being to prove one's agility rather than one's grace.

To an even greater extent than the rest of Spain, this isolated, innocent society was quite unprepared for the new ideas that were to enter the country during the nineteenth century – and in particular the Napoleonic concept of a centralized state whose citizens should all be subject to the same laws. The Basques soon learnt to equate this new way of thinking with antipathy to the *fueros*. They were first abolished by Napoleon himself after the invasion of Spain, and then by the *liberales* when they seized power for a brief period in the 1820s. On each occasion they were re-established by the reactionary Fernando VII, and so it was natural that when his brother, Don Carlos, raised the standard of absolutism, the Basques should be tempted to rally round it. But Don Carlos's fanatical Catholicism, which so appealed to the rural peasantry, appalled the urban bourgeoisie and throughout the Carlist Wars the bulk of the middle class in towns like Bilbao sided with Madrid against Carlism.

As a way of punishing the Basques for supporting the Carlist rebellion, the *fueros* of Biscay and Guipúzcoa were again revoked in 1841 following the First Carlist War, only to be restored subsequently. But at the end of the Second Carlist War in 1876 the government decreed the abolition of the *fueros* of Guipúzcoa, Biscay and Alava – but not those of Navarre – in a move that was never to be rescinded. All that remained of the Basques' traditional privileges in the three western provinces was a special tax-collection system called the *concierto económico*. But the problem with using the abolition of the *fueros* as a punishment was that it affected all Basques and not just those who had supported Carlism. In fact, those whose economic prospects were most severely affected belonged to the urban lower middle class, which had tended to support the central government. Within a few years of the abolition of the *fueros*, moreover, the Basque country was to embark upon a period of rapid industrialization in which this newly disaffected lower middle class was to play a key role.

The origins of the industrialization of the region are to be found in its ample reserves of iron and timber and an abundance of fast-running streams and rivers. The period of fastest growth was between 1877 and 1902 when the industrialization was largely confined to Biscay. It was not until the end of the period that industry began to seep into Guipúzcoa. Although there were, and are, several large factories in the area, the outstanding characteristic of Basque industrialization has been a multitude of small workshops both inside and outside the cities. Whereas the upper-middle-class owners of the factories, together with the owners of the big banking and insurance concerns which grew up alongside them, tended to align themselves with the Spanish economic oligarchy, often acquiring titles of nobility in the process, the lower-middle-class bosses of the workshops came to regard industrialization as a process from which they had gained less than they had lost. It did not make them particularly rich, yet it caused an influx of hundreds of thousands of workers from other parts of Spain – *maketos*, they called them – who threatened the survival of Basque society in its traditional form.

The man who systematized their fears and resentments into the political ideology which we know as Basque nationalism was one Sabino de Arana Goiri. Born in 1865, Arana was the son of a Carlist whose political sympathies had earned him a period of exile in France. Arana first entered the ideological battlefield at the age of thirty, appropriately enough with an article on the spelling in Basque of the word 'Basque'. His earliest writings were all about philology and etymology. In fact, one of his less fortunate legacies was to distort and complicate written Basque in an attempt to cleanse it of what he considered to be Hispanicisms. In his efforts to avoid any taint of centralism, he also invented a series of Basque christian names to replace Spanish ones, so that Luis, for example, became Koldobika. His most useful contribution was to provide the Basques with a word for the land they inhabited. There had always been a word for the Basque-speaking region – *Euskalerría* – but it had the disadvantage of excluding all those areas populated by Basques where Castilian had taken hold. Arana filled the gap with a neologism, *Euskería*. He later changed his mind and opted for *Euskadi* (often spelt *Euzkadi*), which means 'collection of Basques', and this is the word which has been used by Basque nationalists ever since to describe the nation they hope to create.

It was not until 1892 that Arana published his first full-length political work. As a political theorist, he was profoundly reactionary. He wanted to return the Basque country to a state of pre-industrial innocence in which society would be guided by the dictates of religion, and the choice between socialism and capitalism would be irrelevant. At the core of his doctrine was an undisguised hatred for the immigrants – 'They came up here bringing with them their bullfights, their flamenco songs and dances, their "refined" language so abundant in blasphemous and filthy expressions, their fighting knives and so many, so many splendid means of "civilization",' he once wrote in bitterly ironic vein. What Arana sought was a kind of apartheid. In his writings he inveighed against 'mixed' marriages, and in the community centres or *batzokis* which he founded to spread the nationalist faith it was forbidden to play Spanish music or discuss Spanish politics. The rules of the first *batzokis* demonstrate the depth and intensity of Arana's racism − members were divided into three categories according to the number of their Basque grandparents and only those whose four grandparents had Basque surnames were entitled to hold office.

Arana's involvement in practical politics lasted from 1893, when he made a formal declaration of his ideals at a dinner given by a group of friends (the so-called Oath of Larrazábal), until his death in 1903. This period saw the launching of a nationalist newspaper and the birth of the Basque Nationalist Party (PNV) in 1894. At first, Arana and his supporters were ignored by Madrid, but by 1895 the authorities were sufficiently concerned by their activities to jail Arana for a few months. Four years later, the administration initiated a serious clampdown on regional nationalists of all kinds and Arana decided to change tack, with the result that during the latter years of his life his public demands were for autonomy rather than independence. He thus left an ambiguous legacy, but one which has enabled separatists and autonomists alike to find a home within the PNV.

For Basque nationalists, *Euskadi* consists of the French Basque country, which is traditionally (but not officially) divided into the three districts of Soule (Zuberoa), Labourd (Laburdi) and Basse-Navarre (Behe Nafarroa), and the four Spanish provinces which have a Basque population − Alava (Araba), Guipúzcoa (Gipuzkoa), Biscay (Bizkaia) and Navarre (Nafarroa). Nobody in Spain questions the 'Basqueness' of the first three provinces. But the same is not true of Navarre, which is paradoxical since it was the only state ever to be created by the Basques. Navarre has always had a large number of non-Basque inhabitants, but it is also partly due to the failure of nationalism to strike roots there − at least until recently. Since the Navarrese did not lose their *fuero* at the same time as the other provinces, they already enjoyed a considerable measure of autonomy. Moreover, Navarre − in common with Alava − was a predominantly agricultural region, lacking the sort of industrial middle class which provided the PNV with much of its support in the two coastal provinces.

When, in 1932, the Republican government asked the town councils of the Basque country to decide whether they wanted their respective provinces to form part of a self-governing *Euskadi*, the Navarrese chose to stay out. Alava also opted out shortly afterwards. The 1936 uprising widened the gulf between these two inland provinces on the one hand and Guipúzcoa and Biscay on the other. Given the deeply reactionary outlook of the Basque peasantry and the quasi-fascist ideology of the middle-class nationalists, there can be little doubt that – other things being equal – a majority of all four provinces would have come out in support of Franco's rebellion. Indeed that is what did happen in both Alava and Navarre. But by opting for autonomy Guipúzcoa and Biscay had thrown in their lot with the legally constituted government of Spain. They remained loyal to the Republic and the Republic returned the favour by granting them a provisional statute of home rule after the outbreak of the civil war in October 1936.

Guipúzcoa and Biscay were to pay dearly for their choice both during and after the war. Perhaps the most horrific single act committed by either side during the conflict was the systematic pulverization in April 1937 of Guernica – a town which, as has been seen, had a special place in the affections of the Biscayans in particular and the Basques in general. As soon as Guipúzcoa and Biscay had been subdued, moreover, Franco passed a special 'punitive decree', abolishing not only their provisional statute of home rule, but also the *conciertos económicos* of the two provinces – the last vestiges of the *fueros* that had been abolished sixty years earlier. Alava, on the other hand, was allowed to retain its *concierto económico* and Navarre was allowed to keep its *fuero* with all that that entailed. During the thirty-six years that Franco ruled Spain, Navarre remained an outstanding exception – an island of autonomy within a sea of uniformity, boasting its own legislature and government.

Having been publicly singled out for punishment, it is not surprising that Guipúzcoa and Biscay should be the only provinces of Spain in which there was sustained and violent opposition to the regime. The letters ETA – standing for *Euskadi Ta Askatasuna* (Euskadi and Freedom) – first appeared during 1960, daubed on the walls of towns in the two coastal provinces. The movement that lay behind them had coalesced in the late fifties around a clandestine publication called *Ekin* (Action), set up by university students. In 1961, ETA carried out its first terrorist operation when some of its members tried to derail a train taking Francoist veterans to a rally in San Sebastián. The police response was savage. A hundred or so people were arrested. Many were tortured and some were charged, tried and sentenced to up to twenty years in jail. But the leaders of ETA escaped to France.

The early history of the organization is of a succession of internal conflicts. In 1966 the movement split into two groups, ETA-Zarra (Old ETA) and ETA-Berri (Young ETA). The latter forsook violence and eventually became the Movimiento Comunista de España. In 1970 ETA-Zarra divided into ETA 5th Assembly and ETA 6th Assembly. ETA 6th Assembly also gave up the armed struggle and re-named itself the Liga Comunista Revolucionaria. Then, in the mid-seventies, there was yet another parting of the ways when ETA 5th Assembly gave birth to ETA-Military and ETA-Politico-Military. Finally in 1981 ETA-Politico-Military was fatally weakened when it split into ETA-pm (7th Assembly), whose members dissolved their organization the following year, and ETA-pm (8th Assembly). Thereafter, ETA consisted of ETA-Military, plus the rejectionist rump of ETA-pm. The disputes that prompted these splits are too arcane to explain in detail here, but each time the more violent, less intellectual group survived intact.

Although ETA was founded by university students and professional people, the active end of the organization rapidly came to be dominated by Basques from the *caseríos*. This was particularly true of the *Milis*. The region which provided them with more *gudaris* (soldiers) than any other was the Goierri, a Basque-speaking redoubt in Guipúzcoa and an area of strange contrasts between industry and agriculture where it is not unusual to see a *caserío* and a small factory or workshop side by side. The rise of ETA thus saw the reincorporation into the nationalist struggle of the peasant farmers who fought for Carlism. For all its revolutionary rhetoric, ETA – like the IRA – had a strong streak of conventional Roman Catholic morality and from time to time it mounted campaigns against what it regarded as decadent activities – threatening to murder drug-pushers, for example, or planting bombs in bars and discos or in cinemas showing sex films. But, as time went by, the broader radical nationalist movement, which provided ETA with much of its support in the Basque country itself, began to attract ecologists, feminists – and even, bizarrely, pacifists – whose dissatisfactions were not primarily, or even minimally, nationalist in origin.

The spread of violent, radical nationalism in the Basque country coincided with an altogether more peaceful process of cultural reaffirmation, particularly in so far as the language was concerned. Basque had been ceding terrain to Castilian – literally as well as metaphorically – for centuries, not because of repressive measures ordered from Madrid but because Castilian, being the dominant language of the peninsula, was more useful to those who had to maintain contacts with the outside world. It thus became the language of the upper and middle classes and of those such as the Alavese who were not cut off from their neighbours by mountains. But that is not to say that the repression of Basque when it was ordered by Franco was ineffective. Indeed, it was far more savage and enduring than anything put into effect in either Catalonia or Galicia and caused a good deal of linguistic self-censorship among the Basques themselves. Basque not only disappeared from the media, it virtually vanished from the streets as well. I have a friend from San Sebastián who is as Basque as it is possible to be, but who speaks not a word of her mother tongue because her parents, who were both Basque speakers, forbade her to speak it.

The late fifties saw the start of a renaissance. It was then that the first *ikastolas* were founded. An *ikastola* is a primary school at which the lessons are given in Basque. In the early years, many of them were run from private homes. While Franco was still alive they never had access to public funds. But although the authorities viewed the *ikastolas* with immense suspicion, going as far as to get the police to obtain lists of their staff and backers, they never had an argument for banning a movement which, however subversive, was undeniably helping to supplement the lack of state schooling that was characteristic of the entire Spanish education system at that time. Subsequently, many thousands of adult Basques embarked on the arduous task of learning their mother tongue, among them Carlos Garaikoetxea, who was to go on to become the first President of the Basque country's home-rule government.

Teachers reckon that it takes between 300 and 500 hours of study for a Castilian speaker to get to the point where he or she can chat easily. For several years, moreover, the revival of the language was hindered by the existence of no fewer than six – arguably seven – dialects (four in Spain and two or three in France). But in 1968 the Academy of the Basque Language completed the task of codifying a standard literary Basque called *euskera batua*.

A survey published by the Basque government in 2001 found that the number of people in the Basque country who could either speak or understand *euskera* had risen to 50 per cent from just 34 per cent twenty years earlier.

One of ETA's leaders was once asked by *Le Monde* whether in view of the immense political changes that had taken place in Spain they might consider altering their policies. 'Even if the [Spanish state] were to become a model of democracy,' he replied, 'it wouldn't change things as far as we are concerned. We are not, nor have we been, nor shall we ever be Spaniards.' That may be true of him and his fellow-gunmen, but it is no longer true of the population of the Basque country as a whole. Almost a century of economic growth, interrupted only by the civil war, saw Biscay and Guipúzcoa, which were the poorest provinces in Spain in 1877, climb to first and third places respectively on the table of income *per capita* in 1973. Throughout that period, non-Basques in search of work flowed into the Basque country in an almost uninterrupted stream. The sixties saw the process of industrialization extended with even greater rapidity, first to Alava, and then to Navarre. By 1970 a higher proportion of the population of Alava was employed in industry than in any other province in Spain. All the other Basque provinces – and Navarre – were in the top ten.

In Navarre, the new businesses mainly recruited their work-forces within the province, but in Alava they took them from outside, increasing the population by almost 50 per cent in ten years. By the end of the sixties, 30 per cent of the inhabitants of the Basque country had been born outside it.

In spite of the viciously hostile reception their forebears received, the 'immigrants' have integrated well. One reason for this is that more than half came from León and Old Castile, which were not as wretchedly poor as some of the southern regions, and they tended to originate from within the rural lower middle class. By and large, they were better educated and more skilled than the typical migrant to Catalonia and although, for obvious reasons, fewer migrants learn Basque than learn Catalan, the rate of intermarriage between 'natives' and 'immigrants' has always been higher in the Basque country than in the Catalan provinces. A lot of the more recent migrants arrived to take up jobs as technicians, officials and foremen, so that nowadays there is very little difference between the average earnings of Basques and those from outside. A second reason for the relatively harmonious relations between 'natives' and 'immigrants' is that both were equally affected by repression under the dictatorship. Of the eleven 'states of exception' declared by Franco, four were nationwide. But of the remaining seven, no fewer than six applied to Guipúzcoa or Biscay or both. It has been estimated that by the early seventies a quarter of the entire Guardia Civil was stationed in the Basque country. Tear-gas does not discriminate between natives and immigrants. Nor did the police when they stopped people in the street, often submitting them to humiliating searches. A Bilbao or San Sebastián car number-plate was often enough to get you pulled off the road half a dozen times between the Basque country and Madrid.

That, of course, was exactly what ETA and its followers wanted. Immigration had made it increasingly difficult to justify separatism on racial grounds alone, but repression suffered by all sections of the community enabled the separatist left that supported ETA to argue with some credibility that the Basque country was subject to a unique double oppression by both capitalism and centralism. According to the view put forward by these revolutionary nationalists, or *abertzales* (patriots), economic and social liberation could only be attained through national independence.

By the time Franco died, many of the inhabitants of the Basque country, whatever their ethnic origins, felt deeply alienated from other Spaniards. Among children, it showed up in a survey carried out by the Biscay Chamber of Commerce in 1977. Schoolchildren were asked what they most felt themselves to be. Eliminating the 'Don't knows', the answers among native children were: 'Basque', 80 per cent; 'Spanish', 8 per cent; 'European', 12 per cent. The response from the immigrant children was: 'Basque', 48 per cent; 'Spanish', 28 per cent; 'European', 24 per cent. Among adults, it was demonstrated by the much higher than average abstention rates in the Basque country in the referendum held in 1976 to endorse the political reform bill, and by the fact that a majority of the electorate in the Basque country failed to vote in the referendum on the constitution two years later.* Over the years, many a son – and daughter – of immigrant parents has become involved with ETA or the network of organizations which offer it support.

ETA and its supporters were able to draw additional strength from the onset of recession in the late seventies. Its effects were particularly savage in the Basque country. This was partly because of the region's dependence on uncompetitive 'rust-belt' industries, but also partly – and ironically – because ETA's own activities were deterring investment. Between 1973 and 1979, Biscay and Guipúzcoa dropped from first and third place on the table of income *per capita* to ninth and sixth place respectively.

In retrospect, it can be seen that the late seventies and early eighties were ETA's heyday. Its bloodiest year was 1980, when it was responsible for the deaths of 118 people. Since then, various factors have combined to reduce the level of violence – the winding-up of ETA-pm, growing cooperation between the Spanish and French governments, especially since Spain joined France in the European Union, and – partly because of that – increasingly effective police work.

In 1992, ETA was dealt the severest blow it had ever suffered with the arrest in France of its entire leadership. The organization has never truly recovered. The success of that operation prompted ETA into a change of tactics that was to lead it into one blind alley after another. In 1995, it adopted a new and more radical programme, the so-called Democratic Alternative, which declared that the organization would only call a truce after, and not before, the successful conclusion of negotiations with the government. At the same time, it encouraged its supporters in the Basque country to try to wrest control of the streets with a campaign of violence known as the *kale borroka*. This was partly aimed at getting ETA's

* This was also the case in Galicia, but more because of apathy than antipathy. What distinguished the Basque country, moreover, was that it was also the region with the highest 'no' vote – 23.5 per cent.

prisoners moved to jails in the Basque country. The organization also used this to try to justify the kidnapping in 1997 of the PP local councillor, Miguel Angel Blanco.*

His cold-blooded murder made ETA more unpopular than it had ever been. People who had never before dared to do so openly denounced and defied the men and women of violence. Yet, instead of adding its weight to the growing consensus in favour of isolating ETA, the leaders of the biggest nationalist party, the non-violent Basque Nationalist Party (PNV), decided the time had come to negotiate with the terrorists and adopt a more radical approach themselves. The following year, the PNV's tactics won from the guerrillas a fourteen-month truce that cleared the way for secret talks with government representatives at a Swiss hotel. But the talks got nowhere, and it soon became clear that the moderate nationalists were not prepared to go as fast as ETA wanted down the separatist route.

The ceasefire – the longest in ETA's history – was called off. It had saved lives, unquestionably. But it also allowed ETA to retrench. It had often been argued that there was a kind of sinister symbiosis between ETA and the Basque Nationalist Party; that the PNV depended on ETA's violence for its dominant role in Basque politics. The truce left a lingering suspicion among many non-Basques, particularly on the right, that the moderates' motive for calling it was to save ETA from extinction. At all events, when the organization resumed its campaign of murder and mayhem, it did so with redoubled force.

Twenty-three people died in 2000; another fifteen in 2001. But the bloodshed that followed the calling-off of ETA's truce only made it more unpopular and provided the government with the backing it needed to clamp down on ETA's support base within the Basque country. When, in 2002, the lower house of parliament voted on a bill to give the Supreme Court the power to dissolve parties that encouraged terrorism, the vote in favour was 304 to 16. Batasuna, the party accused of being ETA's political arm, was outlawed the following year by a unanimous judgement of the Court. It was the first time a party had been barred from taking part in the democratic process since the end of Spain's dictatorship. Police work aimed at dismantling the organization led in 2004 to another resounding

* See above, p. 71.

success when Mikel Albisu Iriate ('Antxa'), the man alleged to have taken over the leadership of ETA in 1992, was arrested along with his partner and lieutenant, Soledad Iparragirre. That year, for the first time since 1999, ETA failed to carry out a single killing.

The return to power of the Socialists changed matters dramatically, unblocking a situation in which the PP government in Madrid refused to talk to ETA unless it capitulated, while ETA refused to declare another truce until after the successful conclusion of negotiations.

Secret talks between government and ETA representatives were held in Norway and Switzerland, and on 22 March 2006 a video was sent to a Basque television station in which a masked woman, backed by ETA's axe-and-serpent emblem, declared a 'permanent ceasefire'. Since, by then, the organization had not killed for almost three years, there were grounds for believing this might indeed be the beginning of the end of a terrorist campaign that had cost more than 800 lives. But ETA's statement did not include a pledge to give up its weapons, and polls showed the attitude of the majority of Spaniards was one of suspicious caution.

It was expected that two sets of talks would begin as a result of the ceasefire: a 'round table' open to all political parties and a so-called 'peace process' involving ETA on the one hand and the Spanish, and perhaps the French, authorities on the other. The idea was that the 'round table' would decide on the Basque country's political future (so that terrorists were not seen to be having a direct influence), while the 'peace process' would settle the way in which ETA wound up its activities. Despite official denials, it was clear that progress in the 'peace process' would depend, at least in part, on the succcess of the political talks.

Numerous questions remained to be settled: above all, whether the government would be able or willing to agree to the concessions needed for a solution ETA considered acceptable. Its goal remained the wholly unrealistic one of a socialist mini-state straddling the Pyrenees. Arguably, the best chance of peace lay in spinning out the process to the point at which a return to arms became as impractical as it was unthinkable.

CHAPTER 18

The Catalans

At Barcelona's El Prat airport, well-groomed executives march to and fro across the concourse with a serious, purposeful air. On your way into the city you will see that every other hoarding sports an advertisement for this or that *caixa*, or savings bank. And if you have already spent some time in Spain, it will strike you that the Catalans spend less time over their meals than other Spaniards, and that there are more self-service restaurants in Barcelona than in the other major cities. The Catalans' legendary industriousness has always meant that Barcelona has been among the most prosperous cities in Spain.

Its prosperity, taken in conjunction with its location – close by France on the shores of the Mediterranean – has also meant that it has traditionally been the most cosmopolitan of Spanish cities. Most of the ideas that shaped Spain's modern history – republicanism, federalism, anarchism, syndicalism and communism – found their way into Spain by way of Catalonia. Fashions – whether in clothing, philosophy or art – have tended to take hold in Barcelona several years before they gained acceptance in Madrid.

In an ideal world, one feels, the Catalans would not mind swapping places with the Belgians or the Dutch. There is a poem by Catalonia's greatest modern poet, Salvador Espriu, who died in 1985, which captures perfectly the ambivalence of his fellow-countrymen's attitude to the Spain of his time:

> Oh, how tired I am of my cowardly
> old, so savage land!
> How I should like to get away
> to the North,
> where they say that the people are clean,

and decent, refined, rich, free
aware and happy! (. . .)
Yet I am destined never to realize my dream
and here I shall remain until death,
for I too am wild and cowardly.
And, what is more, I love,
with a despairing sorrow,
this my poor,
dirty, sad, hapless homeland.

It is significant, however, that Espriú ended up resigning himself to his lot. Catalan dissatisfaction has, for the most part, tended to be expressed as resentment, indignation and a demand for a substantial say in the running of their own affairs, rather than in terms of outright separatism. Madrid politicians are fond of saying that the difference between an ambitious Basque politician and an ambitious Catalan politician is that the first dreams of being Prime Minister of an independent Euskadi, whereas the second dreams of being Prime Minister of Spain.

One reason why the separatist instinct has been less pronounced in Catalonia is that the Catalans, though they tend to have somewhat fairer skin and lighter hair, would not and could not claim to be racially different from other Spaniards. But it is also a reflection of the Catalans' most highly prized virtue – *seny*. There is no exact translation of *seny*. Perhaps the nearest equivalent is the northern English term 'nous' – good old common sense. Respect for *seny* makes the Catalans realistic, earnest, tolerant and at times a bit censorious. Yet it sits uneasily with their frequently tumultuous history.

Barcelona has come under full-scale military attack by the forces of the central government on numerous occasions, usually as a consequence of uprisings and revolutions. The popularity of anarchism among the workers of Catalonia turned Barcelona into the most violent city in Europe during the early part of the twentieth century, and at the height of the civil war the Catalan capital was the scene of a bloody street war between conflicting Republican factions.

This is how the Catalan writer and academic, Victor Alba, squares the circle: 'The opposite of *seny* is *arrauxment*: an ecstasy of violence. But *arrauxment* is seen as an ultimate consequence of *seny*. Because they [the Catalans] are convinced that when they act impetuously they are being sensible ... When a thing is not the way it ought to be, when a situation is not "sensible", the common-sense thing to do is to oppose it abruptly, violently.' Another explanation I have seen put forward is that the Catalans fall into two very distinct groups – those who are *sorrut* (anti-social) and those who are *trempat* (spontaneous, likeable, *simpático*) – and that the violent changes of direction in Catalan political history are the product of their uneasy co-existence.

A similarly paradoxical pattern can be identified in Catalan culture. For the most part, it is rather prim and humdrum. But from time to time it throws up an outstandingly original figure. In the Middle Ages, there was Ramón Llull, a multilingual Majorcan missionary who opposed the Crusades and put forward the theory that the earth was round, and Anselm Turmeda, a renegade Franciscan who converted to Islam and is regarded as a saint in North Africa. More recently, Catalonia has produced Salvador Dalí and two architects whose works stand out like a string of beacons amid the stolidly bourgeois edifices of Barcelona – Antoni Gaudí, whose giant, eccentric cathedral, the Sagrada Familia, was started in 1882 and is likely to take until about 2020 to complete, and Ricardo Bofill, who has been responsible for, among other things, converting a cement works into an office block that looks like a medieval castle.

What unites this curiously heterogeneous and contradictory people is their language. Their pride in it is well-nigh limitless and they speak it at every opportunity. When two Catalan speakers and a Castilian speaker are talking together, the Catalans will address the Castilian speaker in Castilian, but as often as not they will address each other in Catalan – something that profoundly irritates other Spaniards.

Written down, Catalan looks like a cross between Spanish and French, but spoken it has a ruggedness which is lacking in either. It is unusually rich in monosyllabic words – to the point that Catalan poets have constructed entire poems out of them – and the syllables of multisyllabic words are particularly strongly stressed. The diphthongs 'au', 'eu' and 'iu' crop up with great frequency so that to a foreigner it sounds a bit like Portuguese.

Just about the worst gaffe you can make when speaking to a Catalan is to refer to his or her language as a dialect. Catalan is no more a dialect of Castilian than Castilian is a dialect of Catalan. Or, to put it another way, both – like French and Italian – are dialects of Latin. The first recognizably Catalan words were found in documents written in the ninth century, although the language is thought to have begun to evolve in the seventh or eighth century. It spread in the wake of Catalonia's imperial expansion to an area much bigger than the four provinces of Gerona (Girona), Lérida (Lleida), Tarragona and Barcelona which comprise the Principality of Catalonia itself. It is also spoken along a 15- to 30-kilometre-deep strip of Aragonese territory bordering the Principality; in about two-thirds of the region of Valencia; throughout the Balearic Islands; in the co-Principality of Andorra; and in that part of the French *département* of Pyrénées Orientales historically known as Roussillon. It is also spoken in Alguer, a walled town on the west coast of Sardinia, which was captured and populated by Catalans in the fourteenth century. Until the early 1950s it could still be heard in San Agustín, Florida, a town conquered by Menorcans in the eighteenth century. Catalan is the native language of something like 6,500,000 people, which makes it more widely spoken than several better-known languages such as Danish, Finnish and Norwegian.

As it spread, differences began to arise between Catalan as it was spoken in the eastern and western parts of the Catalan-speaking world. The dividing line runs from a point just to the east of Andorra to a point just to the west of Tarragona. The internal fragmentation of the language does not stop there. Both dialects can be further divided into sub-dialects – at least three within eastern Catalan (central, Roussillonaise and Balearic) and two within western Catalan (north-western and Valencian), according to the pronunciation of the first person singular of the first conjugation indicative. 'I sing' is pronounced 'cant*u*' in Barcelona and most of Catalonia proper, 'canti' in Roussillon, 'cant' in the Balearic Islands, 'canto' in Lérida and along the Aragonese fringe, and 'cant*e*' in Valencia.

It is typical of the rampant localism of Spain that many of the inhabitants of the Balearic Islands and Valencia object to their language being called Catalan at all. But in 2004, the Madrid government caused apoplexy among Catalan nationalists when it asked the EU to make Valencian an official language. A request was eventually submitted for recognition of 'the language known as Catalan in Catalonia and the Balearic Islands and Valencian in Valencia'.

Catalonia was among the most thoroughly Romanized regions of Iberia and had only the briefest contact with the Moslems. It was, moreover, the only area to be repopulated on a large scale by *reconquistadores* from outside the peninsula. The Franks' contribution to the settlement of Catalonia was only the first of the many links which were to be established between the Catalans (who were themselves originally called *francos* by other Spaniards) and the people living in what is now France. The Catalans have always been far more receptive to French ideas and attitudes than other Spaniards, who tend in fact heartily to dislike the French.

The period of Catalonia's greatest glory lasted from the twelfth to the fourteenth centuries, during which time the Catalans were allied with the Aragonese. Their confederacy was a precociously sophisticated union in which the two very different partners were each allowed to retain their own laws, customs and language under the same Crown. As early as the beginning of the thirteenth century, Catalonia had a Corts or parliament consisting of three chambers – one for the nobility, one for the bourgeoisie and another for the clergy. The sovereigns of the confederation subsequently undertook to call the Corts once a year and not to pass any laws without its consent. The Corts set up a committee of twenty-four members (eight from each chamber) whose job it was to collect taxes. In 1359 this body – the *Generalitat* – took over responsibility for the way the money was spent as well as the way it was collected, thus becoming what was arguably the world's first parliamentary government. As one medieval chronicler remarked, the rulers of Catalonia and Aragón were 'not the masters of their subjects, but their co-rulers'.

By the middle of the fourteenth century the Catalan–Aragonese confederation ruled not only the Balearic Islands and the city and region of Valencia, but also Sardinia, Corsica and much of present-day Greece. A member of its royal family sat on the throne of Sicily and it controlled the gold trade with the Sudan. Today the world has all but forgotten Catalonia's golden age, but the memory of her power and influence lives on in the folk-sayings of the Mediterranean. In Sicily, recalcitrant children are told to 'do what I say or I'll call the Catalans' and in Thrace you can do no worse than to wish on your enemy 'the Catalan vengeance'. A number of naval and financial terms in Castilian derive from Catalan, including probably the word *peseta*.

A banking collapse in 1381 caused by the cost of financing too many imperial wars, the rise of the Ottoman Empire and the loss of the gold trade sent Barcelona into decline even before the discovery of America shifted the geographical advantage from the Mediterranean to the Atlantic. When the city's fortunes finally took a turn for the better in the nineteenth century, it was due not so much to commerce as to industry, and in particular the cotton business.

It was during the nineteenth century that the Catalans rediscovered themselves through their language. After the unification of Spain, the ruling class throughout the country had adopted Castilian as a mark of status. Catalan became the language of the peasantry and the culture associated with it died out. But in the nineteenth century it became the medium for a literary revival that succeeded in enhancing the status of the language sufficiently for it to be re-adopted by the middle and upper classes, thereby regaining its respectability and influence.

The Catalan *Renaixença*, as it is called, began in the most curious manner. In 1833, a minor poet, Bonaventura Carles Aribau, published a poem in Catalan called 'Ode to the Fatherland'. He had intended it simply as a birthday present for his patron, another Catalan, called Gaspar Remisa i Niarous, who was at that time head of the Royal Treasury. But the poem was published in a Barcelona newspaper and made a great impact on the intellectual community. Aribau, a dedicated centralist, never again published anything of importance and spent the rest of his life working for the government and the monarchy in Madrid. But the renewed interest in Catalan which he had stimulated grew inexorably. In 1859, an annual poetry competition called the Floral Games was inaugurated and in 1877 it brought to light one of Spain's greatest modern literary figures, Jacint Verdaguer. Several other outstanding writers emerged from Catalonia during the late nineteenth and early twentieth centuries – the playwright Ángel Guimerà, the novelist Narcís Oller and the poet Joan Maragall.

The same period also saw the standardization of the language itself. In 1907, an Institut d'Estudis Catalans was founded and four years later the scientific section of the institute asked the philological section to prepare a report on how the spelling of Catalan might be standardized. This seemingly modest request begged a multitude of questions about grammar and vocabulary, many of which were resolved when the report was published in 1913 with the title of *Normes Ortográfiques*.

The researcher who had made the most decisive contribution to the *Normes* was an engineer-turned-philologist called Pompeu Fabra. Soon afterwards he set about compiling a full-scale dictionary. Published in 1932, it is the cornerstone of modern Catalan.

The *Renaixença* provided the raw material and the driving force for the political movement known as Catalanism, which appeared towards the end of the nineteenth century. Catalanism was a broad church, embracing all those who believed in Catalonia's separate identity and who were keen to see it recognized, whether in the form of autonomy or nationhood. The father of Catalanism, Valentí Almirall, author of *Lo Catalanisme*, was essentially a regionalist. But within a few years his ideas were given a sharper, more nationalistic edge by Enric Prat de la Riba, who provided the movement with its first political programme and whose Catalan Union supplied it with its earliest political organization. Except during its earliest years, Catalanism was never represented by a single party. It provided the inspiration for parties of the right and the left and for parties of all classes, of which by far the most influential was the conservative upper-middle-class Lliga. But what Catalanism lacked in cohesion it more than compensated for in the depth and breadth of its appeal within the community and this point was never lost on Madrid.

The first attempt to solve 'the Catalan problem' was made shortly before the First World War when the Spanish government authorized provincial administrations to pool their functions with those of their neighbours to form *Mancomunidades*. The four Catalan provinces were the only ones in Spain to take advantage of the opportunity. The Catalan *Mancomunidad* lasted for barely a decade until it was suppressed by Primo de Rivera. It was not a particularly successful experiment. The degree of autonomy it offered was extremely limited and at one stage it had to go into debt because of a lack of financial support from the government.

In the brief period between the fall of Primo de Rivera and the resignation of Alfonso XIII, the parties of the Spanish Republican left signed a pact with the main regional nationalist parties (the so-called Pact of San Sebastián), promising that if and when they came to power they would grant home-rule statutes to Catalonia, Galicia and the Basque country. But on 14 April 1931 – two days after the local elections which persuaded the King to flee the country

– nationalists in Barcelona pre-empted orderly progress towards home rule by proclaiming a Catalan Republic as part of an Iberian Federation, even though no such thing existed, nor was envisaged. They were subsequently persuaded by the leaders of the central government to change the name of the administration they had set up to the Government of the *Generalitat* in memory of the medieval institution of the same name. An assembly elected by Catalonia's town councillors later drew up a draft statute which won overwhelming endorsement in a referendum (562,691 votes for, 3,276 votes against, with 195,501 abstentions). A considerably watered-down version of the draft statute (which gave the Catalans control over health and welfare, for example, but not education) was approved by the Cortes on 9 September 1932. However, the financial powers transferred to the *Generalitat* in the ensuing months were severely restricted.

Two years later the demagogic anti-Catalanist, Alejandro Lerroux, succeeded in forcing the *Generalitat* to accept right- as well as left-wing members. This was anathema to the left, who believed that the right would not support the Republic. The President of the *Generalitat*, Lluís Companys, responded by proclaiming 'the Catalan state of the Spanish Federal Republic'. The Civil Governor of Barcelona, himself a Catalan, declared war on the new government, and the offices of the *Generalitat* and the city hall both came under bombardment before Companys surrendered along with his entire government. The Cortes suspended the Catalan parliament and appointed a Governor-General to carry out the functions of the *Generalitat*. In 1935 the members of the *Generalitat* were each sentenced to thirty years in jail, but benefited from an amnesty for political prisoners that was proclaimed when the left-wing Popular Front came to power as a result of the elections in February 1936.

The statute of autonomy was restored and, in the period immediately after the outbreak of civil war, the *Generalitat* was able to grab many of the powers that had been denied it between 1932 and 1934. As Franco and his troops steadily gained the upper hand and the Republicans were pushed back into a progressively smaller area, the capital was moved from Madrid to Valencia and then from Valencia to Barcelona, so that it was in Barcelona that the Republic met its end. Companys fled to France, only to be arrested by the Gestapo after the German invasion. They handed him over to Franco, who ordered him to be executed in secret. It later emerged that the President of the *Generalitat*'s last words – shouted out a matter of seconds before the execution squad opened fire – were '*¡Visca Catalunya!*' ('Long live Catalonia!')

Franco's victory unleashed a campaign against the Catalan language unparalleled in the region's history. Publishing houses, bookshops, and public and private libraries were searched for Catalan books and those that were found were destroyed. Pompeu Fabra's priceless collection was burned in the street. The names of villages and towns were Castilianized. The Street of the Virgin of Monserrat (the patron of Catalonia) became the Street of the Redeemer, and the Library of Catalonia was renamed the Central Library. In the midforties, permission was granted for the publication of books and the staging of plays in Catalan. But it remained banned from radio and television, the daily press and in schools. The Institut maintained a curious half-tolerated, half-clandestine existence under Franco. It held weekly meetings, ran courses on the language, literature and history of Catalonia in private houses, gave receptions, and went as far as to publish books and pamphlets, some of which were even bought by the government for display at international exhibitions.

Throughout the first two decades of Franco's rule, Catalonia was the principal source of opposition to his regime. In 1944 the communists made a disastrous attempt to invade the country from France through the Valle de Arán, and between 1947 and 1949 the anarchists staged a bloody but futile campaign of shootings, bombings and hold-ups in Barcelona. The failure of these attempts to overthrow Franco's regime by force ushered in a period when opposition was characterized by mass public protests. Most of the more successful ones took place in Catalonia. The pattern was set in 1948 when opponents of Franco's rule succeeded in getting 100,000 people to attend a ceremony celebrating the enthronement of the Virgin of Monserrat. In 1951 the first city-wide general strike in post-war Spain was held in Barcelona, which was also the scene of mass public transport boycotts in 1951 and 1956.

But being the focus of opposition and promoting it are two very different things, and the truth is that the role played by Catalan nationalists in fighting Franco was by and large a pretty tame one. There was a Catalan Liberation Front, but it never had a fraction of the support or made one-hundredth of the impact of ETA. Barcelona's students were in the forefront of the search for an independent student movement, but once it had been formed the leadership was exercised from Madrid. The most dramatic acts of resistance to come out of Catalonia were symbolic ones, such as when the audience at the Palau de la Música sang the unofficial national anthem of Catalonia in front of Franco when he was on a visit to the area in 1960.

The virtual absence of violent nationalism meant that the inhabitants of Catalonia were not subjected to the same relentless oppression that helped to homogenize the population of the Basque country, and so the differences between 'native' and 'immigrant' were not erased – or disguised – in Catalonia to the same extent as in the Basque country.

The growth of industry, first in and around Barcelona, and then in the other provincial capitals of Catalonia, had created a demand for labour that the Catalans were quite unable to satisfy by themselves.

Not only did the percentage of immigrants from other parts of Spain grow, but so did the catchment area from which they were drawn. And as it grew, it took in areas which were less and less like Catalonia and whose population was therefore less and less sympathetic to Catalanism. The earliest migration was of rural Catalans to Barcelona in the early part of the nineteenth century. By the end of the century, the immigrants came from Mallorca and Valencia. At the beginning of the twentieth century, they came mostly from Aragón, with which Catalonia has close historic ties. In the 1920s, the newcomers were predominantly from Murcia, which – although Castilian-speaking – was partly conquered by Catalans. But the influx after the civil war and during the *años de desarrollo* consisted of an increasing proportion of Andalusians. Since this was by far the largest and longest 'wave', the Andalusians came to form the biggest single group of 'immigrants' in Catalonia. With their gracious, passionate temperaments and their love of flamenco and bullfighting, the Andalusians were not merely not Catalan but the heirs to a very potent alternative culture.

This is only one of several reasons why it proved more difficult to assimilate the most recent wave of immigrants than it had been to integrate those who arrived before the civil war. The immigrants of the twenties arrived at a rate of between 25,000 and 35,000 a year, their numbers peaking in the period from 1927 to 1929 because of the need for labourers to complete two major public works, the Barcelona Metro and the 1929 Exposición Universal de Montjuic. At the time, it must have seemed as if they would never be absorbed. The 'Murcians' as they were all called – even though a sizeable minority originated elsewhere – were a disorderly and uncouth crowd. Crimes of passion, previously almost unknown in Catalonia, became quite common. Even after they could afford to buy better food, many stuck to the lunch of bread and onion that had sustained them in the fields of the poor south. 'Murcian' acquired a pejorative connotation – first in Catalonia and then in the rest of Spain – that it has never quite lost.

The attitudes and behaviour of the 'Murcians' appalled the native Catalans who dubbed them *Xarnegos* (a word probably derived from *Xarnec*, a pejorative expression for someone who is half Catalan and half French) and accused them of 'coming to take the bread out of our mouths'. This wholly unfair accusation was based on the fact that a tiny minority of immigrants had been imported as strike-breakers – by Catalan businessmen. During the civil war, the denizens of the immigrant quarter of Torrasa put up a famous notice at the entrance to their suburb that read 'Catalonia stops here. This is the start of Murcia.' In one area the anarchists pre-empted Franco by putting up posters forbidding people to speak Catalan in the streets. Nevertheless, by then, most of the immigrants of the twenties had begun to digest influences that would turn them into Catalans. In typically Catalan fashion, their assimilation took place by way of the language.

In the thirties it was not difficult to learn – in fact it would have been hard for a Castilian speaker not to have picked up – a working knowledge of Catalan. The immigrants came to live in districts where the shopkeepers spoke Catalan, and went to work in factories and on sites where in all probability the foremen spoke Catalan. There was Catalan on the radio, and for those who could read there was Catalan in the press. Their children learnt Catalan at school. By the time a further wave of immigrants began to arrive, the 'Murcians' of the twenties were in a position to look down on the benighted newcomers from the standpoint of a common language and shared experiences. The elderly 'Murcian' whose support for Catalan nationalism was more passionate than that of any native and who had christened his eldest daughter Monserrat became a recognized stereo-type in Catalan society.

The most important reason why the post-war immigrants were so difficult to assimilate was their sheer numbers – a quarter of a million in the forties, nearly half a million during the fifties and almost a million during the sixties. The tidal wave swept over Barcelona and into the rest of Catalonia. When Spain's 'economic miracle' came to an end, almost one in five of the population of the other three provinces was of immigrant stock. Because of their numbers, the immigrants of the forties, fifties and sixties often ended up in areas where only the priest, the doctor and perhaps the schoolteachers and the shopkeepers were Catalan by origin.

It is against this background that the freedom the Catalans have acquired since the return of democracy to teach and promote their language must be judged, for it has been the principal factor in making Catalonia more homogeneous again.

By the time that Franco died, the Catalan language had entered a crisis. Research highlighted two specific malaises which, if allowed to continue, would sooner or later finish it off.

The first was that, since Catalan had not been taught in schools, could not be written in the press and was not used by officialdom, a lot of people who could speak Catalan were nevertheless illiterate in it. And even those Catalans who were literate in their own language were so accustomed to a world in which documents, books and newspapers were in Castilian that they found it tiring to read and write in Catalan. The second problem – which only became apparent as the result of a survey published in 1978 – was that, contrary to what one might expect, fewer people spoke Catalan at home than spoke it at work, in the shops and so on. This, the survey found, was because where a native had married an immigrant the couple almost always ended up speaking Castilian, which the Catalan-speaking partner had learned properly at school, rather than Catalan, which the Castilian-speaking partner had picked up unsystematically. It was clear that unless something was done the children of these marriages would grow up using only Castilian.

Since the restoration of the *Generalitat*, immense changes have been brought about. Catalan is to be seen on road and street signs throughout the Principality (and increasingly in the Balearic Islands and Valencia as well). It can be heard on radio and television. Catalans are free to publish newspapers and magazines in their mother tongue. And the vast majority of their children are nowadays not only taught Catalan, but taught *in* Catalan.

The 2001 census indicated that the number of Catalan-speakers in Catalonia itself had risen to 76 per cent from around 60 per cent at the time of General Franco's death. In both the other main Catalan-speaking areas within Spain, however, the proportion appeared to have fallen – from 55 per cent to 50 per cent in Valencia and from 75 per cent to 60 per cent in the Balearic Islands. However, the number of people who could understand Catalan had risen dramatically over the same period in all three areas. It was up from 80 per cent to fully 97 per cent in the Principality, from 70 to 89 per cent in Valencia and from 80 to 95 per cent in the Balearic Islands.[*]

Even so, the figures tend to understate the scale of the changes that have taken place since the return of democracy. An entire generation that is more than simply bilingual has already emerged from schools in Catalonia. The young people who compose it are usually more at ease speaking, and even reading and writing, Catalan.[†] Their speech is frequently shot through with Castilianisms and upsets the purists, who have reproachfully dubbed it 'Catalan light'. But it is Catalan for all that, and a lot of those who speak it make frequent grammatical errors when they have to communicate in Castilian.

Nationalists pooh-pooh the idea that Catalonia is on its way to something closer to monolingualism than bilingualism. They point out that commercial television, for example, broadcasts exclusively in Castilian. Nevertheless, one suspects that their denials are coloured by fear of the reaction in Madrid to Catalonia's rapidly growing *de facto* separateness from the rest of Spain. It is certainly not difficult to imagine that within, say, a quarter of a century Castilian in Catalonia could occupy a position rather like that of English in Scandinavia – a second language that people are able to speak exceptionally well, but a second language nevertheless.

---

[*] The percentages in all cases are calculated as a proportion of the number of Spanish citizens in each Autonomous Community.

[†] A survey carried out for the Barcelona edition of *El País* in 1989 showed that, for the first time since figures had been recorded, a section of the population – those aged between fourteen and seventeen – preferred to read in Catalan.

CHAPTER 19

The Galicians

The *Prestige* tanker disaster* focused attention on one of the least-known corners of Western Europe. Spaniards like Galicia's Atlantic beaches. But, were it not for the pilgrimage route to Santiago de Compostela, few foreign holidaymakers would venture into this damp, poor, dolefully beautiful territory jutting out over Portugal. And, indeed, few ever get to visit the interior.

It was somehow to be expected that when Galicia finally attracted the world's attention it would be because of a tragedy, for there is no part of Spain, not even perhaps Andalusia or Estremadura, which has had such an unhappy history as Galicia.

'Spain's Voltaire', the Benedictine monk Benito Feijóo, who visited the area in the middle of the eighteenth century, has left this account of the typical Galician peasant:

Four rags cover his body or perhaps, given the number of tears in them, it would be better to say *un*cover it. His accommodation is as full of holes as his clothing, to the extent that the wind and the rain enter it at will. His food consists of a bit of black bread accompanied by some kind of milk product or some sort of root vegetable, but in such tiny quantities that there are those who have scarcely ever in their life risen satisfied from the table. Add to these miseries the tough, relentless manual labour which lasts from the first rays of dawn until the onset of night and anyone will be able to see that the life of these wretched peasants is more arduous than that of the criminals whom the courts send to the galleys.

Famines were quite frequent and whenever they occurred, as the local records bear witness, the streets of the major cities echoed to the laments and entreaties of semi-naked walking skeletons.

* See above, pp. 74–5.

The last great famine was in 1853–4, but Galicia remained the scene of considerable hardship. It became the poorest of Spain's seventeen Autonomous Communities and, until just a few years ago, it was not at all uncommon in the inland provinces of Lugo and Orense (Ourense) to see old women trudging along country lanes laden down like pack animals with crops or kindling.

Galicia fell victim to the dynamics of Spanish history. Unlike Catalonia, it was Romanized slowly and incompletely. But in common with the Catalans, the Galicians had very little contact with the Moslems. One of the earliest Asturian monarchs seems to have asserted his control over the coast in the middle of the eighth century, although it was only in the reign of his grandson in the first half of the ninth century that the whole region was finally restored to Christian rule. Thereafter, however, the attention of its rulers was drawn inexorably southwards by the desire to reconquer the peninsula. As power passed to the states to which the Asturian monarchy gave birth – first León and then Castile – the Galicians found themselves progressively more isolated from the centre of power.

The Galicians' frustration at being tied to a Crown whose interests were not their own manifested itself at a very early stage in uprisings organized by the nobility, and it is against this background of discontent within the region that the discovery of St James's tomb ought perhaps to be seen.

According to legend, it was found by a shepherd in a field to which he was guided by a star. The field became the site of a cathedral and of a city which took the name of Sant Iago (St James) de Campus Stellae (of the field of the star). An alternative etymology is offered by the fact that St James's supposed tomb lies in what had previously been a burial ground. Compostela, according to this view, derives from *composta* (burial ground) plus the diminutive *-ela*.

At all events, the discovery provided the Asturian monarchy and its successors with a reason – or perhaps a pretext – for showering gifts and privileges on the town which grew up around the tomb. Right up until the nineteenth century the Spanish monarch paid an annual sum to the city, called the *voto de Santiago*, ostensibly in return for the saint's patronage. The effect was to create within a potentially turbulent province a city with every reason to support the central government.

As early as the fourteenth century, the Galicians were left without any representation in the Cortes. They played no part in the *Mesta*, the sheep-farming cartel whose influence brought such benefit to the farmers of the *meseta*, or in the trade with the Americas which was bestowed on the Andalusians, or in the industrial revolutions that transformed the Catalan and Basque provinces. Instead, they became a favourite target for steep taxes and military levies.

The railway from Madrid did not reach Galicia until 1883 and as the region entered the twentieth century its only industries, apart from the naval dockyard at La Bazán founded in the eighteenth century, were a modest textile industry in Corunna, a few tobacco-manufacturing and food-processing businesses and some canning. Typically, the cans came from elsewhere. The region was perhaps entitled to expect preferential treatment from Franco, who was himself a Galician from El Ferrol. But although the region undoubtedly benefited from the general increase in living standards throughout Spain during the *años de desarrollo*, during which period it acquired some important new factories (notably the Citroën plant at Vigo), the main change was a more efficient exploitation of the region's natural resources – hydroelectricity and timber. As recently as 1989, 34 per cent of the population still worked on the land – by far the highest proportion in any region of Spain.

Galicia's agriculture, moreover, was woefully backward. Unlike most of the other peoples of early northern Spain, the Galicians had been unable to relieve the pressure of population growth by mass migration southwards. The Asturians were able to spread into León and ultimately Estremadura. The Basques and Cantabrians were able to spread into Castile and ultimately Andalusia. The Aragonese and the Catalans had Valencia. But Galicia's southward expansion was blocked by the creation of Portugal, a state with which Galicians had no political ties. The only other people who found themselves in this predicament were the Navarrese. But unlike Galicia, which was bounded by the sea, Navarre could and did expand northwards.

Hemmed in on all sides, the Galicians had no option but to divide the same amount of land into smaller and smaller plots. The majority of farmers came to own only tiny amounts of land consisting of several isolated patches. Time was wasted travelling between plots, land was wasted beneath the walls that separated one plot from another, and the size of the holdings and the variety of the crops frequently made the introduction of machinery uneconomic. It was not very different from strip-farming in the Middle Ages. Indeed, the Galician peasantry had until the twentieth century to pay feudal dues called *foros* – long after other such medieval legacies had disappeared from the rest of the country.

Any people who have been as badly treated as the Galicians are entitled to be mistrustful, and among other Spaniards they have a reputation for caution and guile. In Castilian, an ambiguous statement is a *galleguismo* (Galicianism). In this respect, if in no other, Franco was a true son of Galicia – he was famed for his cryptic remarks and always let his ministers argue out a case before he intervened.

Poverty also breeds superstition and Galicia has long been the heartland of Spanish witchcraft. The foremost textbook of Galician magic, *O antigo e verdadeiro livro de San Cipriano* – better known simply as the *Cipranillo* – has gone through countless editions. Belief in the evil eye is widespread and the region is rich in *meigas* (witches) and *curanderos* (folk doctors). It is a legendary haunt of the werewolf, called *lobis-home* in Galician.

To an even greater extent than in the Basque country, women have traditionally enjoyed a high standing in society and a generous measure of influence. Galicia's national hero is a woman – María Pita, who distinguished herself by her bravery during the English siege of Corunna in 1586; and several of the region's most promi-nent intellectuals – the poet Rosalía de Castro, the novelist Emilia Pardo Bazán and the penal reformer Concepción Arenal – have been women. It could be just another legacy of the matriarchal society which existed in northern Spain in pre-Roman times. But it must also owe something to the fact that women in Galicia, for hundreds of years, assumed responsibilities which in other societies were taken on by the men, simply because their menfolk were away in other parts of the country, at sea or abroad.

An awful lot of nonsense has been written over the years about the Galicians' propensity to emigrate. It used to be fashionable to ascribe it to their typically Celtic thirst for adventure. But as one Spanish writer remarked, 'The next time you see one of those emigrating Celts, give him a potato and you will straight away transform him into a sedentary European. What makes "the adventurous races" adventurous is lack of potatoes, lack of bread and lack of freedom.'

It has been estimated that during the past five centuries one in every three Galician males was forced to abandon his homeland. The earliest permanent emigration was in the sixteenth century, when thousands of Galicians were settled in the Andalusian Sierra Morena in an effort to repopulate areas that had been left deserted by the expulsion of the Moslems and the Jews. Thereafter, the focus shifted to the big towns of Andalusia and to those of León, Castile and Portugal, where the Galicians were only too happy to take on the menial and servile jobs that the locals spurned. Domestic servants, for example, were invariably Galician. But small-scale internal migration could only palliate the pressure on land which has always been at the root of Galicia's problems. As has been seen, the Galicians were blocked on land both to the south and the east. To the north and west lay the ocean, and that – in a sense – is where they finally found an outlet.

For almost two centuries, beginning in the second half of the eighteenth century, after the restrictions on settlement in the New World were lifted, a steady stream of Galicians set off to find a new life in Argentina, Uruguay, Venezuela, Cuba and the other states of Latin America. Such was their desperation – or innocence – that in the 1850s, after the Caribbean plantation-owners had been forced to free their slaves, a Cuban of Galician extraction was able to find some 2,000 of his countrymen to take their places. In much of South America, *gallego* is synonymous with 'Spaniard'. Perhaps the most famous contemporary descendant of Galician immigrants is Fidel Castro, whose surname derives from the Galician word for a Celtic hill-fort.

But not all the emigration was permanent. Every year, until the early part of the last century, between 25,000 and 30,000 Galicians of both sexes marched in great gangs to and from the *meseta* where they brought in the harvest. Each of these gangs was made up of a set number of reapers (*segadores*) and binders (*rapaces*), and headed by a foreman called the *maoral*. As they marched along, with their sickles slung over their shoulders, these weatherbeaten nomads, who have passed into the literature of Castile as well as Galicia, must have been a fearsome sight.

The opportunities for emigration to South America dried up in the fifties at almost exactly the moment when the post-war boom in

Europe began to gather momentum, creating an alternative market for cheap labour. Between 1959 and 1973 about a quarter of all the Spaniards who left to work in other parts of Europe were Galicians. But the onset of recession blocked that route too, and meant that some Galicians would be more easily tempted into earning money by means that were both profitable and pernicious.

With its heavily indented coastline, Galicia has long been closely associated with smuggling. Until recently, the main commodity was tobacco. Cigarettes were unloaded from cargo ships on the high seas, whisked into shallower waters aboard high-powered speedboats, and then unloaded on to little inshore fishing-boats that could thread their way through the *rías*. The trade still continues, but in the eighties it was joined by a vastly more dangerous traffic – in cocaine from Latin America.

It is noteworthy that the two communities where it has proved easiest to find people ready to trade in drugs are those historically most neglected by their fellow-Spaniards – the Gypsies and the Galicians. In the same way as has happened with the Gypsies, drugs have brought a mixed legacy to Galicia. Cocaine has left many addicts in the communities through which it has passed. It has fostered the emergence of organized crime. But it has also undeniably brought prosperity.

The Socialists' return to power in 2004 brought new hope from a less tainted source. José Luis Rodríguez Zapatero comes from another sorely deprived area, León, the territory between Galicia and Old Castile. Soon after taking office, he announced a €6 billion programme that promises to transform the infrastructure of north-western Spain and make Galicia more accessible to the rest of the country.

It is one of the paradoxes of Spain that Catalonia, which was independent (if fragmented) for three centuries, ranks as only a principality, while Galicia, which only enjoyed a separate existence for three brief spells totalling eleven years in the ninth and tenth centuries, is conventionally referred to as a kingdom. Galician nationalists see in the popular rebellions that took place in Galicia during the later Middle Ages – and particularly the great uprising of 1467–9, organized by peasant brotherhoods called *Irmandades* – evidence of a patriotic awareness. Modern historians tend to see them more as anti-feudal outbursts. But it is undeniable that from earliest times there was a consciousness among Galicians of being Galician and this was recognized by Fernando and Isabel when they set up a *Junta General del Reino* comprising representatives from the Galician provinces – one from each – to oversee the region's economic and political affairs.

Galicians themselves often believe the roots of their uniqueness are ethnic. Galicia, they will say, is the region of Spain in which the Celts most comprehensively swamped the indigenous population when they arrived in the peninsula around 1000 BC. Exhibit Number 1 is the *gaita*, or bagpipes – as traditional in Galicia as in Scotland or Ireland. There is a good deal of evidence, though, to suggest that all this is a mid-nineteenth-century myth propagated by Galicia's nationalists. In ancient times, the region seems to have been no more Celtic than the rest of the peninsula, and any Celtic speech there was dead long before the end of Roman rule.

Nevertheless, Galicia does have a language of its own, *galego*. If Catalan looks like a cross between French and Spanish, then Galician looks like a cross between Spanish and Portuguese.

Indeed, defenders of *galego* are divided between those grouped around the Real Academia Gallega, who view it as a language in its own right, and the proponents of *lusismo* and *reintegracionismo*, who regard it as one of the two variants of a common Gallego-Portuguese language. The latter argue that the norms adopted by the Academia are enshrining the Castilianization of a language that is constantly under threat of infiltration by the more widely spoken neighbouring tongue. A form of *galego* littered with Castilianisms, known as *castrapo*, is widely spoken in the bigger cities on the coast. The prevalence of *castrapo* needs to be borne in mind when assessing the figures for language use and comprehension in Galicia.

It is arguably the part of Spain where Castilian Spanish is least widely spoken. But whether what is spoken instead is truly a language, or merely a dialect, is open to debate. At all events, the 2001 census showed that more than 99 per cent of the population said they understood *galego* and 91 per cent said they knew how to speak it. In both cases, the figures were higher than for Catalan in any of the Catalan-speaking territories and far higher than for Basque in the Basque country.

The Galicians may not share with the Irish, Welsh and Bretons a common ancestry, but they do live in a similarly wind-swept, rain-sodden land on the edge of the Atlantic, and so it is not perhaps surprising that they should have many of the characteristics associated with Celtic races – a love of music, a fascination with death, a tendency towards melancholy and a genius for poetry. It is appropriate therefore that the rise of Galician nationalism, like that of Catalan nationalism, should have coincided with a literary revival. Indeed, there was an element of imitation. The Galicians, like the Catalans, had their Floral Games – inaugurated two years after those in Catalonia – and just as Catalonia enjoyed a *Renaixença*, so Galicia had a *Rexurdimento*. But for all that, it is arguable that Galicia's renaissance was of greater literary importance. The outstanding figures of the *Rexurdimento* are the poet Eduardo Pondal, the historians Manuel Murguía and Benito Vicetto, and above all Murguía's wife, Rosalía de Castro. The illegitimate daughter of a priest, rejected by society, unhappily married and, towards the end of her life, racked by cancer, she was a quintessentially Galician figure, who suffered as much in her lifetime as her homeland has in its history. Her *Cantares Gallegos*, published in 1863, is one of the great works of Spanish literature.

It was not, however, until after the publication of Alfredo Brañas's *El Regionalismo* in 1889 that the nationalistic sentiments inherent in the *Rexurdimento* began to assume a political shape, and then only in a relatively timid form. The first truly nationalist group was the Irmandade dos Amigos da Fala, founded in Corunna in 1916 by Antonio Villar Ponte. Forced underground soon afterwards by Primo de Rivera's coup, Galician nationalism surfaced again at the start of the Republic in the form of the Partido Galleguista and it was this movement which negotiated a statute of autonomy for Galicia. The statute was put to the vote on 28 June 1936. The turnout was almost 75 per cent and, of those who took part, more than 99 per cent voted 'yes'. Nineteen days later, the civil war broke out and Galicia's hopes of home rule were dashed.

The referendum nevertheless put the Galicians on the same footing as the Basques and Catalans as a people with a separate culture who had verifiably laid claim to self-rule, and that made it difficult for governments of the post-Franco era to deny them a comparable status. But for the moral authority that that vote accorded them, it is more than likely that Galicia's plaintive lament would have gone unnoticed in the raucous clamour for self-rule that issued from the other regions and peoples of Spain.

CHAPTER 20

Autonomy in Action

The system of self-government that emerged from the hurly-burly of the late seventies, and which the Spanish dubbed the *estado de las autonomías*, was by far the most determined and comprehensive attempt ever made to resolve the internal tensions that have plagued their modern history.

It has been said that its defining characteristic is its 'variable geometry'. In no other country, perhaps, has a solution been applied which, while covering all the regions in that country, permits such wide variations in the nature and scope of the powers allotted to their administrations. At the outset, the constitution divided the various Autonomous Communities into three different sorts: those that reached self-government by way of a 'fast track' set out in article 151; those that reached it on a 'slow track' set out in article 143;* and finally Navarre, which – alone of the Spanish regions – already enjoyed a measure of autonomy.

By 1983, all the regional home-rule statutes had taken effect and the following year legislation to adapt Navarre's existing autonomy provisions came into force. The new laws created substantial differences between the powers of the various regional administrations. The Basque country, Catalonia and, to a more limited extent, Galicia, all got their own police forces, whereas the other 'fast-track' region, Andalusia, did not. All four acquired the right to operate their own television channels, but so too did Valencia, a 'slow-track' region that also won a limited right to police itself. The Canary Islands' statute too was more generous than those granted to the other 'slow-track' regions.

* See above, pp. 38–9.

In the Basque country and Navarre, moreover, a traditional arrangement was re-established whereby the regional authorities collected the taxes and handed over to the central government sums – known in the Basque country as the *cupo* and in Navarre as the *aportación* – which notionally corresponded to the services provided by Madrid. In the rest of Spain, the procedure was the reverse: Madrid collected the taxes and gave to the regional administrations what they were reckoned to need. From the very beginning, it was the 'variable geometry' of the system that aroused most controversy and disquiet.

Those who worried that the *estado de las autonomías* could lead to Spain's disintegration feared it was preparing the way for endless demands from regional politicians that would gradually weaken the bonds between the Autonomous Communities and the state. The specific concern was that politicians in the 'slow-track' regions would seek powers to match those accorded to the 'fast-track' administrations, and that, if they succeeded, it would encourage their counterparts in the 'historical nationalities'* to reinstate their privileged status by seeking powers beyond those conceded in the constitution. This is precisely what has happened.

When confusion over the UCD government's plans for the regions was at its height in 1980, Felipe González – then the leader of the biggest opposition party – had proposed a law to eliminate the ambiguities in the section of the constitution that dealt with regional government. It eventually became a reality and was given the laborious title of the Institutional Law for the Harmonization of the Autonomy Process. It soon became known by its initials, the LOAPA.

At the heart of this much-debated piece of legislation was an attempt to clarify the question of whether state law should prevail over regional law. What distinguished the regions that had achieved a measure of self-government by way of article 151 from those that had attained it via article 143 was that they were entitled to lay claim immediately to powers in certain areas that the constitution reserved in principle for the central government. But the LOAPA stipulated that, where there was a conflict between state and regional law in those areas, state law should always prevail, even after the relevant powers had been delegated to a particular region in its statute of

* See footnote on p. 39.

autonomy. The nationalists of the 'historical' regions – and particularly the Basques – argued that the LOAPA was an attempt to limit the scope of their statutes without having to submit the changes to a referendum, as required by the constitution. The lines were drawn for a bitter and lengthy battle.

Nor did it end with the approval of the LOAPA by parliament in June 1982, because the law's opponents referred it immediately to the Constitutional Court. It took the Court more than a year to reach its decision, but when it was eventually delivered – in August 1983 – it was a bombshell. The judges declared that more than a third of the LOAPA was unconstitutional, including those clauses that guaranteed state law supremacy over regional law in those areas where the Basques, Catalans, Galicians and Andalusians had been given powers denied to the rest.

Reservations about the 'variable geometry' of Spain's new system of self-government were inspired by more than just concern at the threat, whether perceived or real, to the country's unity. There was also a fear that differences between the powers granted to the various regions could exacerbate the disparities that already existed between the richer and poorer parts of Spain. The Autonomous Communities given the broadest powers, the Basque country and Catalonia, were also among those with the highest GDP per capita, and it was argued that unless some kind of corrective mechanism was introduced they would draw apart from the rest of the country economically as much as politically.

In 1985, therefore, a Law on the Financing of the Autonomous Communities (known as the LOFCA) was passed which, among other things, was intended to help close the gap between rich and poor regions. A pool of cash, known as the Inter-territorial Compensation Fund, was created, from which the poorer Autonomous Communities could be provided with assistance. Thereafter, attention switched to the transfer to the regional governments of the powers they had been granted in their statutes, together with the human and financial resources needed to exercise them.

In the case of the regions that came under article 143 of the constitution, the transfer was conceived as a two-stage process. Though they were initially denied powers granted to the Autonomous Communities that came under article 151, they stood to acquire at least some of them once a period of a few years had elapsed. In 1992, following numerous delays, representatives from the PSOE and the PP sat down to negotiate an agreement on how many of these extra powers the 'slow-track' regions should be given. A number of new responsibilities were agreed, of which the most important was perhaps university education.

That still left another big difference between the fast-track administrations and Navarre on the one hand, and the slow-track administrations on the other: the latter, with the exceptions of Valencia and the Canary Islands, did not control public health care or the vast spending power that went with it. Over the next ten years, however, this gap too was whittled away as the remaining Autonomous Communities all acquired their own regional health services and the money to run them.

The fact that the Autonomous Communities were being given far broader powers than had originally been envisaged forced a change in the way they were funded. A deal agreed in 1996 gave the regional administrations automatic access to a far bigger share of the taxes collected in their region, including 33 per cent of income tax, 35 per cent of VAT and 40 per cent of the excise duties on alcohol, tobacco, petrol and the like. This made their financial arrangements more akin to those of the Basque government which, in a separate deal, saw its own powers to raise and spend cash further enhanced.

The construction of the *estado de las autonomías* has still not been finished. But the transfer of responsibility for public health care to the last regions in 2002 meant the bulk of this vast enterprise had been completed. How united or disunited is Spain as a result? Has it become, as you often hear Madrid politicians insisting, the EU's most decentralized nation? Is it true, as they claim, that the 'historical nationalities', and particularly the Basque country, enjoy greater real autonomy than anywhere else in Europe? Or are the regionalist nationalists correct in stressing that Spain is not a federation and arguing that those European countries that are federal – Germany, Austria and Belgium – have more genuinely decentralized forms of government?

There is evidence to support both views. Power in Spain has not been passed upwards to the centre in a true process of federation, but downwards from it, so the Autonomous Communities do not have some of the powers retained by the states that make up Europe's federations, notably the right to take part in the formulation of national government policy. This does not, however, detract from their own capacity for self-government, and there is hard evidence to show that this is very extensive indeed. According to statistics compiled by the OECD, in 2001 Spain's regional administrations were already responsible for a higher percentage of public expenditure than the *Länder* of either Germany or Austria. Since then, the figure has increased considerably with the transfer of public health spending to those Autonomous Communities that did not already have control of it. By 2002, it was higher than the comparable figure for the US states. In fact, by the OECD's reckoning, the only member countries with a more decentralized form of government were Canada and Australia. Not even in Switzerland did the cantons have as much spending power as Spain's Autonomous Communities.

Interestingly, the 'historical nationalities' all opted initially to be governed by the right. The first Basque and Catalan elections handed power to the centre-right nationalists of the Basque Nationalist Party (PNV) and Convergence and Union (CiU). In Galicia, it was not the nationalists who won but the People's Alliance, a Madrid-based party, albeit one founded and led by a Galician, Manuel Fraga.

The turbulent politics of the Basque country, which has increasingly come to be known as Euskadi, have since led to several changes of *Lehendakari*, or President. But the PNV has remained throughout the dominant force in government.

The leadership of the Catalan *Generalitat* went to a former banker, Jordi Pujol, who came to power on the quintessentially Catalan slogan '*Anem per feina!*' ('Let's go to work!'). Pujol was the embodiment of many traditional Catalan values – sober, astute, conventionally Roman Catholic (his wife was the head of the local anti-abortion movement), and above all boundlessly proud of his country's language and culture.

Pujol remained in charge for a quarter of a century and planned to hand over the *Generalitat* to a hand-picked successor. But support for Convergence and Union had gradually eroded, and at the Catalan election of 2003 a rival nationalist party, the pro-independence Esquerra Republicana de Catalunya (ERC), doubled its share of seats in the assembly and put itself in a position to decide the next government.

The ERC chose to ally itself, not with CiU, but with the Catalan wing of the Socialist party. The Socialists' leader, Pasqual Maragall, a highly successful former mayor of Barcelona who had steered the city through the 1992 Olympics, became the new President of the *Generalitat*.

That was an upset. But, for political thrills and spills, none of the Autonomous Communities has so far matched Galicia.

The earliest head of the Galician *Xunta* was a cultured elderly doctor, Gerardo Fernández Albor. However, day-to-day power soon came to be exercised by his conspiratorial deputy, Xosé Luis Barreiro. In 1987, having failed in a plot to unseat Fernández Albor, Barreiro took over a small centrist party. He then linked up with the Socialists to approve a motion of censure that ousted the People's Alliance. A year later, corruption charges were laid against Barreiro – by then re-established as the *Xunta*'s Vice-President – so that it was against a background of seething controversy that the Galicians approached the regional elections of 1989. Manuel Fraga, founder of the People's Alliance (by then re-christened the People's Party), opted to stand as its candidate, having long since accepted that his Francoist background precluded him from the premiership. The result was a landslide, with Fraga winning an absolute majority of seats in the local assembly, largely at the expense of Barreiro's party. He subsequently became an unlikely convert to the cause of regional autonomy, governing Galicia like a patriarch until 2005.

By then, he was 82 years old. Yet nothing could stop him from running for a fifth term that he very nearly secured. The vote was so close that it was decided by Galicia's big emigrant postal ballot. There were claims that Venezuela's president, Hugo Chávez, had held back sacks full of votes to favour the left in Galicia and that Fraga had called on his long-standing – and wholly unlikely – friend, Fidel Castro, to get them released. In the end, Spain's longest-serving elected official and last political link with the Franco era was ousted by just 10,000 votes. The result brought to an end a remarkable career. Manuel Fraga never lost his authoritarian temperament. But he made a priceless contribution to the construction of post-Franco Spain by showing Spaniards of the right – and particularly the hard right – that they could have a role, not just in democratic politics, but in the autonomous regional institutions they so mistrusted.

Could they have been justified in those suspicions, though? Has

Spain, in fact, benefited from the *estado de las autonomías*? Has decentralization enhanced or impaired the efficiency of government? Has it narrowed or widened the gap between rich and poor regions? And could it, as the centralists have long feared, be edging Spain towards break-up?

The first and most important point, I think, is that it had to be tried. This is a point that can only really be grasped by someone who lived in Spain in the period after General Franco's death. Such was the pent-up frustration of the regional nationalists after thirty-six years of unbending centralism that, if the government of the day in Madrid had insisted on retaining the existing system, there would have been a revolt in one or several areas. Almost certainly, someone would have declared independence or proclaimed a republic, and then the army would have stepped in, tipping that part of Spain into civil strife and setting the country as a whole back by years. It is all very well for the PP's leader, Mariano Rajoy, to warn about the threat of 'Balkanization', but the moment at which Spain was really in danger of going the way of the former Yugoslavia was before, and not after, it embarked on its experiment with decentralization. The pros and cons of the *estado de las autonomías* need to be weighed with that in mind.

The problem with striking a balance is that, for the moment at least, the benefits are less easily quantifiable than the drawbacks. And, just to make things more difficult, there is disagreement over which is which. Decentralization has unquestionably led to inequalities. A primary school teacher in the Basque country, for example, nowadays earns 25 per cent more than his or her counterpart in Galicia. But that reflects the need to compensate teachers in the Basque country for the area's higher living costs, and many economists would argue that regionally negotiated pay deals are more likely to arrive at a just wage for the region in question than a nationally negotiated one. However, one advantage of the old system was that it encouraged talented people in all areas of public service in poor regions to remain in them. The danger with the new one is that they will gravitate to the richer, higher-paying Autonomous Communities, leaving their native regions more deprived than they are already.

The creation of seventeen different governments, legislatures and judiciaries has led, not just to unevenness but also to incongruity.

Until the Zapatero government legalized gay marriages, for instance, a same-sex couple living in a village in Navarre could enjoy rights that would be denied to them if they moved a few miles away into La Rioja. Decentralization has undoubtedly made Spain a more complicated place and often complication leads to delay, particularly in cases where two administrations of different political colouring need to reach agreement on shared or disputed responsibilities. There are any number of examples of this, but just to take one: a plan to save the last of Spain's Iberian lynxes was held up for years because of wrangling between the Socialist administration in Andalusia, where the lynxes live, and the then conservative government in Madrid.

There is also a danger that some parts of Spain could become fiefdoms of a single party, or even a single individual. The upsets in, first, Catalonia, and then Galicia, have lessened that risk. But that still leaves Euskadi, which has been run continuously by the PNV for more than a quarter of a century, and where it has become almost impossible to win advancement in public service without a nationalist background. Similar situations have developed with the Socialists in Andalusia and Estremadura.

However, autonomous government also holds out the promise of making Spain a lot more competitive. Being closer to the people they serve, the regional governments ought to be more efficient both at raising and spending cash. What is more, there is a natural tendency for them to compete in the provision of services, both for the sake of regional pride and because they are subject to a degree of comparison by those who live in one part of Spain but regularly visit others. Such comparisons need to be made more widely available, though. The publication of benchmarks in areas like health and education would provide a huge incentive to the less efficient administrations to improve.

The economic impact of autonomy is almost impossible to assess. This is partly because the authorities have so far not published any figures to show which regions emerge as net beneficiaries and contributors. But another reason is that so many other factors have a bearing on whether a region becomes richer or poorer. In the table of per capita regional GDP, Asturias has fallen sharply since being granted its statute. But is that because its autonomous government has not been as adept as others in exploiting the powers at its disposal?

Or is it perhaps because the Principality has been saddled with a dying, 'rust-belt' economy? Almost certainly, it is the latter.

Similar, circumstantial factors may have had a crucial impact on the gap between Spain's best-off and worst-off regions. But it is nevertheless the case that, as the transfer of power from the centre has gathered pace, a drift towards greater inequality has been checked and very slightly reversed. In 1981, the richest part of Spain was the Balearic Islands where per capita GDP was 25 per cent above the national average. The poorest area was Estremadura where the comparable figure was 38 per cent below. The span was 63 per cent. Ten years on, the Balearic Islands and Estremadura, still at the top and bottom of the table respectively, were 72 per cent apart. By 2003, Madrid had taken over as Spain's most prosperous Autonomous Community while Estremadura remained the poorest. Per capita GDP was 35 per cent above the national average in Madrid and 35 per cent below it in Estremadura. The overall gap had shrunk to 70 per cent.

Not that that was much consolation to the people of Estremadura whose situation relative to the rest of the population was scarcely any better than it had been more than twenty years earlier. Their long-serving regional president, Juan Carlos Rodríguez Ibarra, has been a persistent critic of greater decentralization on the grounds that it could allow the richest Spaniards, and particularly the Catalans, to shirk their responsibilities to their poorer compatriots. The Catalans, for their part, point to statistics indicating that since the mid-1990s they have lost ground to other regions, and particularly Madrid.

The figures cited earlier would suggest that Mr Rodríguez Ibarra's fears are unfounded – so long as the present system remains. Things might change, however, if Catalonia, which accounts for a fifth of Spain's total output, were to acquire greater autonomy. This was one of several fears raised in a heated debate over a measure promoted by the new President of the *Generalitat*, Pasqual Maragall, that won the backing of José Luis Rodríguez Zapatero who, like Maragall, depended on support from the radical nationalist Esquerra Republicana de Catalunya. The controversial new legislation amended the Catalans' autonomy statute, gave their government powers similar to those of the Basques and Navarrese to raise taxes and, most emotively of all, included a reference to Catalonia as a 'nation'. It gave the *Generalitat* broader control in several areas and made it a duty for residents of

Catalonia to learn Catalan. The new statute was debated, first, by the Catalan parliament and then by both houses of the Cortes in a process that lasted the best part of a year.

Though it was progressively watered down, conservative politicians continued to warn that the measure would open the way to the break-up of Spain. The PP called for a nationwide referendum and got up a petition in support of its demand that attracted the signatures of 4 million people – 10 per cent of the population. Such were the feelings aroused by the proposals that some Spaniards even took to boycotting Catalan sparkling wine, *cava*. Altogether more disturbingly, the commander of Spain's land forces, Lieutenant-General José Mena Aguado, warned in a speech that the suggested new arrangements could trigger a clause in the constitution that entrusts to the armed forces the duty of defending Spain's 'territorial integrity and constitutional arrangements'. He was immediately put under house arrest and later dismissed.

In June 2006, the new statute was put to a referendum in Catalonia and approved by 74 per cent of those who voted. However, less than half the electorate turned out, so while Maragall and the other supporters of the reform were able to claim a victory, their claims had a slightly hollow ring. There were hopes that the implementation of the new statute would put a cap on Catalan demands for many years to come. But it was equally clear that it would set off new calls for wider powers from the other Autonomous Communities, and that the Basques in particular would press for a new and more comprehensive statute in the talks following ETA's ceasefire.

More than a quarter of a century after Spain began to experiment with autonomy, the issues posed by its ethnic and cultural heterogeneity remained to be resolved. What is more, in the meantime, and for reasons that had nothing to do with Basque blood types or Catalan language usage, Spain had become even more ethnically and culturally heterogeneous.

PART FIVE

A Changing Society

CHAPTER 21

New Arrivals and Old Prejudices

Every morning, the cleaning firm's vans would drive over to Torremolinos from Málaga, arriving in the square at around seven a.m. Waiting for them would be a throng of men from all over the world, illegal immigrants or *sin papeles* ('without papers'), as they are known in Spain. After a quick count and some hurried exchanges, the men would be bundled into the vans to be driven off to various sites on the Costa del Sol.

But on 31 August 2004, when the vans arrived, the waiting immigrants were not alone. The police were there too. They arrested the owner of the company, two of his relatives and several of his employees, along with thirty-two illegal aliens. They included Uruguayans, Romanians, Moroccans, Colombians, Moldavians and Ghanaians.

'I warned him,' the company's lawyer said afterwards of the owner. 'But he always told me he couldn't find the manpower he needed.' The police said in a statement that the workers were being paid miserable wages for a working day that was longer than allowed by law.

The work-hungry clandestine immigrants. The exploitative, but also perhaps genuinely frustrated, employer. It is a story with parallels to be found throughout Europe.

As regards immigration, Spain, as in so many other ways, has come to resemble the rest of the EU. Statistics in this area can be misleading because they often leave out immigrants who have yet to legalize their situation. But in Spain illegal immigrants have an incentive for registering themselves with the local authorities because that way they get access to health care, and so official estimates tend to be more than usually reliable. In 2006, it was reckoned that Spain's immigrant population had reached 3.7 million people, or 8.4 per cent of the whole population. That was higher than the EU average and, proportionally, more than in France. But what really made Spain exceptional was the speed with which its sizeable immigrant community had come into being. It had quadrupled in size since 2000.

Until the mid-1980s, indeed, Spain's cultural and religious make-up was still much as it had been for almost five centuries. The Jews – or rather, those who refused to become *conversos* (converts) – had been expelled in 1492 to become the Sephardim.* The Moslem equivalents of the *conversos*, the *moriscos*, stayed on, pretending, in many cases, to be Christian, for more than a century after the fall of the kingdom of Granada. But between 1608 and 1614, the vast majority† of the *moriscos* too were rounded up and driven out. Over the almost 400 years that followed, those few *conversos* and *moriscos* who remained intermarried with the so-called 'Old Christians', and even where that did not happen most gradually lost their sense, or knowledge, of being different. The only significant exception to this general rule was represented by the Chuetas of Mallorca. The descendants of Jews who had been forcibly converted in 1435, they remained a compact group within island society, fully aware of their origins. They were known to other Mallorcans as *judíos* or *hebreos*. Most lived and owned jewellery shops in Palma on a particular street, Calle de las Platerías, and used a church that was built on the foundations of the old Great Synagogue of Palma. In 1948, following the foundation of the state of Israel, one of their number wrote to the new Prime Minister, David Ben-Gurion: 'Regretfully, we know very little of Jewishness, and therefore urge you to supply us with books on Judaism in Spanish. We Chuetas yearn to return to our people.'

* J. H. Elliott in his *Imperial Spain 1469–1716* (Harmondsworth, Pelican, 1963) put the number of Jews in Castile and Aragón at that time at around 200,000, of whom 120,000–150,000 fled rather than embrace Christianity. Those who remained joined an already considerable number of *conversos* (also known pejoratively as *marranos*) whose ancestors had converted to escape death in the anti-Jewish riots at the end of the previous century. Elliott reckoned that before the expulsions of 1492 the number of *conversos* was at least as great as the number of practising Jews. He estimated the overall population of Castile and Aragón at the end of the fifteenth century to be around 5.5 million, so it would seem that *conversos* and their descendants continued to make up at least 6 per cent of the population of Fernando's and Isabel's ethnically cleansed territories.

† Elliott estimates 275,000 out of a total population of 300,000.

On the mainland, the populations of entire villages in remote parts of the country retained customs such as not eating pork. And, in the 1970s, I was told of families in Madrid in which it was customary to light candles on a Friday night, though nobody understood – or admitted to understanding – why they did it.

Elsewhere there were small communities, normally inhabiting a handful of villages, who faced discrimination from their neighbours and came to be known as the *pueblos malditos* ('damned or cursed peoples'). The most fanciful theories grew up to explain why this should be: that they were fugitive Roman slaves or, in one case, lost Chaldaeans. The truth was usually more prosaic. The Vaquieros of Asturias and the Pasiegos of Cantabria seem to have been discriminated against for no other reason than that they followed a way of life – transhumance – that was different from that of the people around them. In at least one other case, the facts were more bizarre almost than the legend. Research carried out in the 1970s showed that the Agotes of Navarre were the descendants of lepers who had begged along the pilgrimage route to Santiago de Compostela.*

Far from being the uniform nation that the Catholic Monarchs and their successors hankered after, Spain was a patchwork of languages and cultures – Catalan, Basque, Galician, etc. However, the only sizeable minority from outside the peninsula was the Roma.

The first Gypsies arrived in Spain in the early fifteenth century. There is evidence that they were initially well received, possibly because they claimed – or were taken – to be pilgrims. But they soon fell foul of the growing enthusiasm for an ethnically homogenous state. By 1499, Fernando and Isabel were ordering the expulsion of the 'Egyptians who go wandering about our realms'. Any found without a job or a trade after sixty days would be liable to 100 lashes.

---

* Though never classed as *pueblos malditos*, there were also, scattered around western Andalusia, communities made up of the descendants of African slaves who had been brought to Europe in the fifteenth century. The biggest surviving community is at Gibraleón near Huelva. In 1989, the newspaper *Diario 16* reported that there were still some 100 inhabitants who described themselves as *morenos* (coloureds). There were other, smaller communities in Niebla, Moguer, El Chorrito de Huelva and Palos de la Frontera.

Over the next three centuries, numerous efforts were made to force the Roma to conform or leave – much the same choice that had been presented to the Jews and Moslems. Legislation was enacted forbidding Gypsies to use their language, known as *caló*, join guilds, hold public office and even marry among themselves. But it was all to no avail, and the fact that the Roma stayed in Spain in such numbers would seem to indicate that bouts of fierce repression alternated with long periods of resigned inaction.

Around the turn of the nineteenth century, the situation of Spain's Gypsies began to change. The liberal Constitution of Cádiz of 1812 recognized them for the first time as Spanish citizens and, though prejudice and discrimination continued, the country's lawmakers stopped enacting coercive legislation. At the same time, Roma, particularly in Andalusia and Estremadura, began to find roles for themselves in the rural economy, mostly as blacksmiths and horse traders. Many gave up the nomadic life and became fully integrated into local society. Some found their way to the cities, and entire *barrios* like Triana in Seville and Santiago in Jerez became predominantly Gypsy. The growth in popularity of flamenco music* enhanced the status of Romani culture. And while it can scarcely be said that the Roma were freed of oppression, as is clear from the words of so many flamenco songs written during this period, many Spanish Gypsies nevertheless look back on the nineteenth century and the first half of the twentieth as a golden age.

What brought it to an end was the progressive mechanization of the Spanish countryside, which made redundant both the Roma's favoured rural professions. A lot of Gypsies drifted into the cities from the countryside and settled in shanty towns on the outskirts. So too, of course, did millions of *payos* (non-Gypsies). But whereas most of the *payos* moved on to a better and more prosperous life, the *calés* (Gypsies) did not. In the mid-1970s, a book-length study of the Roma who lived in the Madrid shanty towns† found that, contrary to legend, the proportion of Roma who worked was as high as in the rest of the population. However, Gypsies tended to work shorter hours, they were more likely to have more than one profession, and

* See below, Chapter 30.

† *Gitanos al encuentro de la ciudad: del chalaneo al peonaje*, Equipo GIEMS, Madrid, 1976.

the proportion of working women was much higher in the Roma community. Part of the year was often spent harvesting, but the chief normal source of livelihood was scrap dealing, followed by street vending. Only 1.3 per cent of the capital's Gypsies at that time made their living by begging.

What was even more fascinating about this study, though, was that it made absolutely no mention of the two factors that were to have the biggest impact on Romani life in Spain over the next three decades. One was evangelical Protestantism. Back in 1950, a French convert from Catholicism to Protestantism, Clément la Cosset, decided to dedicate his life to winning over the Roma. One of his admirers, Claudio Salazar, brought the movement to northern Spain and in 1969 the Spanish government recognized it as the Iglesia Evangélica de Filadelfia, though it soon came to be known among Gypsies themselves as the Aleluya. Since then its preachers have made steady inroads into what was traditionally a Roman Catholic community. The Aleluya offers the Roma a livelier, noisier, more participatory form of worship and a Church they can justifiably call their own. In what looked suspiciously like a belated counter-attack, the Vatican in 1997 beatified a Gypsy, Ceferino Jiménez Malla, also known as *El Pelé*, who had been executed by Republicans in 1936 for trying to prevent the arrest of a priest.

The other development in Romani life was of a very different kind: the spread of drugs and drug peddling. The latter actually preceded the former. For the narcotics wholesalers, Spain's deprived Roma communities offered ideal territory in which to establish a network of retailers. The technique was to lure just one Gypsy in a particular settlement into peddling drugs. His sudden affluence soon made him the envy of his peers and a chain reaction was set off. Within a short while, a stream of young *payos* would be visiting the settlement. But the chain reaction rarely stopped where it was meant to. Eventually, one of the Gypsies marketing drugs would be tempted to try his own wares. The combined effects of rapidly acquired wealth and growing drug addiction had a devastating effect on Romani society and, in particular, on the authority traditionally exercised by elders.

I suspect that it was drugs more than anything that spurred the government into tackling the age-old problem of what to do about the Roma. Since the coming of democracy, individual local authorities in many parts of Spain had made determined efforts to ensure that the Gypsies in their area were given access to proper schooling and housing. Their efforts frequently encountered determined opposition from the *payo* majority and, on occasions, it degenerated into violent protests. In 1988, the central government stepped in to launch a *Programa de Desarrollo Gitano* (Programme for Gypsy Development), which was intended, among other things, to facilitate access to the many welfare benefits and services to which the Roma were entitled.

By the mid-1980s, when Spain joined the EU, it was an anomaly in the European context. It was culturally highly diverse. There were the Basques, the Catalans, the Galicians and at least half a million Roma.* Yet Spain had almost no foreigners. The only immigrant community of any size was made up of sub-Saharan Africans who had been recruited to work on the farms of the Maresme, a predominantly agricultural area along the coast north of Barcelona. The word *inmigrante* was still used mainly to describe a Spaniard who had moved from the countryside to the town two or three decades earlier. And *racismo* meant prejudice against Gypsies.

Yet, unnoticed at first, the situation was changing. Impressed by the evidence of Spain's new stability, increasingly large numbers of other Europeans were buying retirement homes in coastal and rural areas. Meanwhile, a steady trickle of immigrants from outside the EU was entering the country, both legally and illegally.

By far the largest group consisted of Moroccans entering the country across the Straits of Gibraltar. The most popular method was to pay for a crossing aboard a *patera*, the local Spanish name for a kind of flat-bottomed boat equipped with an outboard motor, which is used for inshore fishing on both sides of the Straits. Most *pateras* are designed for up to seven people, but the immigrant traffickers were soon packing in as many as twenty-five.† In any case, *pateras* are fragile, easily capsized vessels that are not intended for the open

---

* In 2004, the government estimated there were 600,000–650,000 Roma in Spain.

† The earliest gangs were based at Nador in the Rif mountain range of northern Morocco and are thought to have been involved in drug smuggling before they turned their hands to migrant trafficking. Their agents were originally to be found around the Socco Chico, a square in the labyrinthine old quarter of Tangier.

seas, let alone a stretch of water notorious since classical times for its unpredictable winds and idiosyncratic currents. It was not long before the bodies of the unfortunate began to be washed up on the southern coast of Spain.

In the big cities, the demand for cheap domestic labour was attracting growing numbers of Latin Americans. The earliest substantial community came from the Dominican Republic. The Dominicans often took jobs as nannies and gardeners in the more prosperous suburbs. In 1992, a Dominican, Lucrecia Pérez, had the sad distinction of becoming the first person to die in modern Spain as a result of anti-immigrant violence. She was killed when gunmen stormed an immigrant squat in the prosperous Madrid suburb of Aravaca.

The authorities had anticipated the problems of illegal immigration with a seemingly draconian law, passed in 1985, which said that any foreigner found without the required documents was subject to deportation within seventy-two hours and without a right of appeal.

But, as is so often the case in southern Europe, appearance and reality were two different things. The problem was one of identification. Before deporting someone, it was necessary to know where they came from, and if they had torn up their papers on arrival, that – in many cases – was impossible. Moroccans and other North Africans could often be speedily identified and returned. But the sub-Saharan Africans, who were being detained in growing numbers, usually presented an insuperable problem. Politicians announced, and journalists reported, substantial figures for the number of 'expulsions'. But what was actually happening was that the immigrants concerned were being served with expulsion *orders* and then let go. Once freed, they joined the swelling ranks of the earliest *sin papeles*. In 1986, the Socialists declared the first of many amnesties enabling immigrants already in Spain to legalize their situation.

If all this sounds like a rather half-hearted policy for stemming immigration, then it needs to be stressed that the official attitude was profoundly ambivalent. On the one hand, no one could openly condone illegal entry. On the other hand, there was no realistic way in which poor, non-EU citizens could enter legally, and it was increasingly clear to politicians and officials that immigration could be beneficial to a country like Spain with an ultra-low birth-rate. Without it, there was a danger that the active population would become too small to support the inactive population, with the result that Spain's nascent welfare state would collapse.

The PP came to power vowing to clamp down on illegal immigration. José María Aznar's government tightened up surveillance of the Straits of Gibraltar by, among other things, building a line of watchtowers along the coast. But the effect was to divert African emigration away from the Mediterranean and towards the Atlantic. Increasing numbers of migrants began arriving in the Canary Islands, particularly Lanzarote and Fuerteventura. What is more, the numbers arriving from Africa were soon outstripped by those coming in by other routes. Huge numbers of Latin Americans, particularly Ecuadorians, who did not need a visa, were entering Spain by plane and simply overstaying. At the same time, immigrants from Romania and countries further afield, including China, were getting through the EU's eastern frontier and making their way across the continent. As a result of the so-called Schengen agreement, which Spain signed, the EU had been largely free of internal border controls since 1995.

It was not until 2000 that the Aznar government managed to steer a comprehensive new immigration act through parliament. The new law came into effect after two vast regularization processes that saw some 380,000 immigrants obtain their papers, and was meant to put a stop to illegal entries once and for all. It gave those who had become legally resident in the country all the benefits to which Spanish nationals were entitled and set up a quota system so that a small number of immigrants could in future enter the country in an orderly fashion. But the illegal immigrants were a different matter altogether. They were banned from joining trade unions, holding public assemblies and going on strike. The new law denied them access to the housing aid and free schooling they had enjoyed up until then. And it also gave the government the power, not just to order, but to effect, the deportation of illegal immigrants. Once again, however, there was a gap between what was proclaimed and what actually happened. Indeed, there were several.

The quota system failed miserably. Employers found it much easier to hire workers 'on the black'. The act kept open a loophole whereby immigrants could still get access to health care by registering with their local authority. And, once again, tens of thousands of expulsions were ordered but not carried out.

Despite all the 'get-tough' rhetoric, the PP's years in office saw immigration rise on a gradually steepening curve until, in Aznar's second government, it became vertiginous. The increase in arrivals from outside the EU was particularly marked. Over the four years to the end of 2002, the number of non-EU citizens living legally in Spain tripled. In some parts of the country, the suddenness of the increase was astonishing. In 1996, at the start of the PP era, the Valencia region, for example, had a foreign population of fewer than 15,000, or 0.4 per cent of the total, and almost all of them were Europeans. By the beginning of 2003, there were more than 440,000, or 9 per cent, and the vast majority were from outside the EU.

What makes this upsurge all the more remarkable is that it occurred at a time when unemployment in Spain, though falling, was still the highest in the EU. There were, however, several sectors in which the demand for labour was just not being met because Spaniards aspired to better-paid, and less strenuous work. They included catering, agriculture, construction and domestic service.

By far the largest single national group within Spain's immigrant community was from Morocco. But during the second Aznar government, the biggest increases were in the numbers arriving from Latin America. By the end of the period, the Ecuadorians, Colombians and Peruvians all outnumbered the Dominicans.

Every big city now had at least one immigrant *barrio*. In Madrid, a quarter of the population in the Centro district was foreign and there were primary schools where 90 per cent of the children were the sons and daughters of immigrants. Out in the countryside, immigrant labour was being used to cultivate entire areas, like the 200 square miles of Almería that had been covered with plastic sheeting to create the vast hothouse that supplied much of Europe with its winter cucumbers and tomatoes.

Meanwhile, the beneficial effects of immigration were making themselves felt. Spain's birth rate rose for the first time in many years in 2001 entirely because of its immigrant population. Eight per cent of the women who gave birth were foreigners. Two years later, the OECD noted that what legalized immigrants in Spain paid to the state was more than twice what they got back.

Yet few people outside government were aware of these facts, and it was to be wondered how long Spain could go on assimilating immigrants at this rate without a risk of severe racial tension. The EU's statistics office, Eurostat, estimated that, of the half a million immigrants entering Europe each year, slightly less than a quarter – around 115,000 – were settling in Spain. A UN study had earlier concluded that that was not nearly enough. It reckoned that as many as 200,000 immigrants a year were needed to guarantee Spain's continued economic growth and the preservation of its welfare system. But that is looking at things from a standpoint that takes no account of prejudices.

I doubt if Spaniards are inherently more racist than anyone else, and indeed the answers they give to pollsters have long suggested that they are actually less prejudiced than other Europeans. They themselves tend to feel that that is because of their own relatively recent experience of emigration; that it makes them more understanding of others who have decided to leave their homelands and families in search of a better life.

However, many of those now entering the country are Moslems, and Spain in 2004 was the target of a mass bombing by Islamist extremists that provided the worst possible start for a multi-ethnic society.

Spain has not experienced immigration for almost 600 years and, such has been the pace of events, Spaniards have not had much time in which to develop the kind of sensitivity on racial issues that has long been impressed on Britons and Americans. Anyone in Spain today over the age of twenty-five grew up with comic strips in which offensive terms like *kafir* ('Kaffir') were cheerfully bandied around. The clearly pejorative *moro* ('Moor') is commonplace. So is *negrito* ('Darkie'). All one can do is hope that the broad tolerance to which I have alluded before as the outstanding trait of the new Spain can be extended rapidly to the newest Spaniards.

CHAPTER 22

Welfare: The Spanish Exception

At the start of this book, I mentioned a visit I made to Estremadura. I wanted to visit a remote district known as Las Hurdes. For a long time, whenever Spaniards wanted to talk about the underdevelopment in their country or the gross inequalities in their society, they would cite Las Hurdes. This was largely because of Luis Buñuel. In 1932, the surrealist film-maker made a documentary about the area which, though speedily banned, helped spread an awareness of the grotesque deprivation in remote parts of Spain.

Buñuel's 'first surrealist documentary' took more than a few liberties with the truth. It portrayed the *urdanos* as quasi-savages: not just oppressed, but ignorant and superstitious. A lot was nonetheless true. The *urdanos* really did suffer from inbreeding and disfiguring goitres. They lived in hovels with slate roofs that were insufferably hot in summer and miserably cold in winter. The roofs did not even keep out the rain properly, so gradually water seeped into the beams and, from time to time, a hovel would collapse, killing or maiming those inside.

The idea in the back of my mind was that Las Hurdes might provide me with a new introductory chapter. Like so many other parts of Spain in the past thirty years, it would have been transformed beyond recognition, and the changes it had undergone would give me a way to start explaining the transformation of Spain as a whole.

I drove into Las Hurdes from the south on a recently improved, two-lane road and in the towns and villages along it the signs of modernization were evident. I saw several restored houses. The shops seemed well-stocked. There were signs everywhere announcing infrastructure projects co-funded by the European Union.

Caminomorisco, the biggest town in Las Hurdes, had a brand new Casa de Cultura.*

But then I turned off the main road on to one of those lanes asphalted with help from Brussels and climbed up through woodlands till the asphalt ran out and the lane became an unmade track. I pressed on and found myself in a village high in the hills on the steep banks of a gurgling stream. I could have been in, say, Morocco.

The terraced plots on the other side of the stream were mostly untended, but here and there you could see women in traditional straw hats leading donkeys. In the village itself, old ladies sat on their doorsteps, clad in black from head to foot. I saw no one with goitre, but there were still plenty of slate-roofed hovels, though most now – a villager told me – were used for keeping animals. The village did not have any shops but, he said, there was a bar. He directed me to a house on a precipitous slope with nothing about it to suggest it was different from any other in the village, except an open front door. I stepped through the bead curtains and, for a moment, my suspicion that I had made a mistake became a certainty. It was pitch dark. Then something moved in a corner. A voice said 'Buenas tardes'. A light went on and I could see an elderly man shuffling towards a counter on which stood jars of pickled olives and peppers. He had been sitting in the dark, rather than waste electricity, while he waited for a customer. I imagine he had been waiting for a very long time.

He poured me a drink and then – this may have been a great honour – he switched on a little television behind the bar. It happened to be a day on which the late Pope John Paul II was visiting Madrid and the TV was supplying live coverage. As I sipped my beer, we watched as the 'Popemobile' made its way down the Paseo de la Castellana, past the skyscrapers of the AZCA district where many of Spain's financial institutions have their headquarters. Expensively dressed Madrileños waved flags and blew kisses at the cavalcade. It was like seeing a transmission from another planet.

'The young people have all gone,' said a man outside whose own three children all now lived in the capital. 'We used to make our money out of olives, but these days it costs more to get them to market than

* Casas de Cultura serve as meeting-places for the community, but can also be used for concerts, lectures, exhibitions and the like. They often incorporate a library too.

they fetch. Some people grow peppers. Some people gather snails. But what we all really live off are our pensions,' he said.

I certainly hadn't got what I was looking for, but I had had a valuable reminder that Spain remains a country of huge imbalances. The richest region, Madrid, has a per capita income almost twice that of the poorest region, Estremadura. And there are cities in Estremadura that seem like New York when compared to the heart-rendingly desolate village I found in Las Hurdes. Within the big cities themselves, there are equally immense disparities between some of the working-class suburbs and inner-city, 'old money' districts like El Viso at the top of the Calle Serrano in Madrid.

This is to some extent because Spain is a comparative newcomer among the world's developed economies. There has just not been time to iron out the wrinkles. It is also, to a much larger extent, because, alone among European nations, Spain became an advanced, industrialized state under the aegis of a right-wing dictatorship. Some of Franco's ministers, who retained a loyalty to the principles of early fascism or believed sincerely in Christian ideals, did care about social equality. But there were plenty who paid it no more than lip service. By the time the dictatorship ended, Spain had a welfare state of sorts. But it only covered about three-quarters of the population and, in many areas, the benefits it offered were negligible. Since then, welfare provision has been extended. But while the health service is now available to 100 per cent of the population, social services and social security are not.

In this respect, Spain is an anomaly. When Britons and Americans think of Western continental Europe they tend to see a jigsaw of interlocking welfare states, all spending sizeable proportions of their wealth on handouts for the unemployed, the disabled and the sick. It would be a great mistake to view Spain in such terms.

It may be because of its frontier history and the resulting social emphasis on self-reliance. It may be because Spain's post-Franco politicians unconsciously absorbed many of the attitudes and prejudices of latter-day Francoism. But the fact is that successive governments have taken a stand-on-your-own-feet, no-time-for-shirkers approach that would do credit to any US Republican. And, until recently, this was as true of the left as it was of the right. Felipe González's Economics and Finance Minister, Carlos Solchaga, once told a meeting of his fellow-Socialists that 'the state is not there to pay for idlers'.

The Socialists who regained power with José Luis Rodríguez Zapatero are of a different stripe. One of Zapatero's earliest moves was to announce an increase in minimum pensions of twice the rate of inflation. Under his stewardship, Spain looks as if it could start to converge with other 'Old European' welfare states such as France, Germany and Italy. But the cumulative effect of the attitudes held by Zapatero's predecessors is still clearly legible in international statistical comparisons. In 2002, only one other EU nation spent a lower share of its GDP on social security.

Arguably, the biggest gap in Spain's welfare system is in the area where there has long been greatest need. Ever since the seventies, the outstanding characteristic of the economy has been an inordinately high unemployment rate. Not even the job-creation bonanza of the Aznar years succeeded in getting the rate below 10 per cent, and by the time the PP left power Spain was still the only country in the then fifteen-member EU in which it ran to double figures. It was also the one with the highest percentage of insecure jobs: much of the employment created during Aznar's term was based on short-term contracts that allowed workers to be hired and fired with ease.

Yet barely half the unemployed were entitled to unemployment benefits. School-leavers did not qualify at all. The assumption – a very Mediterranean one – was that they could live at home, supported by their parents. To qualify for benefits, workers had to have held down a job for at least twelve months and the duration of the payments to which they were entitled varied according to how long they had been making contributions into the scheme.

This situation, however, was a lot better than at times in the past. In 1983 restrictions imposed by the Centrists pushed the proportion of the unemployed entitled to unemployment benefits down to 26 per cent. In the economic downturn of the early eighties, some people fell in a matter of months from prosperous employment to begging on the streets. It took a general strike in 1988 to force the Socialists to make substantial adjustments to the system, but within five years the proportion of the jobless entitled to unemployment benefit had reached almost 70 per cent. Then it fell back again as the Socialists imposed fresh restrictions – a policy that was redoubled when the PP came to office.

In view of Spain's high unemployment rate, it is understandable that successive governments should have shrunk from the task of providing every jobless man and woman with a living wage. But at no time have they created a 'safety net' benefit comparable to Income Support in the UK or Supplemental Security Income in the US. Once you lose your entitlement to unemployment benefit in Spain, you may be entitled to a so-called *salario social*, offered by the regional government. But it depends on where you live, and many people are unaware of their entitlement. In any case, the sums involved are distinctly modest.

The underlying assumption of successive administrations has always been that unemployed workers without an entitlement to unemployment benefit will be helped by their families. The politicians' reluctance to subsidize the jobless has saved the Treasury many fortunes over the years, but it also entailed a risk, particularly in the south of the country.

Back in the seventies, I was at a lunch with the then Prime Minister, Adolfo Suárez, when he was asked what it was that made him lose sleep at nights. The army? ETA? The price of oil? Or perhaps the runaway social security budget? Suárez began his answer by denying that he ever lost sleep. But he added that, if anything were to make him do so, it would be Andalusia.

It was a wholly unexpected reply. Nothing had happened in Andalusia that had not happened in the rest of Spain, and the movement in support of autonomy for the region had yet to get up a head of steam. But, as I later came to realize, Suárez – in common with every other Spanish politician of his generation – had been brought up to think of lush, balmy Andalusia, not as Spain's flower garden, but as its powder keg.

Traditionally, much of Andalusia and the smaller but even poorer neighbouring region of Estremadura has consisted of vast estates owned by absentee landlords and worked by huge armies of casual labourers. The potential for social unrest among these day-workers, or *jornaleros*, was evident even before mechanization made most of them superfluous. Migration from Andalusia and Estremadura to elsewhere in Spain, and later to other parts of Europe, in the fifties, sixties and seventies, offered a temporary safety-valve. But by the time Suárez came to power it had been closed off, and for some while parts of the south teetered on the edge of destitution. The nub of the problem was a lack of work between harvests – there were villages where, for a month or more each year, people gathered berries to fill their stomachs.

In order to stave off the threat of a peasant revolt, and that is what it came down to, the UCD provided the southerners with a community works programme intended to fill the gaps between harvests. But when the Socialists took office, led by the son of an Andalusian smallholder, they put into effect an altogether more comprehensive, and generous, solution.

Any Andalusian or Estremaduran who could provide evidence that he or she had worked the land for sixty days in a given year would qualify for nine months' of a special benefit, the *subsidio agrario*, to cover the period in which he or she was out of work.* Incredible as it may seem to outsiders, the assumption was that the land in the south of Spain was incapable of providing farm-workers with more than three months' employment in any one year.

And not only that. Fearing some *jornaleros* would be unable to find even sixty days' work on the land, the Socialists instituted a community works scheme of their own, and decreed that days worked for it could be counted towards the required number. *The Plan de Empleo Rural* (PER) sponsored projects for the improvement of local facilities. It enabled ditches to be dug, monuments to be scrubbed, and roads, gutters and pavements to be laid.†

The *subsidio agrario* was to become the outstanding exception to the generalization I made earlier, that Spain is a country in which people are vigorously discouraged from living off the state. Despite the fact that the number of *jornaleros* on the land was falling, the number of beneficiaries of the government's special dole rose to more than 300,000. It soon emerged that mayors in villages the length and breadth of the PSOE's heartland had been signing vouchers falsely crediting local people with however many days' work on the PER were needed for them to collect the *subsidio agrario*. In some cases, the beneficiaries were genuine *jornaleros* for whom there was not enough work. But

---

* Both the qualification and benefit periods were subsequently reduced, to thirty-five days and six months respectively.

† The *subsidio agrario* is often, though quite wrongly, referred to as the PER. This is now doubly mistaken since the PER has since been renamed the *Acuerdo para el Empleo y Protección Social Agraria*, or AEPSA.

most were simply country-dwellers who had seized an opportunity to obtain a steady, if modest, income for part of the year. A former councillor in charge of agriculture in the Socialist-run Andalusian government acknowledged that fewer than a third of all beneficiaries were genuine day-labourers. The majority were women, even though women had never outnumbered men in the fields.

Between them, the *subsidio* and the PER have changed Andalusia profoundly. There are village squares that have been re-paved to such a standard that you could imagine you were in rural California instead of one of the poorest regions in Europe. In villages where all the obvious work has been done, councils have been accused of presenting non-existent projects to the government and then diverting the labour and materials to their own ends. More than one mayor is reckoned to have acquired a new swimming-pool or house extension thanks to the PER.

Two points need to be stressed. The first is that the *subsidio* is no lavish handout. By 2003, it had risen to just €325 ($370 or £225) a month. The second point is that, since it has been brought within Spain's main welfare system, the Seguridad Social, the *subsidio* is not a handout at all. To qualify, claimants have to show that they have made monthly contributions, albeit very modest ones.

Nevertheless, it is fair to say that the *subsidio* has institutionalized underemployment in large parts of Andalusia and Estremadura. It has fostered the creation of an entire class that can use the dole money, combined with odd jobs here and there, to get by. The members of this class have little incentive to move off the land (though it can be argued that, with so few jobs elsewhere in Spain, there is little point in their doing so anyway).

At the same time, the rules laid down by Felipe González's Socialist government created a machine for the distribution of patronage. The mayors of Andalusia and Estremadura, most of them Social-ists, soon began to take over from the landowners as the arbiters of local fortune. Not surprisingly, both regions have remained PSOE strongholds to this day.

Equally unsurprisingly, José María Aznar's conservatives came to office determined to put an end to a system they viewed as both corrupt and the source of a 'culture of dependence' that was sapping the prospects for genuine economic growth in the south of Spain.

Yet – and this is another indication of the sensitivity of the issue – it was not until 2002 that the PP felt confident enough to make a move. By then, some 600,000 people were paying contributions to the scheme within the Seguridad Social under which the *subsidio* was made available. Some 320,000 had benefited from it the previous year. As part of a package of benefit reforms that came to be known as the *decretazo*, the government began dismantling the *subsidio*.* It closed the scheme to new contributors, excluded about a tenth of the existing contributors and made it considerably more difficult for the remainder to claim benefits. The scheme was to be wound up altogether by 2009. Those left out by the new rules were given access to two alternative, but much more restrictive, schemes.

The *decretazo* enraged the unions and prompted them to call a one-day general strike mirroring that of 1988. The 2002 stoppage was just as successful. A few months later, the government did a U-turn, effectively cancelling all its reforms, with the single exception of the phasing-out of the *subsidio*. Despite further protests, it stuck to its guns and, at the beginning of the following year, the necessary legislation came into force. During 2003, the number of claimants dropped to below 260,000. The Socialists vowed to reverse the PP's measures if elected. But after coming to power, they remained coyly silent on the issue.

The Seguridad Social itself was set up in the sixties to replace the various services provided by the *sindicatos*, insurance companies, mutual societies and the state-run Instituto Nacional de Previsión, which was founded shortly after the turn of the century. It is not the only welfare system in Spain – there are separate systems for local government, the civil service and the armed forces. But the Seguridad Social is certainly the biggest and offers a complete range of welfare provision – cash benefits, health care and social services.

The system has once already been in danger of going bankrupt – and could be again. As the recession of the late seventies and early eighties bit deeper, the first thing many companies did in an effort to cut costs was to suspend their social security contributions – something they were able to do then without fear of being penalized.

---

* But not the AEPSA (formerly PER). By 2003, the plan had an annual budget of some €125 million.

At the same time, the system had to cope with an upsurge in the demand for cash benefits. This was partly because a lot of people who had lost, first their jobs, and then their entitlement to unemployment pay had succeeded in wangling disability pensions to which they were not entitled. The main reason, though, was that in common with other developed nations Spain's population was getting older, and its social security system was having to pay out more and more in the way of old age pensions.

The problem was particularly acute in Spain's case because it was in this area that cash benefits were most generous. Generous was hardly the word. As a percentage of former earnings, they were the highest in Europe after Sweden's; nor was there any upper limit.

In 1985, however, the government introduced a comprehensive reform that restricted access to disability pensions and imposed much stricter limits on the value of retirement benefits. The effect was to put the funding of the Seguridad Social on an altogether sounder basis.

The main, contributory pensions are funded by deductions from earnings.* Employees give up 6 per cent of their salaries and employers add in a whacking 24 per cent that has been repeatedly criticized as a disincentive to job creation.

The growth of the economy from the mid-nineties onwards and the incorporation into the official labour market of large swathes of the 'black economy' led to a sharp rise in the number of contributors and, by 1999, the Seguridad Social was receiving more money each year than it was disbursing. Heartened by the turn-around, the PP linked pensions to inflation.

But the problem remains that, on average and allowing for the effects of inflation, pensioners draw more out than they have put in. Retirement pensions, which account for the lion's share, are still fairly generous. They are based on the number of years of contributions, but also on an average of the pensioner's earnings over the fifteen years before retirement. At the time of writing, a Spaniard's average state retirement pension was higher than that of a Briton

---

* There is also a non-contributory pension for those with an insufficient contributions record which is paid for by the state out of taxation. But it needs to be stressed that it is only available for those who are retired, widowed and/or disabled. It is not for able-bodied people of working age who lack other means of support.

notwithstanding the large disparity in average earnings between the two countries.

Experts agree that, as the proportion of elderly people in society climbs inexorably, the current system will become untenable. Most put the day of reckoning somewhere between 2010 and 2015. An ageing population will also start to exert considerable strains on Spain's public health service. Or rather, *services*. Because of the transfer of power to the regions, there are now seventeen of them.

The creation of a comprehensive state health service was one of the outstanding achievements of the Socialists' first spell in office. Yet, characteristically, Felipe González and his ministers did little to make the public aware of it. When they came into office, 86 per cent of the population was entitled to use the public health service and there were still instances of sick or even dying people being turned away from state-run hospitals because they did not qualify for treatment. The Socialists set about extending coverage to the entire population.

A *Ley General de Sanidad*, passed in 1986, was intended to be the keystone of the system for several decades to come. Unlike earlier health legislation, it was based on the premise that citizens should be entitled to use the public health service as of right rather than in return for contributions. As a result of regulations and definitions applied under the *Ley General de Sanidad*, the government achieved its goal of effectively total cover during 1991.*

Yet within barely a decade the entire system had been dismantled and parcelled out between the regions. A Basque police force may be more historically evocative; a Catalan television network more culturally significant. But politically and financially health care is by far the most important aspect of Spain's *estado de las autonomías*. In 2003, it accounted for 13 per cent of all government expenditure and, in several regions, the health budget represented more than half the money spent by the autonomous administration. How the regional politicians administer their health services will, to a very large extent, decide whether Spain's experiment in decentralization comes to be viewed as a success or failure.

* It should not be imagined that medicine in Spain became 100 per cent public as a result. There is still a large private sector, but by the early 2000s barely 10 per cent of Spaniards had private health insurance.

Having said that, there are strict limits to what they can do. The cash they receive for health care comes from an overall, national budget that is determined in Madrid. How much each region gets depends partly on the size of its population and partly on how many people there are on its territory over the age of sixty-five. The autonomous governments must spend their entire allocation on health care. That stops regional politicians from diverting cash from, say, a hospital to an election-winning new road project, but – it can be argued – it also deters them from looking for savings so as to be able to use the money elsewhere. If, however, an autonomous government wants, or needs, to spend more on health care than it has been allotted, it can divert money from other areas (excepting education), or it can levy additional excise on petrol.

Already, significant variations in health spending have emerged. By the time the system was fully decentralized, Navarre was spending 40 per cent more per head of population than Valencia. The Aznar government became increasingly concerned that decentralization might be taking the country backwards, to a situation in which some Spaniards were entitled to better health care than others, not because of the contributions they had paid, but simply because of where they lived. In 2003, parliament approved a government-sponsored law setting up a new agency to recommend common standards and another to monitor the way in which the regions were providing health care. The Act also created a so-called cohesion fund to reimburse those regions, particularly holiday areas, that treated a disproportionate number of patients from elsewhere in Spain.

Not the least of the problems created by decentralization is that doctors in, say, Benidorm now find themselves unable to access the records of a visiting patient from, say, Bilbao, because they are locked away in the computerized archives of a different health service. The Spanish propose to get around this snag by issuing everyone with a health card on which the patient's records will be held in a 'chip'.

The autonomous governments face quite a daunting task in convincing the public it is better off with regionally administered health services, because in the few years that it existed Spain's Sistema Nacional de Salud set high standards. The fear around the time of its birth was that not enough money would be available to cover the increased number of patients and the growing cost of both equipment and drugs. The period in the mid-eighties that saw the health service made fully comprehensive also saw hospital waiting-lists triple. The upswing in the economy in the decade that followed came just in time to fund improvements. By the time the process of decentralization was complete, hardly anyone in Spain had to wait longer than six months for a publicly funded operation, and in most cases the wait was between two and three months.

There were still some glaring imbalances. There were too many doctors (one for every 231 inhabitants compared with one for 595 in the UK) and around 25,000 were either unemployed or under-employed. Proportionately, too much was being spent on drugs. And while hospitals generally offered a high standard of treatment, the same could not be said of the clinics and practices that supplied primary care.*

Nevertheless, polls suggested a high level of public satisfaction and that was borne out by statistics. Spaniards' life expectancy at birth was the third highest in the EU and higher than that of either Britons or Americans. But that, in turn, represented a formidable challenge for Spain's social services.

By the time of the 2004 election, one in six of the population was over the age of sixty-five and more than a third of elderly people were reckoned to have problems of dependence. But although it had been clear for some time that Spain's working women were no longer willing – or indeed able – to fulfil their traditional role as unpaid carers, the authorities had done hardly anything to replace them. There were only enough residential places for 3 per cent of the elderly. As far back as 1993, a much-vaunted *Plan Gerontológico Nacional* had said that places were needed for at least 5 per cent. The PP had encouraged the spread of home help as a way of dealing with the problem without having to build more residential homes, but by 2004 it was available to only about 2 per cent of the over-sixty-fives.

As Spain becomes progressively 'greyer', the problem will only get worse unless vigorous – and costly – action is taken. But the question is – by whom? Part of the responsibility for social services has

---

*This explains the Spaniards' habit of going to hospital casualty units with complaints that, in other countries, would be treated by a general practitioner. It is a custom that has long infuriated, and frustrated, health planners.

always rested with local government and now much of what was once the responsibility of Madrid has been passed to the regions. What is needed is an understanding involving all three levels of government, but it will not be easy to negotiate.

CHAPTER 23

Education: More Aspiration than Achievement

One of the fondest memories I have of the early years of Spain's restored democracy is of the dank night I found myself in a bare, whitewashed storeroom in the shadow of the flyover that channels traffic from Bilbao into Rekaldeberri. Rekaldeberri is one of the satellite towns that sprang up during the industrial revolution that transformed the Basque country at the end of the nineteenth century. Before the civil war, it was known as 'Lenin's Nook', and until much later, when the flyover was built, gangs of youths roamed the borders of the area mugging anyone entering or leaving.

I had gone there to report on a meeting held to discuss the future of the 'People's University of Rekaldeberri'. 'University' was a more-than-somewhat grandiloquent title for what in essence was a scheme for twice-weekly night classes financed by a rag-and-bone operation – every week students toured the neighbourhood collecting jumble, which they then sold off. But it was nevertheless a brave attempt to bring some learning into a community that sorely lacked it and obviously felt the need for it.

I subsequently heard that the experiment collapsed a few years later. But it had not been in vain. Some of the councillors elected when the left took control of many of the towns and cities in the local elections of 1979 had heard about the Rekaldeberri project and decided to imitate it. The first municipally sponsored People's University was set up in San Sebastián de los Reyes near Madrid the following year. Unlike Rekaldeberri, where the curriculum mirrored that of a conventional seat of learning, the new generation of People's Universities tended to concentrate on imparting the basic knowledge, starting with reading and writing, that many working-class Spaniards had never had the chance to acquire.

The People's Universities movement reflected a thirst for education that had long been characteristic of even the most humble Spaniards. Under the Second Republic, it took shape in travelling libraries and in the *ateneos libertarios* and *casas del pueblo*, which were the anarchist and Socialist equivalents respectively of the *casinos* set up by the middle and upper classes so that members could read the newspapers and discuss the affairs of the day.

One can only hazard a guess at the reasons for this desire for learning. Certainly, it goes hand-in-hand with the Spaniards' traditional disdain for manual labour. But perhaps too it is another result of Spain's leap from a pre-industrial to a post-industrial environment. All too often in those parts of Europe which had a lengthy experience of industrialization, 'working-class values' have come to be synonymous with pride in a lack of education and culture.

Such an attitude is wholly lacking in Spain. *Educación* and *cultura*, and the words derived from them, have universally positive connotations in daily speech. *Culto* has come to mean 'educated' and *educado* 'well-mannered'. The opposites – *inculto* and *maleducado* – are really quite serious insults in Spain, and if you ever happen to be in a working-class bar when an argument breaks out, it is odds on that sooner or later you will hear someone tell his adversary that '*Tú no tienes cultura ni educación*' ('You're uncouth and bad-mannered').

A figure who loomed large in modern British writing, the working-class father denouncing his son for having 'betrayed his class' by going to university, has no equivalent in Spain. Quite the contrary. There is nothing the members of that vast 'new middle class' which emerged from twentieth-century Spain's economic, social and political tumult want to do more for their children than '*darles una carrera*' ('give them a university education'; 'put them through college').

This is partly because degrees are seen as badges of social achievement, of prosperity and the *cultura* that is felt to be its necessary accompaniment. However, in the context of the Latin family in which people are expected to share their good fortune with their relatives, a university education also represents a pretty shrewd financial investment. Graduates earn more. They also have lower rates of unemployment, so it is less likely that a son or daughter who has gone to university will be living at home at the age of thirty-odd, draining the family's resources. And Spanish parents do not have to make the same sacrifices as, say, US parents. Fees represent less than a quarter of the actual cost of a college education and Spanish parents do not normally have to pay for their children's accommodation. Since the universities are spread pretty evenly through the country and have more or less identical standards, most students continue to live at home. Nor is there the same temptation that exists in Britain, for example, for parents to urge their children into the labour market so that they make a contribution to the family income, or at least cease to be a burden on it. Unemployment has been so high among the young in Spain that the vast majority of students, if they were not in university, would be without a job anyway.

The Spanish schools system, like most others, is partly private. Just under 30 per cent of schools are outside the state sector and they are attended by slightly more than 30 per cent of pupils. Some are run by the Church. Others are operated for profit by secular proprietors.

By and large, the religious orders offer an excellent education. The Colegio del Pilar, run by the Marian Fathers in the fashionable Madrid *barrio*, or district, of Salamanca, is the closest Spain has to an Eton or Harrow. José María Aznar is an ex-*pilarista*, but so too is Juan Luis Cebrián, the founding editor of *El País*, the centre-left daily that was the PP government's most relentless critic. The most socially prestigious schools for girls in Madrid are both run by nuns: the 'Madres Irland-esas' and the 'Madres Francesas'. But the capital also has a number of first-rate secular schools including the Colegio Rosales, where Crown Prince Felipe was a pupil, those run by SEK, an international firm, and those that teach in a language other than Spanish, such as the Liceo Francés, the Colegio Americano and the Colegio Británico.

Not all private schools are as good and some are not up to the standard of the state schools. But the state schools came into existence to teach those whose parents could not afford to pay fees and they continue to suffer a certain social stigma.

The modern Spanish schools system was built on the 1970 *Ley General de Educación*, often referred to as the *Ley Villar Palasí* after the then Education Minister, José Luis Villar Palasí. The 1970 Act made it compulsory for children to attend school from the ages of six to fourteen. This compulsory education, known as Educación General Básica (EGB), was meant to be available free.

Perhaps the oddest aspect of the 1970 Act was that it made basic schooling compulsory at a time when there were still not enough places to go round. During the *años de desarrollo* the government had initiated a crash programme of school construction, but it had not yet caught up with the demand for new places created by the movement of population from the countryside to the towns, by increased prosperity (and expectations), and by the 'baby boom' which, from the late forties onwards, affected not just Spain but the whole of Europe. As late as 1977 when the UCD took power there was a sizeable gap between the number of children between the ages of six and fourteen and the number of places for them, so that the beginning of each school year saw harrowing scenes as children and parents were turned away from schools that had either not been completed or reached saturation point.

The problem for the UCD was that, at that time, some 40 per cent of the places were being provided by fee-paying private schools. This was a far larger percentage than was required by those families who actually wanted to pay for their children's education. A lot of parents who had to pay would rather have sent their children to state schools. The authorities could claim that there were now enough – or almost enough – places to go round. But the places on offer were not, as Villar Palasí's law required, freely available.

The Centrists' answer to the problem was to enlarge on a solution that had already been tried out by their Francoist predecessors, which was to give money to the private schools to enable them to provide their services free. In the years immediately preceding the Socialists' arrival in government in 1982 the increase in that part of the education budget devoted to private schooling was eight times the increase for the system as a whole. By the time the Centrists left office, only a handful of EGB schools were not receiving state aid.*

The Socialists inherited a situation in which the government was paying the piper, but was unable to call the tune. It was meeting the costs of the private schools, yet it could not, for example, insist that they give preference to local children. Because of the unplanned way in which schools were built and pupils enrolled, children often had

---

* Since then, state funding has been accepted by almost the entire private sector. Those few that have refused government subsidies and still charge fees, like most of the schools run by Opus Dei, constitute a genuine elite.

to travel long distances to get to school when there were schools in the vicinity filled with children from other parts of the city. There were children in Madrid, where the situation was particularly dire, who were spending five hours a day travelling from one side of the city to the other on buses which the government provided specifically for this purpose – 2,000 of them in the capital alone.

The *Ley Orgánica del Derecho a la Educación*, or LODE as it is known, which was passed in 1984, made a government subsidy conditional on the private school in question accepting the same criteria for admissions as those laid down for state schools. It stipulated that every school should have a governing body, called the Consejo Escolar, with the power to appoint the Head. The Consejos are made up of the Head, together with representatives of the proprietor, the teachers, the parents, the pupils and the school's non-teaching staff. The LODE also decreed that teachers' salaries were to be paid directly by the government, rather than – as before – from the government subsidy at the proprietor's discretion.

Not surprisingly, the LODE was regarded by many middle-class parents as a threat to the educational exclusivity of which their children had seemed assured. With the backing of the Church, they set out to block it. No single piece of legislation laid before parliament during the Socialists' first term of office caused as much controversy as the LODE. Demonstrations brought hundreds of thousands of parents on to the streets. More than half the government's total allocation of parliamentary time was taken up debating the numerous amendments to the bill tabled by the opposition, and it was not until after an unsuccessful appeal to the Constitutional Court that it finally came into effect. The government's determination to see it on to the statute book more or less intact was a measure of its conviction that only a radical measure of the kind represented by the LODE could open the way for a more egalitarian, and perhaps more secular, Spain.

The LODE transformed the relationship between the state and the schools, but it did not pretend to tackle shortcomings in the structure and operation of the system which have become increasingly apparent with the years.

Ironically, given the Spaniards' thirst for – one might almost say, obsession with – learning, they have an educational system that falls a long way short of their aspirations. The OECD's so-called PISA survey in 2000, which compared the achievements of fifteen-year-olds, ranked Spain 'well below the average on most scores'. Some 30 per cent of secondary school students finish their courses without any sort of qualification.

The reasons for this widespread failure have become a subject for intense and heated political debate. Though the running of Spain's schools and universities is now a matter for the Autonomous Communities, the central government retains a decisive role in the framing of educational policy, no doubt because politicians sense that it is an issue of such overriding concern for the electorate.

Money, though it is sometimes raised, is not really the issue. When prosperity came to Spain during the *años de desarrollo*, education received the largest share of the new-found wealth. Between 1962 and 1976, the share of the budget given to education more than doubled, whereas the proportion spent on health and social services rose by just over half, and the share allocated to housing actually fell.

Since then, spending on education has continued to climb and, by 2001, it accounted for 11.3 per cent of public spending. That was below the OECD average of 12.7 per cent, but only 0.1 per cent less, for example, than in Britain. It has been pointed out that as a share of the country's annual output, its GDP, government spending on education has failen in recent years from a peak in the early nineties. More could no doubt be spent and, under José Luis Rodríguez Zapatero and the Socialists, it probably will be. But there is a widely held feeling that money is not really at the root of Spain's educational failings and that it will only improve when politicians change the way the system actually functions.

Things start promisingly enough. Pre-primary education, which most experts believe is crucial to a child's educational receptiveness, is very widespread. The late sixties and early seventies saw an upsurge of enthusiasm for nursery education, with first the private and then the public sector racing to fulfil the demand. For some parents, it represented an opportunity to give their children a better start in life than they themselves had had. But for others it was simply a cheap and socially acceptable way of getting the children off their hands so they could work. A lot of nursery schools in Spain are more nurseries than schools. Nevertheless, standards have risen since.

In 2004, almost half the total number of children under six were receiving some form of schooling, a figure well above the OECD average. By then, the PP government, in a move that recalled the UCD government's handling of basic education, had decided to make all pre-primary schooling free, regardless of whether it was made available in a privately owned school. Critics decried it as another means of subsidizing the private sector with public money.

The current organization of Spain's compulsory schooling is the work of the Socialists. In 1990, they steered through parliament a law, the *Ley de Ordenación General del Sistema Educativo*, or LOGSE, that gave the system its biggest shake-up since the days of Villar Palasí. The LOGSE made schooling obligatory to the age of sixteen. Primary education from the ages of six to twelve leads into what is known as Educación Secundaria Obligatoria (ESO) which lasts for four years and is intended to provide students with a high-school certificate known as a *Título de graduado en educación secundaria*. At that point, children can choose between leaving school, doing a one- or two-year further professional training course, or continuing their academic studies with the aim of obtaining a *bachillerato* at the age of eighteen. Those who do not then go on to university have the opportunity to do the advanced part of the vocational training before they start looking for a job.

It is in primary education that the first grounds for concern arise. Educationalists say one of the main reasons for failure among Spanish students at the secondary level is their failure to acquire enough basic skills in primary school. In an attempt to improve the situation, the PP increased the number of hours a week devoted to core subjects.

The nut that remained to be cracked was secondary education itself, particularly in state schools. Part of the problem clearly lies with the teachers. Foreigners who have worked inside the Spanish public system say they find the teachers dedicated, but resistant to change. The OECD has noted that their pay system offers neither incentives for improvement nor rewards for experience. Teachers' starting salaries, proportionate to GDP, are the highest of any developed nation. But they barely increase with the years. In 2003, the OECD found a teacher with fifteen years in the profession was earning on average just 17 per cent more than at the beginning of his or her career. Unsurprisingly, teacher morale is low. A survey in 2004 found three-quarters regarded themselves as 'undervalued by society'.

Some of the other problems can, perhaps, be traced back to that very reverence for learning mentioned at the start of this chapter. One side-effect is a contempt for vocational training that has been evident for decades. In the days before schooling was made compulsory to the age of sixteen, only a quarter of those who successfully completed their basic education at fourteen opted for what was then known as *Formación Profesional*. Nowadays, less than a third of pupils who complete their ESO choose to follow vocational training.

By repeatedly shepherding their sons and daughters towards the most academic options, parents skew the system, ensuring that it turns out too many university students and not enough plumbers and hairdressers. They also seem to be setting up many of their children for failure.

I have a friend who teaches that most intellectual of disciplines, philosophy, to teenagers in the final phase of their secondary education. She recently changed from one state school to another. 'One of the pupils I got was a nice boy, who was trying his best, but just didn't have the intelligence or the enthusiasm to tackle the material,' she told me. 'Anyhow, he thought – quite rightly – that he was never going to need it in the rest of his life. He wanted to be a mechanic. I rang up his mother in a *pueblo* just outside Madrid. She said: "I don't care what it takes. My son's not leaving school without a *bachillerato* [the diploma needed for university entry]." Any teacher at my level will tell you the same. In a class of thirty, say, you will find at least five who ought to be out working and leaving the rest of us to get on with it.'

The failings of secondary education were the prime focus of the PP's main educational reform, the *Ley Orgánica de Calidad de la Educación*, or LOCE, which was passed in 2002 and began to take effect at the start of the 2003–4 academic year. Among other things, it 'streamed' pupils after their second year of ESO in an attempt to steer lower performers on to more vocational paths in the expectation that they would end up doing vocational training. In an effort to maintain standards, it stipulated that pupils who failed in more than two subjects during ESO would have to stay down for a further year unless they could pass a special exam in the autumn. And, finally, the

LOCE made the obtaining of a *bachillerato* dependent on the passing of a national exam, known as the *reválida*, which took the place of seventeen different university entrance exams which, until then, were being set by the various Autonomous Communities.

Whether any of this will really make an impact is questionable. Most of it was criticized by Spanish educationalists and the OECD gave a distinctly lukewarm welcome to both the early 'streaming' and the course repetition. But the LOCE did nonetheless introduce some much-needed change into the teaching profession. It gave more autonomy to schools, provided extra incentives to teachers who showed 'special dedication' and changed the system of appointing head teachers. Incredibly, until the law took effect, 'heads' were appointed by rotation on hardly any extra pay and returned to their previous jobs five years later.

Perhaps the strangest aspect of the Spanish educational system is that, despite the inadequacy of secondary – and, to a lesser extent, primary – schooling, Spain has proportionately one of the biggest university populations in the developed world. In 2002, 38 per cent of twenty-year-olds were at college. That was the same as in the US. In Britain, the comparable figure was 33 per cent, and for the developed world as a whole it was just 31 per cent. Spain had more of its young people receiving tertiary education than Finland, Holland or Switzerland.

The growth of the university system during the *años de desarrollo* was even more rapid than that of the schools system. In the sixties, total enrolment tripled to over 200,000 and the government initially had every intention that it should go on growing at the same rate. Villar Palasí's Act entitled anyone who passed the *bachillerato* to a place at college. Four years later, with the economy facing a recession and the full implications of this undertaking becoming clear, another law was passed reintroducing university entrance exams. Under Franco, the universities were kept firmly under the thumb of the government, which could remove lecturers and professors whose political outlook it disliked. The 1983 *Ley de Reforma Universitaria* gave the universities their autonomy in matters of internal organization. But it left the government to decide how many students they should take in every year. The numbers kept on growing, and rose vertiginously after the PSOE came to power in 1982 as the Socialists extended grants and promoted the building of new universities.

The momentum has been sustained by decentralization. Aware that higher education is a vote winner, the new autonomous governments have been eager to found yet more seats of learning. By 2002, Spain had sixty-six universities* with a total enrolment of more than 1.5 million. The vast majority of students go to state-owned universities. The oldest is Salamanca, which was founded in 1218. More than half the rest have come into existence since 1970.

The oldest private institutions are all run by the Church. Three are owned by the Jesuits, including the well-regarded Deusto in Bilbao. The fourth is Opus Dei's University of Navarre, which also boasts high standards and excellent facilities. In 1991, the Socialists laid out the guidelines for a new generation of private universities. Some were based on existing *colegios universitarios*, privately owned institutions which give courses in the university disciplines but whose students take their exams at, and their degrees from, a public institution to which the *colegio universitario* is attached. The first of this new wave of private universities to open its doors was the Ramón Llull in Barcelona. By 2002, eighteen of Spain's universities were privately run, but they were mostly quite small and accounted for less than 10 per cent of total enrolment.

Under that relentless pressure from aspiring parents that has been the constant theme of this chapter, successive governments expanded the university system, but without always earmarking the funds needed for such an extensive system to prosper. In 2002, spending per student as a proportion of the nation's wealth was barely two-thirds of the average in the developed world.

Money is by no means the only problem, though. Spanish university education may not be in crisis, but it is lacklustre, and many have questioned whether it is performing its essential task of providing society with an intellectual elite. Outside the private sector, there is little pressure on either students or teachers. Students who fail to pass their exams are allowed to take them again – up to six times. The result is that many stay on at university for much longer than the nominal length of their course. Some are over thirty by the time they graduate. Back in the nineties, there was a character known as *El gordo* ('The fat one') who haunted the Sociology faculty of the

---

* Including an 'open university', the Universidad Nacional de Educación de Distancia, with an enrolment in 2002 of 133,591.

Universidad Complutense in Madrid. He was said to have been there so long that no one knew when he had matriculated.

Effectively, moreover, the state universities do not have to compete. Since the early nineties, students have in theory been free to 'shop around'. In practice, the vast majority go to their local university, and the result is a very homogeneous picture. Some of the universities, like Salamanca or the Complutense, which dates from 1499 and can count Cervantes among its alumni, have venerable histories. But Spain does not have a Cambridge or Yale, a Sorbonne or Heidelberg, where an illustrious past is matched by standards that are consistently above average. In the early nineties, the French newspaper *Libération* got some 600 academics from all over Europe to rate the continent's universities subject by subject. Only one Spanish faculty – the Politécnica de Barcelona's architecture school – gained a place in the top five in any discipline. That said, some of the new universities are starting to differentiate themselves from the pack. The Universidad Carlos III was founded in the González years in a converted army barracks in the industrialized, proletarian south of Madrid. At the outset, it could not have been less fashionable. But it has quickly turned itself into one of the most sought-after universities in Spain and now sets exactingly high requirements for entrants.

CHAPTER 24

Housing: Through the Roof

There can be few towns in Spain changed as much by the prosperity of recent years as Valdemoro. It used to be one of several agricultural villages south of Madrid — not as picturesque as nearby Chinchón, maybe, but with an elegant church and a pretty square. Then a series of industrial estates sprang up around Valdemoro and the number of people living there began to climb. As late as 1992, though, it had a population of fewer than 19,000. A decade later, that number had doubled.

One evening in March 2004, more than 1,000 people crammed into the Casa de Cultura in Valdemoro for the drawing of lots for the right to buy 121 subsidized flats developed by the local authority. Except there weren't 121. Part of the way through the draw, those present were told that the council had decided to withdraw twenty-four of the flats so that they could be let instead. You do that sort of thing in Spain at your peril. The fury of the crowd was such that the organizers hurriedly suspended the draw. But, instead of going home, several hundred people, enraged at having been robbed of the chance to own a house, formed into a mob that blocked the traffic before converging on the town hall to pelt it with eggs. Luckily for the mayor, he was not in Valdemoro that night.

There are few issues in Spain today that arouse more passion than housing. And none that offers more insights into the way the country is as it is. Spain's grossly distorted housing market explains why some people with modest incomes seem to have money to burn, while others you would expect to be prosperous seem to be watching every euro. Housing is one of the keys to Spain's prudent transition from dictatorship to democracy. It exerts an influence on matters as diverse as sexual behaviour, artistic creativity and the integration of immigrants.

As with so many things, the origins of these distortions are to be found in the economic and social upheavals of the 1950s and 1960s, and specifically in the migration of millions of Spaniards from the countryside to the towns. It has been calculated that one in seven of the population moved on a permanent basis from one part of the country to another during those years, and a lot set off without any guarantee of accommodation at the other end.

The government, whose experience of housing was limited to a relatively modest programme of reconstruction after the civil war, only became involved with the greatest reluctance. It was not until 1957, in fact, that Spain acquired a separate Housing Ministry, and from the beginning it was clear that the new ministry would not have the resources to build and manage a massive stock of state-owned rented accommodation like the 'council houses' in Britain. In any case, the aim of the technocrats who dominated government thinking from 1957 onwards was to create an economically advanced but politically conservative society in Spain, and one of the keys to this was to encourage property ownership. There is nothing like having to meet monthly mortgage payments for deterring people from going on strike and, in a broader sense, property ownership gives people a stake in the prosperity and stability of the society in which they live. All but a very small proportion of the millions of houses and flats built during the *años de desarrollo* were thus offered for sale rather than rent.

The scheme devised by the Francoist authorities to cope with the hordes of Spaniards who had made themselves homeless by the early sixties was the *Plan Nacional de Vivienda* (National Housing Plan). Its aim was to ensure the construction, between 1961 and 1976, of 4 million new dwellings.

It must be stressed that not all of this accommodation was to be provided at the behest of the state. It was expected that much of it (about half, as it turned out) would be supplied by the private sector on its own terms. The rest was accounted for by subsidized housing – Vivienda de Protección Oficial (VPO). But VPO was not 'state housing' in the sense that the term is understood in much of the rest of Europe. Only a fraction was bought by the state and then let to the occupants at a subsidized rent. The rest was bought by the occupants, and what the state subsidized was merely the rate of interest at which the cost of the property was repaid.

The target of 4 million dwellings set by the *Plan Nacional de Vivienda* was more than fulfilled. Acre by acre, the shanty towns gave way to stark multi-storey blocks standing amid wasteland on the outskirts of most Spanish cities. There were often no leisure facilities in the immediate vicinity and the apartments were usually cramped and noisy. But they were a lot better than a leaky shack.

To pay for them it was often necessary to take in lodgers from among the ranks of those who had not yet been able to find or afford a place of their own. Francesc Candels, a Catalan author who wrote a best-selling book about Barcelona's immigrants, *Els Altres Catalans*, estimated that by the mid-sixties one-fifth of all the working-class families in the city were living in someone else's apartment. If it was simply a matter of a man on his own sleeping in the spare room or, in the case of one-bedroomed apartments, in the sitting-room, it worked reasonably well. It also worked, although to a diminishing extent, with two, three or even four men on their own (and it was by no means uncommon during this period for a family with two or three children to be sharing a two-bedroomed flat in a tower block with several lodgers). It was when the men got together enough money to bring their families that the system usually broke down. Left alone all day, often with children to look after, the wives would often start rowing and then the husbands would get sucked into their disputes. But as more blocks went up, the horrors of lodging became less commonplace.

Because the scale of internal migration turned out to be even greater than expected, the fulfilment of the plan did not solve the problem of homelessness altogether. After it had run its course, there were still some million and a half families without a home of their own. Some still lived in shanty towns, but most were living as lodgers, often with relatives – '*con la suegra*' ('with the mother-in-law'), as the saying went.

The real failing of the *Plan Nacional de Vivienda*, though, was that the housing subsidized by the government went to the wrong people. The problem was that, because they relied on property developers to supply most of the housing they sponsored, the authorities had only a limited say in the type of accommodation produced. And since there were bigger profits to be made from expensive accommodation than from cheap accommodation, there was always a tendency for the property developers to go as far up-market as the guidelines would allow. By contrast, many of the high-rise blocks thrown up to accommodate the shanty-town immigrants were put there without any kind of public subsidy and the apartments in them were sold off on the open market at commercial rates.

While arranging for the bulk of newly built homes to be made available for purchase rather than rental, Franco's ministers perpetuated a ludicrous arrangement which encouraged the owners of existing surplus properties to keep them off the market rather than rent them out.

Back in 1936, with his government still operating from its wartime headquarters in Burgos, Franco had ordered rents throughout Spain to be frozen. Tenants acquired the right to insist that their contracts be renewed with the rent unchanged. And not only that: they could leave their leases, with their rights to automatic renewal, to any relative who happened to be living with them when they died. In the case of an elderly partner, this was admirably humanitarian. But it became manifestly unfair to the landlord or landlady when applied to the tenant's sons, daughters, nephews and nieces. A law introduced in 1964 retained the tenant's entitlement to the automatic renewal of his or her lease, but gave the owner the right to raise the rent by the rate of inflation.

However, this was scant compensation since rents were already very low by comparison with the cost of living. All that the law did was to ensure that, in real terms, they did not get any lower. Not surprisingly, the owners of surplus property became loath to let it out and the stock of housing available for rental shrank with each passing year.

The effect of the policies adopted in the latter years of Franco's rule was to turn Spain into a nation of owner-occupiers, sharing all the cautious inclinations that go with the possession of property. Before 1960, more than half the population lived in rented accommodation. By the time his dictatorship came to an end, less than a quarter did. If Franco and his ministers calculated that a high rate of owner-occupancy would inhibit social conflict, they were right. Strikes became more frequent towards the end of his dictatorship, but they were rarely protracted. And if the growing prevalence of home-ownership was one reason why Franco was able to die peacefully in his bed, then it was also a key to the relatively peaceful transition that ensued. This in turn may help to explain why successive democratic administrations have been loath to reverse the trend he began.

Spain today has the highest rate of owner-occupancy in the European Union. In 1999, it was 86 per cent. In Britain, despite the fact that the authorities had been selling off council houses for almost two decades, the comparable figure was only 69 per cent.

One of the earliest concerns of Spain's democratic governments was to find a way of ensuring that VPO accommodation went to those for whom it was intended. The obvious thing to do would have been to introduce a means test. But in a society where there were no reliable tax returns and almost everybody was doing more than one job, this was not practicable. It was only after Fernández-Ordóñez's tax reforms that the UCD was able to make low income a criterion for access to VPO accommodation.

The Socialists introduced a number of other well-intentioned innovations after 1982. But their housing policy soon bore only the most oblique relation to reality, for it had been overtaken by the most spectacular boom in property prices in Spain's history. Prices began to lift in 1984. Then they climbed. Then they soared. And, finally, they went into orbit. By 1991, it was reckoned that the cost of a house or flat in one of the big cities had risen fivefold in the previous seven years.

What happened was that the end of the long recession that had begun in the mid-seventies freed savings and encouraged borrowing, thereby increasing the potential demand for housing in a society in which many people were living in inadequate accommodation. This was also because investing in property was identified as an ideal way to launder *dinero negro*. It offered not only spectacular capital growth, but also impressive tax efficiency. Under the peculiar arrangements governing property transactions in Spain, the value of a house or flat for tax purposes could be whatever the buyer, with the seller's consent, chose to make it. Overnight, 20 million pesetas of real money could be transformed into 5 million pesetas for the tax records, and while remaining as 5 million on the tax records would have grown, between 1984 and 1991, to 100 million.

The upward spiral in prices was given additional momentum by two other factors. One was a fiscal regime that encouraged property speculation. Until 1989, taxpayers were allowed to set against tax the cost of purchasing an unlimited number of properties, provided the amount they claimed as an allowance did not come to more than 30 per cent of their total liability.

Many relatively well-to-do Spaniards used the tax breaks to take advantage of the property boom and buy a house or a flat they did not need to occupy purely as an investment. This is one reason why Spain, a country with severe housing shortages, also has the EU's highest level of second-home ownership.

Yet while a large proportion of the population had two or more homes, many had none. The vast majority of those living in shanty towns were either Gypsies or immigrants. However, there was a less dramatic, but more widespread, problem hidden from sight by the strength of Spanish family ties. A growing number of young people were unable to move away from home because they could not afford separate accommodation. For all but a minority of young Spaniards – those with rich parents or lucrative jobs – even flat-sharing was out of the question.

The second factor pushing up house prices was land hoarding. Other things being equal, housing ought to be cheap and plentiful in Spain. Unlike most other European countries, it is not exactly short of space. But other things are not equal. Land management in Spain is largely the preserve of local authorities. And high land costs are in their interests because taxes on property account for the bulk of their revenues. The surge in demand for better housing in the mid-1980s offered them a golden opportunity to boost their income by releasing to developers only a fraction of the land available. In some cases, it was worse than that: councils became involved in outright speculation, expropriating land for development, then holding it off the market as they waited for prices to rise.

Despite this, it was several years before an order for the compulsory purchase of land for development ran into serious resistance. When it did, it provoked one of the whackiest episodes in Spain's recent history. In 1990, the Madrid council served notices to quit on the occupants of a collection of humble single-storey dwellings at Cerro Belmonte in the generally prosperous north of the city. The owners of the houses had mostly built them with their own hands when they arrived on the outskirts of the capital in the fifties. The council offered them a choice between either making improvements to the area that were beyond their means or taking as compensation a pittance and a flat in one of the most crime-infested areas of Madrid.

Spurred on by a young lawyer, Esther Castellanos, whose father owned a plot of land in the area, the inhabitants of Cerro Belmonte embarked on a succession of increasingly bizarre publicity stunts culminating in an appeal to the Cuban leader, Fidel Castro. It happened that, at the time, he was locked in a tense and bitter dispute over Spain's refusal to hand over a group of Cuban dissidents who had taken refuge in the Spanish Embassy in Havana. In a speech at the height of the crisis, and to the intense embarrassment of the Spanish government, the Cuban leader cited the goings-on at Cerro Belmonte as evidence of the evils of capitalism. He then invited twenty-four of Cerro Belmonte's residents on a free trip to Cuba. The Cerro Belmontese subsequently began making arrangements to declare themselves independent. Barricades were thrown up around the neighbourhood. And it was only after a flag had been designed and a constitution drafted that the Madrid council was finally embarrassed into making them a better offer.

The rise in property prices of the late eighties transformed Spanish society every bit as much as the educational reforms of the early seventies. Those who had enough money to buy a house or flat in addition to their principal residence enhanced their families' fortunes as handsomely as many a sixteenth-century adventurer returning from the Indies. But just as the gold and silver of the Americas enriched a few in the short term and impoverished so many in the long term, the property boom of the late eighties did considerable damage to the fabric of Spanish society. Because of its differential impact, the rise in prices widened the gaps separating one class from another, and reduced mobility between them.

Poorer families soon found that, even if they were government-subsidized, the rise in prices which began in 1984 made it almost impossible for them to save up the deposit or make the payments that were needed for them to buy a home of their own.

Yet rental was scarcely an option – unless you were lucky enough to have inherited a lease on a flat or house, in which case you were living virtually rent-free. In 1985, in an effort to tempt owners to let out their properties, the then Economics and Finance Minister, Miguel Boyer, issued a decree enabling landlords to make new agreements for a fixed period at whatever price the market would bear. When the lease ran out, the owner could demand an increased rent and evict the tenants if they refused to pay. In a lot of other countries, such an arrangement would normally lead to a reasonable deal. Both sides would have something to lose if the contract were terminated. The tenant would have to pay removal costs, but the owner would have to pay an agent a fee to find a new occupant. In Spain, however, it is the lessee, not the lessor, who has to compensate the agent (normally with one month's rent). So property-owners took to insisting on one-year contracts, knowing that as soon as they expired they could count on the tenant accepting any increase less than one-twelfth of the existing rent plus estimated removal costs. The result was that rents on properties subject to the *decreto Boyer* all rose at well over the rate of inflation.

The advantages bestowed on property-owners by the decree should have ensured that most of the houses and flats bought for speculative purposes during the boom were let out to provide their owners with a regular income as well as capital growth. But a lot were not. In 1991, 15 per cent of the total housing stock was vacant – the highest proportion in the EU after Italy.

Middle-class Spaniards had formed the view that letting was a high-risk venture. Not surprisingly. Hundreds of thousands of landlords had been effectively dispossessed of their houses by rental agreements signed before the *decreto Boyer* took effect. They could not evict their tenants and had no option but to accept an absurdly low recompense for allowing other people to occupy their properties. A body representing these landlords claimed that in 1990 some 830,000 families were paying rent of less than 3,000 pesetas (then $30 or £16) a month.

Vivienda de renta antigua ('Old rent housing'), as it came to be known after the introduction of the *decreto Boyer*, undoubtedly had beneficial social effects. It created a stock of cheap housing in the centre of Spain's cities that allowed people with modest incomes to continue to live there and provide the services that cities need. It ensured affordable accommodation for many an elderly or infirm couple. In that sense, it was a makeshift substitute for the subsidized rental housing that other countries supplied, with the difference that it was a landlord, rather than the government or the council, who was doing the subsidizing. Apart from the iniquity of this situation, the drawback was that a lot of the housing in Spain's city centres was becoming severely dilapidated. Unable to get a decent return on their property, most landlords had long since ceased investing in its upkeep.

In 1994, the Socialists introduced new legislation designed to phase out the old leases. It restricted the bequest of rented property to anyone but the tenant's partner. And it empowered landlords to fix a new rent that took account of inflation since the original agreement was signed.

The Aznar years left the broad outlines of the housing situation unchanged. A country with chronic housing shortages is also one that, according to the 2001 census, is littered with some 2.8 million unoccupied dwellings. Spain is still overwhelmingly a nation of owner-occupiers. Yet the cost of buying is high. The economic boom of the late 1990s sparked another round of price rises. In 2005, *The Economist* calculated that over the previous eight years, the average price of a house or flat in Spain had increased by 145 per cent. The only other countries in Europe that had seen comparable rises were Britain and Ireland. In the US, the increase over the same period was 73 per cent. Incomes went up too, of course. But the rise in the cost of accommodation far outstripped the increase in earnings. By the time the PP left office, the average cost of a home had gone up from four times the average yearly salary to seven times.

There were two new reasons why prices soared under the conservatives: the fall in interest rates as Spain moved towards membership of the euro zone, and the global stock market crash that began in 2000 and scared a lot of Spanish investors out of equities and into bricks and mortar. But the other factors remained broadly as they had been. Land was still scarce. Local authorities were as stingy as ever in allocating land to developers because they were as reliant as ever on property taxes, which in 1999 accounted for more than two-thirds of their revenue. The PP tried to get a deal on land management with the regional authorities, who had acquired important powers over housing as a result of devolution, but failed to clinch it. At the same time, the government was still providing tax breaks for home-ownership. Spaniards may have been barred from setting the cost of a second or third home against their liability, but they still enjoyed incentives for the purchase of their first home, even if under the Aznar government the incentives became slightly less generous.

However, the key reason why prices went up was – as before – that the underlying demand for housing outstripped supply. As had happened under the Socialists, as soon as families acquired new wealth they opted to invest it in new, or rather better, accommodation. Spain, in this respect, is still working through the effects of the massive displacement of population that took place in the middle of the last century. Moving so many people into makeshift accommodation inevitably creates a pent-up demand for adequate housing that takes decades rather than years to meet. And, along the way, a lot of the housing that is thrown up gets pulled down again, so that even a feverish level of building activity may make only a temporary impact on the supply.

According to the professional body that represents Spain's architects, work began in 2004 on 750,000 new homes. That was as many as in France, Germany and Italy combined. Spain was making more housing starts, proportionate to its population, than any country on earth. It was the fourth time in four years that the previous record had been outstripped. Yet, despite this flood of new accommodation on to the market, prices in 2004 rose by more than 17 per cent.

This was partly because the government was no longer playing more than a token role in moderating the cost of buying a home. Under the PP, the volume of new VPO housing dwindled steadily from an already low base. One reason was ideological: the conservatives did not feel the state should be meddling any more than strictly necessary in the workings of the market. But another reason was disillusion with the workings of the entire VPO system. Subsidized homes were meant for the needy and they were meant to remain in the possession of the original buyer for at least fifteen years, unless he or she sold them to another deserving buyer at an officially controlled price. But, in practice, all sorts of scams were perpetrated, and often VPO flats and houses ended up with owners whose sole intention was to resell them on the open market – something they could do with impunity because no proper register was kept of VPO occupants.

As for the rental sector, it was in scarcely better shape than when the Socialists left office in the mid-1990s. The state-owned sector was tiny – a mere 2 per cent of the overall housing stock compared with, for example, 21 per cent in the UK. In the private sector, a gulf still divided properties let under 'new' and 'old' leases. Largely because of continuing difficulties faced by landlords in getting redress through the courts, the 1994 law had not succeeded in doing away with *vivienda de renta antigua*, so several hundred thousand fortunate Spaniards were still paying nominal monthly sums for their accommodation. Other tenants had to cope with rents that were at least as formidable as the costs of buying. The trade union federation Comisiones Obreras calculated that in 2003 the average rent of a new property absorbed nearly 80 per cent of the average salary.

By the time the Socialists returned to power the following year, housing was a burning issue. In his first interview after taking office, José Luis Rodríguez Zapatero put it at the very top of his list of social priorities. 'If there is something that comes up every time I go out on the street and meet people, particularly young people and families with low to medium incomes, then it's housing,' he said.

What the voters he met wanted was access to affordable accommodation. But there was also a growing awareness among economists, politicians and others of another issue. Spain's high rate of owner-occupancy, which had served it so well in the past, was starting to become a handicap. The problem was not the high rate of home-ownership as such, but rather the low availability of rental accommodation that it implied. The shortage of flats and houses to let was getting in the way of a reduction in unemployment because it was discouraging people from looking for work outside their region of origin. A lack of rental accommodation was likewise making it more difficult for the rapidly growing number of immigrants to integrate into society. And it was an important reason why so many young Spaniards were staying at home for much longer than had been usual in the past. This in turn had consequences for the birth-rate. It meant that they were finding partners later in life and having fewer children. The fact that so many Spanish young people lived with their parents also curbed their propensity to challenge the ideas of their elders, with implications for the degree of creativity in a society which, like others in the developed world, was increasingly dependent on innovation.

The most controversial initiative in the Socialists' first, 2005–8, housing plan was for the construction of state-funded *minipisos* (mini-apartments) measuring 30–45 square metres – just enough for a 'bed-sitter' or tiny one-bedroomed flat – to be let to tenants under the age of thirty-five. The plan also provided for an increase in the building of VPO housing and measures to tackle the black market that had sprung up around it. The government was intending to set up a nationwide register of buyers and sellers and extend to thirty years the period during which state-subsidized accommodation had to be held off the free market.

The two most important distortions in the Spanish housing market, though, remained the limited availability of land and the tax incentives to purchase rather than rent. The Socialists made some early progress on the first issue by buying from the armed forces a large site on the outskirts of Madrid and giving it over to development. In the longer term, they were hoping to reform the funding of local authorities in such a way as to make them less dependent on property taxes. So far, though, there is little sign of Zapatero's wanting to grasp the nettle of tax breaks. This is hardly surprising. Now that the process of encouraging home-ownership has gone so far, there is a large section of society – and the electorate – whose attitudes on this issue are deeply ambiguous. They want their children to be able to benefit from the lower prices that abolition of the tax incentives could bring about. But if a change in the tax system were to be outweighed by other factors and prices kept on rising, then all it would have done would be to make things even more difficult for future house-buyers. And, in any case, to the extent that a tax reform succeeded in bringing down prices, it would erode the value of homes that many Spaniards have come to see not just as dwellings, but as endlessly remunerative forms of saving.

In terms of their personal finances, Spaniards have become property junkies. Americans, for example, have almost as much of their money invested in the stock market as they do in real estate.

Using figures from 1998, the OECD calculated that the proportions were 20 and 21 per cent respectively. Britons had 12 per cent of their total household assets tied up in shares and 34 per cent in property. But for Spaniards the comparative figures were 9 per cent and fully 67 per cent.

CHAPTER 25

Law and Disorder

The Madrid bombings of 2004 had a dramatic and violent sequel. Following a trail laid by mobile telephone calls, police tracked the bombers through an area south of Madrid to a block of flats in the working-class dormitory town of Leganés. Children were still playing football in the courtyard when the first shots were exchanged. After a two-hour stand-off that gave time for the evacuation of the surrounding area, a unit of the Spanish police's Grupo Especial de Operaciones (GEO) prepared to storm the apartment where the bombers were holed up. They had just blown open a door leading to the hideout when a massive explosion ripped through the building, killing one of the GEO's officers.

While the police were clearing nearby flats and buildings, the men they were hunting had been busy putting together a huge bomb with which to blow themselves to pieces before they could be seized by the police. Such was the force of the blast that it was some time before investigators were able to establish how many men had been in the flat – and not until six months later that they succeeded in identifying the seventh and last, an Algerian called Allekema Lamari. Police said they believed he had played a leading role in arranging the slaughter on 11 March. They called him 'the emir of the bombings'.

By then, the attention of the world's media had long shifted elsewhere, so a very important, and – for the Spanish authorities – very embarrassing, detail went virtually unnoticed outside Spain. It was that, throughout the period in which Allekema Lamari is thought to have been preparing for the Madrid bombings, he should have been in a Spanish prison cell. He had been arrested and jailed on terrorism charges in 1997. Four years later, he was tried and sentenced to a total of fourteen years. His lawyers appealed to the

Supreme Court. The following year, their appeal had still not been heard and the court that had tried Lamari sent a formal notification – a so-called *auto* – to the Supreme Court pointing out that within a few months he would have spent five years in jail, which is the longest that anyone in Spain can be held without a final and definitive conviction. The *auto* warned that, unless Lamari's case was dealt with soon, he would have to be released. The Supreme Court swiftly arranged for the appeal to be heard and, on 7 June 2002, Lamari's conviction was upheld though his sentence was reduced. Even so, it should have meant that he spent another four years or so in jail. The reason he did not is that the paperwork informing the lower court of the Supreme Court's verdict took more than a month to work its way through the judicial administration with the result that the lower court, believing his appeal had still not been heard, ordered Lamari's release.

Ineptitude and delay are sadly typical of the Spanish courts system, which has been overloaded and under-funded since at least the latter stages of the Franco dictatorship. A study in 2000 by the law faculty of the Complutense University concluded that one problem was inefficiency in the division of work between courts, but that the other was simply that successive governments had not invested enough of the taxpayers' money in the administration of justice. In proportion to its population, Spain had a third as many judges as Germany.

Its recent history is dotted with stories of judicial delay that would be comic were they not so tragic. In 2003, the European Court of Human Rights took up a case that had taken fifteen years to resolve. In 1985, a prosecutor began proceedings against one Francisco López Solé. But the preliminary investigations took nine years and it was not until 1997 – three years after the completion of the preliminary investigations – that the defendant was actually tried and given a three-year prison sentence. Successive appeals to the Supreme Court and the Constitutional Court took a further three years.

Perhaps the most remarkable case was that of Eugenio Peydró Salmerón, who stood trial in 1987 for a property fraud committed in the days when Franco was still alive. By the time his case reached judgement, he was eighty-one years of age. The judges handed down a nine-year jail sentence, and a week later he died of a heart attack.

The backlog first built up at the end of Franco's dictatorship as the result of a growth in crime, and the mounting complexity and litigiousness of society. The Centrists failed to respond to the growing crisis and, although the Socialists after 1982 repeatedly increased the Justice Ministry's budget by more than the rate of inflation, the increases never proved sufficient to cope with the problem.

Delay generates injustice. People can be kept in jail for years on remand for crimes they are later found not to have committed. Under Franco, judges were allowed to grant bail to anyone accused of an offence for which the penalty was less than six years in prison. In most cases, they did. But in response to concern about the increase in crime and, in particular, the suspicion that criminals caught by the police and bailed by the courts were responsible for much of it, a law was passed in 1980 restricting bail to those accused of crimes for which the penalty was less than six *months*. By the time the UCD left office, more than half the inmates of Spain's jails were still awaiting trial.

The Socialists came to power in 1982 determined to make bail once again the norm rather than the exception and ensure that theoretically innocent remand prisoners did not have to spend unduly long periods in jail. Soon after their victory at the polls, they passed a law which stipulated that no one should remain in custody for longer than three years awaiting trial for serious offences, or eighteen months in jail awaiting trial on minor charges.

The trouble was that, because of the delays in the system, huge numbers of prisoners on remand – guilty and innocent alike – qualified for release on the day that the law came into effect and were promptly let out. The results were catastrophic. During 1983, the number of crimes reported to the police soared by a third. The biggest increase was in armed robberies, which went up by 60 per cent. Amid the public outcry that ensued, the government hastily raised the detention limits to four years and two years respectively.

The PP's main attempt to speed up the criminal justice system came in the form of a *Ley de Enjuiciamiento Criminal* passed in 2002 to replace one that had been in force since the nineteenth century. This was meant to streamline the procedures for all but the most serious offences – those with sentences of nine years or more. In addition, it provided for courthouses in the bigger cities that would stay open round the clock to judge petty offences, particularly those where the defendant had been caught *in flagrante*.

The conservatives also introduced a much more comprehensive reform of the civil justice system with a new *Ley de Enjuiciamiento Civil* that aimed to put an end to a different sort of injustice arising from delay. It had always been the case in Spain that, if you committed a serious crime and were caught, then you would pay for it. But if you failed to settle a debt, say, there was until recently a pretty good chance you would never have to make amends. The other party would find it was just not worth the time and cost required to sue you. Better to settle out of court or drop the case altogether.

The clogging up of the judicial machinery gave new life to a kind of Spaniard who first surfaced in the picaresque novels of the sixteenth and seventeenth centuries – an opportunist living, usually in some style, off his wits and one step ahead of his creditors. In his modern guise, he became known as a *buscavidas* or *vividor*. I doubt if he will ever entirely disappear from Spanish life, but it is clear that the reform introduced under the PP will make life more difficult for him.

A key defect of the old law was that orders for, say, the payment of damages did not take effect until after the appeal process had been exhausted and that, on average, took three to four years. The new *Ley de Enjuiciamiento Civil*, which came into effect in 2000, stipulates that a ruling by the court of first instance has to be acted upon immediately. If and when the defendant's appeal is successful, it is revoked. The new law also allows plaintiffs to recover small claims without having to hire a lawyer.

The PP's reforms made a considerable impact on the backlogs in Spain's courthouses. By the end of 2003, there were still more than a million cases pending. But that was half the figure of two years earlier.

Congestion is not the only failing of the Spanish legal system. The corrupting of judges is disturbingly commonplace. Cases of bribery come to light at least once a year. And the system as a whole is more susceptible than it should be to influence by the government of the day. This is scarcely a problem unique to Spain. In Britain, the Lord Chancellor, who is responsible for appointing judges, is a member of the cabinet. In the US, the President names the members of the Supreme Court.

But the subjection of Spain's judges to its politicians is nevertheless blatantly at odds with its constitution. This entrusted the administration of justice to a twenty-member committee known as the Consejo General del Poder Judicial.

At the outset, eight of its members were elected by parliament and twelve by the legal profession. Then in 1985 the Socialists, claiming that Spain's admittedly conservative legal profession was using its control of the Consejo to block change, ordered that the Cortes be made responsible for electing all twenty members. Since the Socialists at that time had an overall parliamentary majority, the government acquired effective control of the judiciary. It should be noted, however, that the opposition People's Party, which apparently saw in the move an opportunity to boost its influence, agreed to the Socialists' proposals.

The insidious effects of this change can be illustrated by the arrangements for dispensing justice at regional level. Each of Spain's seventeen Autonomous Communities has its own High Court. In each of its *Salas*, or divisions – criminal, civil, etc. – there are three judges. One is chosen by the Consejo and another by the regional parliament. So wherever the regional government is of the same political colouration as the national government a majority of the judges in each division owe their jobs to the party in power.

Because of similar systems of parliamentary designation, the government in Spain not only holds sway over the administration of justice but also exercises an influence over the three bodies to which it is meant to be accountable: the office of Spain's Ombudsman (known as the Defensor del Pueblo), the Tribunal de Cuentas, which audits public-sector accounts, and even the Constitutional Court itself.

Spain's highest tribunal has twelve members. The government and the Consejo each choose two. The remaining eight are named by parliament. In 1985, the Socialists changed the ground rules so that laws referred to the Constitutional Court did not have to wait for a verdict from the judges before coming into force. Jurisprudentially, the arrangement is questionable – it allows a *fait accompli* to be created by means of legislation that is later shown to be unconstitutional. Nevertheless, even their opponents will acknowledge that, in this instance, the Socialists were not trying to curb the powers of the judiciary but prevent creeping paralysis of the executive. By referring everything approved by parliament to the Constitutional Court, the opposition could bring the government's legislative programme to a standstill.

The years since the end of Spain's dictatorship have seen changes not only to the way that justice is administered, but also to the law itself. The penal code – that is to say, the text setting out the criminal law – that was inherited from Franco was clearly unsuited to the democratic society that emerged after his death. But the business of framing a thoroughly modern one proved such a monumental task that it was not until 1995 that an entirely new penal code was finally approved by parliament.

The Socialists under González had earlier introduced a partial reform, affecting about one-sixth of the articles in the existing code. Much of it was concerned with adapting Spain's criminal law to the constitution. But the reform also introduced suspended sentences, imposed stiff penalties for failure to comply with the food and drink regulations, made pollution of the environment a crime for the first time and created a clear distinction between 'hard' and 'soft' drugs for the purpose of sentencing. It was this reform that enshrined the de-penalization of drug possession for personal use.*

The full revision did away with much that had long since become anachronistic. Until 1995, for example, slandering or libelling a figure of authority constituted the serious offence of *desacato*, which was abolished. It was also the case that the truth of a defamatory statement was irrelevant if the offended party could establish that his or her honour had been impugned by it. That concept too was jettisoned. But it remained an offence to defame a range of institutions including the legislature, the government, the Constitutional Court and the King. And it was – and still is – a crime to libel or slander the dead.

The 1995 penal code incorporated several new company-related offences. It became a crime, for example, to take money out of a firm to the detriment of its shareholders. The range of offences relating to the environment was further extended. In some areas, there was a relaxation. Pimping ceased to be an offence so long as the prostitutes involved were not handicapped or being forced to sell themselves against their will. But in a number of other areas there was a tightening-up. The penalties for drug trafficking, for instance, were increased.

* See above, p. 152.

337

So too was the overall time that a convicted offender could spend in prison. Previously, this had been limited to fifteen years. The new penal code provided for sentences of up to thirty years, and under the PP, with the agreement of the Socialists, the limit was raised to forty. However, there is still no means by which a judge in Spain can order that an offender, no matter how dangerous, be put in jail for the rest of his or her life.

The PP, which abstained in the vote on the 1995 penal code, later drafted a partial revision of its own, which was approved in 2003. This introduced jail sentences for the first time for drunken and dangerous driving and increased the penalties for child pornography and intellectual property offences. It made violence in sport liable to criminal prosecution. And, at the last minute, as the legislation was making its way through parliament, it was decided to make cruelty to domestic animals – though not other animals – a criminal offence.

Spain has several police forces to uphold the law. Arguably, it has too many. Some operate nationally. Others are run by the regional and municipal authorities, so the scope for rivalry, misunderstanding and the overlap of responsibilities is considerable.

The various municipal police forces, the *policías municipales*, are recruited and administered locally. They are funded by the town or city council concerned and their job is essentially to uphold the local by-laws. Much of their work is concerned with traffic. Most *policías municipales* carry guns (often reluctantly), but they were never regarded as a repressive force, even under Franco.

The Cuerpo Nacional de Policía, on the other hand, was formed in 1986 out of two forces which had been created under the dictatorship to keep order in the cities. The Policía Armada and the Cuerpo General were set up in 1941 with the help of advisers from Nazi Germany to replace two forces created in the 1870s – the Cuerpo de Seguridad and the Cuerpo de Vigilancia – which, in the words of the law that abolished them, had become 'imbued with apoliticism'.

The Policía Armada (literally the 'armed police') was perhaps the most hated body of men in Spain during the Franco era. Whether cradling their sub-machine pistols at the entrance to public buildings or cruising the streets in their white shooting-brakes, the *grises* (greys), as they were called after the colour of their uniforms, were the visible symbols of repression for city-dwellers. In 1978, in an effort to change their image, the government renamed them the Policía Nacional and kitted them out in khaki and beige.*

In 1989, by which time they made up the uniformed branch of the Cuerpo Nacional, they were given another change of uniform, and put into blue. Successive changes of dress have been accompanied by a profound change in outlook and attitude. Between 1979 and 1982, the Policía Nacional was the responsibility of one of those decisive figures of the transition who are virtually unknown outside Spain – Lieutenant-General José Antonio Sáenz de Santa María, a burly moustachioed soldier whose tough professionalism went hand-in-hand with a genuine commitment to democracy. In 1981, when Tejero occupied the Cortes, Sáenz de Santa María sided unhesitatingly with the government and ordered his Policía Nacional to encircle the building. People have not forgotten that. To the average Spaniard today, it is the force which, when the chips were down, took the side of democracy.

Its image improved still further a few months later when the GEO, the close-quarters battle unit of the Policía Nacional, stormed the Banco Central in Barcelona and released more than a hundred hostages unharmed in one of the most spectacular and successful operations of its kind. Men of the same unit later freed the father of the singer Julio Iglesias after he had been kidnapped by criminals.

The Socialists under González saw in the reformed Cuerpo Nacional an organization with which they felt they could do business, and they established friendly relations with a number of up-and-coming young officers. Nowadays, it is by no means unusual for members of the Cuerpo Nacional, particularly those running *comisarías* in the working-class dormitory towns, to be pro-PSOE. Many of the leaks to the pro-Socialist media that undermined the conservative government's version of events in the crucial days that followed the Madrid bombings are believed to have come from PSOE sympathizers in the Cuerpo Nacional.

Although often thought of, and even referred to, as a creation of Franco, the Guardia Civil actually traces its history back to 1844 when it was set up to combat banditry. Richard Ford, who was living in Spain at the time the force was founded, remarked how efficient

---

* This led to them being nicknamed *maderos* ('woodies'), the implication being that they were both brown and dense.

it was. But he added that Civil Guards 'have been quite as much employed ... for political purposes rather than those of pure police, having been used to keep down the expression of indignant public opinion, and, instead of catching thieves, in upholding those first-rate criminals, foreign and domestic, who are now robbing poor Spain of her gold and liberties.' He was not the last commentator to see in the force an instrument for the oppression of the poor by the rich.

Supporters of the Guardia Civil argue that it has merely stood by authority, whatever its political complexion, and they point out that when the civil war divided Spain into two camps, its members gave their loyalty to whichever faction had come out on top in that part of the country. That is true, although it overlooks the fact that in several areas the Guardia Civil was instrumental in ensuring that the uprising succeeded, rather than in defending the legitimately elected authorities. As with the army, the Guardia Civil became ideologically more homogeneous and more reactionary under Franco's influence. But it was always much more popular with the average Spaniard than the Policía Armada. The courtesy and efficiency of the Guardia Civil highway patrols, who not only enforce the traffic laws but also help motorists in distress, enhanced the force's reputation still further.

Yet of all Spain's police forces it was the Guardia Civil that had the greatest difficulty in coming to terms with democracy. As late as 1980, Guardia Civil units received a telex from headquarters – apparently sanctioned at the highest level – stipulating that on all official premises there ought to be, in pride of place, the portrait of 'HM the King and, in a fully visible place, the portrait of Generalísimo Franco'. Tejero's part in the abortive coup was unfortunate in this respect because it provided the most reactionary elements within the service with a hero and martyr.

The reason why the Guardia Civil proved more resistant to change than the police is that it is far closer to the army both sentimentally and organizationally. In spite of its name, the Guardia Civil is, and always has been, an essentially military body. Its members qualify for military decorations. Under Franco, moreover, the Guardia Civil was responsible to the Ministry of Defence, whereas the Policía Armada and the Cuerpo General came under the Ministry of the Interior – a division of authority that made it virtually impossible to co-ordinate the policing of the country. During the early years of the transition there was a lot of talk about having to 'civilianize' the Guardia Civil among politicians who did not perhaps fully appreciate how fiercely proud the force was of its military status. A formula was eventually worked out whereby the Guardia Civil was made responsible to the Ministry of the Interior in time of peace and to the Ministry of Defence in time of war. But, by that time, the ultra-right had had a field day exploiting the force's apprehensions.

In 1983 the Socialist government put the Guardia Civil under the command of General Sáenz de Santa María in the hope that he would be able to bring about the same sort of transformation that he had wrought in the police. The Socialists did their best not to offend the Guardia Civil's corporate sensibilities, while at the same time applying a sort of back-door demilitarization. New standing orders which came into force in 1991 reiterated the 'military nature' of the Guardia Civil, yet were actually very different from those for the army.

The Guardia Civil also has had a change of uniform intended to exorcize the ghosts of the past. Their tricornes, however picturesque they may seem to foreigners, inspire nothing but grim historical memories in the majority of Spaniards. In the late eighties, they were quietly dropped for all but ceremonial occasions and the guarding of public buildings and foreign embassies.

History continues to weigh heavily on the relative strengths of the two forces. The Guardia Civil traditionally patrolled the countryside, the highways and frontiers. The Cuerpo Nacional was responsible for provincial capitals and other large towns. Today, there is far more crime in the cities than there is in the countryside, so you would expect the Cuerpo Nacional to be a much bigger force than the Guardia Civil. Yet the reverse is the case. In 2003, the Guardia Civil had some 69,000 officers and the Cuerpo Nacional only 46,000. In other words, the force that had the experience of urban policing and was responsible for dealing with the bulk of crime was the less well-staffed and funded. What is more, the Cuerpo Nacional was much further below its nominal strength than the Guardia Civil. This was partly because the Guardia Civil has always had less difficulty with recruitment. The force's strong *esprit de corps* attracts more sons – and nowadays daughters – of officers than is the case with the police. And, as a paramilitary force, it also enjoys the advantage of being able to draw recruits directly from the armed services.

What has happened over the years is that, instead of reducing the Guardia Civil in line with the decline in criminality in the areas for which it was originally responsible, successive governments have found other things for it to do. They have put Civil Guards in charge of guarding the prisons and supervising the transport of prisoners. They have agreed to the creation of a close-quarters battle group of the Guardia Civil, a sea-going coastal unit and an environmental protection service. But above all they have deployed the Guardia Civil in city areas which were once the preserve of the police. In 2004, *El Mundo* reported that some 5,500 officers of the paramilitary force were stationed in Madrid, alongside around 7,500 officers of the Cuerpo Nacional. There is a clear danger that Spain could drift into the same situation as Italy, which has two rival national forces with overlapping responsibilities and a higher ratio of police to population than any other nation in Europe.

The other big change in the deployment of the Spanish police has been as a result of decentralization. For more than two decades now, the Cuerpo Nacional and the Guardia Civil have been gradually withdrawing from the regions whose statutes of autonomy give them the right to a police force of their own. The most important of these are the Basque country and Catalonia.

The introduction of the Basque police force, known as the Ertzaintza (pronounced 'Er-chine-cha'), has been particularly sensitive because of ETA. Militant nationalists see them as stooges of an occupying power and refer to them as the *zipaioak* (sepoys), an allusion to the native troops in colonial India. Civil Guard and national police officers regard them with just as much suspicion for the opposite reason. They consider the Ertzaintza to be a creation of the Basque Nationalist Party, which they view as ambivalent in its approach to ETA. Their suspicions were reinforced when it emerged that the guerrillas had succeeded in infiltrating the Ertzaintza. Though the Basque police began to take a role in the fight against ETA in the mid-1980s, the Guardia Civil and the Cuerpo Nacional have never given up their anti-terrorist responsibilities in the Basque country and today share them, somewhat uneasily, with the Ertzaintza, who are prevented from seeing much of their intelligence material.

The Ertzaintza began to be deployed in 1982 when they were given responsibility for traffic and guarding the institutions and members of the Basque government. Then, starting in rural areas, they were assigned to general policing. In 1994, they were deployed in Bilbao and San Sebastián, and the following year the process was completed when they were put into Vitoria. With some 7,500 officers, the Ertzaintza is now the main general police force in the Basque country and statistics show that the public recognizes them as such. In 2001, 55 per cent of all crimes in the region were reported to the Ertzaintza and only 8 per cent to the two national forces. Most of the remainder were reported to local police forces.

The Catalan force, known as the Mossos d'Esquadra, is bigger than the Ertzaintza, but its deployment has been more gradual and it was not until 2005 that it assumed responsibility for the policing of the city of Barcelona. By then, the 8,000 or so *mossos* were responsible for traffic throughout Catalonia. They kept law and order in two of the Principality's four provinces, Gerona and Lérida. And they had begun to take over from the Cuerpo Nacional and the Guardia Civil in the remaining two, Tarragona and Barcelona. It is intended that by the time they are the main force in Catalonia, there will be some 16,000 *mossos*.

As the only autonomous region sanctioned by Franco, Navarre was allowed to keep the tiny regional police force set up in 1928 whose main duties had to do with traffic. Its responsibilities have since been broadened somewhat, but it remains a modest operation involving some 400 officers. The same was until recently true of the other police forces created as a result of devolution after Franco's death. Galicia and Valencia both have their own constabularies, each with a rag-bag of responsibilities that includes protecting the buildings and members of the regional government and investigating cases involving juveniles, domestic violence and alleged infractions of the environmental and heritage laws. In Valencia, there were just 275 officers in the regional force in 2003 and in Galicia some 400. But the Galician authorities were planning a considerable widening of the powers of their police force and an increase in its strength to 1,700. At the same time, some other Autonomous Communities, notably the Canary Islands, which do not currently have forces of their own, were pressing Madrid for the right to set them up.

The combined strength of all Spain's police in 2001 was just below 185,000. This was fewer than when the PP came into office, and one of the sticks which the Socialists used to beat their opponents in the 2004 election campaign was that the conservatives had encouraged the privatization of policing to the detriment of public security. One of the most frequently repeated allegations was that Spain by then had 27,000 more private security guards and 6,000 fewer police officers than when Aznar took office.

But was the overall total for the police less or more than society required? International comparisons suggest that Spain is, in fact, amply supplied with police. According to a study by the UK Home Office, there were 457 officers per 100,000 inhabitants in Spain in 2001, compared with an EU average of only 337. The comparative figure for Britain was 255 and for the United States it was 230.

However, it is important to stress that comparisons in this field are open to all sorts of qualifications, and this one is no exception. Many police officers in Spain do jobs they would not be required to do in other countries. Much of the work undertaken by the municipal police would be done in other countries by traffic wardens, while many of the Guardia Civil are employed on duties that in other countries would fall to prison guards and forestry wardens.

Until recently, Spain's police had to tackle far less crime than their counterparts in countries with smaller police forces. That is no longer true. One of the saddest developments in modern Spain has been a steady, and rapid, increase in the crime rate. It has almost doubled in each of the last three decades and is now much the same as in countries where you might expect crime was much more widespread. In 2001, there were almost 100 reported offences in Spain for every 1,000 inhabitants. In the same year in England and Wales, the comparable figure was 105. In at least one area, Spain is the European leader. In recent years, it has seen more murders than any other EU nation. In 1998, there were more than 1,000 murders. England and Wales, with a population more than 25 per cent higher, had 750 murders that year.

Part of the explanation for Spain's soaring crime rate is that people have been losing their mistrust of the police and reporting offences more readily. But it is clear that there has been an explosion in underlying criminal activity that many Spaniards, particularly older and more conservative ones, blame on the advent of democracy.

It would have been surprising if the disappearance of the dictatorship and the lifting of so many restrictions within such a short time had not had some effect. But if you look at a graph based on the crime figures, you will see that the line begins its ascent in the year *before* Franco's demise, and this suggests that it had less to do with political factors than with the social and economic pressures that built up during the *años de desarrollo*.

Arguably the most worrying trend for the future is the growth of organized crime. This is not really an indigenous phenomenon. Spain, unlike Italy, has never had a home-grown Mafia for reasons that are an endless source of debate among those who know both countries well. My personal view is that Spaniards are just too proud, too defiant and reckless to submit to the extortion that is the life-blood of Sicily's Cosa Nostra and the other 'mafias' of southern Italy. It may also be, though, that their traditional lack of social cohesion has, in this area, worked in their favour. Spaniards are not naturally disposed to joining clubs, let alone swearing to uphold its rules on pain of death. Though a growing number of Spaniards belong to organized crime syndicates, the syndicates themselves are mainly foreign in origin.

British gangsters began to settle along the holiday *costas* and in the islands at a time when there was no extradition treaty between Spain and the UK. Many were later returned when extradition procedures were agreed, but others eluded deportation to become major players in the local underworld, particularly in the Canary Islands. Colombians and Italians linked up with the rudimentary smuggling networks in Galicia to turn the area into the principal route into Europe for cocaine. Moroccans crossed the Straits of Gibraltar to make Andalusia their main base in continental Europe for the wholesale distribution of cannabis. Immigration has brought the Russian and other 'mafias' to Spain. By 2004, the Interior Ministry calculated that there were some 18,000 organized criminals at work in Spain.

PART SIX

New Perspectives

CHAPTER 26

The Press: More Influence than Readers

As was seen in a previous chapter,* it was not until the early sixties that, according to the yardstick then used by the United Nations, Spain ceased to be economically underdeveloped. It could be argued that it was only in the late seventies, when the first free and fair democratic elections were held, that it ceased to be politically backward. However, it was not until the early nineties that Spain reached one of the benchmarks set by the UN for a country to be regarded as culturally developed. In 1992, for the first time, an average of more than one in ten of the population bought a daily newspaper.

Arguably, UNESCO's measure of development was a bit unfair on Spain because the number of readers per copy is higher than in many other countries. Newspapers are more likely to be shared at home, at work and in cafés in Spain than is the case in countries where newspaper reading is more closely associated with commuting and where readers often buy a copy at the start of their journey and throw it away at the end.

Nevertheless, though sales and readership in Spain have both grown in recent years, in 2000 only 36 per cent of the population aged fourteen or over read a newspaper on a typical day, compared with an average of 62 per cent in the then fifteen-member EU and 57 per cent in the US.

To some extent, of course, newspaper-reading is a reflection of a country's wealth and the levels of educational achievement wealth brings. It is no coincidence that Spain was poorer than most of the other countries to which it was compared in 2000. Nor is it any coincidence that Spanish newspaper readership has increased along with the overall

* See above, p. 16.

level of literacy. But the correlation with wealth and literacy is by no means perfect. The British are not as well-off, and maybe not as well-educated, as the French, yet they read more newspapers.

Various theories can be put forward to explain these and other similar discrepancies. In the first place, it is noticeable that newspaper-reading diminishes the closer one gets to the Mediterranean; and the closer one gets to the Mediterranean, the more oral is the nature of the culture. Another possible explanation is that international differences in newspaper sales have something to do with the relative incidence in each country of a popular press. A comparison between Spain and Britain is particularly interesting in this respect since Britain has such a highly developed popular newspaper market, whereas Spain has none. The sort of people who buy a 'serious' daily in Britain also buy a 'serious' daily in Spain, but the kind of people who buy a popular 'red top' in Britain buy nothing at all in Spain, and for the simple reason that there is nothing designed to meet their needs.

Some Spanish newspapers, such as *El Periódico* and *El Mundo*, use the design techniques of popular journalism – eye-catching layouts and jazzy graphics. But even *El Periódico*, which makes a more conscious appeal to working-class readers, is not a popular newspaper in the sense that the term is understood in Britain, Germany or the United States. It gives extensive coverage to 'serious' political and economic news, and although it carries stories about, for instance, the private lives of celebrities, it will rarely lead the paper with them. In fact, it is precisely the sort of non-sensationalist 'popular' paper that middle-class critics elsewhere would like to see replace working-class tabloids such as the *New York Daily News*, the *Sun* and *Bild Zeitung*.

Two attempts have so far been made to establish a comparable product in Spain. The first was *Diario Libre*, which was launched in 1978 and whose demise a few months later is perhaps best explained by one of its more memorable headlines, '*Maricas en el Ministerio de Cultura*' ('Poofters in the Arts Ministry') – not exactly an issue of burning concern in the ground-down workers' suburbs around Spain's big cities.

The second was an altogether more serious effort. *Claro*, backed by a fifty-fifty joint venture between Germany's Axel Springer group, which publishes *Bild*, and Spain's Editorial Española, owners of the conservative daily *ABC*, hit the news-stands in 1991. Its editor and some of his senior staff had spent weeks at *Bild* before the launch, being introduced to the techniques that have made it Europe's best-selling daily newspaper. What they produced was essentially a *Bild* tailored for the Spanish market – more scandalized than scandalous, and using a layout technique once described as 'typographical terror-ism'. It was launched with a cover price thirty pesetas below that of the rest of the national daily press, an initial print-run of 600,000, and a pledge of enough money to keep it on the market for up to three years. In the event, it took just three months for its backers to realize that *Claro* was never going to work. When they pulled the plug, news-stand surveys by rivals estimated that its sales had fallen to just 22,000 copies a day.

Why, then, is Spain seemingly incapable of sustaining a popular press? One explanation points to the comparable absence of popular newspapers in most of the rest of southern Europe. Perhaps there is something unique to Latin societies that makes them inimical to popular journalism, though it is not immediately apparent what that might be. Another theory is that Spain's well-established gossip magazines and sports newspapers already cover in unbeatable depth the stories on which a popular press would depend.

A more convincing argument, in my opinion, is that southern European journalists, unlike their northern European counterparts, have been unable – or unwilling – to come up with a product capable of luring working-class readers. Most of Spain's journalists enter the profession as university graduates, fresh out of the journalism schools that were originally set up under Franco as a way of bringing a traditionally troublesome profession within the framework of his corporatist state. Graduation from a 'Faculty of Information Science' became a precondition for registration as a journalist. An incidental effect was that it restricted the profession to the children of those relatively well-to-do families who were the only ones who could afford to send their children to university.

As the Socialists' policy of grants has taken effect, and more and more working-class graduates have issued from the universities, so more and more working-class youngsters have found their way into journalism. But they nevertheless bring with them an intellectual's interpretation of its nature and purpose. And they continue to regard themselves as members of the intelligentsia, whose mission is to write for other members of the intelligentsia in the sort of terminology both parties understand. Spanish journalists do not choose to write for their readers in the language of everyday speech, nor do they seem bothered about translating for them the technical terms in which stories are relayed to them by their sources.

It was left to foreigners – Scandinavians in the event – to fill the gap left by the absence of a popular press. With its low newspaper sales and growing army of commuters, Spain was an obvious market for the publishers of the new generation of free newspapers that began to appear in the mid-nineties when the first of Metro International's titles was launched in Sweden. The company entered Spain in 2001 when it began publishing a *Metro* for Barcelona, and was followed into the market by *20 Minutos*, published by the Norwegian group Schibsted. Both papers are distributed free of charge and by hand outside train, underground and bus stations, as well as from racks set up at carefully selected points. The content is sparse and bland, but clearly written and attractively presented.

The arrival of the giveaways has revolutionized the press world in Spain. By the middle of 2005, their publishers were putting their circulation at around 2.5 million, which was well over half the total for the country's paid-for dailies. *Metro*'s publishers claimed their paper had become the largest in Spain by circulation and the third most widely read, with a daily 'reach' of almost 1.9 million. However, since the various editions were strongly local in their emphasis it could be argued that *Metro* was a chain rather than a single title. In mid-2005, it was being published in eight cities and three regions. Its main rival, *20 Minutos*, claimed that its Madrid edition was the best-read title in the capital.

So far, the sales of Spain's paid-for papers, already under siege from the Internet, have held up better than in most other countries. This may be because they are underpinned by the steady and continuing rise in the overall level of education in Spain. It may even be that the giveaways are spreading the newspaper-reading habit and creating potential readers for the paid-for dailies. The conventional newspaper publishers' initial response was to invest more time, money and effort in their local sections. But in 2005, Recoletos, which publishes two of Spain's most successful specialist dailies,* opted to try and beat the Scandinavians at their own game with a third giveaway called *Qué!*, specifically and innovatively aimed at capitalizing on the habits of the Internet generation. The online version is directed at younger Internet surfers who can contribute to the paper with their blogs.

Spain's leading paid-for newspapers fall into two distinct categories: those established before the Franco era and those founded after it. Interestingly, not a single paper of any importance created during the dictatorship has survived it.

La Vanguardia was founded in Barcelona in 1881 and became the voice of Catalonia's upper middle class, many of whose members supported Franco's regime after the civil war. But its dependence, for advertising as well as circulation, on the Catalan nationalist middle- and lower-middle classes was brought home to it by a famous episode in 1960. *La Vanguardia's* then editor, outraged at hearing a sermon being delivered in Catalan, interrupted the service and harangued the priest. A boycott organized by the nationalists threatened to put the paper out of business and cost the editor his job.

After his departure, and within the bounds imposed by censorship, *La Vanguardia* gradually acquired a reputation for sound, objective reporting, especially of international news. By the time that democracy returned, it was Spain's best-selling newspaper. The lifting of censorship has permitted the rigorous standards once applied only to foreign coverage to spread to other parts of the paper, and a redesign has put colour on the front page without costing *La Vanguardia* that air of Olympian detachment which is its hallmark.

Yet it has never managed to break out of Catalonia to become the truly national paper it deserves to be. That, more than anything else, explains why its professional stature has not brought it higher sales. Its circulation of just over 200,000 in 2004 was much the same as when Franco died. *La Vanguardia* lost its place as Spain's best-selling newspaper to *El País* at the start of the eighties and, within what might be called the quality conservative market, it was overtaken by *ABC* in 1985. The *La Vanguardia* group's commercial growth has come through diversification into, first, radio and, later, television.

*See below, p. 358.

ABC was founded in 1905 and had established a distinguished reputation for worldwide coverage long before the civil war. It was allowed to continue publishing after Franco's victory because its monarchist proprietors, the Luca de Tena family, favoured the Nationalists during the conflict.

Ever since the return of democracy, it has been a loyal supporter of the People's Party (formerly Alliance). Unlike *La Vanguardia*, it has not always made a virtue of detachment. Under the editorship of Luis María Ansón, its anti-Socialist bias sometimes verged on the hysterical. But his strategy brought *ABC* handsome dividends in the form of circulation increases to above the 300,000 mark. Since Ansón departed in 1997, initially to become chairman of the subsidiary of a Mexican media conglomerate, sales of *ABC* have slipped, and in 2004 the paper was selling under 270,000 copies a day.

This was also partly because, in the year following his departure, *ABC*'s former editor launched a new, aggressively rightist product, *La Razón*. The paper, which was later sold to the Planeta publishing group, has succeeded in carving out a niche for itself, and in 2004 had sales of more than 140,000. *La Razón* was the latest of numerous attempts since the return of democracy to launch new dailies. Most of the others have failed. But two papers born since the end of the dictatorship have gone on to dominate the market.

El País was launched in 1976 to provide Spain with a quality daily untainted by associations with the past. Its parent company, PRISA, had been set up with a broadly based shareholding in which almost every leading personality committed to the consolidation of democracy had a stake. The first editor, Juan Luis Cebrián, who was only thirty-one when he was appointed, was given generous resources that allowed him to take his pick of Spain's most able young journalists. From day one, his newspaper was required reading for anyone seriously interested in the nation's affairs.

Its clean, clear modern format stood out on the news-stands, proclaiming that this was a newspaper that intended to highlight what was noteworthy rather than obscure it. During the UCD's years in power, *El País*'s reporters 'broke' several important stories, but perhaps an even greater contribution was made by its leader-writers who, day in, day out, explained patiently and clearly how this, that and the other was done in a democracy. It was an invaluable contribution in a country whose voters – and leaders – could be forgiven then for failing to grasp such concepts as collective responsibility, ministerial accountability, and where to draw the line between a permanent administration made up of officials and a transitory government made up of politicians.

By the time the Socialists first took power in 1982, *El País* was aligned with the PSOE and has remained broadly supportive ever since. Over the years, the breadth and accuracy of its coverage have earned it a reputation as one of Europe's best centre-left newspapers, comparable with the *Guardian*, *Suddeutsche Zeitung* or *Le Monde*. *El País* has been Spain's best-selling newspaper since the early eighties and in 2004 its average daily sales were more than 440,000.

Its closest rival was *El Mundo*, which was selling some 285,000 copies a day. The story behind its creation is quite as interesting as its subsequent evolution. In 1989, the Chairman of the now-defunct newspaper *Diario 16*, Juan Tomás de Salas, sacked its editor, Pedro J. Ramírez. Ramírez maintained he was dismissed for refusing to tone down the paper's investigations into the GAL.* De Salas insisted it was because he felt *Diario 16* was becoming too sensationalist.

At all events, it was a decision that was to cost his paper dear. First, de Salas's brother Alfonso, a senior executive of the group, threw his weight behind Ramírez's plans to set up a new daily and took on the chairmanship of the company created to launch and manage it. Then Ramírez set about stripping his old newspaper of much of its brightest talent. Among those who joined him were Spain's most original columnist, Francisco Umbral; one of its most popular cartoonists, 'Forges'; the head of the GAL investigation, Melchor Miralles; and several experienced roving correspondents, notably Alfonso Rojo, who in 1991 attracted worldwide attention as the only non-Arab press reporter to stay in Iraq throughout the Gulf War.† Ramírez also signed an agreement with the *Guardian*, one of *El Mundo*'s founding

---

*See above, p. 57.

† *El Mundo*'s journalists have since paid a terrible price for their determination to be at the front line. One of the paper's correspondents, Julio Fuentes, was murdered in Afghanistan in 2001. Another, Julio Anguita Parrado, died in Iraq in 2003. His death brought to three the number of *El Mundo* writers who have given up their lives for their profession: in 2000, a columnist, José Luis López de Lacalle, was assassinated by ETA.

shareholders, which allowed his paper to reprint material from the British daily.*

Within eight months, *El Mundo* was on the news-stands sporting a layout that was to win it more prizes at the following year's US Society of Newspaper Design awards than had ever been given to a European paper. Its relentless criticism of the Socialist government gained it a solid following among the well-educated, disenchanted urban young – precisely that section of the population that holds most attraction for advertisers. With the help of a big cash injection from the Italian publishers of RCS, who took a 45 per cent stake, *El Mundo* overhauled *Diario 16* in 1992. RCS, which owns *Corriere della Sera*, has since increased its stake to some 90 per cent.

Diario 16, by contrast, went into a gradual decline after Ramírez's departure. In 1994, Juan Tomás de Salas himself quit the board and in 2001 the paper finally went out of business.

El Mundo's revelations of corruption under González and the vitriol cast in the Socialists' direction by some other papers and magazines undoubtedly contributed to the PSOE's removal from power. Debate continues to simmer over the role played by journalists in the latter stages of the González era. For some, it was a period in which certain editors, notably Ramírez, went beyond the bounds of what is acceptable in a democracy to become actors on the political stage. Ansón later acknowledged that he and other editors had met to co-ordinate actions against the government. For others, though, this was the Spanish press's finest hour. Rightly or wrongly, many of the then Socialists' critics, to the left as well as the right of the government, believed that the PSOE's corrupt funding, the government's contempt for the law as exemplified in the GAL case, and González's personal disrespect for parliament threatened to warp Spanish democracy irreparably. They concluded that a desperate situation required desperate measures.

If González was the main casualty then Ramírez did not escape unscathed. A year after the Socialists were removed from power, a

* At this point, I should make a 'declaration of interest'. As the *Guardian*'s correspondent in Madrid at the time, Ramírez invited me to move my office to his new newspaper. I remained there until 1994. For part of that time, and until the *Guardian* sold its holding in 1999, I was one of the paper's representatives on the board of *El Mundo*'s parent company.

video showing the editor taking part in sex games with a prostitute was distributed to media offices and leading figures in Spanish life. Ramírez battled through the scandal, albeit with slightly dented authority, and remains today an influential commentator on the nation's affairs.*

His paper retained an ambivalent stance while Felipe González remained in power. It presented itself to its heterogeneous readership as anti-Socialist, but never made it entirely clear whether it was attacking the government from the left or the right. After the PP came to power, *El Mundo* came out more openly in support of José María Aznar and his policies. That did not, though, prevent it from being a fierce critic of his decision to back US policy in Iraq.

Ramírez's paper has often shown itself to be professionally more adroit than its competitors, and never was this more true than in its reaction to the challenge presented by the Internet. Considerable resources were put into giving it what is today by far Spain's most popular newspaper website.

The other journalistic survivor of the post-Franco era is *El Periódico*, which was founded in Barcelona by the Zeta magazine group. It was initially conceived as a national newspaper, but like *La Vanguardia* it failed to win acceptance outside its region of origin. It has since become very much a product aimed at the Catalan market, as its full title – *El Periódico de Catalunya* – makes clear. During the late nineties it lost readership, and by 2004 was selling an average of just over 170,000 copies a day.

The years following the end of the dictatorship also saw the re-creation of a vernacular daily press in Spain. The only newspaper of importance written entirely in a language other than Castilian is *Avui*, published in Catalan, which by 2004 had a circulation that had fallen to below 30,000. *Deia*, also a daily, is written partly in Basque. The more radical *Egin* was closed in 1998 by order of the ubiquitous Judge Baltasar Garzón, who accused the paper of being a part of the infrastructure of ETA. The following year he agreed to the order being lifted, but the debts that *Egin* had accumulated in the meantime made it impossible for it to continue publishing.

* He is also still by far the most controversial figure in Spanish journalism. In 2005, a left-wing parliamentarian led a 'raid' on Ramírez's holiday home in the Balearic Islands to draw attention to an alleged contravention of the planning laws.

By far the most profitable of the specialist dailies are those covering sport. *Marca*, once part of the press empire of Franco's Movimiento Nacional, is the leading title. With sales of more than 390,000 in 2004, it was the second best-selling daily in Spain, after *El País* and ahead of *El Mundo*. Its closest rival was *As*, which ranked between *La Vanguardia* and *El Periódico*. Spain also boasts a lively and highly competitive financial press, led by *Expansión* which, like *Marca*, forms part of the Recoletos group.

No one visiting Spain for the first time can fail to be impressed by the news-stands in the big cities – particularly the ones on the Gran Vía in Madrid and the Ramblas in Barcelona. Shut up at night to form mysterious steel boxes on the pavements, they open out in the morning like variegated tropical blooms. Every available space on the walls, the counter and on the opened-out doors is taken up with the vividly coloured covers of every conceivable kind of magazine. Usually there are so many on sale that the owner of the stall has to set out trestles at the front and sides to accommodate them. There are news magazines and general and special interest magazines, including a good many published elsewhere in Europe and in the States. There are humorous magazines, educational magazines, 'adult' magazines (for gays and lesbians as well as for heterosexuals), literary and scientific reviews, partworks, comics for children and comics for adults.

The news-stands are a tribute not only to the Spaniards' genius for display, but to the resilience of the Spanish magazine trade. Spaniards' enthusiasm for periodicals serves as a corrective to the view, based on a glance at the newspaper circulations alone, that Spaniards are not keen readers.

The overall 'reach' of magazines in Spain is greater than that of the newspapers, or at least it was until the arrival of the free dailies. In 2004, the Estudio General de Medios calculated that 55 per cent of the adult population were magazine readers and only 41 per cent were paid-for newspaper readers.

In Spain, the habit of subscribing to a newspaper or magazine has never taken root. The press is sold almost entirely from news-stands. Magazines suffer more from this than newspapers, because reader loyalty – and this is not just a Spanish phenomenon – tends to be weaker towards weeklies than dailies. The result is that the sales of individual Spanish magazines vary wildly from week to week, depending on the attraction each successive edition holds for the idle browser. Competition is fiercer than in any other section of the media. The lengths to which Spain's magazine journalists will go to secure an exclusive sometimes border on the piratical, and particularly 'hot' photographs can fetch immense sums.

As in most countries, the magazine business inhabits the gaps left by the newspaper industry. None of the Spanish newspapers, for example, has an equivalent of the social diaries or gossip columns you find in the British and American papers. But then Spain has a plethora of highly profitable glossy magazines devoted to the lives and loves of the famous.

The pioneer was *¡Hola!*, an extraordinary enterprise created by the Sánchez Junco family in 1944. Each week's edition was made up in Eduardo Sánchez Junco's front room with the help of his mother, his wife and his niece. It seemed to be a product suited only to a particular time and place. But not so. A magazine that helped its readers to escape from the rigours and the colourlessness of Francoist Spain turned out to have immense appeal elsewhere. The publishers of *¡Hola!* certainly anticipated the worldwide resurgence of interest in celebrities, and may very well have helped to promote it.

In 1988, an English-language edition, *Hello!*, was launched with the same outdated design and cravenly respectful approach to the rich and famous. Within four years it had won a weekly circulation of almost half a million and given the English language a new word – 'helloization'.

¡Hola! has been joined over the years by others such as *Pronto*, Spain's best-selling magazine with a circulation in 2002 of some 970,000, *Diez Minutos*, *Lecturas*, *Semana* and *¡Qué me dices!* These magazines – generically known as the *prensa de corazón* ('Press of the Heart') – occupy all six of the top places in the table of weekly magazine readership and sell more than two and a half million copies a week.

Sensing another gap in newspaper coverage, the magazines did their best to satisfy the clamour for uninhibited reporting of current affairs during the latter years of the dictatorship and the early years of the monarchy, when newspapers were unwilling or unable to do so.

The first opposition current affairs magazine was the quaintly titled *Cuadernos para el diálogo* ('Notebooks for the Dialogue'), founded by a group of Christian Democrats back in 1963. But *Cuadernos* was above all an intellectual publication with a penchant for the results of sociological investigations. The first real news magazine was *Cambio 16*, which hit the news-stands in 1973. Similar to *Time* or *Newsweek*, it rapidly achieved a high standard of professionalism and was followed into the market by a host of similar weeklies. By 1977 there were fifteen of them, selling a total of 2 million copies a week. But as *El País* and the other new newspapers began to assert themselves they started to wilt. *Cuadernos* was one of the first to go. Others followed in rapid succession. Today, *Cambio 16* is the only survivor of those giddy days, although it has since had to face competition from *Tiempo de Hoy* and the conservative *Epoca*.

Cambio 16 was a product of the rather serious, impassioned atmosphere that prevailed in the years leading up to Franco's death. But the magazine which captured and reflected the more liberated spirit of the years that followed was *Interviú*. Founded in Barcelona soon after the end of the dictatorship, *Interviú* set out to provide its readers with two things they had been denied under Franco – uninhibited coverage of politics and pictures of naked women. It did so in a way that proved particularly appealing to the Spanish market. Instead of wrapping its reports in code and metaphor in the way that had been customary until then, *Interviú* went straight to the politicians themselves, asked them blunt, provocative questions and printed the answers word for word. Rather than rely on the professional, usually foreign, models who were beginning to make their appearance in other magazines, *Interviú* approached Spanish actresses and singers with the beguiling proposition that by shedding their clothes they would be putting their democratic credentials beyond question. The message projected to the reader was – and is – that sexual and political liberation are one and the same thing. To anyone who did not live in Spain during the late seventies it is a peculiar concoction, and for the non-Spaniard it is made even more peculiar by the regular inclusion of full-colour photo-features on surgical operations, killings and accidents, often made up of pictures considered too explicit for use in the daily press.

When it hit its peak in 1978, *Interviú* was selling almost three-quarters of a million copies a week. The cash it generated formed the basis on which its proprietor, the late Antonio Asensio, was able to build a formidable media empire, the Zeta group. *Interviú* itself, though, lost circulation steadily and by 2004 it was selling barely 120,000 copies a week.

Tacky though it often is, *Interviú* has helped to fashion a specifically Spanish style of journalism that has evolved in the years since the end of the dictatorship. Perhaps surprisingly, in a country that has borrowed much from the other side of the Pyrenees, it has little in common with the elliptical French approach to reporting in which articles frequently start with a question. In their news stories at least, Spaniards favour the Anglo-Saxon method of beginning with a summary that is then expanded.

The singularity of Spain's journalism is to be found in a high degree of personalization that faithfully reflects the Spanish fascination with individuals and a relative indifference to depersonalized institutions and associations. The proportion of space occupied by signed opinion columns must be among the highest in the world and there is a quite extraordinary degree of concentration on the precise words spoken by news-makers. Interviews are invariably left in their raw 'question-and-answer' form and, if a report is not headlined with a 'quote', it as often as not starts with one. Yet I have rarely, if ever, heard anyone in Spain complain of having been misquoted, or quoted out of context.

CHAPTER 27

New Waves: TV and Radio

Surprisingly perhaps, the Spanish are a nation of TV addicts. The viewing figures for Europe as a whole reveal a situation that is precisely the opposite of what you would expect. By and large the people who watch television least are those with a reputation for being withdrawn and who live in the colder northern countries, whereas the people who watch television most are those who live in the warmer southern nations and have a reputation for being gregarious. One theory is that media preferences are influenced by the prevalence of an 'oral' culture in the Mediterranean.

There is an exception to this general rule. Britain also has very high viewing figures. But not even the British can match the Spanish when it comes to televisual dependence. The Estudio General de Medios calculated that, on an average day in 2002, almost 90 per cent of the population over the age of fourteen watched television. In Britain, the figure was 87 per cent. Spaniards, moreover, watched for much longer. The national statistics institute, INE, estimated that they spent some three and a half hours glued to the box, against two and a half hours in the UK. In 2000, 99.5 per cent of Spanish homes had a television set, compared with 87 per cent in the UK.

I do not know if this is further backing for the 'oral culture' theory or evidence of a link between television-watching and poverty, but the region in Spain with the highest viewing rate of all is Andalusia. I have not been able to find out if it is still true, but in the early eighties in Andalusia, which is the hottest region in Europe, more homes had television sets than refrigerators.

Whether 'watching' is the correct phrase for what the Spanish do with their televisions is open to question, though, because they will often leave them on while they are doing other things. I suspect the amount of undivided attention they give to TV is nothing like as high as the viewing figures suggest.

That said, research also shows that a high proportion of Spaniards form their political views on the basis of what they see on television. It is therefore no exaggeration to say that whoever controls what Spanish intellectuals call *la caja tonta* (the silly box) is in a position to control the mood and outlook of the nation. Though he could not have foreseen the extent of the Spaniards' addiction to television, Franco decided that the medium was too powerful to be left in any other hands but his own.

Televisión Española (TVE) was set up as a state monopoly in 1956. As with every sort of creative activity under the dictatorship, the programmes it transmitted were subject to censorship. But TVE was subject to a unique, double filter. First, the programming plans were scrutinized by 'advisory commissions' made up of judges, priests, officers in the armed forces and the like. Then, the finished product, whether made in Spain or bought from abroad, underwent what was euphemistically described as 'content evaluation'. As a result, things that were permitted in films and on stage were not allowed on to the small screen.

In 1980, *El País* got hold of the reports of one of Franco's censors, a Dominican monk called Antonio Sánchez Vázquez. These are the cuts he ordered in Billy Wilder's *The Lost Weekend*:

1. Kiss at the point of farewell.

2. When he steals the woman's handbag, eliminate the shots in which she and her companion behave with excessive affection (two or three times). At least, temper these shots.

3. Kiss and conversation while holding one another. Temper the kiss.

4. After the nurse says good-night ... one of the patients suffers *delirium tremens*. Allow it to start, cut quickly to when the doctors come in and he makes off with the doctor's coat.

Fr Antonio was not just concerned with sex and violence. After seeing a French comedy film, he wrote that 'Although the intention may be humorous, the Gestapo and their chief in Paris are held up to ridicule in their behaviour and references to the Führer.' Indeed, he seems to have had a remarkably sensitive set of political antennae for a priest. Mindful of Spain's position as a colonial power, he cut from a film called *Jaguar* a phrase about how the English exploited the Africans. Soon afterwards, relations with Britain entered one of their periodic crises over Gibraltar and the records show that Fr Antonio sent in another report suggesting that the phrase be reinserted. Perhaps his most memorable remark, though, accompanied a recommendation not to show a film called *The Morals of Mrs Pulska*. '"Strong" subject,' he wrote. 'Criticism of hypocrisy. I warn you this will cause a rumpus.'

The censors did not disappear with the ending of the dictatorship. Fr Antonio was one of four on the staff of TVE as late as 1980, although by that time their job was not so much cutting material as finding ways of toning it down – substituting 'dung' for 'shit' in subtitles, for instance.

Though the censors were later withdrawn altogether, the advent of democracy did not free TVE from government interference in the political content of its programmes. It was particularly unfortunate that the first Prime Minister of a democratic Spain should have been a man who had held high office under Franco in RTVE, the state corporation that controls both state-run radio and television. Adolfo Suárez had been controller of the first TV channel and subsequently the corporation's Director-General. He was thus thoroughly imbued with the Francoist notion of television as an arm of government.

It was only at the insistence of the Socialists and Communists in 1977 that the Centrists agreed to set up a governing body, responsible for guaranteeing RTVE's objectivity, scrutinizing its finances and – most important of all – drawing up a charter. The charter for RTVE, which came into effect in 1980, created a new governing body, the Consejo de Administración, made up of members elected by the Cortes. Its membership tends therefore to reflect the composition of parliament, which in turn is weighted in favour of the government.

The PSOE's victory in 1982 did not bring about any obvious change in attitude. In the campaign leading up to the NATO referendum, the 'box' was overtly manipulated to bring the electorate around to the Socialists' new-found point of view. During the 1989 general election campaign, the last to be held before the advent of commercial television, *Diario 16* put the stop-watch on TVE's newscasts. It found that the bulletins' special campaign reports had been pretty balanced, with each party receiving air-time more or less in proportion to its share of the vote in the previous election. But the rest of the news was another matter. A total of an hour and forty-three minutes had been spent on coverage of the government and the PSOE, as opposed to just four minutes given to the PP.

In 1990, the Socialists were finally forced to give a public account of the Juan Guerra affair* at a special debate in the Cortes. Ignoring a petition signed by the editors of all its bulletins, TVE refused to televise the debate 'live'. The head of news and current affairs said the scandal, which had been at the centre of public attention for months, 'was only of interest to a specialized audience'.

TVE's usefulness to Franco and his successors helps explain why successive governments were prepared to turn a blind eye to evidence of wholesale abuse in its management.

The earliest allegations came soon after the end of the dictatorship. In 1977, a group of workers set up an 'anti-corruption committee' and the following year *Cambio 16* published a lengthy report exposing some of the worst abuses – inflated salaries, people drawing two salaries for doing (or pretending to do) jobs in both radio and television, members of staff being paid on a freelance rate for work they did in RTVE's time, and so on. Among other things, they unearthed the case of someone who, while living and working in Brazil, where he was the representative of a Spanish company, was earning a handsome salary for 'co-ordinating' a programme which, as the magazine commented, he probably never even saw.

It was partly because of this extravagance and graft that RTVE had asked the government for a subsidy in 1976. It was clear that, unless something was done to sort out the corporation's finances, RTVE would soon get into the habit of taking ever larger handouts from the state. In 1978, Suárez sent in the government's auditors to find out where the money was going. Unfortunately for the government, the report they produced found its way to *El País*, which found enough material in it to fill seven articles.

After nine months of investigation, the government's accountants confessed that they were unable to say for certain how many people worked for RTVE or how much property and equipment it owned.

* See above, p. 59.

Huge numbers of books and records and large amounts of clothing and film were found to be missing. In fact, theft was so widespread that there was a special euphemism for stolen goods at RTVE. They were called *depósitos personales* (personal stores). Theft apart, the auditors noted that there seemed to be genuine confusion in people's minds over where to draw the line between what belonged to the corporation and what belonged to individuals. 'There are cases of directors and producers who regard their programmes as private property and, in extreme cases, flatly refuse to return them.'

The Centrists succeeded in putting the corporation back in the black. But a decade later, *Diario 16* got hold of a draft report on RTVE by the Tribunal de Cuentas, the body responsible for auditing the public sector, which covered the period since the Socialists had been in power. RTVE still did not have a reliable inventory, and different departments within the corporation were operating on different estimates of the number of people who worked for it. 'Investment plans, work programmes and budgets have turned out to be mere formal documents, lacking any kind of follow-up,' said the draft. One programme, with an initial budget of 11 million pesetas, had actually cost 150 million. In some cases, advances had been given for films that had already been made. By then, however, the corporation was operating in an entirely different environment.

Although it had to be pulled out of them like a tooth, the Socialists' decision to allow competition on television is likely to be seen with hindsight as one of their most valuable contributions to the consolidation of democracy, comparable with their taming of the army. The state's television monopoly ended on Christmas Day, 1989. At one o'clock in the afternoon, an announcer, Miguel Angel Nieto, said: 'Antena 3 Television, Spain's first privately owned television channel, has been born.' In the control box, the station's Director-General was so overcome by emotion that there were tears in his eyes as he tried to make a speech to the guests who had come to see the network launched. Characteristically, Spanish commercial television* had been got on the air at breakneck speed

---

* This is a less than satisfactory description of the privately owned channels, since the publicly owned ones also take advertising. But it is the most usual phrase in English and makes the point that the new channels have to make a profit.

– Antena 3 had learnt just four months earlier that it had been awarded a franchise.

Not surprisingly, given the degree of maladministration in state-run television, there were fears in RTVE and the government that Televisión Española would have difficulty competing with the new independent stations. One way in which RTVE reacted was by trying to give both its channels a fair chance in the coming battle. TVE-2, which had been launched in 1965 as a 'minority interests' channel, acquired a broader role, more resources and a new identity as 'La 2'.

In the meantime, the government had set about adding to the number of publicly owned stations in the regions, thereby increasing the competition that the privately owned channels would have to face. The original idea behind regional television had been to offer a vernacular service in those regions where people spoke a language other than Castilian. The autonomy statutes of these regions stipulated that the stations created to provide this service would be run by the regional administrations in much the same way that RTVE was run by central government. Regional television thus became a means of giving additional powers to the governments of those areas with a solid claim to a separate identity, and the issue of whether it should be exclusively vernacular soon became blurred.

The first two channels were launched with a cavalier disregard for the law. The Basque government's television service, Euskal Telebista (ETB), began transmissions on New Year's Eve, 1983, several days before the entry into effect of legislation authorizing the regions to apply for franchises. It now operates two channels – ETB-1, which broadcasts in Basque, and ETB-2, which transmits in Castilian. The Catalan government, which felt obliged to take up the gauntlet thrown down by the Basques, inaugurated TV-3 a few days later. Galicia subsequently got a channel of its own, as did Valencia, where a substantial minority of the population speaks a dialect of Catalan. In 1988, Catalonia acquired a second Catalan-language channel, Canal 33. Its launch was yet another act of defiance: unlike that of the Basque country, Catalonia's statute of autonomy did not entitle the area to more than one channel. Canal 33's earliest broadcasts were actually jammed by Madrid until the row with Catalonia's home-rule government was patched up.

To no one's great surprise, both the regions that got channels of

367

their own in the run-up to the launch of commercial television were in the hands of the Socialists. Canal Sur was launched in Andalusia and the capital acquired Telemadrid, or TM-3.

The three independent television franchises went to Antena 3, Tele 5 and Canal Plus. The Antena 3 consortium was led by the radio network of the same name, which in turn had been created by *La Vanguardia. ABC*'s owners also took a small stake. Tele 5's major shareholders, each with a 25 per cent holding, were the Italian media tycoon, Silvio Berlusconi, the Barcelona publishing house, Anaya, and Spain's financially muscular association for the blind, ONCE. Canal Plus was called after the privately owned French channel of that name, which had a 25 per cent stake. Its leading Spanish shareholder was the *El País*-based media group, PRISA.

It was assumed from the start that each of the privately owned television channels would have an identifiable political bias, like that of the privately owned radio networks in Spain.* Antena 3 could be expected to be critical of the Socialists; Canal Plus could be relied on to support them. The third channel, Tele 5, had made it clear in its prospectus that it did not intend giving much air-time to news and current affairs, aiming instead to build up a mass audience with games shows, variety programmes and popular films. Indeed, it could be argued that the scales were weighted against the government because, unlike Antena 3, which also considered but rejected the idea, Canal Plus opted to become a pay channel, thus restricting its potential audience.

It is against this background that a boardroom *putsch* at Tele 5, only days before it went on the air in early 1990, should be viewed. Berlusconi's representatives joined forces with those of ONCE to remove the channel's Chairman, who had come from Anaya. He was replaced by ONCE's Director-General, Miguel Durán. It was the first time a blind person had ever been given day-to-day control of a television station. A lot of commentators, bearing in mind that ONCE was subject to a government ministry, saw in the row a manoeuvre by the PSOE to redress the balance of commercial television's coverage.

---

* This is the case in much of continental Europe. Within Europe, the idea that the broadcast media do not have the same right as the written media to follow an editorial 'line' is a mainly British concept, inherited from the BBC's first Chairman, Lord Reith.

The ploy – if such it was – did not work. Certainly not for long. As ONCE backed away from its controversial policy of equity investments,* it gradually reduced its stake in Tele 5 and the channel fell under the control of Silvio Berlusconi. But Tele 5 remained more concerned with winning ratings battles than with peddling the right-wing politics of its leading proprietor.

The ownership structure of Antena 3 also underwent a series of changes that eventually handed control to a joint venture between two media groups that had both grown out of publishing – Spain's Planeta and the Italian firm De Agostini. Unlike Tele 5, though, Antena 3 retained an identifiably conservative bias, so free-to-air commercial television in Spain continued to lean to the right.

It is perhaps therefore not surprising, though nevertheless regrettable, that the Socialists should have continued influencing TVE's political coverage right up until 1996 when they were voted out of power. What is more surprising – and even more reprehensible – is that the PP should have continued the same shameful tradition of political control, despite the fact that they could count on the sympathy, if not the outright support, of both the free-to-air commercial channels.

In opposition, the PP had promised to reform RTVE's charter in such a way as to encourage its impartiality and establish a new national radio and television commission to protect its independence. Neither project came to anything, and a year after coming into office the new government gave the clearest possible indication of what to expect when it appointed a PP deputy to be the Director-General. Some of TVE's coverage under the conservatives was reminiscent of the Franco era. One of the most blatant examples, which gave rise to legal action by the trade unions, was a report on the 2002 general strike that included a 'vox pop' of supposedly representative interviews with members of the public. The comments of twenty-one people were aired. Every single one of them was against the strike.

The propaganda value of the state broadcast media helps explain why successive governments were prepared to let them run up vast debts in order to stay afloat. It was not long before the impact of

* See above, p. 151.

369

competition on RTVE's delicate, and chaotic, finances was felt. As early as 1991, RTVE had revealed that for the first time in almost a decade it was in the red. The biggest single contributory factor to its loss was a drop in advertising revenue. The shortfall made inevitable a draconian, though long overdue, rationalization.

Both sides in the battle for viewers and advertisers claimed that they were at an unfair disadvantage. The commercial stations, who took their case to the EU Commission, argued that the two state channels should be paid for out of public funds and ought not to be tapping the private sector by means of advertising sales. RTVE, meanwhile, complained that it had to meet a series of extra costs from which its competitors were freed. TVE has to subsidize the state-owned radio network, Radio Nacional de España (which no longer takes advertising), fund the corporation's external broadcasting services and the national Radio and Television Institute, and make good the losses of RTVE's orchestra and choir. In 1994, for the first time, the government provided RTVE with a subsidy intended to meet these additional costs.

But the subsidy which, by 2005, had grown to €78 million ($97 million or £53 million) proved nowhere near enough to cover RTVE's growing losses. The gross mismanagement of earlier years has disappeared. Nevertheless, year in, year out, the corporation has got deeper and deeper into debt. In 2005, it expected to earn barely half of what it planned to spend, and forecast that by the end of the year its accumulated debts would have reached €7.6 billion ($9.4 billion or £5.2 billion), which was more than 1 per cent of Spain's expected GDP.

TVE's free spending goes some way towards explaining why it managed for so long to hang on to its position as Spain's leading television network. It was not, in fact, until 2004 that a commercial channel, Tele 5, succeeded in notching up a bigger average share of the year's audience than TVE's first channel. Antena 3 was hard on its heels. Canal Plus had a mere 3 per cent of the audience, while La 2, which seemed initially to be offering real competition to the commercial channels, faded in importance during the nineties, and by 2004 had an average share of less than 5 per cent.

Perhaps the biggest surprise in the development of Spanish television has been the resilience of the regional channels. Their share of 17 per cent in 2004 was higher than a decade earlier, though the increase was partly due to the fact that two other regions, the

Canary Islands and Castile–La Mancha, had set up regional channels in the meantime.* The highest viewing figures among the *televisiones autonómicas* were for Catalonia's TV-3.

One of the first weapons to be brandished in the ratings war between the various channels was, perhaps inevitably, sex. It was first brought into play by Tele 5 in the summer of 1990 when the channel launched a thrice-weekly, late-night quiz programme-cum-striptease show that had been bought from an Italian channel. In its dubbed version it went by the title of *¡Uf! ¡Que calor!* which, freely translated, means 'Phew! What a Scorcher!' TVE hit back with a professional striptease routine to round off its chat-and-variety show, *Un día es un día*.† It later showed a series of made-for-TV films based on erotic classics such as *Roxanne*, and resumed the transmission of X-rated films such as *Emmanuelle*, which had been a feature of its programming in the first years of the Socialist administration. Meanwhile, and with a minimum of publicity, Canal Plus began showing hard-core pornographic movies once a week in the early hours.

Sex, though, soon lost its impact, and the ratings war began to be waged mainly with imported Latin American soap operas, known as *culebrones* (serpents),‡ then – more encouragingly – with locally produced variety shows and situation comedies. What gave Antena 3 an early advantage over Tele 5 was the hugely successful *Farmacia de guardia*, a comedy centring on the comings and goings at a local chemist. Tele 5 subsequently wrested back the lead, thanks in part to *Médico de familia*, which achieved the highest ratings of any fictional series since the introduction of commercial TV. Drama series produced in Spain by Spaniards in recent years that have won critical plaudits as well as high ratings include TVE's *Cuéntame cómo pasó*§ and Tele 5's *Periodistas*.

---

* Several other Autonomous Communities, including Aragón, Asturias, Estremadura and Murcia, made failed attempts to implant regional television in their areas. But in both Andalusia and Valencia the experiment was sufficiently successful for the regional authorities to set up second channels.

† TVE took *Un día es un día* from the Catalan channel, TV-3. The last edition broadcast by TV-3 won the programme widespread notoriety: it ended with the presenter persuading the entire audience to take off their clothes in front of the cameras.

‡ Because they go on and on.

§ See above, p. 87.

Meanwhile, however, Spanish viewers were falling under the spell of what soon came to be known as *telebasura* or 'trash telly'. Some of this was simply a rehash in Spanish of voyeuristic 'reality' shows that had already been successful elsewhere like 'Big Brother' (*Gran hermano* in Spain). But some *telebasura* was entirely home-grown – a projection on to the small screen of the Spanish obsession with celebrity that fuels its gossip magazines, the *prensa de corazón*. The archetype was *Crónicas marcianas* ('Martian Chronicles'), which first appeared in 1997 and was put out on Tele 5 in a slot that began late at night and ended early in the morning.* There followed a stream of similar products: Antena 3's *¿Dónde estás corazón?* and *A la carta*, Tele 5's *Aquí hay tomate* and *Salsa rosa*, Valencian Canal 9's *Tómbola*, and many, many more. Like so much else in Spain, the fashion for these so-called *programas de corazón* was taken to an extreme. In 2004, it was calculated that they occupied an average of thirteen hours a day on the three leading channels alone. The attraction for television executives is that they are not just popular, but cheap. Partly, they are talk shows of a stunningly vulgar kind in which participants loudly dispute, for example, the sex lives of reality show contestants or the purported drug addiction of a minor celebrity. The air is thick with rumour, insinuation and sometimes outright defamation. Depending on the format, there can be reports filmed outside the studio, often using the intrusive techniques of the *prensa de corazón*. A typical encounter would see, say, a bullfighter's girlfriend being chased down a street by an interviewer shouting out questions about the most intimate aspects of her private life.

When the Socialists returned to power in 2004, they vowed to tackle what they saw as the two biggest scandals on the Spanish small screen: *telebasura* and the pro-government bias of TVE's news and current affairs. RTVE's new Director-General, Carmen Caffarel, drew up a code of conduct that included a series of norms intended to tone down some of TVE's output and protect children during the hours when they were likely to be watching.† At the same time, government officials began talks with all the major

* Television scheduling in Spain is as idiosyncratic as the Spanish timetable. Prime time starts at 9.00 p.m. and ends at midnight. Peak viewing is between 10.00 p.m. and 11.00 p.m.

† This so-called *horario protegido para menores* lasted until 10.00 p.m.

broadcasters on reining in the *programas de corazón*. The influence of any government is considerable, and nowhere is this truer than in Spain, where public and private interests are still extensively intertwined. Despite blustering about censorship from some TV executives, the tide soon began to turn against *telebasura*. At the start of the 2004–5 season, the producers of *Crónicas marcianas* were already promising a 'change of tone'. The following year, in what may prove to be the beginning of the end for the genre, the programme was withdrawn.

Zapatero's Socialists also showed signs of intending to deliver on their undertaking to make TVE politically impartial. Carmen Caffarel appointed a new news and current affairs director, Fran Llorente, with instructions to give the public bulletins that were *desgubernamentaliza-dos* (de-governmentalized). However, at the same time, in an effort to redress the political imbalance of Spanish television, the government also signalled that it would give a free-to-air licence to the owners of Canal Plus. Their new channel, Cuatro, went on the air for the first time at the end of 2005.

Radio has a place in Spaniards' affections that is very possibly unique in Europe. You will sometimes hear them say with pride that they have the 'best radio in Europe' – and they may well be right. Spaniards are natural broadcasters. They tend to be fluent speakers as well as brilliant improvisers, and the radio professionals among them seem to realize that the medium is at its best when it is spontaneous, flexible and just a little unstructured. There is much less scripting than in Britain or the US, and that applies to current affairs presenters as well as to disc jockeys. The quality of Spanish radio helps explain an audience of more than 19 million a day. Only television has a greater 'reach'. Well over half the population over the age of fourteen listens to radio on an average day – the highest proportion in Europe.

To a greater extent than television, moreover, radio has played a key role at crucial moments in Spain's recent history. Many adult Spaniards' first experience of uncensored news was gained by listening to the SER network's late-night current affairs programme, *Hora 25*, during the transition to democracy. As radio was freed from the constraints imposed on it under the dictatorship, the number of listeners shot up from around 7 million at the time of Franco's death to some 16 million by the late seventies.

But it was the broadcasters' performance during the abortive coup attempt in 1981 that really made the difference. The radio correspondents in the Cortes press gallery stayed on the air until the moment that Tejero ordered his men to loose off their fusillade. Throughout the night that followed, their colleagues elsewhere, in studios and outside-broadcast vehicles, succeeded in conveying urgency and concern without seeming to panic. Spain's most famous radio sports journalist, José María García, climbed on to a car outside the parliament building and kept up a running commentary from there. A lot of Spaniards felt that the broadcasters 'held their hand' during that anguished night, and they have not forgotten it.

Radio made another decisive, but altogether more controversial, intervention in the nation's affairs in the extraordinary hours and days following the Madrid bombings of 2004. With voting due to be held just three days later, José María Aznar's government, terrified the attack would persuade voters to take revenge on the PP for having dragged them into Iraq against their will, did everything it could to keep the finger of suspicion pointed at ETA rather than al-Qaida. Its arguments were demolished, not in print, which is too slow to have made an impact in the brief time that was available for voters to change their minds, but on the air waves, and by radio far more than television.

The bombings took place on a Thursday. For the rest of that day and into the next, the media were so busy reporting on the carnage and the casualties, they barely had time to focus on the causes. But later on the Friday, Cadena SER, Spain's biggest radio network, which is pro-Socialist, started to break a series of exclusives about the investigation that left the government's case in ruins. At times on the Saturday, its reporters were providing new 'scoops' every hour and people were doing their weekly shopping with transistor radios, so as not to miss the latest development. It is sometimes forgotten in the age of the Internet that radio is still the fastest of all mediums. You do not need to mark up a story for a web page, much less arrange a studio or design a newspaper. All you need to do is to speak the facts – or claims – into a microphone to relay them to the public. Spaniards were given a remarkable demonstration of the power of radio in the period leading up to the 2004 election. Those who sympathized with the PP are still smarting from the experience.

The Madrid bombings and their aftermath also, though, highlighted the fact that the Socialists were heavily dependent on radio to get their message across. So Cadena SER has an immense political, as well as social, importance. Its daily audience in 2004 was more than 5 million. Cadena SER's nearest rival, Onda Cero, which is part of the same group as Antena 3, had an audience of fewer than 2 million. It was followed at a short distance by the state-run Radio Nacional and COPE (Cadena de Ondas Populares Españolas), which is the last outlet of real importance belonging to the once-mighty media empire of the Roman Catholic Church.

Competition between these four networks for the big morning audiences* is a contest without respite, fought out with networked magazine programmes whose presenters are national celebrities. For many years, the king of the air waves was Cadena SER's Iñaki Gabilondo, who rose to fame as the anchorman of *Hora 25* during the transition. In 2005, after nineteen years presenting the programme *Hoy por hoy*, Gabilondo left to join the new Cuatro TV channel. The rewards for radio stars in Spain are often greater than for television personalities. When Onda Cero signed up Luis Del Olmo† for its morning programme in 1991, it was reported that he had secured an annual payment of 600 million pesetas ($5.8 million or £3.3 million) *plus* a percentage of his programme's advertising revenue.

It must say something about the Spanish love of debate that Spain is one of the few countries in which programmed radio still has a bigger share of the audience than the specialist stations, which are mostly devoted to music. In the specialist area, too, Cadena SER is dominant. Its Cadena 40 pop network has a daily audience of more than two and a half million. Spain also has a variety of specialist talk

---

* It is another reflection of the Spaniards' unique timetable that listenership does not reach its peak until after 10.00 a.m. when almost 7 million people tune in on an average weekday. Another outstanding idiosyncrasy is the night-time listenership which soars to more than 3 million in the period between midnight and 1.00 a.m.

† Del Olmo has been broadcasting since he was a teenager. His father was the stationmaster of a small town in Galicia at which the trains to and from Madrid had to make a lengthy stop. Armed with a tape-recorder, he would scour the first-class carriages in search of celebrities who, in the circumstances, found it difficult to refuse him an interview.

stations. The leader is Radio Nacional's all-news channel, Radio 5 Todo Noticias. There are others specializing in sport or finance. But none has won a substantial following, and in 2004 all-talk radio had barely 7 per cent of the total audience.

Or rather, it had 7 per cent of the total *legal* audience, because another of the peculiarities of Spanish radio is a vast 'pirate' sector whose audiences are not included in the official figures. In 2004, the professional body that represents Spain's main commercial radio networks, the Asociación Española de Radio Comercial (AERC), presented the results of an investigation into unlicensed radio stations. Its researchers had found 2,279 – more than twice as many as had an authorization to broadcast. In addition, there were 504 municipally owned stations that had been given licences, but were breaking a law that forbade them to form part of a network, and another 124 that were transmitting either from a different place or on a different frequency from the one for which they had been given permission. AERC's study provided remarkable evidence both of Spaniards' enthusiasm for radio and their blithe disregard for official rules. Nothing better illustrates the point made in an earlier chapter that the delays in Spain's judicial system breed disrespect for the law than the anarchy on its air waves. One network had forty unlicensed stations. Then came one with thirty-eight. That was the Roman Catholic religious network, Radio María.

CHAPTER 28

A Cultural Revolution

'When I heard they were going to build it and I saw the plans, I thought it was ghastly,' Gerhard Richter wrote.

Then I went to Bilbao a year or two after the opening. The sight of it made a big impact. It continued to fascinate me. It was incredible. Once there, I could see the pride that people took in the museum, and I realized it fulfilled a social function that questioned the concept of museum architecture I had held until then.

Germany's leading contemporary artist is not the only person to have harboured doubts about Frank Gehry's glowing, metal-clad Guggenheim museum on the banks of the River Nervión. Many Basques, including leading figures in the arts, fiercely opposed the establishment of this outpost of one of America's leading cultural institutions, seeing in it a form of US imperialism. Today, hardly anyone can be found to agree with that view. Within months of the opening, even former critics were acknowledging an *efecto Guggenheim*.

For one thing, the museum had conjured a local tourist industry out of nothing. Ugly, rainy, post-industrial Bilbao, racked by terrorism, had always been a place that any holidaymaker with half a grain of sense would avoid. The Guggenheim's continually changing collection of modern and contemporary art has drawn tourists to the city for the first time in its history.

But, as Richter saw, the building in which it was housed has also had a remarkable effect on the outlook of the *bilbainos*. It is so startlingly contemporary, so shiningly visible and so *big* that it gives the people who live with it little choice but to look to the future. It is as if Gehry's extraordinary building – part ship, part fish – were saying to the Basques that there is a world of bright possibilities beyond their narrow valleys and that the time has come for them to break free from their history. Perhaps some were right to fear its arrival.

The Guggenheim, funded by the local government, but with most of the collection on loan from New York, is more than just an outstanding example of successful collaboration between public and private sectors. It also reflects two of the most important characteristics of cultural policy in Spain since the end of the dictatorship. One is the use of culture to re-brand Spain as a modern country. The other is the extension of an enhanced cultural infrastructure to every part of that country.

What the Spanish sometimes refer to as *demanda cultural* is a palpable, and occasionally awkward, reality. Though it is an attitude more often honoured in word than deed, in the Spanish view of things, culture, like education, is axiomatically good. Elsewhere in Europe, that belief was dented by events in the last century, and in particular by the role the arts played in Hitler's Germany. Spain did not take part in the Second World War, so Spaniards are neither as interested in, nor as familiar with, the awkward questions Nazism raises. Their intellectuals have never wrestled with the conundrum of how the gas-ovens came to be stoked to the strains of Richard Wagner.

Spain also differs from the other big nations in Europe in that most of the country did not experience an industrial revolution. One of the effects of industrialization is to bolster a sense of working-class identity by promoting the formation of trade unions and the spread of collective bargaining. In Spain, that process was largely restricted to Catalonia, Asturias and parts of the Basque country, and even in those areas it was put smartly into reverse when Franco took power, outlawed the unions and imposed a fascist notion of wage-bargaining. The Spain that eventually came out from under his shadow was one almost wholly devoid of working-class consciousness. It is particularly true of the millions who fled the countryside in the fifties and sixties. They may not be ashamed of being, or having been, poor. But the idea that poverty could in any way be a source of pride, or that wealth might be a source of shame, would strike them as just plain silly. And, just as there is no real questioning of 'bourgeois values', nor is there any real objection to 'bourgeois culture'. You rarely if ever hear working-class Spaniards talk disparagingly about, say, Cervantes in the way that their British or American equivalents will sometimes refer to Shakespeare. What happens in practice is that most choose to watch Tele 5 rather than go to the theatre, but what rejection exists is passive rather than active, silent rather than vocal.

The need for 'culture' is something to which everyone, but everyone, in Spanish society pays lip-service. Talk to the mayor of any godforsaken little *pueblo*, and he will invariably round off his list of the village's grievances and deficiencies by saying, '... *y hay un terrible déficit cultural*'. As if he were talking about a shortage of drinkable water. Or telegraph poles.

Indeed, the single biggest problem in this area by the time Franco died was one of geographical imbalance. Spain's cultural resources were concentrated almost exclusively in Madrid and Barcelona. The rest of the country was largely neglected. Andalusia, for example, has much the same population as Switzerland. It is a region with a rich cultural tradition and a huge cultural appetite. Yet, as late as 1982, it had not a single functioning theatre or orchestra.

The change wrought since then has been truly astonishing. A full list of the theatres, concert halls, orchestras, festivals and art galleries that have come into existence in the Spanish regions over the past twenty-odd years is beyond the scope of this book, and would no doubt bore the reader anyway. But a few examples may give an idea of the cultural revolution that has swept through the provinces.

Murcia and Estremadura, both areas once associated with back-breaking labour, parched landscapes and dreadful poverty, now have their own youth orchestras. Valladolid, a city that used to epitomize Old Castilian conservatism, has a museum of Spanish contemporary art. At one time, the only arts festival of any real importance outside Madrid and Barcelona was the annual San Sebastián film festival. Today, it seems as if every provincial capital in Spain has its movie festival and some, like the one in Gijón, are attracting interest from abroad. But then the map of Spain nowadays is smothered with arts festivals. There are more than 400 of them: some specialist, some generalist; some more ambitious than successful, but others of genuine international significance in their respective fields.

The outstanding achievement among Spain's regional arts initiatives, though, has not been a festival but a museum, the Institut Valencià d'Art Modern (IVAM). It first began to make news in the eighties when it acquired a collection of works by the early twentieth-century sculptor, Julio González. Since then, the museum has won widespread respect for a focused collection that aims to balance the local with the global.

There may be an element of hypocrisy in Spaniards' professed reverence for *cultura,* particularly in view of their enthusiasm for *telebasura.* But it is also the case that, given theatres, concert halls, art galleries and the like, Spaniards have used them. As new wealth poured into Spain in the late nineties, a disproportionate share was spent by the public on the arts. Between 1998 and 2000, in fact, annual expenditure on cultural activities leapt by 20 per cent. In 2005, the Touring Club Italiano conducted a highly original survey into the degree of what you might term cultural aversion in each of the twelve states then making up the European Union. The aim was to establish what proportion of the population in each country had never taken part in a range of cultural activities, such as going to a concert or visiting a library. Spaniards were found to be slightly less culturally active than the average, which is what you would expect of a country that is less prosperous than most in the EU. But, altogether more surprisingly, the Spanish were found to be more culturally active in general than either the French or the Italians. *Telebasura* is by no means the whole story.

Clearly, the spread of institutions and activities to the Spanish regions is in large part a product of decentralization. All the Autonomous Communities were given the arts as part of their bundle of responsibilities and it has sparked the healthiest sort of competition. If one region funds, say, a new art museum, it is not long before its neighbours are planning one too. But perhaps the area in which decentralization has played the most valuable role of all has been in promoting the spread of public libraries. This was the biggest single cultural deficiency in Spain at the time of Franco's death. As late as 1982, the number of library books per 100 inhabitants in Spain was lower than it was in Morocco. The progress since then has been remarkable.

By 2000, Spain had more than 4,000 public libraries and almost 8 million people – a fifth of the population – were enrolled users. Over the previous ten years, the number of libraries had risen by 60 per cent, but the number of enrolled users had gone up by 140 per cent, suggesting that the authorities were still struggling to meet the demand. That said, the volume of loans was proportionately much lower than in other, comparable nations. In 1998, the most recent year for which I was able to find an international comparison, French library-goers took out about ten books a year. In Spain, the figure was only six, though that may also have had something to do with the fact that Spanish public libraries have just not had the time or resources to build up the same, vast collections that are to be found in France. The number of library books per 100 of the population was still only half that in France.

Overall, the assumption by the autonomous governments of responsibility for culture has been a success. But it has not been free of controversy. One accusation has been that of narrow-mindedness: that, in deciding the allocation of funds, regional administrations judge projects less on their intrinsic cultural merits than on how much they will further the cause of that area's regional, or 'national', culture.

The Basque administration, for example, was criticized in the early years for earmarking a quarter of its arts funds for the creation of Basque-speaking media. 'We can get by without Basque song, music or theatre for ten years,' a senior official retorted, 'but if we spend ten years without speaking Basque and without offering a real solution to the problem of our language, it'll be lost.' Elsewhere, critics have deplored a tendency to give undue prominence to mediocre local artists, composers, performers and so on.

As the transfer of responsibilities and funds went ahead, the budget of the Arts Ministry in Madrid shrank steadily. As the Catalans in particular never tire of pointing out, more than half of all the central government's spending on culture goes to Madrid. But then Madrid, being the capital, is also where most of Spain's national cultural institutions are based, and over the years quite a lot of money has been needed to bring them up to scratch or, in some cases, into existence.

After Franco's death, one of the most pressing tasks was to provide Madrid with a contemporary art museum of international standing. The existing one, which had been opened in 1969, stood forlornly on the outskirts of the capital – a monument to the dictatorship's indifference to contemporary trends, and visited only by interested Madrileños and the occasional, really determined tourist.

For years, Spaniards' attitude to modern art had been much the same blend of majority hostility and minority enthusiasm that was to be found in other Western nations. But at some point in the early eighties it underwent a profound change. It is difficult to say exactly when that change took place, but it is possible to pinpoint the moment when it began to manifest itself – February 1983, when the second government-sponsored International Festival of Contemporary Art, held in Madrid under the title of *Arco-83*, was almost overwhelmed by the number of people who packed in to see it. When I visited Madrid a year later, I was struck by an atmosphere that I had never encountered before – that of a city gripped by art fever. Everywhere I went, in cafés, bars and restaurants, there were posters advertising exhibitions, and on all sides friends and acquaintances had a story to tell of how they had had to queue for hours to get into this or that show. As the Professor of History of Art at the Complutense University, Antonio Bonet Correa, wrote at about that time:

All of a sudden, the Spaniards – who for years knew nothing of the art world and were deprived of contemporary international art – have woken up to discover a new terrain. The habit of going to exhibitions in order to know about modern art has entered into the customs of those professional people who would wish to be considered as cultured.

According to an Arts Ministry survey carried out in 1985, 20 per cent of all Spaniards over the age of fourteen were going to a public or commercial art gallery at least once a fortnight. One can only guess at the reasons for this remarkable level of interest. History shows that painting is an art form for which the Spanish have shown a special genius, and it may simply be that they have an innate attraction to it that was stifled under Franco's dictatorship. To some extent, art in Spain may also have benefited from the worldwide surge of interest in painting and sculpture during the eighties, much of it inspired by the investment possibilities fine art offers.

But it also seems to me that when a society manifests a passionate interest in contemporary art it is telling us something about itself. There was a similar change in Britain in the nineties when people stopped decrying contemporary art and began to be, if not appreciative, then at least intrigued by it; when even popular newspapers began to take an interest in the Young British Artists movement, and conferred on those such as Damien Hirst and Tracey Emin a celebrity status that would have been unthinkable for their counterparts of an earlier generation. Perhaps the British, like the Spanish a decade earlier, were saying that they were ready for a new start; that, after years of dwelling on the past, they were all of a sudden more interested in the future.

At all events, the degree of interest in contemporary art shown by the public in Spain put considerable pressure on the authorities to equip Madrid with a museum that would bear comparison with the Pompidou Centre in Paris or the Tate in London. The plans for what was to become the Museo Nacional Centro de Arte Reina Sofía were hotly debated from the outset.

Work had begun in 1981 on the conversion of an eighteenth-century hospital near the end of the wide avenue on which Spain's great classical art museum, the Prado, stands. But when it was opened in 1986 – many felt precipitately, to win votes at the general election of that year – the building did not even have proper air-conditioning. Works by the American artist Cy Twombly were put on display and started to warp. A new round of repairs was begun three years later, and in 1990 the museum was closed down for seven months for refurbishment, which eventually cost over 50 per cent more than initially budgeted. By the time it was re-opened, the Reina Sofía had acquired – among many other additions – three controversial glass towers on the outside of the building to accommodate lifts.

It still lacked a permanent collection, and as its curators' plans for one began to leak out, the Reina Sofía found itself plunged into yet more controversy. The director was accused of attempting the impossible in trying to assemble a collection that explained the development of twentieth-century Spanish art. The painter Antonio López, the 'star' of Victor Erice's film *El sol del membrillo* (*The Quince Tree Sun*), complained bitterly that it did not do justice to Spain's figurative artists. And then there was the most heated row of all, over what was to become the centrepiece of the museum's permanent collection – the most celebrated work of twentieth-century Spanish art, Picasso's *Guernica*.

In 1981, it had travelled all the way from New York's Museum of Modern Art in compliance with its creator's wish that it be given to the Spanish people once democracy was restored. After eleven years spent in an annexe of the Prado, it was moved again, against the wishes of many of Picasso's surviving relatives, to the new Reina Sofía art centre.

Some critics feared the already flawed canvas would suffer further damage. Others believed the move ran counter to the artist's stated intention, which was to have his masterwork hung in the Prado and thereby open a bridgehead for contemporary art in a collection which otherwise came to a halt in the nineteenth century. For the government, though, getting *Guernica* moved to the Reina Sofía was essential to the scheme of things they had devised. This was that the Prado and its annexes should be retained for pre-twentieth-century painting and sculpture, while the Reina Sofía was given over to modern art. It was also a way of providing the controversial new gallery with a work that would bring in the visitors and finally justify the immense sums of money that had been spent on it.

During 1993, the Reina Sofía enjoyed a much-needed respite from controversy as the focus of attention switched to another eighteenth-century building at the opposite end of the Paseo del Prado.

The Villahermosa Palace had by then become home to most of what was widely regarded as the world's finest private art collection after that of the British royal family. By the mid-eighties, Baron Heinrich von Thyssen, the Dutch-born steel tycoon, had expanded the art collection he had inherited from his father to the point where it included some 1,500 paintings and sculptures of note. Faced with the impossibility of displaying them adequately at his home in Lugano, he began casting around for a new home for his treasures and set off a sort of international competition for the privilege of providing one. The Prince of Wales was even said to have flown to the Baron's Swiss home in an attempt to talk him into handing over his collection to Britain. The Baron's Spanish wife, Carmen 'Tita' Cervera – an ex-Miss Spain and former wife of the screen Tarzan, Lex Barker – proved more persuasive. In 1988, the Baron chose Spain instead, undertaking to loan some 800 of the best works for an initial period of nine and a half years.

It was agreed that the bulk of the collection should be housed in the Villahermosa Palace, and that the remainder should go to the medieval Pedralbes monastery in Barcelona. Both buildings were specially refurbished for the purpose. The deal was made permanent in 1993, with the Spanish government effectively buying the collection for 44,000 million pesetas ($315 million or £210 million). Six years earlier, a panel of Spanish experts had concluded that the part of the collection that had come to Spain was worth almost seven times as much. Art prices had – it is true – dropped in the meantime, but by any reckoning the deal was a bargain for Spain.

The Thyssen Collection complements the other two. It is strong in areas such as the German Renaissance, Impressionism, post-Impressionism, German Expressionism and the early twentieth-century avant-garde in which the Prado and Reina Sofía are weak.

Quite apart from its cultural value, the acquisition of the Thyssen Collection, together with the creation of the Reina Sofía centre, gave Madrid a new dimension as a tourist destination. It could be argued convincingly that the triangle formed by the Villahermosa Palace, the Reina Sofía and the Prado held one of the greatest treasures of fine art anywhere in the world.*

Yet more has since been added. In 2004, a modern, glass-and-steel extension to the Villahermosa Palace was inaugurated, mainly to house the collection of Baron Thyssen's widow.† The following year, the Reina Sofía opened a wing designed by the French architect Jean Nouvel that increased the available space by more than half and turned the centre into one of the world's biggest galleries of modern art. Nouvel's wing will be used for temporary exhibitions, freeing up the whole of the old hospital for the permanent collection.

Work had meanwhile begun on an ambitious three-year plan to allow the Prado to show many more works than previously, and exhibit together in a single building its Old Masters and a less often seen collection of nineteenth-century works.

The Prado's problem had long been a perverse one for a museum: it had too many good things. At any one time only about one-seventh of its total collection was on display. The rest formed the *Prado oculto* (the hidden Prado) and the *Prado disperso* (the scattered Prado): the first made up of works confined to the store-rooms beneath the gallery; the second comprising the paintings, sculptures and drawings the Prado

---

* The Thyssen Collection has not, however, proved to be as much of a tourist attraction as originally forecast. Initial projections put the number of visitors per year at around a million. But in recent years it has been no more than about 500,000. In 2004, the Prado drew 2 million and the Reina Sofía 1.5 million.

† Baron Thyssen died in 2002.

loans out to government buildings. Between them, the *Prado oculto* and the *Prado disperso* added up to a collection that could well be as valuable as Baron Thyssen's, yet the acquisition of the latter made their eventual display much more problematic. By putting the Thyssen Collection in the Villahermosa Palace, the authorities deprived the Prado of a building that had previously been used for temporary exhibitions of some of the treasures in its basement or on loan.

After a series of controversies and delays, contracts were awarded in 2001 for the creation of what the architect, Rafael Moneo, termed a 'campus', a four-site complex that would double the museum's floor space and provide it with the definitive solution it had needed for years. The central idea was to free up the main building, the Edificio Villanueva, so that it could be used exclusively for the exhibition of the permanent collection, including nineteenth-century works that had previously hung in an annexe, the Casón del Buen Retiro. This is being turned into a research and teaching centre. Temporary exhibitions are to be moved to a complex of galleries built around the reconstructed Renaissance cloister of the nearby church of Los Jerónimos. But it is hoped that, eventually, this too can be freed up for the permanent collection. The plan is to shift the temporary displays once again, this time to the nearby Salón de Reinos. Work on its conversion is due to start in 2008.

It is expected that, ultimately, part of the traffic-clogged Paseo del Prado will be turned into a pedestrian precinct joining all three museums in an 'art walk' similar to the Museum Quarter in London or the Museum Mall in Washington.

The Prado played a unique role under the dictatorship. It was a beacon of Spanish culture in general and of its painting and sculpture in particular. It reminded people – Spaniards and foreigners alike – that, no matter how hateful they found the regime, no matter how backward they found the society, they could not deny that Spain had an artistic tradition that mattered. Sadly, no such beacon shone for its performing arts, and the consequences are still being felt today.

Spain is sometimes credited with possessing the richest theatrical tradition in the world after England. Yet the country that produced Lope de Vega, Tirso de Molina and Calderón did not have a repertory company dedicated solely to staging the classics until 1986, when the Compañía Nacional de Teatro Clásico came into being under the direction of the actor and producer Adolfo Marsillach. Though he was often criticized in his lifetime for trivializing the classics in an effort to draw the crowds, his death in 2002 pitched the company into a period of debilitating ups and downs from which it has yet to emerge.

Marsillach was a key figure in the 'cultural transition' that followed the death of Franco, having also been the first director of Spain's leading institution for contemporary theatre, the Centro Dramático Nacional, founded in 1978. The CDN, which is based at the Teatro María Guerrero in Madrid, is not a repertory company like, say, the National Theatre in Britain. It is a production centre, headed by a director, which vets original scripts and ideas for revivals and then puts on a season of quality productions, contracting different actors for each of them. The María Guerrero is used for staging mainstream plays, while experimental works are put on at another theatre run by the state, the Teatro Olimpia.

Shortly after coming to power in 1982, the Socialists took the adventurous step of appointing a thirty-year-old Catalan producer, Lluís Pasqual, as director of the CDN. His work there was widely acclaimed. In 1989, he left to take up an offer from Jack Lang to become director of the Paris-based Théâtre de l'Europe. Since then, the outstanding director has been Juan Carlos Pérez de la Fuente, another young talent, appointed under the PP.

State aid was essential in helping the theatre to survive a profound crisis that began in the mid-eighties and almost destroyed the private sector. As in many countries, the vast majority of private theatres are in the capital. In 1984, Madrid – a city of only 4 million people – had thirty-nine theatres. Its stage life was comparable with that of London or Paris and much livelier than, say, that of Rome. Nine years later, the number of theatres had dropped to twenty-two. The difference between the two figures was accounted for almost entirely by the closure of commercial venues.

By 1993, there were only thirteen left, of which one was given over exclusively to musicals. Several Madrid theatres had been turned into cinemas showing pornographic films. One became a discothèque; another a fast-food restaurant. One reason for the slump was the leap in Madrid property prices: the profits to be gained from selling out to developers dwarfed the income to be made from staging plays.

But the other reason is simply that Spaniards stopped going to theatres. In *En ciernes*, published the year after Franco's death, the Catalan novelist Juan Benet wrote that:

Literature ... evolves in a different way from society. It has its gods and cults and it likes nothing less than for its ritual offices to be used for purposes other than purely literary ones. The White Goddess is fairly spiteful, and sooner or later, she takes her revenge on those who claim to love or worship her, but whose thoughts are, in fact, fixed on another deity.

For the theatre, his words were to prove chillingly prophetic. Under Franco, drama was widely employed for political ends. The censors were less concerned with what was put on stage than with what was shown on screens, no doubt because the theatre had a smaller audience than either cinema or television. Stage authors were not free to write whatever they pleased, but provided they wrapped up their criticism in metaphors they stood a much better chance of seeing their work performed than the writers of critical screenplays or TV scripts. During the last years of the dictatorship, the theatre acquired an enthusiastic and sizeable following among those members of the middle class who opposed Franco's rule. But with the end of the dictatorship and the freeing-up of so many other areas of public and cultural life, that following melted away.

What eventually rescued audiences from their nadir was the gradual growth in the number of provincial playhouses. But it was not until the mid-nineties that theatre-going really became fashionable again. Drama was the outstanding beneficiary of the resurgence in spending on cultural activities mentioned earlier in this chapter. Middle-class Spaniards, enriched by the economic boom of the Aznar years, poured money into box offices the length of Spain. Most of what they were paying to see was a far cry from the politically audacious, intellectually demanding work of twenty years earlier. They particularly liked musicals, for example. Between 1997 and 2000, the total audience shot up by almost 30 per cent. In Madrid, by 2003, the number of theatres had risen again to twenty-seven, of which twenty-four were privately owned.

Among the many distortions introduced into Spanish life by Franco's dictatorship was that it turned an essentially racy nation into a profoundly tedious one. One way in which Spaniards tried to inject some glamour and excitement into their lives was by going to the movies. They did so in remarkable numbers. At one time, Spain had more cinema seats per 1,000 of the population than any country in the world except the United States.

That alone made Spain a gold mine for foreign distributors. But, in addition, foreign-language films had to be dubbed. Dubbing was made compulsory in 1941 so as to give the censors total control over the content of imported movies. Dubbing, rather than sub-titling, foreign-made films makes them much more accessible to a society, such as Spain at the time, with a high rate of illiteracy.

Without protection, it is almost certain that the introduction of compulsory dubbing would have put Spain's own film industry out of business. But Franco liked Spanish films – he even wrote the screenplay for one, called *Raza* (*Race*) – and he saw that they offered a way of propagating the regime's ideas. In 1955, the Spanish government was so firm in its insistence on protectionist measures that the American Motion Picture Export Association called a boycott that lasted three years. But, in the end, it was the MPEA that had to capitulate. It reluctantly accepted a stipulation that the number of foreign films distributed in Spain must not be more than four times the number of Spanish ones. It also agreed to a tax on the takings of dubbed films, the proceeds of which went into financing Spanish productions. By the end of the dictatorship, domestically directed and produced works accounted for almost 30 per cent of box-office receipts – a healthy figure by any standard.

In 1977, however, a decree that eased censorship in the cinema and largely replaced it with a classification system also did away with the four-to-one distribution rule and replaced it with a much stricter condition – that one day had to be allotted for the showing of Spanish films for every two days of foreign films. This so-called *cuota de pantalla*, or screen quota, was intended to strengthen the industry, but it was enacted at a time when – for a variety of reasons including the chaotic state of the financial arrangements for domestic film production – Spain's film-makers were unable to rise to the challenge. The cinema owners and managers, who had to dredge up films from the Franco era to meet the demands of the decree, appealed to the courts and in 1979 the Supreme Court abolished the screen quota altogether.

The Supreme Court's decision brought the industry face to face with disaster. It was only saved by a law passed the following year which, while re-introducing the screen quota, fixed it at the more reasonable ratio of three days of foreign films to one day of Spanish. It also set up a complex system whereby the number of dubbing permits granted to a distribution company was dependent on the success of the Spanish films financed by that firm, the aim being to make it impossible for foreign distributors to get foreign movies into Spain by financing the production of low-cost, low-quality Spanish ones.

When the Socialists swept to power in 1982, another of their bold moves was to appoint Pilar Miró to be the official in charge of the movie business. Miró, a rising young director, had spent more than a year in the period before Tejero's coup battling with the authorities to get permission for the showing of a film of hers, *El crimen de Cuenca*, which had upset the military. For better or worse, Miró was to make a huge impact on the Spanish film industry.

Within a year of taking over, she had given Spain one of the most liberal film censorship laws in Europe. As a consequence, though hard-porn films could not be shown to under-eighteens, all the other ratings were simply for guidance. Miró also brokered the first-ever agreement between the movie business and state-run Televisión Española. Under the deal, TVE undertook to show a certain minimum percentage of Spanish films and underwrote a framework for joint projects.

But the law with which Pilar Miró was most closely identified – to the point where it came to be known simply as the *ley Miró* – was a decree that came into force at the start of 1984. This added to the existing protectionist measures a quite extraordinarily generous system of subsidies. Producers could get an advance from the authorities of as much as half the estimated cost of their films. All Spanish-made films qualified for a grant equivalent to 15 per cent of gross receipts. But a further 25 per cent was available if they were judged to be of 'special quality', and 25 per cent more was provided for high-cost enterprises. The government only stopped doling out the cash when the subsidies came to more than the cost of the film. But even then, the excess was set aside for the producer's next project. As an official of the European Commission commented: 'If I were a Spaniard, I'd resign from my job and go and make films.'

One of the effects of the Miró decree was to tip the balance of advantage towards art-house movies and away from the silly, vulgar, but popular, sex comedies that had been the bread-and-butter of the industry since the early seventies. Another outcome was inflated production budgets. The years in which the *ley Miró* was in force saw the rise to fame of Pedro Almodóvar, but – crucial to any argument over its pros and cons – they also saw the number of films made in Spain drop by more than half.

By 1988, when Jorge Semprún* took over as Arts Minister, Spain's cinema industry had never been held in such high esteem. Almodóvar's *Mujeres al borde de un ataque de nervios* (*Women on the Verge of a Nervous Breakdown*) was playing to packed houses around the world. Yet that year Spanish films accounted for barely 11 per cent of box-office takings. In the background, EU officials were warning Madrid that the *ley Miró* appeared to contravene Community law.

In 1989, it was replaced by a *ley Semprún*. The level of financial support for the industry was maintained, but less of it was channelled towards producers. The 15 per cent subsidy based on box-office takings was kept, but a limit was set on the advance. Three years later, the *cuota de pantalla* was re-cast in such a way as to conform with EU legislation. For every three days of non-EU (i.e. mainly American) movies, cinema managers had to project one day of EU material. Neither measure succeeded in reviving the industry, which in 1994 hit a historic low when just 7 per cent of box-office takings came from Spanish films.

An important reason for this was a lack of support from television. In 1990, TVE, bracing itself to cope for the first time with competition from commercial television, slid out of the deal it had been strong-armed into making by Pilar Miró.

That said, not everything can be blamed on a shortage of protection or a lack of support from TV. The global success of Pedro

---

* Semprún, who held the job until 1991, is among the most remarkable ministers ever to sit at a Spanish cabinet table. An ex-member of the wartime French resistance, he survived Buchenwald to become the leader of the Communist underground resistance in Madrid under Franco. Expelled from the Communist Party for advocating many of the ideas that subsequently formed the basis of 'Eurocommunism', Semprún turned to full-time writing. He is the author of novels written in both French and Spanish, and co-scripted the Oscar-winning movie 'Z'.

Almodóvar obscured the fact that, with rare exceptions, his fellow Spanish directors were just not making the sort of movies their compatriots wanted to see. It was not until a new generation of film-makers began to make its appearance in the mid-nineties that the share of Spanish movies in overall box-office takings began to lift. It has been an erratic recovery, but in most years since 1997 the figure has hovered between 11 and 14 per cent. By the turn of the century, the number of feature films being made in Spain was almost as high as in the early eighties.

As more and more directors able to make films of interest to the public came on the scene, so the television companies found that it was more and more in their interests to take advantage of their talents. But the level of their investments tended to oscillate wildly from year to year and in 2004 Zapatero's government imposed a new rule forcing the companies to set aside 5 per cent of their pre-tax profits for the production of domestic and European movies.

Traditionally, music has been the Cinderella of the Spanish arts. Concerts, operas and ballets require large premises, sizeable numbers of performers and a lot of costly equipment. The Spanish monarchy and aristocracy were always reluctant to patronize music, and in this respect Franco was a typically Spanish ruler. The amount of money allocated to music while he was in power was pitiful. As the conductor Jesús López-Cobos once remarked, being born a conductor in Spain was a bit like being born a bullfighter in Finland. By the time Franco died, Spain had no classical ballet; there were only two state-aided orchestras, the Orquesta Nacional de España and the Orquesta Sinfónica de RTVE, and the capital had no proper opera-house or concert hall.

The Teatro Real, opposite the Royal Palace, had begun its eventful life as an opera-house in 1850. In the 1920s, it was closed by fire. During the civil war, it was blown up after someone hit on the idea of using it as a magazine. It was not re-opened until 1966, and then solely for concerts and recitals.

Madrid's only other musical forum was the Teatro de la Zarzuela, which opened two years after the Teatro Real. As its name suggests, it had been intended for the staging of Spanish home-grown light opera, or *zarzuela*,* but of necessity it came to be used for what little opera and ballet was staged in Madrid, as well as for operetta.

The logical first step in any rearrangement was to erect a purpose-built concert hall. The Teatro Real could then be closed down for the changes needed to turn it back into an opera-house. In 1984, work began at a site in the eastern part of the city, and four years later Spain's first-ever Auditorio Nacional was ready for its ceremonial inauguration. Its acoustics have since won lavish praise from visiting conductors.

The Teatro Real was meant to be ready in 1992, but repeated setbacks forced the deadline to be put back. That left the Barcelona Liceo, or Liceu as it is called in Catalan, as the only building in Spain built solely for, and devoted exclusively to, opera. In 1994, it burned down. A fire started by a welder's torch reduced the nineteenth-century structure to a pile of smouldering rubble. For several years, then, Spain, which had given the world some of its greatest opera singers, had not a single opera-house of any importance.

The Real lurched from one mishap to the next. Such was the air of calamity that enveloped it, there was even talk of a 'phantom'. The architect originally in charge died of a heart attack as he was giving details of his plans to journalists. The builders went into receivership. All 1,800 seats had to be re-upholstered after it was found they were not flameproof. And the centrepiece of the auditorium, a two-and-a-half-ton chandelier, crashed to the ground. But eventually, in 1997, after a programme of works that ended up more than three times over budget, a truly grand opera-house was reborn. Two years later, after a less eventful restoration, the Liceu came back from the dead – re-equipped, refurbished and reorganized. Nobody ever doubted that, if the Liceu could be rebuilt, it would recapture a leading place on the international circuit. But few were as confident about the Teatro Real, and doubts grew after it was put under severe financial constraints by the Aznar government. Nevertheless, it has won through. In 2002, it received an important boost when Jesús López-Cobos

---

* *Zarzuela* is so called because it was originally staged, in the early seventeenth century, at the palace of that name outside Madrid. The present Palacio de la Zarzuela, where King Juan Carlos and his family now live, stands on the same site. The word *zarzuela* means 'little bramble'.

agreed to return to Spain to be musical director. Three years later, the American Record Guide felt able to refer to the Real as 'one of the world's great opera houses'.

The recent story of dance in Spain has been almost as dramatic as that of opera, but without the same happy endings. Until after Franco's death, the only ballet companies in Spain were devoted exclusively to *ballet español* – a fusion of flamenco, classical and modern influences. There were schools of conventional Western dance, most notably the one run by María de Avila in Saragossa. But promising young dancers who, after graduating, wanted to pursue a career on stage had to go abroad.

In 1978, the Arts Ministry set up a Ballet Nacional de España consisting of two companies – one for *ballet español* and the other for classical ballet, each directed by a leading dancer in the field. Antonio Gades was recruited to head the first and Víctor Ullate, the principal male dancer in Maurice Béjart's Ballet of the Twentieth Century, returned at the height of his career to direct the second. His original idea was to reunite the many talented dancers who, like himself, had been forced to work abroad. But it soon became apparent that most of them had other commitments, and Ullate was left to do the best he could with the youngsters emerging from the schools, in particular the state-funded school that was set up at the same time as the Ballet Nacional, and run by his wife, Carmen Rocha. Given these inauspicious beginnings, it is to his immense credit that within the space of a mere five years Ullate managed to form a national ballet company worthy of the name. In 1983, the incoming Socialist government – apparently concerned that the two supposedly national companies were becoming the fiefdoms of their respective directors – sacked Ullate together with Antonio Gades's successor, Antonio Ruiz, and put María de Avila, Ullate's old tutor, in charge of both companies. It was an unseemly and unjust reward for the man who had single-handedly resurrected Spanish classical ballet. Ullate's parting words were: 'I shall go away saddened because I do not understand a great deal of what has happened. Or rather, I do understand, but it seems impossible.'

María de Avila's directorship of the combined company was surprisingly undistinguished. In 1986, she left following a bizarre scandal in which three of the male classical dancers were expelled for turning up at an official reception in Germany dressed in women's clothes. On her departure, the BNE was again split. But this time the Spanish ballet kept the title of Ballet Nacional de España and classical dance in Spain began to fall back gradually into irrelevance.

After several years of indecision and uncertainty, the rest of the old joint company was entrusted to another returning 'exile', the choreographer and former dancer in the Nederlands Dans Theater, Nacho Duato.

The Compañía Nacional de Danza, as it is known, has since evolved into a company that uses both classical and modern techniques. So Spain, uniquely among the big European nations, has no national classical ballet, and scant prospect of acquiring one in the near future. The only classical dance company is Víctor Ullate's Ballet de la Comunidad de Madrid. But it is a distinctly modest enterprise whose performances in recent years have been, at best, unexceptional.

None of this, of course, means that dance enthusiasts in Spain have nothing to see. There are performances by visiting foreign companies and the capital even has a theatre, the Teatro de Madrid, devoted solely to dance. But, to all intents and purposes, the dance performed in Spain by Spaniards now is *ballet español*, an art form that is still very much in the making.

In the past, Spanish dance-lovers could at least console themselves with the fact that the schools were constantly turning out new talent. But during the 1990s, at a time when the number of music students was soaring, the number of dance students actually dropped, by almost 10 per cent. In a cultural panorama exploding with vitality and enthusiasm, dance stands out as a moribund exception.

As far as orchestral music is concerned, the key break with the past came when López-Cobos first returned to take over the Orquesta Nacional de España in 1983. Like France and Italy, Spain is not a country with a great orchestral tradition. Perhaps it has something to do with Latin society, which values spontaneity more than discipline, and rewards individual rather than collective achievement. At all events, the conservatories of southern Europe have traditionally aimed to turn out soloists rather than rank-and-file players. A former member of the ONE once said that the problem with tuning up in a Spanish orchestra was that 'everyone has his or her own conception of *la*'. López-Cobos, who had spent much of his career conducting

German and British orchestras, set his sights on inculcating what he called 'musical discipline'.

In 1988, however, he resigned the conductorship of the ONE in somewhat perplexing circumstances. A newspaper article had anonymously quoted members of the orchestra as criticizing him for, among other things, taking on too much work outside Spain. Since coming back from America in 2002, he has raised the standard of the Orquesta del Teatro Real, also known as the Orquesta Sinfónica de Madrid, to such an extent that some regard it as Spain's finest orchestra.

The early eighties saw the creation of a national youth orchestra, the Joven Orquesta Nacional de España. Since then, there have been substantial increases in the number and value of grants and prizes for the young. That, together with the gradual spread of an awareness of classical music, has helped bring about one of the most heartening recent developments in the Spanish arts. Not so very long ago, you almost never saw a schoolchild in a Spanish street carrying an instrument case. That is no longer so. Many of today's parents are keen for their children to learn music at school, and the nineties saw an astonishing rise in the number of students reaching a level at which they could seriously contemplate music as a career. In the ten academic years to 2000/2001, the number attaining *grado superior* rose by 80 per cent. Somewhere among them there could even be a Murray Perahia, an Anne-Sophie Mutter or a Simon Rattle.

CHAPTER 29

Arts and Artists: No Limits

When Ramona Maneiro mixed up a cyanide cocktail and left it at her partner's bedside, she must have known she was taking a considerable risk and fuelling a national controversy. But she could not have imagined she was also setting in train a chain of events that would lead, seven years later, to the Academy of Motion Picture Arts and Sciences in Beverly Hills and one of modern Spain's greatest creative triumphs.

Soon after the death of her partner, Ramón Sampedro, who had wanted passionately to die ever since a diving accident left him paralysed from the neck down, Maneiro was charged by police with assisting a suicide. Her case became a *cause célèbre* and rekindled a nationwide debate on euthanasia first lit by Sampedro himself. Thousands of Spaniards came forward to shield her by claiming that they, and not she, had prepared the fatal potion. In the end, the police were unable to prove anything and the charges against Maneiro were dropped.*

By then her story – and, to an even greater extent, her partner's story – had attracted the attention of one of Spain's most promising young movie directors, Alejandro Amenábar. It is hard to think of a subject less obviously appealing than paralysis and euthanasia. But, with the help of the actor Javier Bardem, who played Sampedro, Amenábar succeeded in making a stunning movie. Bardem won the prize for best actor at the Venice film festival in September 2004 and five months later *Mar adentro* (*The Sea Inside*) took the Oscar for best foreign movie. In his acceptance speech, Amenábar dedicated the award to Sampedro 'wherever you are'.

---

* It was not until 2005, by which time she was covered by a statute of limitations, that Maneiro admitted to having prepared the concoction that killed her lover.

Any film industry with at least one outstanding director and a handful of good actors can hope to hit the jackpot in Hollywood with a screenplay that connects with American sensibilities. Over the years Oscars have been handed to directors from Hungary, the Ivory Coast and Bosnia-Herzegovina. What Amenábar's Oscar put beyond doubt was that Spain had joined a quite different category. In just over twenty years, it had brought home no fewer than five Oscars – more than any other non-English speaking country over the same period.

The first went in 1983 to José Luis Garci for *Volver a empezar* (*Starting Over* or *Begin the Beguine*). Spaniards were inclined, perhaps unfairly, to dismiss that as a bit of a fluke. Garci's film had been a box-office flop in Spain itself and its popularity with the Hollywood jury no doubt owed something to its strongly American flavour – the principal character had spent much of his life in the United States and the theme music was Cole Porter's 'Begin the Beguine'. But then Fernando Trueba's *Belle Époque* took the Oscar for best foreign film in 1993 and, six years later, Pedro Almodóvar won what many critics felt was long overdue recognition from Hollywood when he was given the same award for *Todo sobre mi madre* (*All About My Mother*). In 2002, he picked up a second Oscar for the screenplay of *Hable con ella* (*Talk to Her*).

Garci belongs to a post-Franco generation of directors including Manuel Gutiérrez Aragón and Mario Camus, whose best work may now be behind them. But Trueba is several years younger and Almodóvar has entered a hugely productive mature phase characterized by films that are less quirky, but more thoughtful, than those he made in his early years. As for Amenábar, the son of a Chilean father and Spanish mother, he has scarcely begun. His first full-length feature was made only nine years before he won his Oscar, at the age of just thirty-one. To a greater extent than any of his contemporaries, he has succeeded in carving out a place for himself in the English-language movie business, yet without noticeably compromising his commitment to make quality cinema. His second feature film, *Abre los ojos* (*Open Your Eyes*), made in 1997, resulted in the Hollywood movie *Vanilla Sky*, for which Amenábar co-wrote the script, and four years later he directed Nicole Kidman in his first English-language movie, *The Others*.

Amenábar, though, is one of a raft of talented directors of the post-Almodóvar generation who have won recognition beyond Spain. They include Julio Medem, Juanma Bajo Ulloa and Alex de la Iglesia, one of whose earliest productions, *Acción Mutante*, attained international cult status. Between 1997 and 2000, the number of awards given to Spanish movies in foreign film festivals tripled.

What is more, as Paul Julian Smith has pointed out,* 'Spanish cinema has, with the help of the print media, begun to evolve a successful star system.' Two Spanish actors, Antonio Banderas and Penélope Cruz, are now firmly established as Hollywood stars. Carmen Maura, the star of *Mujeres al borde de un ataque de nervios*, has a solid international reputation. And several other younger actors, including Bardem, Elena Anaya and Paz Vega, are beginning to break into English-language movies.

The achievements of Spanish cinema are perhaps the best evidence that Spain is beginning to recover the extraordinary standing it once enjoyed in the arts. No other area of society perhaps was affected to such a degree by the civil war and its aftermath.

In 1936 Spain was a creative superpower. It had given the world three of its greatest contemporary painters – Picasso, Dalí and Miró. It could lay claim to one of the finest established composers – Manuel de Falla – and to several of the more promising younger ones such as the Catalan, Roberto Gerhard, and the Valencian, Joaquín Rodrigo. Its fledgling film industry had already managed to produce a director of the calibre of Buñuel. In literature, the leading figures of the celebrated 'Generation of '98' – the philosophers Unamuno and Ortega y Gasset, the novelist Pío Baroja, the playwrights Benavente and Valle-Inclán, and the poets Machado and Jiménez – were all still alive. But more importantly, a further generation, the 'Generation of '27', was just reaching maturity. Outside Spain, the best known of the writers who belonged to it is Federico García Lorca. But there were many others considered by Spaniards to be of equal stature – poets such as Rafael Alberti, Vicente Aleixandre and Luis Cernuda. The achievements of the entire 'Generation of '27' were finally recognized by the award of the 1977 Nobel Prize for Literature to Aleixandre.

The vast majority of Spain's artists and intellectuals took the side of the Republic against the Nationalists. Some, like Lorca, were killed. Of those who survived, most fled into exile. Once the fiercest

* *Contemporary Spanish Culture*, Cambridge, 2003.

period of retribution was over, they faced a grim choice. Returning home offered an opportunity to re-establish contact with the cultural traditions of their homeland, but it also meant handing the regime a propaganda victory and resigning themselves to a lifetime of censorship. Staying abroad meant losing touch with their roots, but it did guarantee them their creative integrity. Miró returned, but the majority opted to remain in exile. Seen as a set of individual, personal decisions it was understandable. Seen as a development in the nation's cultural history it was catastrophic. Most of what the exiles wrote, painted, sculpted and filmed went completely unnoticed within Spain until the sixties, when Manuel Fraga as Minister of Information and Tourism eased the restrictions on imported works. But by then, much of it was ten, fifteen, even twenty years old and of little or no use as a stimulus or inspiration.

The intellectuals' opposition to Franco meant that, throughout his dictatorship, he and his supporters harboured a deep suspicion of all things intellectual. Culture *per se* became dangerous. 'At home, we didn't even listen to the radio,' the Catalan folk-rock singer Pau Riba later recalled. 'Books were simply bound objects that you didn't touch.' What makes his reminiscence all the more remarkable is that Pau Riba did not come from a family of shopkeepers or factory-workers, but from a line of eminent literary figures – his grandfather was the poet and philologist, Carles Riba.

The artists and intellectuals born in the twenties, thirties and forties had to make their way as best they could without guides or maps. In retrospect, what is surprising about Franco's Spain is not that there was so little good music, art and literature, but that there was so much. Probably the best-known creative work of the Franco era was Rodrigo's popular classic, the *Concierto de Aranjuez*. But the same period also saw the emergence of a number of outstanding painters such as Antoni Tàpies, Antonio Saura, Luis Gordillo and Manuel Millares, and at least one internationally renowned sculptor in Eduardo Chillida. Alternately duping and defying the censors, playwrights such as Antonio Buero Vallejo and film-makers such as Luis García Berlanga, Juan Bardem and Carlos Saura managed to create works of depth and integrity. The printed word became a medium of protest – a way of recording the shallowness and hypocrisy of Franco's Spain. The pioneers were the poet Dámaso Alonso and the novelists Camilo José Cela and Miguel

Delibes, who began to make an impact in the late forties. Then came an entire generation of writers committed to 'social realism', of whom perhaps the most talented representative was Juan Goytisolo.

The period immediately following Franco's death was one of tremendous disorientation and introspection. A regime that had provided so many creative Spaniards with a target on which to unleash their energies had been whisked away overnight. While its supporters were complaining that '*Con Franco vivíamos mejor*' ('We lived better with Franco'), the novelist Manuel Vázquez Montalbán spoke for many of his fellow-intellectuals when he remarked that '*Contra Franco vivíamos mejor*' ('We lived better *against* Franco'). At the same time, there were new freedoms to exploit and influences to absorb. Sex was no longer taboo and the temptation to describe or depict it proved irresistible to all but the most ascetic. Then there were the exiles who returned to Spain in considerable numbers and whose work, many felt, had to be published or exhibited and then assessed before any further progress could be made. As for the public, a lot of Spaniards found that they were too worried about the fate of democracy to be over-concerned with the fate of the arts.

This rather abnormal period ended in the early eighties. To some extent, it was simply that people had grown tired of sexploitation and had begun to decide what of the exiles' experience and output was worth incorporating. But it also had something to do with Tejero's abortive coup which, while it may have fulfilled people's worst fears, also dispelled them – like the cloudburst that comes at the end of a thundery day.

The most obvious sign of a new mood was to be found in the phenomenon known as the *movida madrileña*. *Movida* is not an easy word to translate. Perhaps the nearest approximation in English is 'scene'. The *movida madrileña*, 'the Madrid scene', came into being at a time when Spain's newly liberated young were getting into the habit of *salir de copas* – going out to drink until the early hours, usually from Friday into Saturday or Saturday into Sunday. By the late seventies, even the smallest provincial capital had its *movida*, its network of bars and discos that stayed open till dawn at the weekends. Madrid's was not only the most extensive but also the most exciting, and gradually the term *movida madrileña* came to be used as a description of the people who inhabited it. There are parallels between the *movida madrileña* of the 1980s and 'Cool Britannia' in the London of the 1990s. Both reflected or channelled a certain amount of artistic creativity. But to a greater extent than with 'Cool Britannia', the *movida madrileña*'s centre of gravity was to be found in the nightspots of the city from which it took its name, particularly the now-defunct Rock-Ola Club. Those who were at the centre of the *movida madrileña* trace its origins back to 1977, the year in which Spain became a democracy again. It was not until about 1982, however, that non-initiates became aware of its existence or that the people identified with it began to exercise an influence on the rest of society.

Foremost among them was the son of a petrol-station attendant, born in 1949 in the parched and backward Don Quixote country of La Mancha. Recalling his childhood, Pedro Almodóvar once remarked, 'I felt as if I'd fallen from another planet.' In 1969, he moved to the capital and set about making Super-8 underground movies while earning a living at the national telephone monopoly, Telefónica. His first full-length film, *Pepi, Luci, Bom y otras chicas del montón* (*Pepi, Luci, Bom and Other Girls on the Heap*), was released in 1980. The movies that followed, filled with candy-bright colours and packed with improbable events and personalities, are quintessentially a product of the frenetic mood that took hold of Spain in the eighties. What made them so popular outside the country was perhaps that they were so utterly at variance with the earnest, bloodstained tragedies people had come to expect of Spanish directors. *Mujeres al borde de un ataque de nervios* was the highest-grossing foreign film in the United States in 1989.

Apart from the work of Almodóvar, though, the creative fruits of the *movida madrileña* have been modest. Among those once associated with it is one of Spain's leading fashion designers, Agatha Ruiz de la Prada, together with a handful of rock and pop musicians. Overall, it is difficult to argue with the verdict of José Luis Gallero, the author of a book on the *movida* called *Sólo se vive una vez* (*You Only Live Once*). 'What has endured,' he wrote, 'is the *salir de copas* habit' – and that had caught on even before Franco's death.

Almodóvar, however, remains an emblematic figure in the Spanish arts, not only because of the widespread international recognition he has been accorded, but also because the work that made him famous caught – and encouraged – a style that can be made out in a lot of the creative output of post-Franco Spain.

A number of Spain's contemporary creative talents have been captivated by melodrama and kitsch; entranced by the outlandish and the outrageous. It is a fascination that has deep roots in Spain's cultural history: Spanish baroque, Gaudí's modernism, Dalí's surrealism, and the *tremendismo* to be found in the work of novelists like Cela have all involved taking a good idea one step – or many more – beyond what good taste might deem to be prudent.

It may be hazardous in these post-modernist times to moot a Spanish school of anything, but I think you can argue persuasively for a link between the studied excesses of Alex de la Iglesia, the lurid use of colour to be found in much of the figurative painting done in Spain in the eighties and nineties, and the Goya-esque touches that run through what is perhaps the most internationally successful novel to be published by a Spaniard since Franco's death, Carlos Ruiz Zafón's *The Shadow of the Wind*.

What is striking about *The Shadow of the Wind* is that it came almost out of nowhere. Its author had worked as a scriptwriter in the US and written some books aimed at a young market before settling down to pen his tale of mystery and obsession in post-war Barcelona. He did not form part of contemporary Spain's literary establishment, responsible for what is known as the *nueva narrativa española*. The term was first coined for a series launched by Ediciones Libertarias in 1985, and doubts have often been expressed as to whether it really describes a movement or school in any meaningful sense. Those identified with the *nueva narrativa española* include authors as diverse as Almudena Grandes, Javier Marías, Juan José Millás, Antonio Muñoz Molina and the widely translated Arturo Pérez-Reverte. Some depict contemporary society. Others have ranged into historical fiction or fantasy.

But what unites the writers of the *nueva narrativa española* is a combination of serious intent and popular appeal unlike anything that had been achieved in Spain for decades, if not centuries. Until the mid-eighties, Spanish novelists were intellectuals writing for a tiny band of other intellectuals in print runs of a few thousand. Almost all the thrillers you saw on bookshop shelves were written abroad. There was scarcely anyone in the tradition of, say, Graham Greene capable of bridging the gap between the two genres, and no one writing intellectually stimulating prose in Spanish for a mass audience. Or at least no one in Spain. That space in the market was being filled, brilliantly, by Latin American authors such as Gabriel García Márquez.

One of the very few writers of intellectual stature with a wide readership was Manuel Vázquez Montalbán, formerly an avant-garde poet, whose fictional private detective, Pepe Carvalho, was to win him a following in many countries beyond Spain. Some other authors too were using thrillers to do more than just thrill – authors such as Eduardo Mendoza and Juan Madrid.

What happened in the mid-eighties, though, was a sea change in the status of the novel. As with so many developments in contemporary Spain, it seemed to happen overnight. In 1986, it became apparent that Spanish novelists were consistently making it into their own country's best-seller list with plots and subjects that appealed to a new readership – middle-class Spaniards, products of the 1970 Education Act, who did not think it odd to read a book on the beach or the train.

For the first time in Spain, authors started to be treated as celebrities. The profits to be gained from novel-writing soared. Established authors such as the late Juan Benet, accustomed to minute sales, suddenly found themselves allotted print runs of 25,000 or more. Every month seemed to bring a new and more lucrative literary award. The playwright Antonio Gala decided to try his hand at novel-writing. His first book, *El manuscrito carmesí* (*The Crimson Manuscript*), won him the 1990 Planeta prize and an initial print run of 200,000. He remains one of Spain's best-selling novelists.

Within a few years, authorship in Spain ceased to be a hobby and became a profession. By writing articles as well as books and *haciendo bolos* (working the lecture circuit), authors nowadays can make a decent living. In fact, overall readership declined in the nineties, but a core public, representing around 20 per cent of the population and comprising more women than men, remains eager to buy the sort of intelligent but readable novels that contemporary Spanish writers seem capable of producing in abundance.

The other important development in recent years has been the growth in the reputation of literature written in languages other than Castilian. The short-story writer Quim Monzó is perhaps the best regarded of several talented authors who publish in Catalan. But it is a Basque, Joseba Irazu, writing under the name of Bernardo Atxaga, who has so far made the biggest impact, and stirred the greatest controversy. His key novels are set in the Basque hinterland where he was born, portrayed in his books through the fictional locality of Obaba. In 1990, Atxaga's *Obabakoak* became the first non-Castilian-language novel to win Spain's highest official award for fiction, the Premio Nacional de Narrativa. In 2003 he returned to the uplands of Guipúzcoa with a more political work, *Soinujolearen semea* (*The Accordionist's Son*), implicitly, but searingly, critical of ETA's terrorists, their historical myths and their self-deluding attachment to a world that no longer exists. Critics were divided. Some hailed it as the first great Basque novel, but *El País*'s reviewer accused Atxaga of 'Jurassic sentimentality'.

The succulent earnings to be gained from novel-writing have understandably lured talent away from other forms of writing. Antonio Gala is the archetype of a playwright diverted to book-writing. What no one can know is the dimensions of the invisible drift – how many potential playwrights, seeing the fame and fortune heaped on successful authors, have chosen to invest their plots and dialogue in novels instead. Of those who have chosen to stay with drama, the outstanding name in the post-Franco generation is José Sanchis Sinisterra. His earliest big success was the civil war tragi-comedy *¡Ay, Carmela!*, which Carlos Saura made into a highly successful film. Since then, Sanchis Sinisterra has written a substantial body of work and earned himself a place as one of Spain's foremost contemporary writers.

Cinema may have exerted the same pull on actors as the novel has on writers. Since the renowned Catalan actress Nuria Espert faded from the stage, there is no one acting primarily in the theatre who enjoys the same degree of international recognition as Penélope Cruz or Antonio Banderas in cinema. The best-known names in off-screen acting are those of groups rather than individuals. Both are Catalan: the satirical company Els Joglars which nobly refuses subsidies for fear they could blunt its edge, and the experimental troupe Fura dels Baus whose visually arresting, intensely physical work lies somewhere between theatre and circus.

Poetry in Spain, as in many countries these days, is a minority enthusiasm. There again, recent years have not brought to the fore poets able to engage the interest of a wider audience. The most important poets to emerge in the latter part of Franco's rule were the so-called *novísimos*, whose work was characterized by an adventurous mixture of antiquated and vernacular language, an interest in symbolism and a fascination with the media culture. Unrepentant social realists regarded them as decadent, reactionary *señoritos*,* but the *novísimos* saw themselves as successors to the Generation of '27 and seem to have been regarded as such by the older poets – or at least by Aleixandre, who wrote a prologue to one of their earliest anthologies.

So far, no one group or single voice has emerged to replace them, though a name that has attracted attention recently is that of Luis García Montero, the husband of the novelist Almudena Grandes.

Among the painters who have risen to prominence in the last few decades, a stands out as having a genuinely international reputation. Mallorcan-born Miquel Barceló is comparable to Almodóvar as one of the iconic figures of creative endeavour in post-Franco Spain. He is celebrated as such by his compatriots, though they easily disagree on whether his homeland is, in fact, Spain, the Catalan-speaking world or the Balearic Islands. The issue is made more complicated by the fact that Barceló, like Picasso before him, is an exile. The Mallorcan painter's exile is voluntary and intermittent, but over the years he has produced work from studios in Lisbon, Naples, Tunis, Marrakesh, Paris, as well as on his native island. In between, he has made lengthy visits to Africa, particularly Mali. Though much of his work reflects Mediterranean themes and influences, some of it is intensely African in inspiration.

The parallels between Almodóvar and Barceló are not confined to the standing of each in their respective fields. Both men, though often regarded as quintessentially contemporary, choose to operate within traditions that many regarded as having run their course. Just as Almodóvar has succeeded in breathing new life into the art-house movie, so Barceló has shown that there is still much to say with paint at a time when the emphasis in contemporary art has shifted towards conceptualism, video and photography.

His canvases, abstract and figurative alike, show a masterly command of colour and texture. And while he frequently uses found objects in his work, they are usually deployed in a context of superb draughtsmanship. Many of those found objects can be grim or gory – skulls,

---

* Although strictly speaking no more or less than the masculine equivalent of *señorita*, *señorito* has acquired a distinctively pejorative connotation. It is used to denote a rich, idle young man – a playboy or a dilettante.

dead plants, eviscerated animals. Indeed, there is a wild energy and a fascination with decay and death in Barceló's work that has persuaded some critics to fit him into a tradition that also encompasses Goya and the newly reassessed Miró.

Sculpture has proved surprisingly resilient in Spain and attracted a number of talented artists, many of them women. Susana Solano emerged as an important figure in the late eighties but has since tended to be overshadowed by younger sculptors such as Cristina Iglesias. In contrast to the trend worldwide, conceptual art, video and photography all still have relatively low profiles in Spain.

The expansion of museum and gallery space has provided Spanish curators with unprecedented opportunities to play a role on the international art scene. In 2002, Vicent – he is normally known in Britain as Vicente – Todolí, one of the driving forces behind the IVAM,* was appointed to take over the Tate Modern in London. Two years later, María de Corral, a former director of the Reina Sofía, and the critic and curator Rosa Martínez were jointly entrusted with organizing the 2005 Venice Biennial.

In architecture, as is also true of painting, one Spanish name is now globally renowned, though not necessarily for designing buildings. Valencian-born Santiago Calatrava first studied architecture, but went on to win his international reputation as an engineer with a singular aesthetic sensibility. Though he was already firmly established before 1992, the festivities of that year gave him a unique showcase for presenting his work to the world. One of his many elegant bridges was the gateway to Expo. His graceful communications tower, set beside the Olympic stadium, became the structure most readily identified with the Barcelona Games. Among his most successful recent works is Bilbao's slick new Sondika airport terminal.

The Barcelona Olympics, or rather the opening and closing ceremonies, also gave the Spanish a chance to point out to the rest of the world that their country was the source of a quite remarkable array of operatic talent. Plácido Domingo, Monserrat Caballé, José Carreras, Teresa Berganza and Alfredo Kraus were all then still active.

Today, only Domingo and Carreras are still performing, and the spotlight is shifting gradually to younger singers. Of these, the most

* See above, pp. 379–80.

celebrated is the Navarrese soprano María Bayo. Recent years have also seen the emergence of an original, and hugely controversial, director, Calixto Bieito, who came to opera from the theatre. His first production, in 1999, was of Haydn's *Il Mondo della Luna* set in a Moulin Rouge-style cabaret. He has since left behind a trail of audience walk-outs and scandalized newspaper headlines on his way to being dubbed the Quentin Tarantino of opera because of the violence of his productions. His London staging of Verdi's *Un ballo in maschera* opened with the conspirators straining on lavatories with their trousers round their ankles. In Berlin, he hired real prostitutes to simulate sex for *Entführung aus dem Serail*. And when he brought a production of *Il Trovatore* to Edinburgh, *The Times* critic described it as 'without doubt, the most unpleasant evening I have spent in the theatre'. Among many other things, the Anvil Chorus was sung as Manrico, the troubadour, was being subjected to a homosexual rape at the back of the stage.

As mentioned in the previous chapter, opera in Spain was characterized by a grotesque imbalance. There was an abundance of great singers but almost nowhere in their native country for them to perform. Sadly, much the same is now true of ballet. The list of Spaniards dancing major roles for foreign companies is a long one. It includes Tamara Rojo and Angel Corella, principal dancers of, respectively, the Royal Ballet and the American Ballet Theater, and Víctor Jiménez of the Béjart. All three were trained by Víctor Ullate in Madrid, but went abroad because of a lack of opportunities in Spain. Another figure who has attracted considerable attention is the innovative contemporary dancer and choreographer, María José Ribot.

Spanish rock music, I always feel, is rather like the Norwegians' fondness for eating three-month-old fish – something with a strictly local appeal. In almost thirty years of association with Spain, I doubt if I have heard more than half a dozen numbers I would want to listen to again. It may have something to do with the language. Spanish is an intensely melodious tongue to which the abrupt rhythms of rock and pop can be adapted only with difficulty. Somewhere on the blurred frontier between rock and pop things start to improve, and from time to time Spanish groups have notched up an international success. Back in the sixties, Los Bravos had a hit with a song called

'Black is Black'. Between the eighties and nineties, Mecano, a slick trio from Madrid, achieved some success in France. And in 2002, a new group, Las Ketchup, made up of the daughters of a well-known flamenco guitarist,* had a global hit with 'Aserejé', a catchy, nonsensical song that began life in a word-game played by the composer, Manuel Ruiz Queco, with his then five- and six-year-old sons. But it is at the point that pop shades into ballad that Spanish singers have made the biggest consistent impact.

Julio Iglesias's 'Begin the Beguine', released in 1981, was the first single recorded (though not titled) in a language other than English to sell more than a million copies worldwide, and Iglesias himself became unquestionably an international rather than just a Spanish, or Hispanic, star. Yet his success was no fluke – he was simply the best of numerous talented Spanish ballad-singers, many of whom have sold huge numbers of records both in Spain and in the Hispanic communities of the US.

For years, it would have been fair to say that the bulk of the light music produced in Spain was derivative. Whether it was rock, pop or crooning in the style of Julio Iglesias, it was largely rooted in English-speaking, and specifically US, traditions, as indeed was what little jazz got played in Spain. But, over the past few years, and in several different areas, Spanish musicians have found a voice of their own, thanks to increasing fusion with that most potent of musical idioms, flamenco.

---

* Juan Muñoz, *El Tomate*, hence, Las Ketchup.

CHAPTER 30

Changing Traditions: Flamenco and Bullfighting

'The night draws on,' wrote José María Caballero Bonald of a gathering at a wayside inn in the midst of the undulating Andalusian countryside.

Already daylight has begun to show over the trees. At the inn, there is a group of seven or eight people. They are drinking wine parsimoniously, calmly. The guitarist is tuning his instrument. All of a sudden, the notes coincide with the beginning of a song and someone utters the preliminary wails. The singer clears his throat and searches for the beat. Everyone maintains a respectful, religious silence. At length, the lyrics emerge. Hands begin to clap miraculously in time with the guitar. The singer, gazing into infinity, moves his face and contorts his body in response to the difficulties of the song and raises his hand in a gesture of majesty.

True flamenco* offers Spaniards much the same as it offers tourists – a dash of the unusual in an increasingly drab world. The songs are exotic, the dances are dramatic and flamenco history is dotted with performers sporting gloriously improbable names like 'The Child of the Combs', 'Frasco, the Coloured One' and 'Mad Matthew'. But the flamenco tradition also offers one of those links with the world of a younger mankind in which Spain is so rich, for it is capable of generating that feeling of ecstasy, the inculcation of which is thought to have been the object of all early music. A flamenco singer ought not to perform until he or she has drifted into something approaching a trance – a state of suppressed emotion in which the need for expression gradually becomes so strong that it can no longer be contained.

Though its origins are obscure, it is thought that flamenco began in the late eighteenth century among the Gypsies of the provinces

---

* Often referred to as *flamenco jondo* (deep flamenco).

of Seville and Cádiz. What is indisputable is that Gypsy music has remained at the core of the flamenco tradition even though a number of southern Spanish songs such as the fandango, which is of Moorish origin, have been absorbed into the repertory. In the same way, many non-Gypsies have become masters of the art as *cantaores* (singers), *bailaores* (dancers) and *tocaores* ('players' – i.e. guitarists). The vast majority of flamenco songs are true folk songs – devised by some now forgotten villager and modified by endless repetition until they settle into the form that is considered most attractive. All attempts to transcribe the music have proved abortive, so the flamenco tradition is reliant entirely on word of mouth, instruction and example. But it also means that there is great scope for individual interpretation.

The songs, or *coplas*, vary between three and six lines in length, but because each word is drawn out by wails and ululations they take several minutes to sing. The language is always very simple and direct. There are about forty different types of song. Some are intended for specific occasions, such as weddings. Of the remainder, the exuberant ones, which can be danced to and which the tourist is most likely to come across, comprise only a relatively small proportion. Most are agonized laments for the death of a loved one, particularly a mother (a figure who is even more important among the Gypsies than among their Latin neighbours), or for the loss of freedom (for the Spanish Gypsies have spent more than their fair share of time in the country's jails), for the transience of life's pleasures and the persistence of its miseries. As the flamenco critic and researcher Ricardo Molina wrote, flamenco is 'the response of a people repressed for centuries', and this may explain why it became so popular among the non-Gypsy peasants of Andalusia in the nineteenth century as they too fell victim to another kind of oppression when their commons were enclosed and they were left as landless labourers.

The spread of flamenco in modern times has been uneven. Twice it has seemed to be on the point of going into a permanent decline, and twice its fortunes have been revived by organized competitions – those of Granada in 1922 and of Córdoba in 1955. These inspired a succession of smaller contests that rekindled interest and unearthed talent. The second revival was less dramatic than the first but proved to be more enduring. It was largely due to the work of just one man, the *cantaor* Antonio Mairena, who died in 1983. Flamenco loses its impetus when it loses its integrity. Mairena insisted on singing an unadorned, undiluted repertoire. He was also tireless in promoting festivals of authentic flamenco. The spread of the purified idiom that Mairena and his disciples rediscovered, or rather reinforced, was helped by social, economic and even political factors. The recovery of 'genuine' flamenco came at just the moment when hundreds of thousands of Andalusians were preparing to pack their bags and start a new life in Madrid or the industrial cities of the north. Their migration to other parts of Spain gave flamenco a following in every region of the country, except perhaps the north-west and the Balearic and Canary Islands.

The last years of the dictatorship also saw the emergence of two of the greatest performers in flamenco history: the *tocaor* Francisco Sánchez Gómez, 'Paco de Lucía', and the *cantaor* José Monge, 'Camarón de la Isla'. With his spare frame and thick mane of hair, there was more than a touch of the Mick Jagger about 'The Shrimp from the Island', who became an idol for many of the younger generation of Spanish Gypsies. Just like some rock stars, though, Camarón found immense difficulty in coping with fame and it was not long before he was battling an acute drug habit. However, it was cancer rather than heroin that claimed him in 1992, at the tragically early age of forty-one. It was reckoned that more than 100,000 people attended his funeral.

Paco de Lucía, who first met Camarón in 1968, had also been a child prodigy. At the age of just fifteen he was signed up to tour the world as a member of the company formed by José Greco. In New York, he met the exiled *tocaor* Sabicas, who had a profound influence on his style. Paco de Lucía gradually emerged not just as an outstandingly talented musician, but as an intellectual pioneer of flamenco. From an early stage, he was enthusiastically involved in a process that, in many respects, has come to dominate the genre – its fusion with other musical idioms.

There had long been occasional two-way traffic. The guitarist Ramón Montoya's incorporation of classical guitar techniques revolutionized the art of the *tocaor* in the first half of the twentieth century and enabled him to found the school of playing to which Paco de Lucía initially belonged. Flamenco provided the inspiration for much of the folkloric music that was popular in the Spain of the late forties and early fifties. Leonard Bernstein used the rhythm of the flamenco form known as *bulerías* for the song 'America' in *West Side Story*. Miles Davis melded jazz and flamenco in his classic 1959 recordings, *Kind of Blue* and *Sketches of Spain*.

But Paco de Lucía's exploration of the possibilities for fusion has been unparalleled in its rigour, duration and intensity. It has won him a place as the most influential single musician in the flamenco world. As early as 1967, he played with Miles Davis and Thelonius Monk at the Berlin jazz festival. In 1976, he released *Almoraima*, an album dedicated to Manuel de Falla, on which he tapped into the classical tradition of orchestral music. That recording brought him into contact with the group Dolores and inspired him to form the sextet with which he toured the world playing experimental flamenco.

At about the same time, other young Andalusian musicians were fired by the idea of trying to blend flamenco with rock. The earliest groups to experiment with this form of fusion were Triana and Veneno. Somewhat later, a number of musicians and singers began playing a kind of 'flamenco pop' consisting of variations on *rumba*, one of the more joyful styles making up the flamenco canon.*

In the late seventies and early eighties, flamenco derived a further boost from the growth of a sense of Andalusian identity – a process that fed off the granting of a generous measure of autonomy to the area. Andalusia's regional government, the Junta, was soon putting money into a month-long flamenco competition, the Bienal, held every two years in Seville. Smaller festivals, dedicated to the preservation – or recovery – of the style characteristic of each locality, sprang up in scores of towns and villages across Andalusia.

By then, however, the flamenco world was being transformed. Film directors love to depict flamenco being sung or danced in the shadow of a caravan round a blazing open fire, but in fact it is largely an urban phenomenon. It emerged from poor *barrios* in the towns and cities of the south where Gypsies settled alongside non-Gypsies, many of whom had drifted in from the countryside in search of work following the enclosures. The exchange of influences between the two groups has been decisive in the evolution of flamenco. The quintessential flamenco *barrio*

---

* However, the musicians who succeeded in giving *rumba* in this form a global audience were French, not Spanish: The Gypsy Kings.

was Triana in the centre of Seville. In recent decades, many such areas have been gentrified and their inhabitants moved to notionally better accommodation in the suburbs. A lot of Triana's inhabitants ended up in an area known as Las Tres Mil Viviendas, which has become one of Spain's most notorious housing estates.

At the same time, the venues for the performance of flamenco were changing too. Traditionally, if you wanted to hear flamenco you went either to a *venta* (a rural inn), or to a *tablao* (an urban bar), or to a festival. Increasingly, the performance of flamenco has shifted to television, radio and recorded media.

Just as the sixties saw flamenco become a Spanish rather than a solely Andalusian art form, so the nineties saw flamenco projected internationally as never before. The Gypsy Kings unquestionably had a hand in this. But so too did the emergence of a spectacular new talent – Joaquín Cortés, who had much the same impact on flamenco dance as Camarón and Paco de Lucía had had in each of their respective fields. For a while, he was a truly international celebrity, squiring the 'supermodel' Naomi Campbell and dancing in a video with Madonna.

The growing international appreciation of flamenco* had at least two effects. The first was on the government. Despite the fact that Felipe González and many of his ministers were from Andalusia, the Socialist administrations of the eighties and nineties were wary of flamenco. Partly, this was because of its growing association with drugs. But partly, I think, the misgivings of ministers and officials in Madrid arose for subtler reasons. Government publications often betrayed just a hint of embarrassment that something as unrefined as flamenco should have survived into the Spain of EU summits, six-lane highways and satellite television receivers. Raucous, rasping laments squared even less with the image of Spain the PP wished to project. But the international respectability being accorded flamenco persuaded the authorities to extend it a sort of grudging respect, if not much in the way of funds or promotion.

There again, it could be argued that the last thing flamenco lacked

---

* A survey carried out for the Andalusian Junta at the 12th Flamenco Biennial in 2002 found 19 per cent of the visitors were from North America, 14 per cent from Japan and 11 per cent from Germany. Less than a quarter were Spaniards.

was cash. The internationalization of the genre was encouraging the big multinational record companies to invest as never before in a form of music that was, at the same time, making itself accessible as never before.

The last few years have not, perhaps, been especially fruitful for *flamenco jondo*. But for as long as there are singers like José Mercé, dancers like Eva Yerbabuena and guitarists like her partner, Paco Jarana,* the cause of purism will be in pretty good shape. Indeed, one of the hallmarks of the latest generation of flamenco musicians is a new seriousness and scholarliness. The death of Camarón had a traumatic effect on the flamenco world and provoked a widespread revulsion against drugs and the bohemian lifestyle of which they formed a part. Today's aspiring young flamencos are quite likely to have studied in a conservatory and steeped themselves in tradition, not by talking to members of their family, but by listening for hours to digital remasterings of recordings made before the civil war.

The patron of this approach is the *cantaor* Enrique Morente. But, like many of his followers and admirers, he sees no contradiction between purism and experimentation. He has collaborated with the late opera star Alfredo Kraus, Heavy Metal rock groups and the Canadian poet and songwriter Leonard Cohen.

His endeavours underline the biggest change in recent years: the cause of fusion, once pursued almost single-handedly by Paco de Lucía, has become central to what contemporary flamenco is about. Not all of it involves dipping into highbrow musical forms.

So-called *nuevo flamenco*, which emerged in the nineties, is the latest form of flamenco-influenced pop – jaunty, syncopated and wholly listener-friendly. Leading exponents include the *tocaor* Vicente Amigo, widely regarded as the natural successor to Paco de Lucía, and the singer Niña Pastor. Their singles, and those of other *nuevo flamenco* musicians, are rarely far from the top of the Spanish charts.

In some other areas, the influence of flamenco has been so powerful that it raises the question of whether it is fusing with the other style or taking it over. It is heady stuff, flamenco. And in at least two areas, it has sidelined traditional genres. As has been seen in the last

* His baptismal name was Francisco Franco Fernández but nobody born in 1966 could go on being called that for long.

chapter, flamenco-influenced dance (*ballet español*) has eclipsed every other form in Spain since the return of democracy, despite official efforts to encourage the spread of the classical and modern styles. Something similar is now happening in jazz where several – arguably most – of the home-grown stars are flamenco-influenced: musicians such as the pianist Chano Domínguez, the bassist Carles Benavent and the flautist and saxophonist Jorge Pardo. Some critics have even begun to argue that, since all other forms of jazz are irremediably American in origin and inspiration, the only jazz that deserves to be called Spanish is flamenco-jazz fusion. It is a contention that outrages Spaniards who wish to play jazz in other styles. Nevertheless, there is a growing case for arguing that flamenco is taking over as Spain's 'national' art form from the one with which it is most often linked – bullfighting.

Some readers will no doubt be appalled to see bullfighting described as an art form, but it has been considered as such in Spain ever since the revolution effected by the *torero** Juan Belmonte in the early years of the twentieth century. The journalists who write about *corridas* in Spanish newspapers, for example, are critics, not reporters. They usually write reviews on some other art form outside the bullfighting season and they come under the *jefe de sección de cultura* (i.e. the arts editor). Until the twentieth century, bullfighting was a spectacle comparable to bear-baiting, albeit with the difference that it was a human being rather than a dog who was being pitted against a dangerous wild animal. Since Belmonte, however, the aim of bullfighters has been, not simply to demonstrate their courage, but to create an artistic spectacle that draws intensity from the risks involved. In that sense, it is comparable with trapeze artistry, but with the signal difference that trapeze artists do not torture and kill a dumb animal in order to achieve their effect.

What makes bullfighting unique among creative spectacles is the participation, however involuntary, of the animal. Foreigners attending

---

* A *torero* is a bullfighter. A *torero* may be a *picador*, responsible for lancing the bull from on horseback during the first stage of the fight, a *banderillero*, responsible for placing the darts in the second stage of the fight, or a *matador* (literally 'killer'), the senior member of the team who puts the bull to death in the third and final stage. He may even be a *rejoneador*, a mounted *matador*. But he is never, in Spanish at least, a 'toreador'.

a bullfight often find themselves baffled by the reaction of the crowd. This is usually because they fail to realize that *aficionados* are not just watching – and applauding or deploring – the bullfighter, but also the bull. There is an entire, more or less untranslatable, vocabulary in Spanish used to describe the qualities of the fighting bull. *Nobleza*, for example, does not mean 'nobility' in this context, but the tendency of a bull to run directly at the lure. *Aficionados* often divide themselves into *toreristas* and *toristas* according to whether they are more interested in watching the performance of the man or the animal. There are extreme cases of bullfight fans who are mesmerized by the bull to the extent that they are wholly indifferent to the performance of the *toreros*. Such extreme *toristas* can easily be found in the days leading up to the San Isidro festival in Madrid, wandering between the pens in which the bulls are kept in the Casa de Campo.

Bullfighting can be justifiably regarded as either an art form or a bloody spectacle, but it is simply misleading to see it, as so many non-Spaniards do, as a sport. In this sense, the English term 'bullfighting' is very misleading. The aim of the *toreros* is not to kill the bull as swiftly as possible, as would be the case with genuine combat, but to enact a ritual in which the plot is identical, but the variations infinite. The point of the ritual is a source of endless debate among *aficionados*, scholars and critics. Perhaps the most widespread view is that it is a drama, a tragedy, in which the brute force of a wild animal is pitted hopelessly against the superior intelligence and cunning of a human being. The only elements of competition in this ritual are the same as to be found in, say, ballet.

Bullfighters, like dancers, will normally try to perform better than their peers. If a *matador* does particularly well, the official who presides over the *corrida* can award him (or her) one or two ears or the tail of the bull as a trophy. At the end of each season, tallies are made of the number of bulls fought, and trophies obtained, by each *matador* and *novillero*,* but they serve largely as a measure of popularity (and influence with the people who organize bullfights). Often, the most critically acclaimed bullfighter will be some way down the list.

---

* A novice who has yet to graduate to the status of *matador* and may only fight smaller bulls.

It is difficult to imagine Spain without 'the bulls'. Bullfighting has inspired some excellent writing as well as some brilliant art.* Everyday speech is crammed with expressions that would become meaningless without it. We have all heard of *la hora de la verdad*, if only in its English version of 'the moment of truth'. But there are hundreds of others, some of which I suspect have no equivalent in any other language. *Dar largas*, for example, derives from the term for one of the most spectacular manoeuvres in bullfighting, the *larga cambiada*. The *matador* kneels in front of the gate through which the bull charges into the ring, then sends him careering harmlessly out of the way with a wide sweep of his cape. In its metaphorical sense, *dar largas* provides Spaniards with a single, immensely expressive phrase to describe the way in which people get out of a difficult situation by talking at length about something quite different. An outstanding example of the way Spaniards borrow from the culture and imagery of bullfighting to express their ideas came when Manuel Fraga was asked why he had chosen to defy the odds and stand for a fifth term as governor of Galicia. 'Good *toreros*,' he declared, 'die in the ring.'

It needs to be stressed that the *fiesta nacional*, as the taurine lobby likes to call it, has – and always has had – a limited following. Surprisingly few opinion polls have been carried out on the subject of 'the bulls', perhaps because the issue arouses such passionate disagreement among Spaniards themselves. What all of them point to, though, is that about half the population shows no interest or enthusiasm. Indeed, there is firm evidence to suggest that the Spanish as a whole are more 'anti' than 'pro'. The only poll I know that asked people whether they actually liked bullfighting was published by the magazine *Tiempo* in 1985. The 'No' response exceeded the 'Yes' by 51 per cent to 35 per cent, with the remainder indifferent. In recent years, around 2 million tickets are reckoned to have been sold annually for the thousand or so first- and second-class bullfights held in a season. That compares with over 10 million tickets to first- and second-division football matches.

The annual number of *corridas*† began to rise sharply in the late fifties, and the increase continued throughout the following decade.

* The latest great Spanish painter to be inspired by the drama of the *corrida* is Miquel Barceló.

† The statistics that follow refer solely to fights in first- and second-class rings.

Higher disposable incomes and increased leisure both seem to have contributed to the boom, as did the emergence of an outstandingly controversial *torero* in the person of Manuel Benítez, *El Cordobés*, whose antics in the ring horrified purists but lured the crowds. But these were also the years in which large numbers of fights were being staged primarily for the tourists who were flooding into Spain, and that meant the upward curve was much steeper than it would otherwise have been. The number of *corridas* peaked in 1971 at 682 and then began to fall rapidly to below 400 ten years later.

With the return of prosperity, the total grew during the eighties and nineties, surpassing the previous record in 1994 and reaching a new peak of 958 in 1998. But despite the economic boom of the Aznar years, the annual number of *corridas* staged has since diminished slightly. Nevertheless, three times as many first- and second-class bull-fights are being held in Spain today as in the days when Hemingway first wrote about them.

What is more, there has been a steep rise in the number of *corridas* of all kinds held during village, town and city festivals. This is a direct result of the return of democracy. It was not long before Spain's local politicians worked out that one way to improve their chances of re-election was to invest ratepayers' money in making a success of the local *fiesta*. Since, in most parts of the country, bullfights are traditional at festival time, one of the easiest ways to do this is to increase the quantity, or more rarely the quality, of the *corridas*.

Initially, indeed, democracy seemed to be doing 'the bulls' no end of good. The 1982 election brought to power one of the most pro-taurine administrations ever to have governed Spain, led by a man from bullfighting's Andalusian heartland. All of a sudden, bullfighting became fashionable. Madrid's month-long San Isidro festival became a social occasion of the first magnitude. Show-business personalities were spotted among the crowd, along with avant-garde designers and the owners of fashionable discos. PR companies began buying season tickets so as to be able to offer clients a ringside seat.

In 1988, moreover, Felipe González handed responsibility for 'the bulls' to a lifelong *aficionado*. As Minister of the Interior, José Luis Corcuera provided bullfighting with an entirely new legal framework. His 1991 *Ley de Espectáculos Taurinos* was, remarkably, the first law ever to be enacted by a Spanish parliament to deal exclusively with bullfighting. It defined it as a 'cultural tradition', thereby strengthening the hand of those who seek to identify bullfighting with patriotism. It provided much-needed statutory backing for penalties imposed by the authorities for infringements of the rules. And it paved the way for the introduction of an updated rule-book, or *reglamento*, to replace the one that had been in force since 1962. The new *reglamento* took effect soon after the start of the 1992 season, and at once set off a raging controversy.

Perhaps the most remarkable thing about it, in view of mounting pressure from outside for the abolition of bullfighting, was that its authors should not have seen fit to include more than a nod in the direction of animal rights. The conditions for the transportation of bulls were improved. But reports at the time suggested that this was to make sure they reached the ring in a satisfactory condition, rather than to save them from unnecessary suffering. The first stage of the *corrida*, in which the bull is lanced by mounted *picadores*, was modified – but not with any evident intention of reducing the suffering involved.

This has always been the most hotly debated phase of the fight. One reason is that, whatever changes are made, they lead either to more punishment for the bull or to greater risk for the horses. In the old days, when the *picador* had a more or less ordinary and unprotected mount, it was the norm for horses to be gored, and to be stumbling over their own entrails by the time they left the ring. Half a dozen or more were usually killed every afternoon. To reduce the amount of gore, it was decided in 1928 to equip the horses with a mattress-like covering known as a *peto*. At first, it was quite light and covered only the belly and flanks. But it soon grew in size and weight to the point at which it was impeding the horse's mobility. In the meantime, and in order to make things easier and safer for themselves, the *picadores* gradually ensured that their mounts became progressively heavier and stronger, to the point at which they were using virtual – if not actual – carthorses. Sitting atop these equine tanks, the *picadores* were in a position to mete out severe punishment to the bull, while the *matadores*, who were just as keen to limit the risks they were going to have to run in the second and third stages of the fight, often encouraged them to do so.

Corcuera's *reglamento* tried to redress the balance. It made the lancehead smaller, set a maximum weight for the *peto* of 30 kilos, banned carthorses and reduced the top weight for a *picador*'s mount from 900 to 650 kilos. The first *corrida* held under the new rules took place in Seville on May Day, 1992, and there was keen interest to see what effect the new rules would have. The first bull, after lifting one of the *picador*'s horses into the air and dropping its rider on to the sand, ended the opening phase only slightly weaker than when it began. As the *banderillero* Manolo Montoliú raised his arms over the bull's head to thrust the darts into his back, the bull drove his horns through his chest, splitting his heart and killing him almost instantly. The *picadores* and *banderilleros* blamed the new regulations and immediately called a strike which, if it had been allowed to continue, would have forced the cancellation of that year's San Isidro festival a few weeks later. It was only called off after a climb-down by the government. Corcuera stuck by the upper weight limit for the *picador*'s mount, but allowed the ban on carthorses to be interpreted in such a way as to allow back into the ring the *percherones* (Breton horses, often interbred with Spanish or English strains) which had been used before.

A further ostensible aim of the new *reglamento*, as of the *Ley de Espectáculos Taurinos*, was to tackle what is unquestionably the biggest single abuse in modern bullfighting: the shaving of the bulls' horns. To a bull, horns are what claws are to a cat. But they are more than that. To extend the analogy, they are his 'whiskers' and his 'tail' too – they help him judge distance and maintain balance. Shaving involves trimming the horns so as to put him at a disadvantage in the ring. It is done with a hacksaw, and finished off with a file or even, it is said, with a blow-torch. So skilled have its practitioners become that the signs of shaving can usually only be detected under a microscope. Nowadays, the animal is invariably tranquillized before being shaved, and unless the 'barber' accidentally cuts into the nerve which runs through the horn, a 'shave' is as painless for a bull as a manicure is for a human. However, the doping, confinement and tampering are all immensely traumatic for the bull, and he often emerges psychologically beaten. At all events his horns are more sensitive, as well as shorter and blunter, and he may well have been given a false sense of balance.

The problem is that shaving has come to be in the interests of almost everyone involved in the business – except, of course, the fans, who pay to see the equivalent of a rigged fight. The *matador* gets an opponent who is less likely to kill or maim him (gorings are less common, and less severe, with a blunted horn). And the more a *matador* fights, the more his manager, or *apoderado*, earns. As for the *empresario*, who runs the ring, stages the fight and actually buys the bulls, it is nowadays highly likely that he will himself be the manager of one or more of the *matadores* on any given afternoon. The bull ranchers, or *ganaderos*, may not be the instigators of the fraud, but they can be put under intense pressure by their customers, the manager-promoters, to let their bulls be tampered with.

Shaving has been going on since at least the forties. But it could never be proved that breeders had consented to the shaving, and in any case the rules did not have proper statutory backing. The 1991 law, which specified penalties of up to 25 million pesetas ($240,000 or £140,000), provided that backing. It also seemed to offer a way round the jurisprudential problem by which someone – in this case, the breeder – could be held responsible for something that he or she did not do or incite others to do. Under the new rules, a rancher could overrule the objections of the veterinarians at the pre-*corrida* inspection and insist that a suspect bull be fought, provided he or she accepted full responsibility if – in the post-*corrida* analysis – the horns were shown to have been shaved. However, horns are rarely sent for analysis in the conditions stipulated, and fines under the new arrangements have so far been few and far between.

Shaving, though, is only one symptom of a broader phenomenon – the taming of the Iberian fighting bull. The historic decline can be traced back at least as far as the civil war. So many fighting bulls were slaughtered either for meat or vengeance during the conflict that breeders were unable, during the years immediately after the war, to provide enough bulls of the right age and quality. Though the stock was later to recover, the improvement came at a time when the *empresarios* were gaining ascendancy within the world of bullfighting, often becoming managers, or *apoderados*, to 'strings' or 'stables' of *toreros*, each subject to an exclusive contract with the promoter-manager. In a process that paralleled the spread of shaving, the *empresarios* began to exert pressure on the *ganaderos* to supply them with bulls that looked impressive, but were predictable and lacked the *casta* ('breeding', 'spirit') to present any serious challenge to the bullfighters on their books. In an earlier age, when rearing bulls was simply a pastime of the aristocracy, the *ganaderos* might have been able to resist, but it had become an increasingly commercial activity and since, at that time, more bulls were being bred than was necessary, the *ganaderos* were in no position to put up a fight. The post-war bulls, although small and young, had at least been fiery. Those of the sixties became progressively more docile, and by the seventies some were actually falling over in the ring before the fight had run its normal course.

That problem has never gone away. Some veterinarians now believe that a certain proportion of bulls actually have a genetic propensity to collapse which has been brought to the fore by selective breeding.

In recent years, a different sort of pressure has weighed on the ranchers – a growing demand for big, heavy bulls. This seems to be largely a result of television coverage of the *corridas* held in the top rings like Las Ventas in Madrid. Viewers in the provinces see impressive-looking animals on their screens and want similar bulls in their local festivals.

Among the few exceptions to the general rule of relative docility and predictability are the bulls produced by Victorino Martín. The outstanding breeder of recent years, Martín is not an aristocratic landowner, but a self-made man – a former butcher's assistant from Galapagar, between Madrid and the Guadarrama mountains. In 1989, though, a shadow was cast over his spirited *Victorinos* when he too was accused by the veterinary inspectors of allowing the horns of his bulls to be tampered with. Martín vigorously denied the charge, and for two years refused to let his animals be fought in Spain.

Traditionally, bullfighters were poor country boys. Indeed, it was assumed that only someone who had known hunger would have the incentive to get into a ring and risk a goring (*cornada*). As the saying went, '*Mas cornadas da el hambre*' ('Hunger gives more gorings [than the bulls do]'). So one of the great surprises of recent years has been the emergence of an entirely new breed of *matador* from a well-to-do background, with sophisticated tastes and a good education, sometimes even a university education. In many cases, they are the sons of *matadores* who amassed fortunes that were beyond the reach of their predecessors. But in some instances, they are complete outsiders. At all events, bullfighters have become socially acceptable, indeed desirable, as never before.

The growing sophistication of *matadores* has gone hand-in-hand with a process of increasing professionalism. In the old days, aspiring bullfighters often got their earliest practice by stealing into bull ranches at night and encouraging the animals to run at their improvised capes by the light of the moon. This was extremely perilous – and not just for the youngsters involved. It meant the bulls reached the ring with experience, and were less likely to be taken in by the *matador's* ruses.

The earliest bullfighting schools date only from the early 1970s. One of the most respected was founded in Madrid by a then unemployed *novillero*, Enrique Martín Arranz, who has since gone on to become a leading *apoderado*. The spread of schools, often funded by local authorities, has stimulated a more scholarly interest in bullfighting among those who actually practise it. Many of the *novilleros* issuing from the schools know passes that had long fallen into disuse.

Julián López, *El Juli*, the most successful *matador* in recent years and a graduate of the Madrid school, is an outstanding example. But he is nevertheless regarded as more of a technician than an artist. That coveted title has had two claimants of late.

The first was not a Spaniard, but a Colombian. César Rincón burst out of obscurity in 1991 and was carried shoulder-high from the arena in Las Ventas four times in a season, a feat never previously achieved. But by the following year, he was beginning to succumb to the effects of Hepatitis C, the result of a blood transfusion he had received after a goring in his native Colombia in 1990. His career drifted slowly down and in 2000 he went into retirement to try to beat the disease. It was not until three years later that he recovered sufficiently to attempt a comeback. Since then, he has again impressed and thrilled *aficionados*, though without so far attaining quite the heights he reached in his Spanish debut season.

By the time Rincón returned, however, there had been a new *revelación* (discovery): Victorino Martín's nephew, José Tomás. Publicity-shy, unpredictable, enigmatic, eccentric and withdrawn, he matches exactly the stereotype of the creative genius. His friends include the flamenco guitarist Vicente Amigo and the singer-songwriter Joaquín Sabino. Some *aficionados* believe José Tomás has it in him to be the greatest bullfighter since the late Antonio Ordóñez.

But after a disappointing season in 2002, José Tomás astonished his *cuadrilla** by announcing to them that he was giving up bullfighting after a couple of winter *corridas* in Mexico.

Bullfighting has been at risk for almost as long as it has been known to exist. Torquemada was against it. So was Isabel the Catholic. In the eighteenth century, Felipe V and Carlos III both banned the nobility from taking part. But in the last few years something has happened that had never happened before: parts of Spain in which support for the *corrida* is weak have announced a ban on 'the bulls'.

The first was declared in 1990 in the Catalan resort of Tossa de Mar. The next year, the regional assembly of the Canary Islands voted for prohibition. The move was ridiculed by *aficionados* who pointed out that the last big bullring in the Canaries, at Santa Cruz de Tenerife, had closed in 1986. The vote, they said, was a blatant attempt to curry favour with foreign tour-operators and distract their attention from the fact that the very legislation that outlawed bullfighting legalized cockfighting, a pastime that has a much stronger tradition on the Islands.

That, though, missed the point that a precedent had been set, and that there are several other Spanish regions – Catalonia and Galicia, for instance – whose bullfighting traditions are almost as feeble as those of the Canary Islands.

The prospect of bullfighting withering away in Catalonia is by no means remote. The regional government, the *Generalitat*, has already banned mobile rings. One of Barcelona's two *plazas de toros*, Las Arenas, is no longer used for bullfights. And, in 2003, a survey was published suggesting that 63 per cent of the city's population wanted bullfighting in the city to be stopped.

In Catalonia, and to a lesser extent the Canary Islands, anti-taurine attitudes draw strength from anti-centralist sentiment – bullfighting is seen as something for the amusement of uncouth mesetarians and hot-blooded southerners. If other peripheral regions were to follow the lead given by the Canary Islands, it would severely undermine a key argument of the bullfighting lobby: that the *corrida* is a *fiesta nacional*, quintessential to Spanishness.

Other things being equal, this would still leave bullfighting impreg-

---

* The team of bullfighters who assist the *matador*.

nable in its Castilian and Andalusian heartlands. But in 1992, something happened (and went almost unnoticed) that suggested that other things may not in fact be equal. Tres Cantos is a new town built to the north of Madrid, within sight of several bull ranches. It is an impressive, if soulless, place that has attracted quite a number of firms operating in the new, 'clean' industries, as well as hundreds of thousands of the new sort of suburbanite Spaniards who work in them. In 1992, the town council decided to drop *corridas* from the annual festivities in view of the lack of spectators at the previous year's bullfights and 'the anti-taurine character of the majority of the population'.

Since then, there has been evidence of a growing reluctance to provide bullfighting with a wider audience through the media. In 2003, for the first time, the annual Seville festival was not televised. The following year, the new Director-General of RTVE agreed to a suggestion from a Socialist deputy that, whenever there was a *corrida* on the first channel, Televisión Española should broadcast programmes specifically aimed at children on the second channel to provide them with an attractive alternative.

The long-term threat to bullfighting is that it will come to be seen by Spaniards in the way it is seen by many foreigners, as something less than respectable: bloody, archaic and not at all representative of the new Spain.

CHAPTER 31

The New Spaniards

When I arrived in Madrid in 1976 as a newly appointed correspondent for the *Guardian*, one of the first things I did was to go to see the bureau. It turned out to be a room with a couple of desks tucked away in a dingy corner of a now-defunct Madrid evening newspaper, *Informaciones*. Some of the other British papers holed up there too, and after I had chatted to the other correspondents for a while we adjourned to a bar across the road.

We had been there for maybe half an hour when a big grey estate car drew up in the street outside. Some men in raincoats got out and headed purposefully for a house across the road. They re-emerged a few minutes later with three shocked young men in handcuffs. I got a good look at one of them just before they crammed him into the back of the estate car. With his unkempt hair, his pallid complexion and spectacles, he looked every inch the student intellectual.

People in the street were pretending nothing was happening. Nobody in the bar said a word. We watched through the window as the car sped off towards the Puerta del Sol where, in those days, the police had their headquarters, and where a deeply unpleasant interrogation no doubt awaited the three young men.

Those were the days when you could be walking through a passage in the Metro and suddenly one of your fellow-passengers would throw a bundle of illegal pamphlets into the air and run like crazy; when a peaceful, if unauthorized, May Day gathering in a park could end with hundreds of men, women and children fleeing before mounted, club-wielding police.

Today, those images feel as if they ought to be locked away in sepia tints. In the relatively short space of thirty years, Spain has succeeded in transforming itself into a stable democracy. And how.

The same two parties have dominated politics continuously since 1982, sometimes governing alone and, at other times, making deals with regional nationalist parties. At the same time, Spanish political life has shown a considerable capacity for renewal. Just four years before he became Prime Minister, José Luis Rodríguez Zapatero was an unknown backbencher who had never served in government. His deputy, María Teresa Fernández de la Vega, had at that time only been an MP for four years.

Any assessment of modern Spain must give wholehearted recognition to its achievement of political stability, if only because so much else flows from it. It is the reason why successive Spanish governments have been able to implement the bulk of their legislative programmes. It is the reason why ministers can devote themselves fully to the tasks of government, instead of having constantly to manoeuvre for advantage – or survival – in rancorously divided coalitions. Above all, it has given to the rest of the world an image of Spain as a serious place, and that in turn has buoyed inward foreign investment.

Prospective foreign investors have also been encouraged by the gradual erosion of both corruption and terrorism, for which the governments of José María Aznar and José Luis Rodríguez Zapatero must take much of the credit. Transparency International's 2005 Corruption Perceptions Index ranked Spain twenty-third, just behind Japan and seventeen places ahead of Italy. At the time of writing, ETA has not killed since 2003; there is a ceasefire in force, and the government has announced that it plans to begin talks.

What happens now will depend in part on how politicians in Madrid and elsewhere manage the issue of regional nationalism. This remains the single biggest imponderable in Spain's future.

If there is a criticism to be made of Spain's stable, more or less two-party politics, it is that they have become rather *too* bi-partisan; too rigidly divided between left and right, too toxically infused with a 'with us or against us' mentality. This has been particularly true since the 2004 elections, which one of the two sides felt it lost unfairly. Of late, moreover, the acrimonious confrontation between them has taken on a new aspect, with the conservatives in the PP adopting the role of champions of Spain's unity and depicting the Socialists as fellow-travellers of separatism whose commitments to the regional nationalists who keep them in power could doom the nation to disintegration.

History would suggest that this is potentially a very dangerous situation. Spain's past is littered with examples of how defence of the nation's unity turned to violence. On this occasion, it may be that history is a bad teacher. It seems highly improbable that, with Spain prospering to such a degree from its current stability, the armed forces could be persuaded to intervene, by toppling the government, let alone marching on, say, the Basque country.

But the sensitivity within the armed forces on this issue should not be underestimated, and it was highlighted in 2006 as the new Catalan statute of autonomy was being debated when Lieutenant-General José Mena Aguado, warned of 'serious consequences for the armed forces' if the statute were approved without modification.* Subsequently, the controversial new statute was, anyhow, watered down. But it would be unwise to dismiss the affair as an isolated abnormality.

Part of what the general said was merely a statement of fact. He reminded his audience that the 1978 constitution entrusted to the armed forces the defence of Spain's territorial integrity. It is perfectly clear on that point. Unfortunately, it is far less clear about who should decide when Spain's unity is at risk. The King? The Prime Minister? The Chief of Defence Staff? The constitution does not say. As anyone who has a chance to look back at successive editions of this book will see, I have long been voicing the opinion that this creates a potentially very dangerous situation – and one that successive governments have been all too keen to ignore. Modern Spanish politicians tend to stress that the constitution was written in an entirely different context at a time when the politicians were keen to appease the military. That is true – but irrelevant. What matters is that the officers of Spain's armed forces have sworn to uphold a document that lays upon them, not a right, but a duty to protect Spain from disintegration, and – it could be argued – leaves it up to them to decide when they should act. Before going much further down the road towards yet broader self-government for the various peoples of Spain, it seems to me only common sense that its politicians should think about altering the constitution in such a

* See p. 282.

way as to remove any doubt that the armed forces have a case for intervention.

Ultimately, the issue of Spain's future ought not to be just about clauses in constitutions, or indeed rights to referendums. It should also be about such things as the languages people speak and the communities to which they feel they belong. For more than twenty years now, parts of Spain have been becoming progressively more singular and it may not be long before the Basque country and Catalonia start to feel foreign to people from other parts of the country. The point may not be far off when they will no longer care so much if the Basques or Catalans are given a status that corresponds to their objective singularity.

In all of this, however, there is – or rather, could be – another factor. Attitudes in society go in cycles. The solemn preoccupations of one generation become a target of derision for the next. For the moment, for example, Basques and Catalans of all ages listen without complaint as their leaders perform absurd linguistic acrobatics to avoid pronouncing the word 'Spain'. But I do not discount that a moment could be reached, perhaps, when Basque and Catalan self-government are taken for granted, at which this sort of earnestness will start to look just a little ridiculous, a bit unsophisticated and unfashionable. And, at that point, social prejudice being so much more effective than legal proscription, a whole range of problems that now seem so intractable could silently melt away.

For the time being, however, both areas remain largely inward-looking and – to some extent – the same can be said of Spain as a whole. In view of all that has happened over the past three decades, this is scarcely to be wondered at. Spaniards have had an extraordinary number of problems of their own to tackle without having to look abroad for more.

But there is also, I believe, something deeper at work here. Since the collapse of most of its empire in the early nineteenth century, Spain, alone among the big European nations, has been remarkably isolated from the rest of the world. It had only the most marginal experience of colonialism. It played no part in either of the two world wars.

For whatever reason, Spain's growing economic stature has not been matched by a corresponding level of diplomatic engagement.

Its representatives have been notoriously uncompromising in their defence of Spain's financial and other interests within the European Union, but rather less forthcoming in contributing to projects of common interest. As mentioned earlier,* Spain's defence spending is proportionately the second lowest in NATO. It is also the case, for example, that its overseas aid expenditure as a share of gross national income was lower in 2004 than that of all but three of the fifteen states then belonging to the EU.

Spain is a big country, but with a small country inside just bursting to get out. I have referred on more than one occasion to the ambitions that some Spaniards unquestionably harbour for their country to become a 'Sweden of the Mediterranean'. But there are also many who, one suspects, would be even more content were it to turn into a sort of Latin Switzerland instead, left alone by everyone to get on with the business of getting richer.

The same reclusiveness was until recently a feature of business too. As late as the eighties, almost the only Spanish company with a truly global presence was the Chupa Chups lollipop firm, founded by a Catalan, Enric Bernat.† Spanish executives were slow to exploit the opportunities provided by their country's emergence from pariah status after Franco's death, and when they did begin to invest overseas it was largely in the Spanish-speaking countries of Latin America.

To a considerable extent, I suspect, that was because many spoke no other language but Spanish. As they are gradually replaced by a new generation, comfortable in the international business language of English, Spanish companies are becoming more adventurous. The Galician fashion business, Zara, has showrooms as far afield as the US and Japan. In 2000, Telefónica acquired the big US web portal Lycos Inc., and four years later the Santander Central Hispano (SCH) bought into Britain's Abbey in what was, at the time, Europe's biggest cross-border bank merger.

At first glance, the new Spaniards' economic achievements seem to be at least as dazzling as their political successes. Today, they are about 75 per cent better off in real terms than they were when Franco died.

* See above, pp. 197–8.
†The logo for the earliest Chupa Chups was designed by Bernat's friend, Salvador Dalí.

However, it is worth stressing that the country's economic progress relative to the rest of Europe has been anything but steady in the intervening years. There is a tendency for outsiders to think Spain has been catching up inexorably with the other member states of the EU ever since 1975. That is not true.

The boom unleashed at the start of the sixties lifted Spain's GDP per head at an extraordinary rate. By the time Franco died, it was more than 80 per cent of the average in the twelve nations that were later to form the EU of which Spain too was to be a member. But then the figure dropped sharply. Eleven years later, when the recession ended, it had been whittled down to 72 per cent of the average in the EU of twelve, a figure that was equivalent to 74 per cent of the average in what was later to become the EU of fifteen. Since then, Spain has again been catching up fast and, by 2004, its GDP per head was 89 per cent of the average in the unexpanded EU of fifteen.

Those figures make a couple of very important points. One is that, though Spaniards are indeed a lot richer than they used to be, so are other Europeans. Even with the furious progress of recent years, in which Spain's GDP growth has been consistently above the EU average, their *relative* economic standing in Europe has improved quite modestly. Compared to other Europeans, Spaniards are still only about five percentage points better off than when the dictatorship came to an end. They have done well, but not as well as, for example, the Irish, who as recently as the early eighties were poorer than the Spanish and are now almost 50 per cent richer.

The other point is that all of Spain's real economic progress since Franco's death has come since joining the EU. Membership not only provided Spain with preferential access to a hugely enlarged market, but also an opportunity to tap in to the so-called 'cohesion funds' that were set aside by the richer states to enable the poorer ones to catch up.

Spaniards have expended a considerable amount of hard work on growing their economy. But it is also true that they have had a fairly generous helping of luck. The sixties boom was made possible thanks in part to an influx of foreign tourists, who would not have come to Spain had it not had sunny weather and sandy beaches; that of the eighties was prompted by EU entry. Recently, moreover, growth has been sustained by social rather than economic factors, and in particular the expansion of Spain's workforce by the incorporation of women on a vast scale.

That process still has some way to go. But with the expansion of the EU to include several much poorer nations, Spain will lose some of the advantages it has hitherto enjoyed. It is set to become a net contributor to the budget and, at the same time, it will find itself having to compete head-on with countries that can offer lower wage and other costs to foreign investors from inside and outside the EU. The going, in other words, is about to get tougher, and it could start to expose some of the flaws in the Spanish economy that have been disguised till now: insufficient competition, too much state intervention, and a dearth of skills in the labour force.

It may be too that the Spanish are going to have to accept further changes to their way of life – and even to their outlook on life – if they are to fulfil their dream of one day catching up with countries such as Britain, France and Germany.

They are not inhibited, in the way that so many Italians are, by a fierce attachment to the past and traditional ways of doing things. Spaniards are keen to embrace modernity. There is a high level of enthusiasm for contemporary art. And they are fascinated by new gadgetry. But gadgetry is one thing, and the intelligent, productive use of new technology is another. Statistics suggest Spaniards have been relatively slow in their uptake of the Internet and of information technology generally.

Their ability to act quickly and decisively when the need arises, to 'think big', take risks, and not let themselves be hidebound by rules – all these are of the essence in a successful post-industrial economy. But there are also a number of habits and attitudes to be found in Spain that act as a brake on its development: an aversion to planning, unpunctuality, procrastination, and a reluctance among many subordinates to take responsibility – a trait that goes hand in hand with the compulsion among many bosses to take all but the most trivial decisions. In an age of service cultures and information technology, moreover, the difficulties a lot of Spaniards seem to have in putting themselves in the position of the other person, and dealing with people other than face to face, must also be regarded as handicaps.

Lorca's biographer, Ian Gibson, once remarked that 'the Spanish work hard, but have no work ethic'. If they feel it necessary, either to make money or keep their jobs, they will put in hours that would astonish trade unionists and company bosses in other parts of Europe. Yet their attitude to what they produce is frequently indifferent and the results often slapdash. Except among the Catalans, labour is usually regarded as a necessary evil rather than a source of pride or satisfaction. Indeed, other Spaniards often take the rise out of the Catalans for the way in which they regard work as something honourable and pleasurable. Outside Catalonia, leisure tends to be seen more as a right than a privilege, and as unquestionably more worthwhile than the means of funding it. For those who live among them, this set of attitudes constitutes one of the Spaniards' most engaging – and frustrating – characteristics. It is the reason why there is so much fun to be had in Spain, but also the explanation for that most ubiquitous of figures in Spanish life, the *chapucero*, or bodger.

How the Spanish will deal with the political and economic challenges awaiting them is impossible to foresee. But what can be said with certainty is that they are going to have to meet those challenges against the background of a greatly changed society.

Within just a few years, Spain has been transformed from an ethnically more or less homogeneous society into a multicultural one. So far, there has been remarkably little friction. In a lot of countries with more experience of integration, an attack on the scale of the 2004 Madrid bombings, apparently carried out by immigrants, would have provoked widespread and vicious reprisals. The fact that that did not happen is a tribute to the good sense, tolerance and restraint of today's Spaniards. But I think it is also true to say that, in Spain, the lack of conflict so far has been due to what you might call 'constructive indifference'. It is something I have seen in other Latin societies: the Spanish, like the Italians, may not actively discriminate against the new arrivals, but nor do they take much of an interest in them or their problems. The lesson of the 2005 riots in the French *banlieues* would seem to be that that is not enough to prevent communities sliding inexorably towards violent confrontation.

The steady flow of immigrants into Spain can be expected to reverse the decline in its birth-rate in the way that is just beginning to happen in Italy. But it remains the case that, for the first time since at least the nineteenth century, families in the south of Europe are now smaller than in the north, and in southern Europe they are smaller than they have ever been anywhere. The effects of this on attitudes and lifestyles in Mediterranean Europe will be immense. Family affiliations are at the root of a lot of the favouritism and corruption that is characteristic of Mediterranean societies. So it would seem logical, as families become smaller, that nepotism will recede: you cannot, for example, give a job to your son-in-law if you do not have one, and you are not going to have one unless you have at least one daughter.

I would feel more confident if it were not for the emergence of a generation in which the only child is – if not the norm – then certainly not a rarity. At the root of a tendency to favour those who are closest to you there is always, it seems to me, an element of egocentricity: you give them preference specifically because they are closer to you. The generation now approaching maturity, made up of children belonging to very small nuclear families, has been pampered like no other and may turn out to be more, not less, prone to egocentricity, or what the Spanish themselves term *individualismo*.

This is what linguists call a 'false friend' – a word that resembles one in another language but actually has a very different meaning. When the Spanish talk about *individualismo*, they are not referring to what Britons and Americans mean by 'individualism' (i.e. something bordering on eccentricity). Individualism in that sense is quite rare in Spain. There are plenty of flamboyant, provocative and outspoken Spaniards, but they usually take care to move within the limits of what is considered to be right, proper and decent. *Individualismo* in its Spanish guise means putting your own interests first, and those of the rest of society nowhere. *Individualismo* is parking your car so that it blocks someone else's, and then strolling off to watch a ninety-minute football match – something I have seen people do outside the Real Madrid stadium. At its worst, *individualismo* prompts that intolerance of other people's ideas that has repeatedly driven the Spanish to arms. At its best, it is self-reliance, self-respect and the bedrock underlying that personal dignity which I personally find to be one of the Spaniards' most appealing characteristics. *Individualismo* is what leads the humblest waitress to carry herself like a princess, and the poorest shopkeeper to stop you from hunting for small change with an '*es igual*' and a magnanimous, dismissive wave of the hand.

Individualismo nevertheless made Spain what Ortega y Gasset, writing in the last century, called 'invertebrate' – lacking the backbone of a civil society. Almost the only organization that did not depend on the state was the Roman Catholic Church. People did not join voluntary associations, whether charitable foundations, mutual societies or pressure groups. It was often remarked too that, outside Catalonia, Spaniards did not show much interest in that quintessentially collaborative activity, choral singing. 'Invertebration' made Spain vulnerable. Anyone who succeeded in grasping the levers of power faced much less resistance than in a society with a plethora of organized interest groups.

The opposites of *individualismo* are *solidaridad*, which means doing things for the good of others, and *convivencia*, a word that may have equivalents in other languages, but which takes on unique connotations in Spain. Literally translated, it means co-existence, but with overtones of tolerance and trying to see the other person's point of view.

Because Spaniards were acutely conscious of the fact that a lack of *convivencia* had led them into their civil war, it became the watchword of the transition. It was what made sense of the painful compromises and the deliberate forgetfulness. In my first book on Spain, published in 1986, I wrote that while *convivencia* had become a reality, *solidaridad* was 'still more of an aspiration than a fact'. That has since changed. Indeed, the spread of what is nowadays more often called *civismo* is one of the most striking developments in contemporary Spain to anyone who knew it twenty, or even ten, years ago.

Civismo is the other side of a coin first examined in chapter 12. There is unquestionably a wild side to the Spaniards. But a tamer side is also emerging as they accept that it is reasonable to make personal sacrifices for social gains, as they sort their rubbish, use bottle-banks, respect smoking bans, make organ donations and even stop their cars to give pedestrians right of way at 'zebra' crossings. While I was researching this book, I read an article in *El País* that recounted in a rather disapproving tone how a recent study had revealed that 40 per cent of drivers do not stop voluntarily if someone on foot is waiting at a pedestrian crossing. But just ten years earlier, as I can assure you from personal experience, that figure was somewhere between 90 and 100 per cent, as it is in today's Italy.

In the years leading up to the introduction of the euro, there was a lot of talk about 'convergence' between the states making up the

EU. What it referred to was economic convergence. The economies of the EU had to come into line so that they formed a more or less homogeneous currency area. Thousands of pages of newsprint were devoted to reporting the efforts made by various governments to trim their budget deficits and reduce their national debt.

Yet almost nothing has been written, either before or since, about social convergence; about the way in which, often without the need for legislation or regulation, the EU's member states are growing together in a common acceptance of norms and practices that are at least as important as long-term interest rates. In this sense, Spain is converging as rapidly as anywhere and, in the process, it is reinventing itself yet again.

Change, change and more change. A nation that was once a byword for *machismo* today has a cabinet of which half the members are women. A country that, until recently, was almost devoid of immigrants now has more than the European average. A state once ruled with an iron rod from its invented capital in the dead geographic centre today faces a real, if still remote, prospect of disintegration.

I have a friend who is in her mid-fifties. She was born at a time when Spain was all but closed to the rest of the world and, like the rest of her generation, she has witnessed the entire sweep of its transformation in the years since.

'You know,' she once said, 'there are times when I think back to my childhood and what things were like in those days, and I say to myself "My God! I must be 200 years old." But I'm not. It's just that Spain has changed so much.'

INDEX

439

He just wanted a decent book to read ...

Not too much to ask, is it? It was in 1935 when Allen Lane, Managing Director of Bodley Head Publishers, stood on a platform at Exeter railway station looking for something good to read on his journey back to London. His choice was limited to popular magazines and poor-quality paperbacks – the same choice faced every day by the vast majority of readers, few of whom could afford hardbacks. Lane's disappointment and subsequent anger at the range of books generally available led him to found a company – and change the world.

'We believed in the existence in this country of a vast reading public for intelligent books at a low price, and staked everything on it'
Sir Allen Lane, 1902–1970, founder of Penguin Books

The quality paperback had arrived – and not just in bookshops. Lane was adamant that his Penguins should appear in chain stores and tobacconists, and should cost no more than a packet of cigarettes.

Reading habits (and cigarette prices) have changed since 1935, but Penguin still believes in publishing the best books for everybody to enjoy. We still believe that good design costs no more than bad design, and we still believe that quality books published passionately and responsibly make the world a better place.

So wherever you see the little bird – whether it's on a piece of prize-winning literary fiction or a celebrity autobiography, political tour de force or historical masterpiece, a serial-killer thriller, reference book, world classic or a piece of pure escapism – you can bet that it represents the very best that the genre has to offer.

Whatever you like to read – trust Penguin.